Hazen "Kiki" Cuyler

ALSO BY RONALD T. WALDO

The Battling Bucs of 1925: How the Pittsburgh Pirates Pulled Off the Greatest Comeback in World Series History (McFarland, 2012)

Fred Clarke: A Biography of the Baseball Hall of Fame Player-Manager (McFarland, 2011)

Hazen "Kiki" Cuyler
A Baseball Biography
Ronald T. Waldo

McFarland & Company, Inc., Publishers
Jefferson, North Carolina, and London

LIBRARY OF CONGRESS CATALOGUING-IN-PUBLICATION DATA

Waldo, Ronald T., 1961–
    Hazen "Kiki" Cuyler : a baseball biography / Ronald T. Waldo.
    p.   cm.
    Includes bibliographical references and index.

    ISBN 978-0-7864-6885-0
    softcover : acid free paper ∞

    1. Cuyler, Kiki, 1898–1950. 2. Baseball players — United States — Biography. I. Title.
GV865.C88W35 2012
796.357092 — dc23   2012032479
[B]

BRITISH LIBRARY CATALOGUING DATA ARE AVAILABLE

© 2012 Ronald T. Waldo. All rights reserved

No part of this book may be reproduced or transmitted in any form or by any means, electronic or mechanical, including photocopying or recording, or by any information storage and retrieval system, without permission in writing from the publisher.

On the cover: Hazen "Kiki" Cuyler (National Baseball Hall of Fame Library Cooperstown, New York)

Manufactured in the United States of America

McFarland & Company, Inc., Publishers
  Box 611, Jefferson, North Carolina 28640
  www.mcfarlandpub.com

Table of Contents

Acknowledgments vi
Preface 1

1 • Growing Up in Harrisville 5
2 • From Humble Beginnings in Bay City to Stardom with Nashville 13
3 • The Greatest Rookie Class in Baseball History 30
4 • The Flint Flash Becomes a World Series Hero 47
5 • Pennant Hopes Crushed by the ABC Affair 66
6 • Manager Donie Bush Banishes Cuyler to the Bench 83
7 • Joe McCarthy Steals Kiki Cuyler from Barney Dreyfuss 101
8 • A Comeback Season and World Series Appearance 118
9 • Hazen Cuyler Sets the Table for Hack Wilson 138
10 • Rogers Hornsby, Violet Valli and Another Pennant 155
11 • Babe Ruth's Called Shot and Cuyler's Last World Series Appearance 174
12 • A Great Career in Chicago Comes to an End 193
13 • The Dream of Becoming a Big League Manager 210
14 • An Enduring Legacy and Baseball's Highest Honor 228

Appendix: Statistics 241
Chapter Notes 243
Bibliography 269
Index 271

Acknowledgments

In the months that I worked on this project, several people offered information and guidance so that this book might accurately represent Cuyler's story. The first two people I would like to thank are Cuyler's daughter, Kelly Kruttlin, and granddaughter, KiAnn Kruttlin, who patiently responded to my many questions. This project could not have been completed without them, as they steered me in the proper direction when contradictions sometimes arose.

I also wish to extend sincere thanks to John D. Boufford of the *Alcona County Review* from Cuyler's hometown of Harrisville, Michigan. John's information about Cuyler's early life and photos from the player's life outside of baseball were invaluable to me.

Photo archivists Jenny Ambrose and Pat Kelly from the Baseball Hall of Fame responded quickly and fully to my photo queries. As always, thank you very much, Jenny and Pat, for all of your help.

Lastly, I would also like to thank Jerel Patch, Clifton Blue Parker, David Finoli and David L. Fleitz for offering their time and assistance looking over draft chapters of the Cuyler biography. Thank you, gentlemen, for all of your help checking these chapters for accuracy and for offering suggestions for their improvement.

Preface

I was fortunate to grow up when and where I did. The early 1970s was a great time to be a baseball fan in Pittsburgh as the Steel City was in the thick of the pennant race every season. Under the guidance of men like Danny Murtaugh and Bill Virdon, the Pirates brought home three Eastern Division titles and a World Series victory. I was nine years old when Pittsburgh defeated the Baltimore Orioles in 1971 and claimed their first championship since 1960. Even though I had followed baseball for only two years, I knew the names of every player in each league and loyally followed the exploits of favorite Pirates such as Willie Stargell, Roberto Clemente, Bob Robertson and Luke Walker.

I was not fortunate enough to attend any of the World Series games at Three Rivers Stadium in 1971, but my uncle did give me the official program that was sold at the games. A statistics nut at even that young age, I spent weeks thoroughly digesting each page. I was particularly interested in the section that chronicled all of the Pirates' World Series appearances prior to the meeting against Baltimore in 1971. I spent countless hours scouring the box scores, poring over the photos and reading the stories about Pittsburgh's past postseason glories—1903, 1909, 1925, 1927 and 1960. There was one picture in particular, and one man within it, that I came back to repeatedly. It was the 1927 team photo, and the man stood in the back row. The bill of his cap pointed skyward in such a way that a shock of curly locks on his head was visible. His hands rested on the shoulders of teammate Glenn Wright, who was standing in front of him. The player's name also fascinated me. Kiki Cuyler seemed to be the perfect moniker for a baseball player.

From that point forward, Hazen "Kiki" Cuyler was my favorite baseball player. Even though I had never seen Cuyler play a game, and never would, he quickly became a hero to me after I read about his phenomenal exploits during the 1925 World Series against the Washington Senators. As a young boy unaware that players were sometimes sidelined because of injuries or disagreements with team management, I was puzzled by the fact that Cuyler did not appear in the 1927 World Series against the New York Yankees. When a little digging on my part revealed that Cuyler was traded to Chicago after the 1927 season, it brought on the same profound disappointment I felt when the Pirates traded Freddie Patek to Kansas City for Bob Johnson and Jackie Hernandez in 1970. As the years went by and I grew older, recognition that Cuyler had issues with Pirate manager Donie Bush in 1927 over where he should bat in the lineup and play in the field helped explain why my hero was pushed out of Pittsburgh.

During the past few decades, my frame of reference for Kiki Cuyler's career has expanded, thanks in large part to the diligent efforts of fellow authors. Many books covering the history of the Pittsburgh Pirates have done a fine job covering his short career in the Smoky City and the events which led to him joining the Cubs for the 1928 season. But as time went by, questions about his career remained unanswered in my mind. For this reason, 40 years after Kiki Cuyler first piqued my curiosity, I decided to write about him. In doing so, I answered many of those questions and stumbled across answers to others that it hadn't occurred to me to ask.

In a sense, Kiki Cuyler's biography is a storybook tale about a man whose determination and perseverance inevitably brought good things his way. Cuyler married his childhood sweetheart, joined the military service and toiled as a roof assembler in an auto plant. After Kiki seized the opportunity to play professional baseball, he worked hard to improve as a player while laboring in the minors for three-and-a-half years. When Cuyler was given a chance to show what he could do playing for Pittsburgh in 1924, he quickly rose to the status of an All-Star performer in the National League. His quick rise to stardom was interrupted during the 1927 season when disagreements with Pirates management forced him to the bench. But when it seemed that Cuyler was destined to be added to the list of players that burned brightly and then fizzled out, he resurrected his career in Chicago and continued to play baseball in a manner that eventually gained him entry into the Baseball Hall of Fame.

Kiki Cuyler was one of the greatest money players of his era: he was a man who did his best work in the clutch when National League pennants were on the line. From 1924 to 1934, when Cuyler played for Pittsburgh and Chicago, his teams won four National League pennants, finished in second place once and placed third six times. When Cuyler played for Joe McCarthy in Chicago, the Cubs' manager believed there was no more valuable team player in baseball. McCarthy also considered Kiki the smartest base runner he ever saw. Throughout his playing career, Cuyler was a favorite of baseball fans across America and is still considered an icon in his hometown of Harrisville, Michigan, today.

Every generation of baseball fans needs their heroes. Whether it's the player who hits a game-winning homer in the final contest of a World Series or a pitcher who tosses a no-hitter in a playoff game, there is always someone the fans want to designate as their latest conquering hero. For many rooters in Pittsburgh and Chicago during the 1920s and 1930s, Hazen "Kiki" Cuyler was that player.

1. Growing Up in Harrisville

Throughout baseball's illustrious history, the game has always grown in a way that parallels America's growth as a nation. As the United States prepared to enter the 20th century, immigrants from across the world made this land their permanent home. These post–Civil War settlers helped build this country with immeasurable effort in making it a better place for their children and grandchildren. America's melting pot was the vital fabric that made the nation special after we experienced one of the country's darkest hours during a war in which brothers opposed each other over what they believed was right.

Many of the men who played baseball in the late 19th century and early 20th century also came from a diverse melting pot. During the game's early days, it was filled with rough and tumble players like John McGraw, Cap Anson and Fred Clarke. Collegiate players like Christy Mathewson and Eddie Collins began coming on to the scene during the first decade of the 20th century. Youngsters who were farmers, laborers and teachers also played major league baseball, carving out a niche in their own unique way. Included in this melting pot were characters such as Rube Waddell, Rabbit Maranville and Bugs Raymond, who certainly did not believe in a doctrine of clean living and ordinary behavior. It was these types of dissimilar players that helped baseball grow during its infancy just as America achieved greatness due to the efforts of its unique citizenry.

In 1885, a young man named George Alonzo Cuyler emigrated from Canada to the United States. The 22-year-old took up residence at a small town in Michigan called Black River.[1] While living in Kincardine, Ontario, Cuyler excelled as an amateur athlete.[2]

He was born on October 6, 1863, to George Canning Cuyler and Margaret (Gauley) Cuyler. While George, Jr. was a toddler, his father died on March 12, 1866, at the age of 37.[3] Young George Cuyler was the fifth of six children and was one of four sons who eventually left Canada to search for fortune in the United States.[4] One of the sports in which Cuyler showed great proficiency was baseball, as he performed in a semi-professional league during his last few years in Canada.⁵ A strong, strapping young man of Dutch and Irish heritage, George had the physical make-up to continue his athletic endeavors in America if he so desired.⁶

As it turned out, it was not the game of baseball that motivated Cuyler to make the residency switch from Ontario to Michigan. Cuyler came to America so that he could achieve the dream of achieving great accomplishments on his own in a new country. The United States likely seemed new and intimidating to George, just as it had to his ancestors centuries earlier when they came from Europe to a new land. The original Cuylers had settled in New York over 350 years ago. When the Revolutionary War between England and the colonists began in the 1770s, some of George Cuyler's ancestors wanted to remain and fight, while others had no dispute with King George III. Those Cuylers who supported the actions of America's Founding Fathers assisted in the war effort. The other descendants who were not angry decided to make the move north into Canada.⁷

The Black River area of Alcona County in which George Cuyler decided to make his home was originally a fishing station. In 1849, William Cullings was the first person to settle in Black River after he purchased 40 acres of land from the United States government. Cullings was followed by Willie Roe, who built a cabin; he was a fisherman and trapper for many years before moving to Detroit. The lumbering industry quickly became prominent in 1868, when the Moore & Alger Company started logging in that area of the northern woods in Michigan's Lower Peninsula. This corporation was succeeded by R. A. Alger & Company in 1874. After some changes within the company's hierarchy in 1881, the lumber interest became known as Alger, Smith & Company. General R. A. Alger was named president of the company, and the capital stock was increased to $1.5 million that year. The company, whose central office was located in Detroit, owned 50,000 acres of timberland near Black River.⁸

A large number of the residents from Alcona County were either farmers, fishermen or lumber mill workers.⁹ George Cuyler, like many of his fellow Canadians who emigrated to this area of Michigan, showed an earnest interest in the lumber industry and accepted employment working for a company in Black River.¹⁰ It was while he lived there, toiling and sweating daily as a laborer in the Northern Michigan timber country, that Cuyler met a young lady who had also moved to the United States from Canada. Anna Rosalind Shirley was born in Perth, Ontario, on February 14, 1867.¹¹ After being liberally educated in Canada, Shirley came to the United States in 1888.¹² In 1889, she moved to live with her sister, Mrs. James Tovey, in Harrisville. After a few years, Shirley moved to Black River and became employed as a dress maker.¹³ It was here that she met George and quickly fell in love. On December 30, 1891, she and

George Cuyler were married in Au Sable, Michigan. Charles A. Winter, rector of the Roman Catholic Church, officiated the proceeding. Anna's parents and George's mother attended the wedding, as did witnesses John Nicholson and Martha Shirley.[14]

The two newlyweds continued to live in Black River for a few months until a phenomenal job opportunity dictated that the Cuylers make the move to a nearby locality. In the spring of 1892, George joined the Life Saving Service at Sturgeon Point under the guidance of Captain J.E. Henderson.[15] The Cuylers actually moved their house from Black River to a new location in nearby Sturgeon Point so that George could accept this appointment.[16] Cuyler joined forces with a group of men under Captain Henderson who were responsible for providing 24-hour rescue service for any ships that experienced distress. During that time period, Michigan counted on the waterways of the Great Lakes to bring commerce in and out of the state.[17]

Thousands of ships and steamers traveled the Great Lakes through this area during a time period when sufficient navigational tools were not yet available to warn crew members of dangerous situations. On many occasions, ships were not alerted to the coastline's hazardous reefs, rocks and shoals until they had encountered danger. Sturgeon Point's Lighthouse was built as a warning marker near a dangerous reef that extended a mile and a half out into Lake Huron at that location.[18] The lighthouse, which was situated five miles north of Harrisville, stood 70 feet, nine inches tall, and acted as a beacon of safety for vessels that traveled along Lake Huron.[19]

George Cuyler immediately began work as a dedicated member of this 1890s group, which was considered the Coast Guard of its day. During the fall of

George Alonzo Cuyler and Anna Rosalind Shirley were married on December 30, 1891, in Au Sable, Michigan (courtesy the *Alcona County Review*).

that same year, George and Anna Cuyler experienced another important moment. Anna gave birth to the Cuylers' first child on September 16, 1892. She was christened Edna May Cuyler.[20] Another momentous occasion for George and Anna occurred in 1895 when they both became naturalized citizens.[21] The Cuylers had taken a risk by uprooting their lives in Canada. Like many families in America near the end of the 19th century, their hard work reaped positive benefits with each day.

A second addition to the Cuyler family arrived when Anna gave birth to a baby boy in 1898; Hazen Shirley Cuyler was born on August 30, 1898, at Sturgeon Point.[22] As a means to show respect for both sides of the family, Hazen was christened with the middle name of Shirley, his mother's maiden name. With the birth of son Hazen, George now had a male heir to carry on the family name. Given George's interest in sports and his past experience as a baseball player in Canada, it seemed only logical that the youngest member of the Cuyler family would be exposed to athletic endeavors during his formative years.

During Hazen Cuyler's early childhood, George guided his son in the arena of athletics.[23] Of course, George Cuyler's tutelage was not isolated to teaching Hazen the finer points of athletic competition. Daughter Edna had absorbed her father's wisdom over the years, as he assisted in her athletic development as well. Since George Cuyler had been an accomplished semi-professional baseball player in Canada, he was able to instruct both of his children on the game's finer points at a time when it was rising in popularity throughout America. Hazen Cuyler's love for baseball emerged at a relatively young age, as he constantly joined the neighborhood children to play at Sturgeon Point's sandlot.[24] Cuyler enjoyed playing the game even though his two main interests as a boy remained fishing and swimming.[25]

In 1906, just as Hazen was starting to develop his skills as a baseball player, the Cuyler family uprooted itself from Sturgeon Point and moved to a town called Harrisville located five miles south.[26] The housing structure where the Cuylers lived was moved once again to a new neighborhood.[27] This change occurred because George Cuyler was forced to retire from Sturgeon Point's Life Saving Service due to a disability suffered while participating in a winter rescue.[28] Shortly after the family moved to Harrisville, George was elected to the office of Register of Deeds in Alcona County.[29]

Harrisville was a beautiful community that had been founded in 1854 by fishermen S.M. Holden and Crosier Davison. That year, they purchased the area's valuable pine lands and mill privileges and proceeded to build Alcona County's first small water mill. Holden supervised the mill's activities personally and Davison shut down his fishing business so that he could divert all of his investments into Harrisville's fertile timberland. Once they built up the business, Holden and Davison sold their interests in the mill to Harris & Sons from New York. This company consisted of Benjamin Harris and his sons, Levi and Henry of East Bloomfield, Ontario County, who complemented their father's business savvy as millwrights and carpenters.[30]

Harrisville quickly grew in size and stature. By 1883, the village had Methodist, Presbyterian and Catholic churches, with organized Sunday Schools attached to each. The main part of town also had six stores, two drug stores, two shoe shops, three hotels, one sawmill, one gristmill, one planing mill, three shingle mills, three blacksmith shops, one wagon and repair shop, one tin shop and two agricultural implement stores. Agricultural Hall, a two-story building at the north end of the village, was the property of the agricultural society and housed both the Glen Alger Rifle Association and the Harrisville Driving Park Association.[31] Harrisville was incorporated as a village in 1887 and listed a population of 852 people, according to the 1900 United States Census. Harrisville officially received designation as a city in 1905, three decades after it had been named as the county seat of Alcona County.[32]

George Cuyler quickly became a prominent member of Harrisville after being elected to public office in 1907. Cuyler was a staunch Republican who pledged allegiance to the principles of the party. George was also a loyal citizen who believed in serving the public. Cuyler was affiliated with the Knights of the Tented Maccabees and the Independent Order of Odd Fellows. George and wife Anna were also active members of Harrisville's Methodist Episcopal Church who worked intensely and fervently advancing their religious faith.[33] Despite his busy life, George Cuyler still found time to positively influence his children. Cuyler took great delight in assisting Edna and Hazen with their athletic activities.

When Hazen Cuyler was nine years old, he began to apply himself seriously to the game of baseball.[34] He played for various county league teams.[35] Hazen initially dreamed of being a major league pitcher, but this aspiration was trampled somewhat thanks to his older sister. During a game one year on the Fourth of July, Hazen was pitching for a team of young boys against a squad of girls that included Edna. Pitching well, Cuyler took the mound in the bottom of the ninth inning, his team holding a three-run lead. It was at this point that young Hazen hit the wall. The girl's team quickly loaded the bases. Edna stepped up to the plate and crushed one of Hazen's offerings over the fence for a game-winning grand slam. This course of events slightly damaged his determination to become a big league pitcher.[36]

This type of friendly competition did not diminish Hazen and Edna's healthy relationship. Their interests sometimes varied given that Edna was six years older. When Hazen was 10 years old, his sister left the family nest and embarked on a life of her own. On September 21, 1908, 16-year-old Edna Cuyler married 18-year-old Peter Medor, Jr., in Harrisville. The ceremony was officiated by Louis Bouchard of the Roman Catholic Church, while Howard Kell and Lena Medor stood by as witnesses.[37] Edna and Peter Medor started a life of their own in Iosco, located in Oscoda County, Michigan, as the groom gained employment as a blacksmith at a local power dam.[38]

With his sister now out on her own, young Hazen Cuyler continued to passionately pursue his interest in baseball. The final years of the 20th century's first decade represented good times for a baseball fan and aspiring player in Michigan. The Detroit Tigers won three consecutive American League pennants from 1907 to 1909. The fact that Detroit lost all three World Series, first against the Chicago Cubs in 1907 and 1908 and then versus Pittsburgh in 1909, did little to diminish the excitement that Michigan youngsters felt for the Tigers. The Tigers were an all-star aggregation made up of topflight players like Sam Crawford, George Mullin, Wild Bill Donovan and Donie Bush. This thriving Michigan metropolis was also the home to baseball's newest sensation, a youngster from Georgia named Ty Cobb, who hit the ball hard and ran the bases with abandon.

Hazen Cuyler's first big break as a baseball professional occurred when he was 14 years old. Despite the experience of allowing his sister to hit a game-winning home run, Cuyler received $5 to pitch in a game at the Alcona County Fair.[39] This led to Hazen receiving a more permanent stipend for playing baseball. While Cuyler was a member of the Harrisville High School team, he also played semi-professional baseball on Sundays and received $5 a day plus expenses. Hazen played left field professionally on the Sabbath and pitched for his high school squad when they competed in games.[40]

George Cuyler continued to assist Hazen advance his baseball career. Every night, George spent hours hitting fly balls to his son. On one occasion, the elder Cuyler suggested to his son that he change the type of shoes he wore. Up to that point, Hazen had always worn rubber sneakers when playing baseball. His father, possibly sensing that speed was one of his son's greatest assets, convinced Hazen that he would be even faster wearing spiked shoes. The younger Cuyler followed his father's advice and made spiked shoes a permanent part of his uniform.[41]

It was around this time that Hazen offered some sound advice to his father as well. In doing so, he also made the kind of promise that someone his age usually was not bold enough to do. Hazen was concerned for his father, a man who weighed over 200 pounds and smoked excessively. One day, Hazen approached his father and offered him a proposition. Hazen told the elder Cuyler that he promised he would never drink, smoke or chew tobacco if his father was willing to stop smoking. George Cuyler accepted these terms and shook hands on his promise with Hazen. Even though George was tempted, he never broke this pledge.⁴²

During his time at Harrisville High School, Hazen was both an excellent student and a phenomenal athlete. He was a four-sport performer who excelled in baseball, basketball, football and track. Cuyler was also a polite, quiet young man who showed respect to others, and a clean-cut youngster whose shyness tended to be one of his most endearing qualities.⁴³ When Cuyler completed his studies at Harrisville High School on May 30, 1917, he graduated as the valedictorian of a class that was comprised of five people.⁴⁴

After graduation, Cuyler took a job working as a timekeeper with the Consumers' Power Company, which was building a dam on the Au Sable River. In exchange for receiving the job, he played for the company baseball team.⁴⁵ Further proof of Hazen's diligence and sense of responsibility could be found in his decision to join the Army before reaching the age of draft eligibility. To do so, he needed to obtain parental consent. George and Anna gave their son permission to enlist in the Army shortly after he finished high school.⁴⁶

When Hazen Cuyler reported for permanent military duty, he was assigned to Company A of the Army's 48th Infantry Regiment.⁴⁷ This unit had been established by the military service only a few weeks prior to the time that Cuyler reported. During the summer of 1918, the 48th Infantry Unit was attached to the 20th Division, which was a regular Army division intended for service in World War I. Yet, this detachment never went overseas to Europe and was demobilized in February of 1919.⁴⁸ In the meantime, Cuyler rose to the rank of sergeant while he served with the 48th Infantry.⁴⁹ During the final stages of World War I, Hazen pursued a special course at West Point for enlisted men.⁵⁰ After devoting several months to diligent study, Cuyler was selected as part of a group of 50 soldiers to take a West Point examination. Hazen was one of only two men who actually passed the test.⁵¹

Cuyler did not stay at West Point for long after earning his appointment to the United States Military Academy. After about three months, he realized that he was not suited for military life on a permanent basis.⁵² Officials at the military academy tried to convince him to remain there after the war ended because of his speed and dexterity as a ball carrier on the football squad.⁵³

Cuyler seemed to be yearning and pining to return to his home in Michigan. There were two things that Hazen passionately missed while he spent time fulfilling his military obligation. The first was a woman by the name of Bertha Kelly, who was Hazen's sweetheart while the two attended Harrisville High School. The second consideration that drew Cuyler back to Michigan involved baseball.⁵⁴ He missed the game and now realized that his attraction to baseball was as powerful as any of his basic desires.

Shortly after Hazen Cuyler returned to Harrisville, the 20-year-old youngster quickly began to chart his own course. On January 8, 1919, Cuyler married Bertha M. Kelly during a ceremony in Harrisville. Born on December 20, 1897, Bertha was the daughter of Arthur Kelly and Clennie (Calumier) Kelly from Au Sable, Michigan.[55] Just as Hazen's parents, George and Anna Cuyler, were born in Canada, so too did Bertha's mother hail from America's northern neighbor.[56]

Hazen Cuyler, just as his father had done after his wedding years earlier, moved to a new city in order to find employment. The Cuylers moved to Flint, Michigan, so that Hazen could take a job working as an automobile roof assembler at the Buick Motors Plant. Unlike his father, Hazen decided to branch out much farther from his hometown; Flint was roughly 150 miles away from Harrisville.[57]

Besides performing his duties inside the plant, Cuyler also played semi-professional baseball and excelled for the Buick Big Red's basketball team.[58] Cuyler played as a guard for the company basketball team.[59] Hazen also earned some extra money playing professional football in the area.[60]

It did not take long for Cuyler to establish himself as one of the fastest and strongest players competing in industrial league games in Flint and Detroit.[61] Now 21 years of age, Cuyler possessed the body of a prototypical, chiseled athlete. He stood five feet, ten inches tall and weighed 180 pounds. Hazen batted right handed and threw right-handed while pitching or playing the outfield. Cuyler quickly became a league star as he posted sterling numbers as both a pitcher and hitter.[62] Hazen was particularly potent at the plate. A free-swinging batter who met the ball with resounding force, Hazen continued to torment opposing pitchers throughout the summer of 1919.

Hazen Cuyler continued to develop as a solid, proficient baseball player during his time in the Michigan Industrial League. Up to this point, Cuyler had not made a final decision as to whether baseball could become his permanent job. As a child, Cuyler had dreamed of playing major league baseball. Given his huge success playing at the industrial league level, Cuyler began to ponder the possibility of playing in the big leagues.

Taking a chance on baseball may not have been the wisest choice since the Cuyler family grew by one in the summer of 1919. Bertha gave birth to a boy on August 8, 1919; he was christened Harold S. Cuyler.[63] Now that Hazen Cuyler had more family responsibility, it did not seem prudent for him to pursue a career playing major league baseball. Perhaps he needed to continue his steady job at the Buick Plant in order to receive a guaranteed paycheck. In spite of this level-headed approach, tough economic times would soon dictate that Hazen Cuyler consider a life-changing decision.

2. From Humble Beginnings in Bay City to Stardom with Nashville

Hazen Cuyler continued to work diligently at the Buick Plant in Flint. He also pursued his cherished athletic endeavors by playing baseball and basketball for the company team in 1919. Since Cuyler was becoming accomplished as a baseball player, Hazen gravitated more toward this sport because he could earn extra money playing for semi-professional teams. He needed extra money because he was responsible for supporting both a wife and son. The additional cash was also crucial due to the fact that times were tough for families during this period in American history. In 1919, the United States had slipped into a recession, which morphed into a minor depression the following year.

Various businesses began to feel the sting of tough economic times late in 1919. The food and leather industries were the first to experience hardship, as companies saw a sharp decline in business between December of 1919 and February of 1920. More corporations felt the negative effects of the depression as the boots, shoes and clothing industries saw a decline in April, and woolens followed suit in June. After a brief period of stability, major industry was crippled as cotton manufacturers and wood manufacturers suffered a decline in August. This was followed by economic hits to those companies that dealt in iron and steel, papers, printing and book-making, and chemicals, causing further decline from October through December.[1]

The depression quickly affected Cuyler. The automobile industry was one of the first entities that felt the crunch of tough times, experiencing a sharp decline in productivity in April of 1920. From an employment standpoint, the automobile and woolen industries were hit the hardest by the harsh economic conditions. The situation was not quite as severe in the automobile assembly industry, where Cuyler worked, but business had declined to the point where many workers lost their jobs.² Cuyler did not lose his job as an auto roof assembler, but he saw his position at the plant reduced to part-time status. Hazen's hours dwindled to the point that he no longer earned enough money to support his family.³ His status as a star player on the company baseball team had not saved him from losing his full-time classification at the Buick Plant. Young Hazen decided that the time was right to find out about his ability and potential as a baseball player.

Cuyler was confident that he would be able to carve out a successful career in baseball. He had played the outfield and pitched, both in high school and while playing for the Buick team. Fears of playing professional baseball did not faze Hazen at all, largely because he had been successful playing the game since he was a child.⁴

Cuyler was able to find additional work when he joined Chevrolet and built automobile tops for the company. He also played on the factory's entry in the Industrial League and led the league in hitting.⁵ Following this positive experience, Cuyler did not venture far to begin the process of realizing his dream of professional baseball. He signed with Bay City of the Michigan-Ontario League in the summer of 1920.⁶ During salary negotiations, Cuyler asked for $50 a week. George H. Maines, president of the Michigan-Ontario League, handled the Cuyler signing personally for Bay City. Maines was a baseball fanatic who was interested in promoting the game at the sandlot level so that young boys would become interested in the national pastime. Maines took notice of the fact that Cuyler had also helped support his mother and father, along with his new family, while playing for the Buick Motor Company. Maines made sure that Cuyler received $225 a month playing for Bay City.⁷

The opportunity to play close to his home was something that would not have been possible if the Michigan-Ontario League had made changes that were rumored following the 1919 season. In January of 1920, the four clubs from Michigan that made up half of the eight-team league held a conference to determine whether they would continue to participate in the "Mint League" (as the Michigan-Ontario League was referred to) with their Canadian counterparts. The Michigan teams decided to renew their affiliation when representatives of the four clubs attended the annual league meeting on January 11. The outlook seemed brighter for these teams in 1920, as Saginaw made a small sum of money the previous season, Flint and Battle Creek broke even, and Bay City fulfilled all of its debt obligations. It was no secret that the league's Canadian franchises in London, Hamilton, Brantford and Kitchener had prospered financially in 1919.⁸

Cuyler's first season playing professional ball in Bay City could best be described as uneventful. Bay City manager Cal Wenger intended to use Cuyler as a pitcher, until he was badly spiked while sliding into second base. Wenger then shifted Cuyler to the outfield on a permanent basis.[9] Hazen showed flashes of brilliance as he appeared in 69 games and hit .258 for the Wolves. Even though the 1920 Mint League season brought a summer of growing pains for Cuyler, president George Maines saw enough potential in the youngster to start making sales pitches to major league ball clubs. Maines tried to sell Cuyler to the Detroit Tigers for $500, but Detroit president Frank J. Navin stated that he had no need for a rookie since the Tigers' outfield consisted of Ty Cobb, Harry Heilmann and Bobby Veach, with Heinie Manush and Bob "Fatty" Fothergill waiting in the wings.[10]

The Bay City Wolves' 1920 season was just about as inspiring as Cuyler's debut effort in Organized Baseball. They finished sixth in the Mint League race and drew just over 30,000 fans during the 1920 campaign.[11] The only two major events surrounding the team that received press coverage had nothing to do with player performance. The first incident involved a dispute between first baseman Charley Donnelly and umpire Bill Shuster during a game in June. After Donnelly took a swipe at the umpire, he was immediately arrested. Initially, it was reported that Donnelly had jumped bail and gone into hiding.[12] Even though this story was proven to be false since Donnelly never actually left Bay City, Shuster told reporters that Chicago detectives were pursuing the player.[13] Shuster also threatened to have Donnelly jailed for life once his investigators found him. Donnelly finally went on trial in July for assault. The judge sentenced him to 90 days in jail, but the punishment was suspended when Donnelly promised the judge that he would behave. Donnelly rejoined the Wolves and became a folk hero in Bay City.[14]

A second bizarre story surrounding a Bay City ballplayer surfaced in August when Albert Newman was found dead in Chicago. Newman played first base for the Wolves until he quit the team on August 16. In 1919, he had played for London and was secured by Bay City in a trade that sent catcher Joseph Briger to the Canadian city. Suffering a blow to the head, Newman died under mysterious circumstances in his hometown of Chicago. The police report stated that Newman was picked up by a taxicab driver at two o'clock in the morning, unconscious with a concussion to his brain. Newman was taken to a hospital, where he later died.[15]

Off-season baseball talk as it related to Bay City eventually shifted back to on-the-field concerns. The monetary gap between the Michigan and Ontario teams had widened even more during the Mint League's second season. Flint was the only Michigan city in which fans came out and gave their team the support it needed to remain viable. Owners from the teams that played in Ontario began talking about an all-Canadian Class-A League, while the Michigan squads were considering a move to the Central League.[16]

Despite all of the Mint League's uncertainty heading into 1921, Hazen Cuyler received good news in November when Bay City included the young outfielder on its reserve list for the upcoming season.[17] Cuyler's development as a player was also given a boost when the team announced in December that Cal Wenger would be back as Bay City's manager in 1921.[18]

League president George Maines wanted to institute some changes for the Mint League in 1921 in order to make it a more sustainable operation. Maines hoped to eliminate Battle Creek from the league so that Montreal could be added. He reasoned that the addition of a large city like Montreal would allow the Mint League to move up to Class-AA classification. By bumping his league up to this level, Maines would then be able to secure $5,000 for any player drafted from the Mint League.[19] But his hopes of having the league make the jump from Class-B to Class-AA were crushed by club directors who realized they would be unable to compete financially and logistically with a large city like Montreal. They also felt that Montreal's addition to the circuit would drive up travel costs for the other teams.[20] The only change that occurred before the start of the 1921 season involved Battle Creek shifting its franchise to Port Huron. With Canadian businessmen purchasing one-quarter of the capital in the Port Huron team, it was decided that the team would play some of its games in Sarnia, Ontario.[21]

Mint League officials made a crucial decision prior to the 1921 season with a goal of improving attendance figures. They had experimented with playing twilight baseball in 1920 and decided to do it once again in 1921. Most of the cities in the league were factory towns whose shops did not close until five o'clock. Since it was these men that Mint League owners relied upon to attend games, they scheduled the contests to begin an hour after the factories closed.[22]

Fans from all walks of life who attended games at the nine Mint League cities were treated to a show when the Bay City Wolves came to town. Hazen Cuyler showed himself to be the league's brightest rising star. Cuyler had a sensational season in 1921, as he firmly established his credentials as a legitimate major league prospect. Hazen appeared in 116 games for the Wolves, posting a solid .317 average. He scored 79 runs, while smacking 18 doubles, 16 triples, and eight home runs. He also recorded 82 RBIs and stole 32 bases. He totaled 271 putouts in center field and gunned down 13 opposing runners with his powerful arm.

It became obviously apparent to the Bay City club owners that they owned a true, big league prospect.[23] Shortly after Ty Cobb took control of the Detroit Tigers as manager for the 1921 season, Mint League president George Maines believed that he had sold Cuyler to the Georgia Peach for $1,000, but the deal was scuttled, as Detroit president Frank Navin rejected

2. From Humble Beginnings in Bay City to Stardom with Nashville

Cuyler's purchase by Cobb.[24] Despite the fact that Navin had refused to sanction a deal involving Cuyler, a Detroit scout was among those invited by Bay City's ownership to watch the young phenom during a summer doubleheader. Cuyler put on an impressive hitting display for various major league scouts as he hit a ball over the left field fence for the first and only time during his two seasons with Bay City. Cuyler also drove in most of the Wolves' runs in each game. In spite of this sensational performance, Detroit's scout remained skeptical because he believed that Cuyler could not hit a curve ball.[25]

This assessment of Hazen Cuyler's one shortcoming was accurate. Cuyler could not hit a curve ball because he had been instructed by his manager to stand near the front of the batter's box. Other teams also watched Cuyler. A scout for the St. Louis Cardinals observed Cuyler, but his grading of the Bay City star remained a mystery.[26] Frank Haller, a veteran scout for the Pittsburgh Pirates, was also in attendance for the special viewing of Cuyler.[27] Haller liked what he saw of Cuyler, both at the plate and in the outfield. He filed his scouting report and recommended to Pirates owner Barney Dreyfuss that the team purchase Cuyler.[28]

During the summer, Mint League officials decided to split the season into two phases, due to the fact that London was running away with the race. It was determined that the first half of the campaign would end on July 10.[29] Bay City benefitted immensely from this decision, as the team caught fire during the second half of the season. At a meeting in Detroit on August 14, the league decided to close the season on September 6, rather than two weeks later as originally planned. This was done on the recommendation of the league's Canadian clubs, who argued that attendance dropped dramatically after the first week of September.[30] When the dust finally settled during the final days of the season, Bay City swept a doubleheader against Saginaw on Labor Day and was crowned second-half champions.[31]

The thrill of securing a pennant brought exhilaration to Hazen Cuyler. However, this event paled in comparison to the news that Cuyler received at the end of August. On September 1, *The Sporting News* reported that the Bay City Club had sold outfielder Hazen Cuyler to the Pittsburgh Pirates.[32] Mint League president George Maines had finally moved his hottest piece of property to a major league team. It was reported that Barney Dreyfuss paid $2,500 to purchase Cuyler.[33]

The joy of finally realizing his dream of reaching the major leagues helped to ease the sting of Bay City's showing in the post-season series with London. Canada's top team claimed the Mint League championship by defeating Bay City in six games.[34]

Cuyler's signing by the Pirates received little fanfare in the city of Pittsburgh. Faithful rooters of the Smoky City squad were not informed of his purchase by *The Pittsburgh Press* until September 16. The Pittsburgh newspaper printed a list of players who had either been purchased or repurchased by Pirates management. At the bottom of the list was the name "Cuyler," with Bay City next to his name. Hazen was included in this directory of potential future National League stars, along with such names as Whitehill, Bates, Hughes, Wheeler, Blake, Gooch, Traynor, Stewart, Summa and Mokan.[35] Pittsburgh fans who had never heard of Hazen Cuyler were going to receive an opportunity to catch a glimpse of this young outfielder from Michigan. Pirates management requested that Cuyler join the squad for the last few weeks of the 1921 season.

The Pirates looked like the team to beat in the National League throughout the summer of 1921. On August 23, the Pirates held a seven and a half game lead over second-place New York. When the Pirates returned home from an Eastern swing in early September, their lead had been chopped down to a game and a half. During a doubleheader sweep by the St. Louis Cardinals at Forbes Field on September 1, fans razzed the Pirates players throughout the afternoon. At the root of the fans' disgust was the belief that many of the players did not seem to be adhering to their responsibilities as professionals. Tales of wild night parties and persistent disregard for training rules filtered throughout the city.[36] Some reports classified the Pittsburgh squad as the hardest drinking team in the National League. Such an atmosphere did not seem conducive for a young man like Hazen Cuyler, who did not drink or smoke.

By the time the New York Giants rolled into town for the first game of a crucial series on September 16, the Pirates had been overtaken by the defending National League champions. While the Pittsburgh players seemed to be more interested in amusement and merriment, the Giants took a businesslike approach. New York manager John McGraw took no chances with his players being distracted in the Smoky City. The New York club arranged to have special drinking water supplied to its players at Forbes Field. Giants management ordered its own bottles of water and demanded that they were still sealed upon delivery. McGraw also directed his players to avoid any association with Pittsburgh's fans or players. He kept the team sequestered during the morning and evening. The only time that Pittsburgh's inhabitants caught a glimpse of McGraw's team occurred when they appeared at Forbes Field.[37]

The Giants claimed victory in two of the three games and opened up a solid lead of three and a half games over the second-place Pirates with roughly two weeks left in the 1921 season. Pittsburgh's collapse was not sitting well with the fans, who believed the players had sacrificed a pennant for good times. One player who fell under the public's microscope was shortstop Walter "Rabbit" Maranville. Rabbit, in his first season as a Pirate after Barney Drey-

2. From Humble Beginnings in Bay City to Stardom with Nashville   19

fuss acquired him from the Boston Braves, was the player most often mentioned in connection with drinking and carousing.[38] As Pittsburgh's painful season played out in its final days, Pirate manager George Gibson addressed some of these rumors regarding his ballclub.

> Fans are liable to say anything when a team is losing. I want to state that I am not opposed to one of the players taking a glass of beer, but it is a positive fact that not one of the Pirates this entire season has appeared on the ball field when he was not in condition to give his best efforts to the team.
>
> While I do not lay claim to having a Sunday school team, I know that the Pirates take better care of themselves than 90 percent of all the ball clubs in the business.
>
> There have been a lot of stories floating around about Walter Maranville. Let me say that he has done more individually for the team than anybody imagines. It would be impossible to give him too much credit for his work.[39]

Pittsburgh's failure at maintaining a pennant-winning pace during the month of September worked to Hazen Cuyler's advantage as the team finished its schedule. Gibson finally gave the youngster from Michigan a chance in a game against St. Louis at Sportsman's Park on September 29. Gibson penciled Cuyler into the clean-up spot as his starting right fielder against Cardinals southpaw Bill Sherdel. During his first major league at-bat in the second inning, Cuyler could muster nothing better than a popup to catcher Verne Clemons in foul territory. In the fourth inning, Hazen struck out with one out and Max Carey on second base. During his final at-bat in the sixth inning, Cuyler's speed worked to his benefit as he reached first base on St. Louis third baseman Milt Stock's error.

The Pirates were officially eliminated from pennant contention when they dropped this shortened game to St. Louis by a score of 3–1. Sherdel reduced the once brutal attack of the Pirates to rubble as he mixed in an array of slow balls, crossfire slants and fastballs. Pittsburgh's players had just finished taking their turn at bat in the sixth inning when umpire Bill Klem decided to call the game. Klem determined the contest had to be stopped since darkness was descending upon the field, making it difficult to follow the flight of the baseball from the grandstand. St. Louis' players quickly went to their locker room, but the Pirates remained on the field. They stood there with dazed looks for a few minutes before hustling off to the showers in small groups.[40] The scene had to be a bit puzzling to young Hazen Cuyler, who had not been with the team long enough to experience the humiliation of being called "quitters" by Pittsburgh's fans.

Cuyler's first experience playing in a major league game did not transpire quite as he dreamed it would. Young boys who dedicated themselves to becoming professional base players usually envisioned producing a hit during their first trip to the plate, or even hitting a home run. Hazen Cuyler's dreams probably did not include popping out to the catcher and striking out in his first two major league at-bats. Yet, Hazen realized that this game was only the first step of a long journey to establish himself in the National League. Cuyler heartily believed he possessed the ability to achieve this goal. The next step in this huge learning process would be to experience training camp with a major league club for the first time in the spring of 1922.

Under the guidance of manager George Gibson, the Pirates divided their spring training work at two camps. The initial work was done in West Baden, Indiana, while the crucial preparation for the upcoming season occurred at Hot Springs, Arkansas. The Pirates had trained at these two sites for many years since the team's glory days in the early 1900s, when Fred Clarke won four National League pennants. On the first day of training at West Baden in early March, Gibson split his squad into two groups. The first unit consisted of veteran players who were given an opportunity to get in their normal work. After the veterans' light workout was completed, Gibson devoted a significant portion of the day working with a group of recruits that included Hazen Cuyler. Gibson hoped to give these youngsters constant tutelage even after the team moved on to Hot Springs.[41]

Pittsburgh's veteran players made sure this group of rookies received the proper rights of initiation that had been part of spring training for many years. All of the newcomers were introduced to a specially wired bench in the atrium at the team's hotel. Once a rookie was firmly seated on the bench, a button was pushed that sent enough electric current through the seat to make the young man jump to his feet. The veteran players also planned on choosing a man from this group of rookies to act as a referee for a badger fight that was scheduled for the first night of spring training.[42]

These initial workouts at West Baden gave Gibson's men a chance to work out their winter kinks and begin executing basic baseball fundamentals. Once the team reached Hot Springs for the second round of training, players were expected to perform under actual game conditions. Cuyler was placed with a group of players called the "Yanigans." This unit was made up mainly of rookie players who were not expected to make the squad as regulars. In the first game of the spring on March 15, the Yanigans defeated the "Regulars" by a score of 15–4. Hazen Cuyler went 1-for-5 in the game as he batted fourth and played center field for the Yanigans. Cuyler was praised, along with Pie Traynor, Carson Bigbee and Walter Mueller for making several nifty plays in the field during the game.[43]

Cuyler continued to put on a show for Pittsburgh management a few days later when he made a sensational catch in a 12–10 loss against the veteran players. In the third inning, Hazen denied Ray Rohwer's home run bid when he leaned over a slight precipice in the deepest part of the ballpark and tumbled down an embankment to the woods below, with the ball nestled in his glove. When Cuyler reached the bottom of the ravine, he heaved a perfect toss back to the infield even though he was unable to see the diamond. Cuyler also sizzled at the plate as he went 3-for-3, scored two runs, smacked a home run and stole a base.[44]

The Yanigans gained revenge against their veteran counterparts on March 21, defeating the Regulars by a score of 14 to 5. As had been the custom at Pirates training camp for years, owner Barney Dreyfuss handed out cigars to the Yanigan players whenever they secured victory over the veteran players.[45] Even though he did not smoke, Cuyler appreciated the trophy since it was a reward for a job well done.

One day after the Yanigans' crushing victory over the Regulars, manager Carlton Molesworth of the Southern Association's Birmingham club was on hand to look over some of the Pittsburgh prospects. During the past few years, Molesworth helped develop recruits such as Pie Traynor, Johnny Morrison, Johnny Gooch and Clyde Barnhart, who were touted as future baseball stars. Cuyler hoped to receive one year of schooling under Molesworth, so that his ascent to regular duty in the National League could be realized in rapid fashion.[46]

Hazen Cuyler continued to do everything in his power to prove that he was a valuable prospect. During an intra-squad game at Hot Springs, Cuyler made another spectacular catch over the embankment in center field and disappeared from sight, with the sphere tightly held in his glove.[47] During his first major league training camp, Hazen showed Pittsburgh management that he played the game of baseball with a level of effort not always shown by rookie players. Cuyler took lusty cuts at the plate and played the outfield with abandon as he leapt to catch drives that seemed destined to be hits. But Cuyler's stellar play was not enough to impress Molesworth, who left the Pirates' camp without grabbing the former Bay City player for his Birmingham squad.

Newspaper correspondents who covered Pittsburgh's training trip gave glowing reports about the play of outfielders Walter Mueller and Hazen Cuyler. They were labeled as good outfield prospects who needed only a little more seasoning.[48] After the Pirates finished their exhibition tour, with the main squad traveling to St. Louis to play the season opener on April 12, Cuyler and six other youngsters headed back to Pittsburgh. These seven players went through workouts at Forbes Field under the guidance of scouts Bill Hinchman and Chick Fraser.[49] Cuyler's presence with this group in Pittsburgh rather than with the veterans in St. Louis indicated that Pittsburgh's management wanted to place him with a minor league team.

George Gibson decided to give youngsters Johnny Mokan and Mueller the first opportunity to replace departed right fielder George "Possum" Whitted. After being entrenched in Barney Dreyfuss' doghouse, the Pittsburgh outfielder was sold to Brooklyn on March 14, 1922. Dreyfuss believed Whitted was the main troublemaker on Pittsburgh's squad in 1921. During the first week of the new season, Whitted ripped Dreyfuss in an interview with a Philadelphia reporter. Whitted claimed he had been demoted by being sold to Brooklyn. Dreyfuss wasted no time responding to this allegation, claiming that Whitted was treated fairly when he played in Pittsburgh.[50]

> We had some trouble on our team at a certain stage of the 1921 season because all our rules were not lived up to. I have never discussed that matter fully, because I did not care to show up any of the men who failed to do right.
> However, Whitted was the ringleader of that gang. One notable incident occurred while we were playing in New York. Whitted took several other members of the team with him on a gay expedition. That settled him with me. We were in the thick of the pennant fight at the time, and I was naturally angered when I heard the details.
> I made up my mind then that Whitted was through as a Pirate, and I got rid of him at the first opportunity. I do not want to go into details, for there are certain men still on our roster who are mixed up in that defiance of the rules.
> They will remain with us as long as they do what is right, but the moment there is a break on their part, they will be dealt with as they deserve.[51]

The day after Dreyfuss' sharp reprimand, the Pirates made a few moves aimed at reducing the size of their roster. Infielder Suffy Stewart was returned to Birmingham under option.[52] Catcher Mike Wilson was released outright after Pittsburgh management failed to place him with a minor league team. Pitcher Fred Blake was sent to Rochester of the International League while Hazen Cuyler was shipped to Charleston of the Sally League. Blake and Cuyler were both under option agreements, with the likelihood of returning to Pittsburgh in the fall.[53]

Cuyler quickly left Pittsburgh and hustled off to join his new team, which was playing in Augusta, Georgia. Hazen arrived in time for Charleston manager Jimmy Hamilton to insert the outfielder into his lineup for the game on April 24. Cuyler wasted little time doing damage as he collected a triple, double and single in the Charleston Pals' 5–4 win over Augusta in ten innings.[54] Because of Cuyler's late arrival, he did not have a current uniform to wear. The Michigan youngster played the game in an old style jersey that nearly ripped to shreds when he slid into third base after his triple. Cuyler's fifth-inning triple drove home two runs and knotted the score at 3–3. The following day, a Charleston newspaper marveled at Hazen Cuyler's hitting prowess and described him as playing a superb game in center field.[55]

When Cuyler finally received a chance to play before the hometown fans at Charleston, his name had become commonplace in the city. In a relatively short period of time, fans began flocking to games and paid the price of admission just to watch him hit.⁵⁶ The season soon became a rollercoaster for Hazen filled with both great performances and hitless days. On May 8, Cuyler banged out four hits and smacked three triples in a loss against Columbia. He went 3-for-4 with two doubles in a 7–6 loss to Greenville on June 10. Hazen smacked a home run and went 3-for-4 in a victory over Columbia on June 30. Cuyler emerged as the galvanizing force behind Charleston's successful season, with manager Jimmy Hamilton's team well out in front of the South Atlantic League race by the middle of June.⁵⁷

While Cuyler was helping his team to a Sally League pennant, big changes were happening in Pittsburgh. Manager George Gibson tendered his resignation at the end of June and was replaced by coach Bill McKechnie. Many observers in Pittsburgh believed that Gibson walked away after a firestorm of criticism was levied against him concerning the conduct of his players. It was no secret that members of the team had been breaking team rules since the previous year. The players took advantage of an easygoing manager. When Gibson finally tried to restore some semblance of discipline, the situation had fallen out of control.⁵⁸

Back in Charleston, Hazen Cuyler continued to belt baseballs. In a doubleheader against Charlotte on July 29, Cuyler recorded multiple hits in both games, homering in the first contest and blasting a double in the nightcap. Hazen followed this performance by going 2-for-5 against Columbia on August 2. On August 21, he went 3-for-4 with a double in a 5–0 victory over Columbia. Hazen continued his onslaught the following day, when he went 4-for-5. The youngster twice hit a home run in the second game of a doubleheader in late August. It happened the first time on August 23 during a 10–3 win over Columbia and was followed by a repeat performance during a 4–3 victory against Charlotte on August 29.

Hazen Cuyler enjoyed a solid season in 1922 as Charleston claimed the South Atlantic League pennant. He batted .309, scored 84 runs and stole 35 bases. Cuyler also showed good power numbers as he smacked 29 doubles, 15 triples and 12 home runs. Cuyler ended up with only 46 RBIs due to manager Hamilton hitting him anywhere from first to seventh in the batting order.

After claiming the Sally League pennant, it was determined that Charleston would face the Wilson, North Carolina, entry of the Virginia League to decide superiority among the Southern League teams. Charleston claimed the best-of-seven series by winning the championship, four games to two. Cuyler starred throughout the series for Charleston. In the first game, his home run over the left field wall helped secure a 4–3 victory in 13 innings. One of the longest drives ever hit at the Wilson ballpark, it left the fans amazed and gasping for breath.⁵⁹

Cuyler displays the batting stance that helped contribute to his great season for Charleston in 1922. He hit .309 in 131 games as the Pals won the Sally League pennant (courtesy the *Alcona County Review*).

Cuyler deeply appreciated the support the fans of Charleston gave him in 1922. When Hazen first arrived in the South Carolina city, he was a shy stranger who did not know anybody. The locals quickly went out of their way to make him feel welcome. The family of Dr. Melchers of Rose Garden Pharmacy was particularly kind to the young man from Michigan.[60]

Cuyler was not afforded much time to join in celebration with the fans after the Pals claimed victory over Wilson. He was ordered to report immediately to Pittsburgh. Cuyler, along with Charleston teammate Claude Rowher and catcher Firman Warwick, joined the Pirates in Philadelphia on September 17.[61] With Pittsburgh still in the hunt to secure second place in the National League behind the pennant-winning Giants, manager Bill McKechnie was reluctant to use youngsters like Cuyler in a game.[62] Cuyler saw his only action during a loss in Brooklyn on September 23, when he pinch ran for Johnny Gooch in the ninth inning. After the game, Cuyler was among a group of six young players sent back to Pittsburgh until second place money had been won or lost.[63]

The Pirates ended up finishing third in the National

2. From Humble Beginnings in Bay City to Stardom with Nashville   25

League standings, eight games behind the pennant-winning Giants. The right field position, which had been manned by Mokan and Mueller early in the season, was a problem for Pittsburgh until McKechnie arrived as the team's skipper. Former Chicago White Sox pitcher Ewell "Reb" Russell joined the Pirates in July after McKechnie purchased him from Minneapolis. Russell enjoyed a phenomenal year at the plate in 1922, as he hit .368, smacked 12 home runs and drove home 75 runs while appearing in only 60 games. Despite the fact that Russell had shown he was capable of being a middle-of-the-order thumper, McKechnie still planned on platooning the left-handed batter with another player in 1923. Before the Pirates left for spring training, a Pittsburgh newspaper claimed that Clyde Barnhart, Walter Mueller, Art Jahn and Hazen Cuyler would compete to share time with Russell in right field.[64]

Barnhart was considered a solid hitter whose defensive work in the outfield was poor. Mueller had missed time during the 1922 season due to a dislocated vertebrae in his neck, and was considered a fine batsman and a good outfielder who was only fair on the basepaths. From a fielding standpoint Cuyler definitely had an advantage over these two men. Hazen had served notice during his first training camp in 1921 that he was very fast and as polished a fielder as some of his veteran counterparts. The only concern on the minds of Pittsburgh's management team was whether Cuyler could hit consistently.[65]

Cuyler received a wonderful opportunity during the Pirates' 1923 spring training trip to Hot Springs when veterans Max Carey and Carson Bigbee missed time due to injuries. Carey pulled up lame in the first game of a special exhibition series against the Boston Red Sox. Bigbee displaced a muscle during the Pirates' first workout, resulting in him suffering severe headaches.[66] Cuyler received a chance to play with Pittsburgh's regular players in one of the Boston games when he replaced Walter Mueller, who had pulled up lame.[67] Hazen finished the game by going 0-for-1, scoring a run and striking out in the eighth inning.[68] Cuyler started the next game in left field as Pittsburgh defeated Boston, 12–11. Hazen went 3-for-5 at the plate, stroking three doubles. He also made a phenomenal catch that brought the 2,500 Hot Springs spectators to their feet. As Cuyler came running in for a short drive to left, he slipped on the wet grass and fell to the ground. He never panicked, instead keeping his eye on the ball while sitting on the turf and making the catch.[69]

Cuyler continued his blistering hitting in a loss against Boston the following day. He rapped out three singles, but nearly killed one of his teammates. In the ninth inning, Rabbit Maranville was knocked unconscious running from second to third when a drive from Cuyler's bat struck the diminutive shortstop.[70] A week later on April 1, Cuyler continued tormenting Red Sox pitchers during a 10–9 Pittsburgh loss. Once again, Hazen showed his power by pounding a double and a home run.

When the Pirates finally broke camp at Hot Springs and began their exhibition tour by moving northward for the season opener in Chicago on April 17, Cuyler was one of the 25 players that manager Bill McKechnie took with him. This meant that the battle for the two outfield utility roles still involved Cuyler, Barnhart and Mueller.[71]

When the Pirates arrived in Nashville for a game against the Southern Association team, McKechnie decided to turn over three players to manager Jimmy Hamilton.[72] Pitcher John Wright, infielder Ralph Michaels and Hazen Cuyler were farmed out to Nashville for the 1923 season.[73] Cuyler's demotion to the minors meant that McKechnie had decided to retain Barnhart and Mueller as extra outfielders. The move surprised many observers who believed Cuyler had shown enough during training camp to remain with the Pittsburgh club. McKechnie did not agree, deciding that another year as a starting outfielder in a quality minor league would be beneficial. Yet, all three of these demoted players could be recalled to Pittsburgh whenever they were needed.[74]

Cuyler received the chance to play under Jimmy Hamilton for a second consecutive season. After Charleston won its playoff series against Wilson in 1921, Hamilton became so disgusted with the lack of support given his team by the fans that he decided not to return to the South Carolina city for another season.[75] Hamilton signed on with Nashville and did not waste time grabbing Cuyler when the opportunity presented itself. Hazen immediately treated Southern Association pitchers with contempt as he went 4-for-5 with a triple and a homer during a 19–8 loss against Birmingham on April 21. Hazen followed this up with a strong performance a few days later when he went 3-for-5 as Nashville fell to Memphis on April 26, 19–18.

Nashville's newest young star immediately became a favorite of the local fans. In late May, team owners decided to add temporary seating in order to handle the overflow crowds attending games. During one ten-game stretch, the Volunteers drew 35,000 fans. If Jimmy Hamilton could keep his team going at such a strong pace, it seemed likely that Nashville attendance would reach over 200,000 in 1923.[76] Cuyler continued to do his part to bring the fans into the ballpark. On May 29, Cuyler went 3-for-4 with a home run in a 10–6 victory over New Orleans. He followed this up by going 3-for-5 with a double as Nashville defeated Chattanooga, 17–4, on June 1. On June 3, Cuyler went 2-for-4 with a triple in Nashville's win over the Lookouts, this time by a score of 5–4. The Volunteers' star outfielder completed his personal vendetta against Chattanooga on June 5 by going 2-for-3 during a 12–2 win.

During the middle of June Cuyler did fall into a minor batting slump that forced manager Hamilton to drop him to sixth in the batting order. Hazen quickly shook off these batting doldrums and was once again hitting third by June 18, as he recorded five multiple-hit games during the final weeks of the month. Cuyler went 5-for-5 during a 15–1 victory over Little Rock on July 1 and continued to hit robustly for Nashville throughout the summer. When official batting averages were posted on August 2, Cuyler was batting .319, had scored 83 runs, stolen 42 bases and accounted for 208 total bases. By August 23, Cuyler's average had jumped to .330, as he now had 289 total bases and 55 steals.

Nashville's star player had become a base stealing demon by using a technique that would likely be ridiculed in baseball today. Whenever Cuyler reached first base after ripping a single or drawing a walk, he always took an enormously long lead off the bag. He stood with his back toward second as he faced the first baseman. Cuyler, who was able to watch the pitcher out of the corner of his eye, seemed to glide effortlessly when he made his move to steal second. Cuyler's speed also helped him become one of the most accomplished outfielders in the Southern Association. At the crack of the bat, Hazen was able to turn his back as the ball flew to the outfield and run with extraordinary speed while maintaining graceful form in his pursuit. At the final moment, when the ball was within his reach, Hazen then turned and efficiently grabbed the ball with his glove.[77]

Cuyler's outfield prowess had a hand in the young star acquiring a nickname that stuck with him throughout his career. When Cuyler was a youngster growing up at Sturgeon Point and Harrisville, his friends used to call him "Cuy."[78] After Cuyler began his professional career in 1920 at Bay City, catcher Benny Stumpf also began to refer to him as Cuy. Area newspapers shortened the moniker to "Ki."[79] Shortly after Hazen began playing for Nashville in 1923, the team's second baseman and shortstop started yelling Cuy in unison when they wanted the outfielder to grab a fly ball. Nashville newspapers and fans quickly grasped the repeated references to Cuy during games. Nashville's faithful rooters soon began referring to Cuyler as Kiki.[80]

Hazen "Kiki" Cuyler had a dream season playing for the Volunteers in 1923. Major league scouts who watched Southern Association games proclaimed him the best ballplayer in Dixieland. Since he was property of the Pirates, these scouts could only lower their heads in disappointment as they quietly coveted the untouchable star outfielder.[81] Cuyler had a spectacular season for the sixth-place Volunteers in 1923 as he hit .340 while appearing in 149 games. He hit 39 doubles, 17 triples, and nine home runs while scoring 114 runs. He led the Southern Association in runs, stolen bases and doubles.[82] His speed accounted for 63 steals and his powerful arm allowed him to throw out 35 baserunners from the outfield. He also accumulated 285 total bases.[83]

Cuyler was named the Most Valuable Player of the Southern Association and earned a special trophy that was presented by Commissioner Kenesaw Mountain Landis.[84] Landis also honored the Southern Association's best player by presenting him with a Gardner automobile.[85] Though Cuyler appreciated receiving an automobile as a reward for his great 1923 season, he was not prepared to rest on his laurels. He feverishly anticipated his next opportunity to show Pittsburgh management what he was capable of achieving at the major league level.

Hazen Cuyler played his last game for Nashville on September 18. Five days prior to this game, it was reported that Cuyler and other recruits like Everett Barnes, Delmar Lundgren, Ralph Michaels, Dudley Foulk and Jackson Matthews were recalled by the Pirates.[86] Pittsburgh was basically out of the running for the National League pennant as the Giants seemed poised to capture their third straight championship. Manager Bill McKechnie sought a jump on the 1924 season by looking over some of the organization's younger players. McKechnie's outfield was so decimated by injuries that he wanted

Cuyler stands next to the automobile that was presented to him in 1923 by Commissioner Kenesaw Mountain Landis for being named the Southern Association's Most Valuable Player (courtesy the *Alcona County Review*).

Cuyler to replace one of the ailing veterans once he arrived from Nashville. The manner in which Cuyler conducted himself during this trial was expected to influence his placement on the outfield depth chart prior to spring training.[87] The time had finally come for Kiki Cuyler to prove to Pittsburgh management that he was ready to play in the National League.

3. The Greatest Rookie Class in Baseball History

Pirate fans who had read glowing spring training reports about Hazen Cuyler in Pittsburgh newspapers for the past two years would now see this youngster in live action. Rooters throughout the city wanted to draw their own conclusions about the ability of this hazel-eyed, curly-haired outfielder from Nashville. Cuyler wired Pittsburgh management that he hoped to arrive in Pittsburgh on September 19.[1] If Cuyler made it in time for the game against Boston that afternoon, manager Bill McKechnie planned on starting him in left field.[2] As nighttime descended upon the Smoky City's inhabitants, Cuyler had still not arrived in Pittsburgh. There was no reason given for this delay as new reports indicated that Cuyler would arrive in Pittsburgh the following morning.[3] He finally reached the city on September 20 and reported to McKechnie that afternoon.[4]

Excited fans who had followed Cuyler's stellar work at Nashville throughout the 1923 Southern Association season were able to watch him for the first time at Forbes Field on September 21.[5] Cuyler started in left field in both games of a doubleheader sweep by the New York Giants. Hazen had a tough day at the plate during his Forbes Field debut, as he went 0-for-3 with a walk and a strikeout in the first game. He followed that up by going 0-for-4 in the nightcap. Hazen's performance in the field proved difficult as well. In the second inning of the first game, Emil "Irish" Meusel made it to third with a triple after Cuyler misjudged a fly ball. On another occasion, the young outfielder dropped a wicked liner after he had made a mad dash to reach the ball.[6]

Some of Cuyler's poor performance could be attributed to nerves and fatigue due to the long trip to the Smoky City. Cuyler's performance in the outfield was also likely the result of unfamiliarity with playing left field after spending the whole season as Nashville's center fielder.

Cuyler showed better form for the Pirates during their 4–3 defeat at

New York's hands on September 22. He made a spectacular catch after Frankie Frisch drilled a liner that seemed destined to fall safely in left field. At the plate, Cuyler recorded his first major league hit when he blasted a triple to the right-field screen. He also displayed his competitive zeal by sticking out his spikes as he tore into third base. Heinie Groh, who attempted to block the bag as Cuyler slid into it, barely escaped before receiving potential spike wounds to both of his legs.[7] Pittsburgh rooters who were enthusiastic over Cuyler's potential quickly realized one thing after watching him play three games: Hazen possessed the kind of game-breaking speed that could alter the outcomes of games.

Cuyler was not the only recruit that Bill McKechnie used during the final days of the 1923 season. Eddie Moore, a young shortstop from Atlanta who played against Hazen in the Southern Association, was given the opportunity to replace Rabbit Maranville. In an 18–5 victory over the Philadelphia Phillies at Forbes Field on September 25, Moore went 3-for-4 and scored five runs. In the field, Moore looked like he had been playing shortstop in the majors for years, but was charged with an error when second baseman Johnny Rawlings was unable to handle a throw from the youngster. Newspaper scribes in the press box who believed that Rawlings normally would have handled such a toss with ease felt that Moore's play at shortstop was a little too fast for the veteran second baseman.[8]

Cuyler continued to play in left field as Pittsburgh's season wound down. In the ninth inning of a game against Philadelphia on September 26, Cuyler made a great catch that helped preserve Johnny Morrison's shutout. The Nashville phenom ran toward the fence and hauled in Curt Walker's prodigious blast.[9]

Cuyler finished up his short trial at the end of the 1923 season on a strong note. On October 6, he went 2-for-4 and scored a run as Pittsburgh defeated the Cincinnati Reds, 7-to-1. Cuyler was then afforded the opportunity to start in center field for the Pirates in the season finale on October 7. Hazen went 1-for-4 and stroked a double as Johnny Morrison secured his 25th victory in a win over Cincinnati, 7–5.

Cuyler had appeared in 11 games for Pittsburgh during the season's final weeks and hit a respectable .250. This was not a bad showing considering his rough start in the first two games against New York.

The Giants claimed their third consecutive National League pennant in 1923 as Pittsburgh finished in third place, eight and a half games behind the league leaders. Once again, many players on Pittsburgh's roster persisted in displaying complete disregard for team rules. Rabbit Maranville's unsavory off-field activities continued to infuriate owner Barney Dreyfuss. Other players followed the diminutive shortstop's lead by failing to keep themselves in condition throughout the season. Star pitcher Johnny Morrison was another player who circumvented team rules on many occasions. Prior to a crucial series against New York in July, Morrison boasted of his pitching ability while drinking heavily in a Pittsburgh saloon. The intoxicated hurler claimed he would vanquish the Giants in a few days and offered to make wagers on the outcome of the game he was scheduled to pitch. Two days later, the Giants hammered the Pirates as Morrison was banished to the showers in the third inning.[10]

Players like Maranville and Morrison who had disregarded discipline were slowing falling into the minority category, as Bill McKechnie and Barney Dreyfuss continued to rebuild the Pirates with an infusion of youth. Harold "Pie" Traynor, Johnny Gooch and Clyde Barnhart had been added during the past few seasons. Additional players like Hazen Cuyler and Eddie Moore were expected to take part in this rebirth as Pittsburgh management made further moves to strengthen the roster. Pittsburgh's pitching staff received a major boost for the 1924 season when McKechnie and Dreyfuss purchased two top-notch minor league hurlers. Young southpaw Emil Yde came from Oklahoma City of the Western Association on December 1, 1923. Prior to Yde's acquisition, McKechnie procured veteran Pacific Coast leaguer Ray Kremer from Oakland.

Dreyfuss and McKechnie passed up attending the Subway World Series in New York so that they could catch a glimpse of their hottest prospect, who was playing in the Junior World Series. Shortstop Glenn Wright and the Kansas City Blues of the American Association played the Baltimore Orioles of the International League. Pittsburgh's management team was there to watch Wright, for whom the local club recently paid Kansas City ownership $40,000 to secure his services.[11] Wright was rated as the best player in the minors by most major league baseball scouts. Nearly every team in both the National and American leagues showed interest in adding Wright to their club. Pittsburgh held a huge advantage over these teams because Dreyfuss had a

Glenn Wright was the most prominent member of a group of 1924 Pirates rookies that included Hazen Cuyler, Eddie Moore, Ray Kremer and Emil Yde (courtesy the National Baseball Hall of Fame Library, Cooperstown, New York).

good relationship with Kansas City president George Muehlebach. When the Blues were in need of players, Dreyfuss was able to offer assistance by assigning recruits to that squad on three occasions.[12] Former Philadelphia Phillies outfielder Sherwood Magee, now a member of the American Association's Milwaukee team, gave Wright his personal stamp of approval.[13]

"There is no doubt that Pittsburgh got the best infielder in our circuit in Wright," said Magee. "You remember Mike Doolin of the Phillies, don't you? Well, Wright is a second edition of Mickey when it comes to throwing from any angle, but he is a much better heaver than was Mike, and there are other things that he can do better. He is quite a hitter. I don't think Bill McKechnie will have to look any further for a shortstop. Glenn will fill the bill."[14]

Every writer who covered American Association games believed Glenn Wright would do wonderful things for the Pirates. Former Pirate great Fred Clarke was a big booster of Eddie Moore; he felt the young infielder was destined to flourish once he was given an opportunity to perform on a daily basis.[15] Pittsburgh manager Bill McKechnie was confident that pitcher Ray Kremer possessed enough quality stuff to become a star in the National League. McKechnie held this opinion in spite of the fact that some within the organization felt Kremer looked like he was 50 years old rather than his actual age of 30.[16] In contrast, as Pittsburgh's players prepared to embark for spring training prior to the start of the 1924 season, it was obvious to Smoky City inhabitants that local fans were Hazen Cuyler's biggest boosters.

Pittsburgh's squad was heading to a new destination for their spring training work in 1924. After spending countless years preparing for their pennant campaigns in Hot Springs, the Pirates switched to Paso Robles, California. In February, the players journeyed aboard a Santa Fe railroad flyer called "Navajo" toward their destination on the Pacific Coast. When the train arrived in Chicago after leaving Pittsburgh, six members of the Pirates' entourage joined those members who had boarded the flyer in the Smoky City. Johnny Morrison, Emil Yde, Johnny Gooch, scout Bill Hinchman, and Hazen Cuyler were part of this group that joined the Pirates in Chicago as they continued on their journey to California.[17] For Cuyler, this was not his first trip to the West Coast. During the winter following his first season playing for Bay City in 1920, Cuyler had traveled west to play for a team in the California Winter League. Hazen appeared in only one game for the Pacific Redi-Cuts during the league's short season and went 1-for-4 at the plate.[18]

Those who followed the Pirates believed that Cuyler was poised to make a strong bid for a berth on the team.[19] Cuyler, who would be participating in his third spring session with the major league club, was focused on the task at hand. He had been with the Pirates before, but it now seemed that his development reached the stage where permanent employment in the National League was guaranteed. Cuyler had played superbly for Nashville in 1923. His friends were confident that this prodigy from Michigan would receive his big chance in 1924 and make fans throughout the country take notice.[20]

The release of former Pirates starting outfielder Reb Russell to the minor leagues resulted in an opening on Pittsburgh's roster. Hazen Cuyler quickly showed that he had every intention of claiming that spot. On March 7, McKechnie batted Cuyler in the leadoff spot for the Regulars against the Yanigans during a 5–3 loss. He also held down that spot in the batting order when the Yanigans prevailed again the following day by a score of 5–4. Spring training was taking on a new perspective for Cuyler as he continued to play for the Regulars. In years past, Hazen tried to do everything in his power to open the eyes of Pirate management by making unbelievable plays. Cuyler took a more businesslike approach to preparing for the season during the 1924 training session. Cuyler, confident that he would be on the opening day roster, wanted to be ready to contribute once the regular season began.

At times, Cuyler also performed for the Yanigans in order to receive more work during practice sessions. During one game on March 19, Cuyler delivered the phenomenal feat of blasting a home run that skipped over the left field fence on one bounce. The drive, which was estimated to have traveled about 404 feet, occurred while two teammates were on base and accounted for the Yanigans' only runs of the day.[21] Hard hitting, along with loose pitching and ragged fielding, was a feature throughout many of the team's intra-squad games. Despite the shoddy fielding in general, Cuyler received accolades for his work in the field, along with Glenn Wright, Johnny Rawlings and Walter Mueller.[22] Fellow rookie Frank Luce seemed to be Cuyler's direct competition for a permanent roster spot. Although Luce was heralded as a true power hitter due to his minor league work, Cuyler exhibited sufficient skill throughout spring training to be included on Pittsburgh's team for the 1924 season.

The training session would not be completed without incident as Pittsburgh's players prepared for the upcoming season. Coach Jewel Ens was confined to Atascadero Hospital after a doctor diagnosed that he had contracted scarlet fever. A few young players also angered manager Bill McKechnie when they took an airplane ride. During a Sunday training break on March 9, Glenn Wright, Emil Yde and Ray Steineder decided to spend the afternoon enjoying a mid-air outing. When word reached McKechnie that these players had done this without asking his permission, he reprimanded the three men for their recklessness. He believed that such a risk was far too great and reminded the men that owner Barney Dreyfuss had made huge investments in each player. McKechnie decreed that Pirate players would only be permitted to travel by vehicles that stayed on the ground.[23]

3. The Greatest Rookie Class in Baseball History 35

As the Pirates prepared to open the 1924 season in Cincinnati on April 15, McKechnie was faced with a dilemma regarding his starting lineup. During the early stages of spring training, veteran outfielder Carson "Skeeter" Bigbee seemed to be ready to have a comeback season in 1924. By the end of the exhibition tour that finally reached Ohio prior to the opener, Carson again resembled the man who struggled mightily in 1923 due to a sinus problem. Bigbee had difficulty putting the ball in play. It seemed that when his bat did meekly make contact with a ball, he could not push the ball past the infield. Still, McKechnie planned on giving Bigbee ample opportunity to work out of this slump. If Bigbee was unable to do the job, Pittsburgh's manager would be hard-pressed not to replace him with the hustling and free-swinging Hazen Cuyler.[24]

Despite the uncertainty surrounding his starting lineup, McKechnie was confident his team would put on a good show for Pittsburgh's fans in 1924. "I believe my boys will be in the fight all the way," said McKechnie prior to the opener. "I am not predicting any pennants, but I will say that it will take a great club to beat us out. We are much better than last year. My new infield suits me perfectly, and I am confident several of our young pitchers will deliver the goods. Our reserves are first class. We are ready for a battle all the way."[25]

When the opening bell sounded in Cincinnati on April 15, Cuyler was part of the aforementioned group of Pittsburgh reserves. Bigbee started in left field and recorded one hit in a 6–5 opening day loss to the Reds. Rookie Glenn Wright was christened as Pittsburgh's starting shortstop while veteran infielder Rabbit Maranville made the switch to second base. Unfortunately, McKechnie's squad played uninspired ball throughout the early stages of the 1924 season. By the end of April, Pittsburgh found itself in fifth place with a 6–8 record. Making matters worse from Hazen Cuyler's perspective was the fact that he remained chained to the bench during the season's first two weeks. In the meantime, Bigbee was hitting .309 and seemed capable of sustaining his solid start even though Pittsburgh's veteran outfielder had recorded only one extra-base hit in the first 14 games.

Cuyler did not see his first game action until the Pirates played Cincinnati on May 4. He was inserted as a pinch hitter for catcher Johnny Gooch in the ninth inning, but struck out in his first appearance of the season as the Reds defeated the Pirates by a score of 5–4. Cuyler finally received a chance to start in a game two days later when he replaced center fielder Max Carey, who was feeling sick.[26] Cuyler put on a spectacular show for the fans at Forbes Field as the Pirates defeated the Chicago Cubs, 2–0. Hazen batted in the second slot of the lineup and went 3-for-4. He scored one run, smacked a double and stroked a triple during his inaugural game of the 1924 season. Cuyler seemed determined to make up for lost time as he brutalized opposing pitchers by going 9-for-13 in the three games he manned Carey's center field post. On May 9 in a 10–7 loss to Boston, Cuyler keyed Pittsburgh's offense by pounding out four hits and smacking a double.[27] When Max returned to the lineup, Cuyler was shifted to left field in order to give Bigbee a break due to a minor ailment.[28]

Pittsburgh's young outfielder continued to assault National League pitching after he replaced Bigbee in left field. Cuyler went 2-for-4 as the Pirates' leadoff hitter in a 2–0 loss against Boston on May 10. Hazen was collared for the first time by an opposing pitcher during Pittsburgh's 5–1 victory over the Braves in their next game. He rebounded quite nicely by going 3-for-5 at the plate when the Philadelphia Phillies strolled into Forbes Field on May 15. Cuyler also gained deep admiration from Pittsburgh's fans by drilling a single in the ninth inning with the bases loaded and two out and driving home the winning run for a 4–3 victory.[29]

Cuyler batted fourth and played right field after Clyde Barnhart was benched for two games against Philadelphia. Cuyler's timely hitting after being inserted into the starting lineup resulted in several Pirates victories.[30]

Bill McKechnie continued to shift Cuyler, Bigbee and Barnhart around the outfield in order to achieve maximum results. Cuyler certainly looked like an accomplished hitter, but he still needed to learn the vital nuances of playing the outfield, where he seemed shaky at judging fly balls.[31] Cuyler's phenomenal speed helped him out of numerous tight spots in the outfield. That speed also intimidated opposing players when he was tearing around the base paths. In a game against the arch rival Giants on May 20, Cuyler's running ability became the feature item during a 12–3 Pittsburgh victory. In the third inning, Cuyler dashed from first to third after New York's Frankie Frisch knocked down Clyde Barnhart's infield single behind second base. Cuyler and Barnhart then pulled off a nifty double steal, as Hazen delayed heading to the plate but then crossed the dish before Frisch's desperate relay throw reached catcher Frank Snyder. In the third inning, Cuyler once again showed the value of his blazing speed when he reached third base with a triple to deep left field. Most mortals were usually held to two bases on such a blast.[32]

Even though Cuyler's batting average stood at .388 when the Giants left Pittsburgh on May 21 after their series at Forbes Field, he found himself back on the bench as the Pirates prepared to play Brooklyn. Carson Bigbee returned to his outfield post and recorded two hits while handling four chances without trouble during his first game back. Despite the fact that Cuyler had done brilliant work running the bases in the series against New York, his overall play against the Giants was not stellar. McKechnie believed this switch would be beneficial for Pittsburgh's rookie outfielder. Pittsburgh's manager would not commit to when Cuyler would return to the lineup, but he stated that the youngster might play when the Pirates faced southpaw hurlers.[33]

Hazen Cuyler saw very limited duty during the next three weeks, as he was only used as a pinch hitter in two games against the St. Louis Cardinals on May 30 and June 2. While Cuyler continued to languish on the bench, three other Pirates rookies received praise for their work during the season's first two months. After a tough start, shortstop Glenn Wright improved daily as a batter and was now one of the Pirates' timeliest hitters. Wright made a number of errors in the field, but he also covered a huge amount of territory. Pitcher Ray Kremer had enjoyed a great start during his rookie season and seemed to pitch with the poise of a veteran. Southpaw Emil Yde had not been used much by McKechnie to this point, but he was simply terrific when he recorded a shutout victory over St. Louis on May 21 in only his second start. McKechnie believed that Yde's puzzling delivery, solid control and excellent speed would incapacitate opposing batters throughout the summer.[34]

As Cuyler remained in the dugout, the Pirates continued to struggle on the field. Following a 4–1 loss against Brooklyn on June 7, Pittsburgh occupied fifth place with a 20–23 record, seven games behind the National League-leading New York Giants. The Smoky City's natives were starting to get restless due to the Pirates' disappointing showing thus far in 1924. Manager Bill McKechnie received his fair share of criticism as the troops continued to underachieve. McKechnie, who seemed as puzzled as everyone else that the Pittsburgh Pirates were performing so horribly, vented some of his frustration during an interview.

> I know it is asking a whole lot of the fans back home to believe that I am doing everything in my power to put the Pirates on a winning track. They, no doubt, are as thoroughly disgusted with the team as I am, and that is saying a lot. Four straight defeats on a trip that I, and the rest of us, expected would see the team gain its true stride.
> But what can I do? What should anyone do? What players can I substitute for the ones I am now using to better the lineup? What team in the National League, taken man for man, looks better than the one I throw out onto the field day after day with success that is far worse than ordinary? I mean it when I say that not in all my experience as a player and manager have I seen an aggregation of players that looks so classy on paper and performs so raggedly on the diamond.[35]

McKechnie discussed his team's fielding and pitching a bit before he resumed the interview by saying that a dearth of hitting had caused most of Pittsburgh's problems.[36]

> It all simmers down to a question of hitting. Of all the players, Wright, a new man and rated as somewhat of a weakling with the war club, has been about the only one who has delivered valuable blows, those that come with men on bases. Take Wright's noble work out of our games so far and you will see how many more would have been entered on the wrong side of the ledger.

Who before the season opened, figured that Traynor, Barnhart and Grimm, our three offensive threats, would fall down? Yet they have, and it is due to their inability to get going with the willow that we are so far down in the standing as we are today. But do not take it to mean that they are not trying. Every one of them is as deeply concerned over the sorrowful showing as I am, and God knows that I have gone through hell in the last few weeks planning and figuring only to have my calculations shot to pieces.

And, let me say, once and for all, that there is no internal friction in the club. Of all the years I have been in the game, I have never seen a club where the feeling of one player towards the other is as fine as in the 1924 Pirates. The players are trying, they are in the best of condition. There has been no dissipation among them. I am sure I have their earnest cooperation and that sooner or later they will come through in the style we all hope for.[37]

Hazen Cuyler's name was not mentioned during McKechnie's impromptu state of the union address regarding his team. This was not surprising since a player could not be properly critiqued while he was sitting on the bench. The fact that Cuyler had injured his wrist while sliding into a base also interfered with the rookie outfielder's desire to return to Pittsburgh's starting lineup.[38] McKechnie finally decided to give Cuyler another chance as a starter when he returned to right field in a five-inning loss to New York on June 8. Hazen recorded multiple hits in back-to-back games against the Giants on June 9 and 10, as Pittsburgh gained a split against its greatest rival. Cuyler went 6-for-19 at the plate during the remainder of the team's eastern invasion, while Pittsburgh fashioned a 3–3 record during those six games.

Pittsburgh returned home for a short two-game series against the Reds before both teams headed to Cincinnati for a three-game engagement. Cuyler went 2-for-4 and scored three runs during the first game of the series at Forbes Field on June 20, with Pittsburgh winning 9–4. Following a tight 1–0 win by the Pirates the following day, both teams boarded a train so that they could compete in a Sunday matinee at Redland Field on June 22. The getaway from the Smoky City that Saturday evening became a turbulent one for both teams as the train wrecked near Watkins Mills, Pennsylvania.[39] The Pennsylvania line train destined for Cincinnati crashed shortly after it left Pittsburgh at a location near Carnegie, the hometown of former Pirate great Honus Wagner. Two railroad cars jumped the tracks.[40] None of the athletes from either squad were injured in the wreck, but it seemed to shake most everyone involved.[41] Pittsburgh's players did not seem to play their best the following day as Cincinnati crushed the Pirates, 9–4.

After Cuyler was held hitless in this game against the Reds on June 22, he proceeded to hit safely in nine out of the next 10 contests. When Hazen did not record a hit in either game of a doubleheader against Cincinnati at Forbes Field on Independence Day, there was concern that the young outfielder might fall into a slump. Pittsburgh's knowledgeable fans were worried that the constant shuffling of Cuyler between left and right field by Bill McKechnie was having an adverse effect on the rookie. They also believed that these shifts were responsible for Cuyler's recent subpar play in the outfield.[42] Opposing players, however, did not seem to buy into the idea that Cuyler's game was destined to decline. Utility infielder Joe Klugmann of the Brooklyn Robins, known as a smart ballplayer throughout his career, made a straightforward observation of Cuyler's ability.[43] "Pittsburgh's new outfielder, Cuyler, looks like a coming star to me," said Klugmann. "He can do anything — bat, field and runs bases and will fit in nicely with the rest of the outfield."[44]

Hazen Cuyler continued to sizzle as Pittsburgh's summer heated up. After being shut out at the plate during the two games on July 4, he reeled off another stretch of torrid hitting as he recorded hits in eight out of nine games from July 5 to July 12. Pittsburgh won both ends of a doubleheader over Philadelphia in dramatic fashion at Forbes Field on July 12. The Pirates claimed the first game, 6–5, when Charlie Grimm's triple drove home the winning run in the tenth inning. Hazen Cuyler, Glenn Wright and Pie Traynor then supplied the critical 11th inning heroics as Pittsburgh claimed the nightcap, 3–2.[45] Pittsburgh's ascension in the National League standings seemed to coincide with Cuyler's rise to stardom. After the doubleheader sweep over the Phillies on July 12, the Pirates found themselves in third place with a 41–35 record that left them nine and a half games behind the league-leading New York Giants.

After being held hitless against the Phillies on July 14, Cuyler went on another tear as he went 12-for-19 and drilled five triples in the next four games against Philadelphia and New York. Cuyler's spectacular play during the past month was now earning him accolades alongside fellow Pirate rookies Glenn Wright, Ray Kremer and Emil Yde.[46] During the first game of a crucial series against New York at Forbes Field on July 16, Cuyler showed off his ability to manhandle opposing pitchers. Hazen proved that he could smack the ball to all fields by blasting a triple to right, a triple to left and a single to center.[47] Cuyler also drove home four runs as the Pirates lost to New York, 8–7.[48] Pittsburgh fared better against New York the following day, when Pie Traynor's walk-off home run in the 13th inning secured a 4–3 victory. Cuyler starred at the plate once again as he hit a single, a double and a triple while scoring two runs.[49] He also made a great catch on a low liner to left, stole two bases and scored Pittsburgh's first run when he pilfered home.[50]

Pittsburgh crushed New York decisively by a 9–2 score on July 18, as Cuyler slammed three more hits and bagged another triple.[51] This brought his hit total for the three-game series against New York to nine. The loyal

Pirate patrons in Forbes Field's left field stands had now grown so accustomed to Cuyler's heroics that they gave him a round of cheers every time he took his position in the outfield.[52] In a relatively short period of time, Cuyler had become the idol of Forbes Field's fans.[53] They loved his free-swinging style at the plate and his non-stop hustling on the bases and in the field. He feared no mound opponent and was not vulnerable to any kind of pitch.[54] The relationship between Cuyler and Pittsburgh's baseball faithful had developed to the point that fans were now calling the rookie outfielder "Kiki" just as fans and teammates did in Nashville.

All was not perfect as the Pirates continued to forge ahead in their quest to overtake New York and claim the National League pennant. While Kiki Cuyler was receiving adulation from Pittsburgh's fans, another rookie was being booed vociferously. During the Brooklyn series following Pittsburgh's two triumphs over New York, rooters at Forbes Field razzed shortstop Glenn Wright after he butchered a play during the first game of a doubleheader on July 21. Most of these jeers originated from a particular area of the grandstand where low-level gamblers from the Smoky City were permitted to pursue their illegal activities while local law enforcement turned a blind eye. When Wright made a sensational play during the second game, the unsavory inhabitants occupying that area of Forbes Field were suspiciously silent.[55] While Wright's psyche was damaged by disloyal Pittsburghers, outfielder Clyde Barnhart was knocked out of the lineup for a few days when he was confined to a bed with bronchitis.[56]

The Pirates continued their climb in the standings as they began a long eastern trip in Boston on July 25. The Pirates swept four games from the Braves as articles in Pittsburgh newspapers continued to write about the exploits of Hazen Cuyler. Pittsburgh won the first six games on the trip before New York held them in check on August 1 by a 3–1 score. Prior to that defeat, Cuyler had recorded 12 hits during those six games. Included among those safeties were three doubles and a triple. He also lost a home run on July 31, when rain shortened the game with New York batting in the seventh inning. The final score reverted back to the sixth, thereby wiping out Hazen's seventh inning smash.[57]

In a victory against the Giants on August 2, Cuyler had to leave the game after Frankie Frisch aggressively tagged the young outfielder on his head. Frisch's rough tactics almost resulted in major injury as he slid hard into the keystone sack. Hazen had to retire to Pittsburgh's dugout for the remainder of the afternoon as he tried to regain his faculties. His Pittsburgh teammates vowed to extract revenge against Frisch at Forbes Field, when New York traveled to Pittsburgh in a few weeks. But Cuyler never complained about the incident and took it in stride.[58] Hazen did not miss a beat as he returned to

Pittsburgh's lineup the following day against Brooklyn and continued his rise as the National League's brightest young star.

During a 9–6 defeat against the Robins on August 7, Cuyler made two exceptional plays in the outfield. In the first inning, he grabbed Eddie Brown's fly in left field and gunned down Johnny Mitchell at the plate after he tagged up from third. Cuyler turned the trick once again in the eighth inning, when he threw even more accurately to catcher Walter Schmidt and nailed Burleigh Grimes after snagging Bernie Neis' drive to left.[59] Two days later, Cuyler starred during a doubleheader sweep over the Philadelphia Phillies. In the first contest, the Nashville phenom banged out six hits as Pittsburgh crushed Philadelphia, 16–4.[60] He smacked three doubles and a triple, for a total of 11 bases. Cuyler also scored three runs and performed flawlessly in left field during the first game. During the nightcap, Hazen only recorded one hit but his fine defensive play, which ended the game, was the highlight of the afternoon. Cuyler dashed at full speed and made a dazzling play to capture Walter Holke's sizzling liner to left, securing Pittsburgh's 7–0 victory.[61]

Pittsburgh ended their long swing through the East by sweeping five games from the Phillies. The Pirates had a sensational road trip as they posted a 15–3 record. When the Pirates returned home after their final game in Philadelphia on August 11, they stood in second place with a 61–44 record and trailed league-leading New York by seven games. Once the players arrived in town after being away from the Smoky City for almost three weeks, four of them hustled off to Youngstown, Ohio, to consult with physician "Bonesetter" Reese about various injuries. Catcher Walter Schmidt sought treatment for his stiffened fingers while Lee Meadows, Johnny Morrison and Hazen Cuyler hoped the famous muscle-twister could relieve pain in their shoulders and arms.[62]

Even though Cuyler was playing with a banged-up shoulder, his pillaging of opposing hurlers throughout the East helped raise the youngster's batting average to .372. Kiki saw that mark climb 13 points higher during a four-game sweep over New York, which helped push Pittsburgh closer to the top of the National League race. On August 13, Cuyler went 3-for-4 as Pittsburgh prevailed against its fiercest rival, 4–2. He was then given a day off to rest his shoulder on August 14 as Pittsburgh beat New York, 3–1. The Pirates made it three straight wins over John McGraw's squad on August 15, as they claimed a 6–4 victory. New York scored four runs in the top of the third inning, but saw that lead quickly evaporate when Pittsburgh tallied five markers of its own during the bottom frame. Cuyler, back in the lineup after one game, struck the crucial blow when he blasted an inside-the-park home run with two men on base.[63]

Kiki Cuyler did his best work against New York during the series' final game on August 16. Cuyler's play moved front and center as Pittsburgh won a tight, 12-inning affair by the score of 5–4. Cuyler continued his impressive work by rapping out five hits in six tries. He personally demoralized the Giants in the eighth inning and swung the game in Pittsburgh's favor by crushing a triple over Irish Meusel's head into the overflow crowd in left field and bringing home one teammate. Moments later, Kiki scampered home with the tying run. Cuyler also made two fine defensive plays that brought rousing cheers from the crowd. In the fourth inning with men on base, Cuyler robbed Meusel of a triple when he raced to deep left and grabbed the ball near the outfield stands. Hazen then traveled in the opposite direction to rob Hack Wilson of a hit in the eighth inning, when he snatched a drive just before it hit the grass behind the infield. After the game fans showed their appreciation for Cuyler's work by carrying him on their shoulders to the Pirates' clubhouse door.[64]

Pennant fever gripped Pittsburgh fans as the four-game sweep over New York pulled their beloved Pirates within three games of first place. Players were hailed as heroes while the city began to dream of a National League pennant. The names of Cuyler, Wright, Carey, Maranville, Kremer and Traynor were on the minds of fans throughout Western Pennsylvania. The sudden adulation did not, however, mean that everyone in Pittsburgh had been focusing on the success of the Pirates. On two different occasions, fans gave priceless responses when some of these players' names popped up during a conversation.

Pittsburgh sportswriter Chilly Doyle relayed a tale about a young Pittsburgh boy named Johnny who was given a fine birthday party during the summer of 1924. One of the boy's aunts came up to Johnny and asked him what he wanted to be when he grew up. When Johnny responded that he aspired to be a big league ball player, the female guests at the celebration expressed their disapproval and stated that such a goal was not a very lofty ambition.[65] Undaunted by this negative response, Johnny pleaded his case to the female relatives.

"But, mother," protested Johnny, "wouldn't you like it even if I got to be Pie Traynor?"

"Good gracious," spoke up Johnny's grandmother. "A boy of mine working in a bakery?"[66]

Johnny and most Pittsburgh fans loved Pie Traynor, but the boy's grandmother could not make the connection. Hazen Cuyler had a similar experience when the Pirates traveled by train to Warren, Ohio, for a Sunday afternoon exhibition game on August 17. Shortly after the Pennsylvania and Lake Erie train left Pittsburgh at 11 o'clock, word made its way to other passengers that baseball's hottest team was onboard. Throughout the trip to Youngstown, a steady stream of passengers traveled back to the parlor car in order to catch a glimpse of the exceptional Kiki Cuyler. After one father took his boy back to see the young star, the child came back to his seat and expressed absolute elation to his mother.[67]

"Oh, Mother, I saw Cuyler!" exclaimed the excited lad.

"CUYLER? Cuyler? Who is he?" asked the mother.[68]

For people like her who were not aware of Kiki Cuyler's exploits, he was 178 pounds of energy and action, and was rapidly challenging veteran Rogers Hornsby for the title of best hitter in the National League.[69] As Cuyler's play on the diamond improved and his popularity in Pittsburgh rose, interview requests became more frequent. During his first full season in the National League, Cuyler had shown signs of becoming a future base stealing champion; veteran teammate Max Carey was the reigning champion in that category and one of the greatest base thieves in National League history. During an interview with a Pittsburgh scribe, Cuyler stated that base stealing at the minor league level was a relatively easy task. He then offered insight into learning the tendencies of National League pitchers and his own approach to hitting.[70]

> Major league pitchers are altogether a different proposition. Practically all pitchers in the majors are smart. If they are not so when they come up, the managers drill them until they acquire the trick of hiding their intentions. As every major league club has from seven to nine pitchers, all more or less skilled in hiding their intentions, and every one of them having his own peculiarities, you have a steady problem of from 50 to 60 pitchers confronting you if you want to steal bases.
>
> Of course, the batter meets regular pitchers more often than second string men, but even the regulars are not regular. The young player in his first year might play at home and abroad against a certain team and not face one or two of its best pitchers, the kind that would hold down scores by his own side and make base stealing doubly useful. They might be out of shape, or their manager might be holding them out for a couple of series or more. Then, all of a sudden, you face those high class artists who are high class because they have all the tricks of the trade, including concealment of intentions, and the very time you ought to steal is the time when you have so done on which to proceed.[71]

The conversation then shifted to hitting, as Cuyler explained his philosophy at the plate. Hazen did not believe in taking a third strike. He reasoned that the task of banging out hits became more difficult when the bat remained on a player's shoulders. Many of Cuyler's safeties during the 1924 season occurred when the opposing pitcher had reached two strikes on him.[72]

"Let the opposing pitcher get two strikes on me," continued Cuyler, "and then put the next one over the plate or near enough to it for me to hit it, and I'm going to take a smash at it."[73]

Cuyler continued to do solid work at the plate in spite of a sore shoulder. Hazen hit safely in 19 out of 20 games between August 11 and September 1.

Some of the highlights during that stretch occurred during two games as Pittsburgh played Boston at Forbes Field. During a 7–6 loss in the first game of a doubleheader on August 21, Cuyler crushed a home run with two men on in the fifth inning. Two days later, Kiki's work with a bat helped Pittsburgh defeat Boston, 3–2, as Ray Kremer and Al Yeargin locked up in a tight pitcher's duel. Cuyler scored Pittsburgh's first run when he drilled a drive to deep center field and circled the bases with an inside-the-park home run during the opening frame. A double by Max Carey in the third followed by Cuyler's single accounted for Pittsburgh's second run of the day.[74]

After the Pirates swept both games of a Labor Day doubleheader against the Cubs on September 1, they stood in second place in the National League with a record of 75–51. They trailed the first-place Giants by only one game. When official batting averages were released on September 4, they showed that Kiki Cuyler was second in the National League with a .378 average and trailed only Rogers Hornsby, who was hitting at a .432 clip. The improved fortunes of the Pittsburgh baseball team had coincided with Cuyler bursting onto the scene as a legitimate star. It seemed only appropriate that the Pirates twisted into a tailspin at the exact time Cuyler experienced his worst batting slump of the year. Following their glorious victory at Forbes Field on Labor Day, the Pirates proceeded to go 15–12 over the remainder of the campaign and finished third in the National League standings with a 90–63 record.

Throughout the final weeks of the 1924 season, Cuyler's slump troubled him. Pittsburgh's star rookie found it difficult to place the ball in safe territory. In a victory over Boston on September 12, Kiki was able to hit the ball out of the infield on only one occasion. To make matters worse, he left teammates stranded on the bases during three different trips to the plate.[75] Cuyler's injured shoulder seemed to be the culprit, as he had difficulty lifting his arm, especially on days when the weather was cold. Because of this, Cuyler was swinging late and producing nothing but harmless infield taps.[76] During the second game of a crucial series against New York at the Polo Grounds on September 24, Carson Bigbee replaced Cuyler in the starting lineup when cold weather caused the pain in his shoulder to become too unbearable to play.[77]

New York finished off a three-game sweep and officially ended Pittsburgh's pennant hopes by defeating the Pirates on September 25 by a 5–4 score. The Pirates went down fighting as they nearly rallied against starter Art Nehf to tie the game in the ninth inning. With two runners on base and two out, Max Carey hit a majestic home run that scored Walter Schmidt and Eddie Moore. But Nehf quickly settled down and stopped Pittsburgh's rally as he struck out Hazen Cuyler for the second time that afternoon.[78] With the pennant now lost, Bill McKechnie decided to keep Cuyler on the bench for the remainder of the schedule in order to rest his injured shoulder. While the

Pirates played out their string of games, New York claimed its fourth consecutive National League crown by nosing out Brooklyn at the finish.

Hazen Cuyler returned to Flint for the winter and reflected on his first glorious season playing in the major leagues. Despite the fact that he had slumped horribly during the final stages of the campaign, Cuyler performed admirably throughout the 1924 season and established himself as a National League star. Cuyler appeared in 117 games and batted .354 for the third-place Pirates. Hazen scored 94 runs, smacked 27 doubles, drilled 16 triples, stole 32 bases and recorded 85 RBIs. He emerged as the top performer from the greatest rookie class in baseball history. Fellow freshmen Glenn Wright (.287 average with 111 RBIs), Eddie Moore (.359), Ray Kremer (18–10, 3.19 ERA) and Emil Yde (16–3, 2.83 ERA) all gave commanding performances during their inaugural big league season.

After spending the first few weeks of the 1924 season on the bench, Cuyler was finally given an opportunity to show manager Bill McKechnie his talent. Cuyler, shown here in his Pirates uniform, responded in splendid fashion as he helped spark Pittsburgh in their battle with New York for the National League pennant (courtesy the National Baseball Hall of Fame Library, Cooperstown, New York).

Shortly after Pittsburgh's season ended, two stories were unearthed that led many fans to believe the upcoming off-season might be a tumultuous one. The first story involved a tip that owner Barney Dreyfuss had received regarding salary demands from two of his young players. One youngster claimed that he was paid a mere pittance in 1924 and planned on being rewarded handsomely in 1925. The second player stated he was just beginning in the game and was young enough to pursue another occupation in life if he was not paid a salary commensurate to his ability. No names were attached to this report, but some people perhaps thought that Cuyler was one of the players because the story's author pondered what Dreyfuss would do when fans realized he was unable to reach salary terms with the previous summer's baseball sensation.[79]

The second tale that made its way into print was the tiresome, repeated narrative about certain players on the Pirates spending too much time in local saloons. Residents from the suburbs of Bellevue, Etna and Braddock could attest to the fact that some Pittsburgh players needed to have a temperance clause resurrected so that it could be included in their 1925 contracts. The story went on to say that some of the players had a wild drinking party when the Pirates made their exhibition jaunt to Youngstown, Ohio, in August.[80] Johnny Morrison was singled out as being one of these players. Morrison was considered a man of the careless nature who did not take his baseball seriously. These stories surrounding the escapades of Morrison and other veteran Pirate players lent credence to the belief that Bill McKechnie needed to become a stern disciplinarian.[81]

McKechnie wasted no time trying to eliminate this problem while reshaping the positive spirit and morale on his team. On October 27, 1924, McKechnie shipped infielder Rabbit Maranville, first baseman Charlie Grimm and pitcher Wilbur Cooper to the Chicago Cubs for pitcher Vic Aldridge, second baseman George Grantham and first baseman Al Niehaus. By trading Maranville and Grimm, McKechnie was ridding himself of two problem players. Maranville's drinking escapades had become legendary during his four seasons with Pittsburgh, while McKechnie and Dreyfuss believed that the banjo-playing Grimm had a tendency to clown around too often. Pittsburgh management felt that it was receiving both good players and solid citizens in the trade with Chicago.

Ten days prior to Christmas, McKechnie gave his assessment of the blockbuster deal with the Cubs. "When I sent Maranville, Cooper and Grimm to Chicago," said McKechnie, "I broke up a good combination, but I did so in the hope that in another year or so I will have a better one. We have come close to winning the pennant three times since I have had charge of the club, but I realized we never would win it unless I made a shakeup. Frankly, I didn't want to part with Grimm, but I had to include him in the deal or see it fall through."[82]

During the interview, McKechnie also stated that he preferred to use Grantham in the outfield rather than at second base. If George showed potential during spring training, McKechnie planned on alternating him with Kiki Cuyler and Clyde Barnhart.[83] This news probably came as a surprise to Cuyler, who believed that he had established himself as a starting outfielder during the 1924 season. Hazen was the National League's fourth best hitter in 1924 and had placed eighth in voting for league MVP. Cuyler had done everything in his power to help lead Pittsburgh to its first pennant in 15 years.

Hazen Cuyler had some unfinished goals on the diamond in 1925; he certainly did not plan on achieving those goals as a platoon player.

4. The Flint Flash Becomes a World Series Hero

Pittsburgh fans continued to discuss Bill McKechnie's blockbuster trade throughout the winter. Local fandom seemed to be split on its opinions as opponents of the deal reasoned that the Pirates gave up more quality than they received in return.[1] Veteran eastern sports writer John B. Foster believed that Pittsburgh came out on top with this trade since a solid young prospect like Al Niehaus was included in the transaction.[2] Rabbit Maranville, one of the principle players in the huge swap, remained in Pittsburgh during the off-season and worked as an employee for a local newspaper. At the end of November, Maranville's name made headlines in many Pittsburgh broadsheets for the second time in the past month. Maranville was arrested and released on $1,000 bond when the automobile he was driving ran over a small boy, injuring him seriously.[3]

According to witnesses who saw the accident, they claimed the incident was unavoidable.[4] The victim of the accident was a five-year-old youngster named Frank Smayda who was struck by Maranville's vehicle while he stood in front of his home at 75 Bates Street. The young boy was confined to Mercy Hospital for a month with a fractured skull. In the middle of January, Maranville's insurance company brokered a $700 cash settlement with Smayda's parents. Despite the fact that both parties came to an agreement in order to avoid a lawsuit, Maranville was still out on bond awaiting a hearing in an Oakland police court on the charge of reckless driving.[5] Considering all of his problems during the off-season, Maranville was ecstatic when the time came for the Cubs to report for spring training at Catalina Island off the coast of California.

The three players acquired in the deal that saw Maranville shipped to Chicago were expected to be vital performers for Pittsburgh in 1925. Vic Aldridge was a right-handed hurler coming off a season in which he went 15–12 with a 3.50 ERA. Aldridge was being asked to replace veteran Wilbur Cooper, who was a 20-game winner on four occasions. Prospect Al Niehaus still had not played a major league game, but Bill McKechnie expected great things from the young first baseman who batted .366 in 1924 for Chattanooga of the Southern Association. George Grantham was a left-handed, free-swinging infielder who hit at a .316 clip for Chicago in 1924. Grantham's aggressive style at the plate contributed to him leading the league with 63 strikeouts. Pittsburgh now had the National League's two players most frequently victimized by the strikeout in 1924. The Pirates' resident fence-buster, Hazen Cuyler, finished second to Grantham in 1924 by fanning 62 times.

In 1924, much of the talk leading up to spring training had centered on prospect Glenn Wright and his $40,000 purchase price. Prior to the 1925 campaign, fans now discussed a player who made it to the major leagues after being acquired for considerably less than Barney Dreyfuss' purchase price for Hazen Cuyler. In December of 1921, Chicago manager Bill Killefer and owner William Wrigley, Jr., had been involved in negotiations to acquire Arnold "Jigger" Statz from Los Angeles of the Pacific Coast League. When Killefer asked Los Angeles president J.H. Patrick what it would take to include Vic Aldridge in the deal, the Angels' magnate stated that he could accommodate Chicago's manager. Patrick said he would accept a pound of tea for Aldridge as long as the Cubs agreed with him on the amount of cash and the players to be exchanged for Statz.[6] As Pittsburgh rooters pondered the addition of a strikeout king, a rookie first baseman, and a pitcher who was exchanged for tea, New York manager John McGraw stated that the Pirates had strengthened their squad more than any other National League outfit.[7] "Pittsburgh will give the Giants the hardest test the coming season," proclaimed McGraw.[8]

The Pirates' squad trained at Paso Robles once again in 1925 and arrived at the California town in early March to prepare for the upcoming campaign. Before Hazen Cuyler left his Michigan home to begin another season, he was presented with a diamond-studded watch fob by some of his admirers in Flint. The memento was given to Cuyler by the Industrial Mutual Association of Flint, where he worked during the winter as a physical director. Flint's fans gave the gift to show both their deep appreciation for the work Cuyler did for the association and to show how proud they were of the National League's newest star.[9] Prior to the first training session at Paso Robles, Bill McKechnie issued an edict that delighted Cuyler and those fellow teammates who lived a clean life.

> The drinking of liquor will not be permitted on the club this year. If boozing is discovered among any of you — I care not whether veteran or youngster is found guilty — he will be suspended at once. No matter what the cost may be — if I have to break up my entire club — I am going to see that such rule is strictly adhered to.
>
> In the past three or four years, our chances have been hurt by such actions on

the part of some of the players. During that time I have shielded them. I have never fined nor suspended a player since I became manager of the Pittsburgh club. But I am through covering up the faults of others. It has got me nowhere in the past and I fail to see where it will obtain better results in the future. Therefore, the guilty one, even if he is the best player I have on the club, will be dropped immediately.[10]

McKechnie certainly did not have to worry about Kiki Cuyler's behavior during the season. Cuyler's only weak moment occurred when he was tempted by the desire of drinking an ice cream soda at times. Even this kind of beverage was ignored by Cuyler during the training season's crucial work. Unfazed by rumors of a possible outfield platoon with either George Grantham or Carson Bigbee, Cuyler picked up where he left off in 1924 by becoming Pittsburgh's heaviest hitter during intra-squad games. His hot hitting continued during an exhibition game against Seattle on March 14, when he belted two doubles, a triple and a home run during a 19–4 victory.[11] But shortly after this game, Cuyler fell into a minor batting slump. McKechnie made a surprising change against San Francisco on March 25, when he benched Cuyler and replaced him with Grantham, largely because the Seals were using a right-handed hurler.[12]

Grantham was no improvement over Cuyler as the former Cub fanned twice during an 11–7 loss to San Francisco.[13] Cuyler returned to the starting lineup the following day, coming back and crushing a home run into the center field bleachers. Hazen had now hit safely in each of the six exhibition contests he played in and was third on the team with nine hits.[14] Cuyler continued to brutalize opposing pitchers as the Pirates made their way on their 1925 cross-country exhibition tour. In a game against Oklahoma City on April 9, Cuyler waltzed in to third base with a triple after his prodigious smash caromed off the fence in left-center on the fly; it was a distance similar to the farthest reaches of Forbes Field. Cuyler also smacked a double that day.[15]

When spring training ended, the player whom Pittsburgh fans now referred to as the "Flint Flash," was penciled into Bill McKechnie's lineup as the starting right fielder. McKechnie did make a few alterations to his starting nine as Pittsburgh prepared to open against Chicago on April 14. Eddie Moore took over Rabbit Maranville's spot at second base. George Grantham grabbed a first baseman's mitt and served as a replacement for Al Niehaus. The rookie first baseman from Chattanooga was unable to play due to suffering a strained muscle in his leg near the end of the exhibition tour.[16] New pitcher Vic Aldridge was also not expected to be of much use during the first few weeks of the season since he did not end his holdout until the eve of the opener.[17]

Hazen Cuyler's season almost began ominously prior to the opening game. During batting practice, catcher Earl Smith allowed his bat to slip from his hands. The bat flew past the batting cage, with the knob end of the projectile grazing Cuyler's forehead. Luckily for the Pirates, Kiki suffered nothing more than a slight contusion to his head.[18]

Cuyler could not be blamed for Pittsburgh dropping its opening game to Chicago, 8–2. He batted fifth, went 2-for-4, smacked a double and drove home one of the Pirates' two runs. The following day, Cuyler went 3-for-5, smacked two triples and drove home three runs as Pittsburgh claimed its first victory of the season by beating Chicago, 8–4. The Pirates treated ex-teammate Wilbur Cooper rather rudely as they chased him after only two innings. Cuyler started off the second stanza with a triple and scored on first baseman Jewel Ens' home run into the left field seats. Glenn Wright followed that up by drilling his first homer into the bleachers at Cubs Park.[19]

Yet, Pittsburgh's fortunes were far from good during the season opening road trip in Chicago and Cincinnati. When the Pirates returned to Pittsburgh for their home opener at Forbes Field on April 22, their record stood at 2–5. Kiki Cuyler was suddenly not performing any better than his teammates as he endured four consecutive hitless games against the Cubs and Reds, pulling his average down to .238 before he responded with a two-hit day on April 20.

Two months before the opener, a Pittsburgh fan had sent a letter to the editor of *The Pittsburgh Press* asking that owner Barney Dreyfuss make changes at Forbes Field for the upcoming season. The woman in question was a member of Pittsburgh's "Flapper Club"; she wanted the games to be conducted under the most favorable conditions.[20] She penned the following letter to *The Pittsburgh Press:*

> Please ask Barney Dreyfuss to have a band at every game this season. It is wonderful, you know, when they beat the drum when the Pirates make a hit. It makes you feel so good.
> Please, Mr. Dreyfuss, have a band at every game.
> We are steady customers.
> (Signed) Flappers Club, per Miss Stedmore.[21]

If Dreyfuss had complied with Miss Stedmore's request, the Forbes Field band would have been busy striking up a song every time that Kiki Cuyler finished a trip at the plate during the Chicago series. Despite the fact that Pittsburgh dropped three out of four games against the Cubs and saw its record plummet to 3–8, Cuyler annihilated Chicago's pitching. Hazen went 8-for-14 during the four-game set and raised his batting average to .385. Cuyler's hitting aside, poor weather and sloppy play kept Pittsburgh mired in the National League's second division as the season moved into May. After the Pirates won three out of four games against St. Louis and Cincinnati, they found themselves in sixth place with a 6–9 record. It was at just about this time of the season that players other than Cuyler began to inject some enthusiasm and spirit into the Pittsburgh aggregation.

In a loss against the Cardinals on May 7, shortstop Glenn Wright was involved in the type of play that can galvanize a club. During the ninth inning, Wright pulled off the unusual trick of executing an unassisted triple play. The inning started gloomily for Pittsburgh as Vic Aldridge walked both Jimmy Cooney and Rogers Hornsby. Aldridge then worked the count to two balls and two strikes on Jim Bottomley before the Cardinals' first baseman struck a vicious drive that seemed headed for the outfield. Cooney and Hornsby, both of whom started running instantly, were shocked when they saw Wright leap in the air to snag Bottomley's smash. Wright touched second to double up Cooney and then tagged Hornsby for the third out as he sprinted toward second base.[22]

One week after Wright pulled off this rare play, catcher Earl Smith showed some misguided fighting spirit while the Pirates were defeating Boston, 7–1, on May 14 at Braves Field. Although the game was a rather one-sided affair, police experienced difficulty handling the crowd.[23] Smith was the target of verbal abuse as a fan heckled him throughout the afternoon.[24] The situation reached a boiling point in the eighth inning, when Smith came face-to-face with his tormentor after failing to grab a foul ball near the grandstand. Smith started to argue with a W.J. Lewis of Boston and landed a glancing blow against the fan's face as the two combatants squared off. Police officers quickly intervened, removing Smith from the game.[25] As Smith left the field and walked down the runway to the visitor's clubhouse, another spectator threw a chair at him. The chair struck his head with so much force that he suffered a gash to his scalp.[26]

Lewis swore out a warrant for Smith's arrest. The catcher was charged with assault and ordered to appear in a Boston court on July 16.[27] Smith also received a minor suspension from National League President John Heydler for his egregious act.[28]

While Smith decided to use his fists to stress a point, Hazen Cuyler continued to let his bat provide anguish for opposing teams. During a six-game stretch in the middle of May as the Pirates made their first trip through the East, Cuyler went 15-for-25 and scored 14 runs, raising his batting average to .394 on the season. His streak started after he failed to collect a hit in the first game of a doubleheader against Philadelphia on May 12. During the Pirates' 13–8 victory in the nightcap, Cuyler banged out two singles and two doubles. He also walked, was hit by a pitch and scored five runs.[29] The following day, Cuyler and Pie Traynor delivered consecutive singles in the seventh inning to score the deciding run in Pittsburgh's 5–4 win over Boston.[30]

As the Pirates attempted to climb the standings while traipsing through the National League's Eastern cities, writer Davis Walsh of the International News wrote a story that discussed how disappointed Pittsburgh fans were with the team's performance. Walsh claimed that Pirate rooters were upset with owner Barney Dreyfuss for sanctioning the huge deal with Chicago during the winter. Smoky City writers believed that Walsh's assessment was incorrect since they had not witnessed any public vendetta against Dreyfuss.[31]

While scribes from various cities pondered the attitude of Pittsburgh's fans, Hazen Cuyler continued to hit prodigiously as the Pirates posted an 8–6 record on their Eastern swing. Cuyler smacked one of the longest hits of the season at the Polo Grounds during a 5–4 loss against New York on May 21. Hazen's two-run, inside-the-park homer eclipsed Bill Terry's 402-foot blast a few days earlier by landing ten feet closer to the ballpark's clubhouse in center field.[32]

When the Pirates returned home to begin a series with Chicago on May 25, they found themselves in fifth place with a 14–16 record, trailing first-place New York by nine games. Home cooking then rejuvenated the Pirates as they reeled off seven straight victories, moved up two places in the standings and cut the Giants' lead in half. While Pittsburgh quickly rose up the National League's leaderboard, Cuyler became mired in his first batting slump of the season. After going hitless in a victory over St. Louis on May 29, Cuyler saw his average drop to .336. But Hazen's hitting woes were short-lived as he responded the following day by going 3-for-9 and scoring four runs during a doubleheader sweep of the Cardinals.

As Cuyler regained his batting eye, Pittsburgh management made two roster moves aimed at strengthening the team. McKechnie gave up on Al Niehaus and traded him to Cincinnati for pitcher Tom Sheehan. The Pirates then signed veteran first baseman Stuffy McInnis to replace Niehaus.

Cuyler had a great day at the plate during a 16–3 rout over the Phillies on June 4. Cuyler hit for the cycle as he went 4-for-5, drew a walk, stole a base, scored four runs and drove home three runs. Hazen also made the defensive gem of the game in the third inning, when he raced to right-center field and snagged George Harper's sizzling drive by making a one-handed leaping grab near a new set of stands that were under construction. Cuyler then made a perfect throw to second that doubled up Lew Fonseca.[33]

On June 6, Cuyler and his teammates had the opportunity to play a special, three-inning exhibition game against members of the 1901 Pirates. The game was played as the Pirates' franchise took its turn celebrating the National League's "Fiftieth Jubilee." Bill McKechnie's 1925 squad defeated the 1901 group, which included Fred Clarke and Honus Wagner, by a score of 5–3.[34] Following this special event at Forbes Field, Pittsburgh then defeated Philadelphia, 9–3 as Cuyler went 1-for-4 and scored two runs.

4. The Flint Flash Becomes a World Series Hero

Shortly after Barney Dreyfuss held his huge Golden Jubilee celebration at Forbes Field, Pittsburgh's owner brought back former player and skipper Fred Clarke to work within the organization as his assistant. Clarke was named team vice-president and also assumed the task of acting as Bill McKechnie's assistant in Pittsburgh's dugout. Clarke was permitted to purchase a small amount of stock in the team as part of the contractual arrangement with Dreyfuss.[35]

Clarke joined McKechnie and his squad on the Pirates' bench in time to watch Pittsburgh sweep four games from their most hated rival during a mid–June series at Forbes Field. Pittsburgh blitzed the New York Giants and moved to within two and a half games of the league leaders. Emotions reached a breaking point during the series. During the game on June 15, George Grantham was ejected from the contest when he threw his bat toward Jack Scott after the New York pitcher had beaned Pittsburgh's first baseman.[36]

Brushback pitches had been a huge topic of discussion among fans and friends of Hazen Cuyler during the first half of the 1925 season. A significant portion of Pittsburgh's fans believed that National League hurlers had entered into a conspiracy to maim Cuyler in order to force him to the sidelines. Such a charge seemed exaggerated since Hazen was a pleasant, engaging young man who was never disrespectful to opposing players. Furthermore, Cuyler was not being dusted off by rival pitchers any more than other star counterparts in the National League.[37] It did not seem to affect Cuyler when an opposing hurler plunked him with a pitch. Unfazed, Hazen continued to hit the ball hard throughout the summer as Pittsburgh battled to unseat New York from atop the National League standings.

On June 20, the Flint Flash did his fair share of damage during a 21–5 win over Brooklyn at Forbes Field. Pittsburgh collected 25 hits as Cuyler launched two home runs.[38] Hazen drilled a two-run shot off pitcher Jesse Petty in the first inning and then legged out an inside-the-park homer with the bases loaded against a Nelson Greene in the sixth stanza. He collected three extra base hits on the day and scored five runs.[39] Following his great performance that afternoon, Cuyler took his son Harold to watch an evening semi-pro game between the Homestead Grays and Homewood at Forbes Field.[40] After a one-day break, Cuyler continued his slugging during a 24–6 victory against St. Louis at Sportsman's Park on June 22. He went 2-for-6, scored three runs and smacked a two-run homer in the first inning.

The Pirates found themselves in a virtual tie for first place with New York by the end of June. The Pirates finally stood alone at the top of the National League on July 2 as they defeated Cincinnati, 2–1 while New York was idle. Max Carey's walk, Kiki Cuyler's triple and Clyde Barnhart's sacrifice fly in the sixth inning gave the Pirates all the runs they needed.[41]

The Pirates and Giants continued to take turns in first place as the season moved through July. Pittsburgh's second Eastern swing was far from successful as McKechnie's squad posted a 6–8 record against New York, Brooklyn, Boston and Philadelphia. After pulling out a few wins over St. Louis and Chicago late in the month, Pittsburgh led second-place New York by one game with a record of 53–35 on the morning of July 27.

Hazen Cuyler entered the game against Boston on July 27 with a .347 average. In recent games, Cuyler's hitting had been good, but not outstanding, as he and other hefty smashers like Glenn Wright and George Grantham slumped considerably at the plate.[42] Fans hoped that the Pirates could start a winning streak against the last-place Braves even though McKechnie's squad had struggled against Dave Bancroft's team during the 1925 season. The game was tightly contested as Cuyler uncharacteristically let his temper and emotions get the best of him. Kiki was a deeply earnest young man who always displayed great intensity on the field. Cuyler was not temperamental, but the youngster possessed a fighting spirit that he wore on his sleeve at times.[43]

Cuyler did everything within his power to bring home a victory for the Pirates as he banged out three hits through nine innings. Despite Hazen's usual stellar effort, the game was tied after regulation. In the top of the tenth inning, Boston's Dave Harris blasted a home run into Forbes Field's right field stands after Johnny Morrison grooved a pitch. After the third out, Cuyler criticized catcher Johnny Gooch as they both walked to the dugout. He questioned signaling for that kind of pitch in such a crucial situation. Gooch, who was a fierce competitor like Cuyler, did not appreciate his teammate's critique. Gooch's hot-blooded temper quickly flared and both men began throwing punches. Bill McKechnie, Fred Clarke and a few Pittsburgh players then separated the two fiery combatants and restored order.[44]

Pittsburgh quickly went to work against pitcher Jesse Barnes in the bottom of the tenth inning. Eddie Moore started the frame by drawing a walk. He then scored the game's tying run when Cuyler crushed a double. After Clyde Barnhart sacrificed Cuyler to third, Barnes walked Pie Traynor and Glenn Wright to load the bases. Cuyler scored the winning run moments later when he scampered home on Stuffy McInnis' sacrifice.[45]

When Cuyler made his way to the bench after scoring the game's winning run, McKechnie brought him and Gooch together. The two men, who were actually good friends and roommates, shook hands and declared their mutual admiration for each other. The incident showed a fighting spirit on the ballclub that had not been seen in years. In the past, most players had not shown interest in the kind of pitch called for by a catcher. The incident involving Cuyler and Gooch demonstrated that Pittsburgh's players had a deep desire to win the pennant.[46]

Pittsburgh continued to battle in an effort to claim the National League flag. Two days after Cuyler scuffled with Gooch, Hazen became the first player in either league to score 100 runs when he crossed home plate during an 8–6 victory over Boston.[47] Cuyler's unrelenting dominance on the diamond had helped Pittsburgh build a small lead over second-place New York as the season moved through August. When the Giants left town on August 13 after splitting a four-game series at Forbes Field, Pittsburgh's record stood at 64–41, enough to lead the Giants by four and a half games.

Loyal Pirate fans in Pittsburgh and other parts of the country were starting to believe a trip to the World Series was a foregone conclusion. Four Pittsburgh patrons who were touring Alaska with the Knights Templar came across numerous fans who were rooting for the Pirates. When the men returned to Vancouver after their trip, they wired Barney Dreyfuss and Bill McKechnie that many in Alaska, the Yukon and Western Canada were pulling for the Buccaneers.[48]

Fans throughout the Smoky City continued to read stories about Pittsburgh victories and Kiki Cuyler's exploits in local newspapers each day. In a game against Brooklyn on August 20, Cuyler made a spectacular play to rob the Robins' Eddie Brown of an extra-base hit. Brooklyn had the bases loaded with two out in the fifth inning when Brown launched a drive to right-center that seemed destined to land for a triple. All of a sudden, the Flint Flash raced over to haul in the long drive. When Cuyler came to the plate in the top of the sixth inning, he hit an inside-the-park home run on a line drive past Brown in center field; the homer turned out to be the winning tally in Pittsburgh's 2–1 victory.[49] When the Pirates rolled into the Polo Grounds after the Brooklyn series and claimed four out of five games from New York, the six-game lead they now held over the Giants as of August 24 seemed insurmountable.

Pittsburgh continued its all-out blitz toward the National League pennant by reeling off a nine-game winning streak from August 26 through September 3. But the situation became tense during the season's final month, as the Pirates lost seven out of eight games to Chicago and St. Louis. Luck, however, seemed to be on Pittsburgh's side since New York was also mired in a woeful slump. Bill McKechnie's squad quickly righted the ship and embarked on a rampage during another nine-game winning streak as the season wound down. During this pennant-clinching stretch, Hazen Cuyler showed why he was Pittsburgh's star player, the National League's best outfielder, and a legitimate candidate for the league's Most Valuable Player award. From September 18 through September 22, Cuyler performed at the level of other great ballplayers when he carried the Pirates and pulled them across the finish line.

On September 18, Cuyler was a perfect 4-for-4, as Pittsburgh defeated the Boston Braves, 9–7. Included among the quartet of safeties was a double and triple. Cuyler also gunned down Gus Felix at the plate in the eighth inning after hauling in Mickey O'Neil's fly ball.[50] Cuyler maintained his perfection at the plate on September 19 as he garnered four hits and a walk in Pittsburgh's 2–1 victory over Boston. Pittsburgh's star outfielder continued his torrid stretch against Philadelphia on September 21, as the Pirates won a loosely played, hard-hitting contest, 9–7. When Cuyler singled twice during his first two at-bats, he equaled the National League record of achieving ten consecutive hits. During his third trip to the plate, Cuyler fouled out and ended his run.[51]

Kiki Cuyler started another small streak the following day when he went 4-for-4 during Pittsburgh's 14–4 victory at Forbes Field. Cuyler also performed the rare feat of smacking two inside-the-park home runs in the same game. Cuyler's recent batting spree placed him third among hitters in the National League with a .361 batting average.[52]

The Pirates clinched the National League pennant on September 23 when they defeated the Phillies, 2–1, and New York lost a doubleheader to St. Louis. As the players celebrated the clinching in their Forbes Field clubhouse, Bill McKechnie made a short speech to his troops in which he gave the players full credit for their outstanding accomplishment. McKechnie also thanked his players for their hard work and dedication and referred to them as the finest group of young men he had ever met. This pennant served as vindication for McKechnie, who was chastised and criticized during the previous winter and spring after making the highly publicized trade with Chicago.[53]

Many Pittsburgh fans attributed the team's successful rise to Fred Clarke's presence on the Pirate bench. There was no doubt that Clarke's wise counsel supplied a steadying influence, but those who minimized McKechnie's contributions were mistaken. Clarke was not responsible for developing players like Glenn Wright, Pie Traynor and Hazen Cuyler. Still, McKechnie and Clarke worked in perfect harmony and neither man attempted to claim any personal glory for Pittsburgh's pennant.[54] Cuyler was another member of the Pirates who always tried to deflect praise away from himself. Cuyler's modesty would not permit him to speak of his own accomplishments, but he enthusiastically discussed the role he played in helping bring home the pennant as a member of the Pirates.[55]

Cuyler's effort during the season was impressive as the Pirates finished eight and a half games ahead of second-place New York with a 95–58 record. He led the team in hitting with a .357 average as he appeared in every game for the Pirates. Cuyler led the National League in runs scored and triples. He crossed the plate 144 times, with 43 doubles, 26 triples, 18 home runs, 41 stolen bases and 102 RBIs. Cuyler certainly received plenty of support from

The 1925 Pittsburgh Pirates. *Front row, left to right*: Johnny Gooch, Roy Spencer, Bud Culloton, Jewel Ens, Bill McKechnie, Jr. (mascot), Cuyler, Ray Kremer, Tom Sheehan. *Middle row*: Earl Smith, Mule Haas, Red Oldham, Fresco Thompson, Stuffy McInnis, Max Carey, Bill McKechnie, Fred Clarke, Glenn Wright, George Grantham, Carson Bigbee, Pie Traynor. *Rear row*: Chick Fraser, Bill Hinchman, Jack Onslow, Clyde Barnhart, Eddie Moore, Emil Yde, Sam Watters, Barney Dreyfuss, Sam Dreyfuss, Johnny Rawlings, Vic Aldridge, Babe Adams, Johnny Morrison, Lee Meadows. (courtesy the National Baseball Hall of Fame Library, Cooperstown, New York).

his teammates as Glenn Wright, Clyde Barnhart and Pie Traynor joined him in the 100-RBI club, while Traynor, Eddie Moore and Max Carey also scored over 100 runs. Moore was the only regular who did not hit over .300, as he barely missed the milestone with a .298 average. Wright and Cuyler were able to set a new franchise mark by hitting 18 homers apiece. Cuyler also established a team record that still stands today by accumulating 369 total bases during the season.

Pittsburgh's opponent in the 1925 World Series would be the defending world champion Washington Senators. The Fall Classic was viewed by many experts as a battle between a veteran Washington team steeped in strong pitching against Bill McKechnie's young hitting machine. Excited fans throughout Pittsburgh waited in anticipation for the first game at Forbes Field on October 7. The night before the series opener, Kiki Cuyler, his teammates and the Washington players were guests of general manager Henry Davis for "Baseball Night at the Davis Theater." All of the boxes on both the orchestra and balcony levels were reserved so that members of each organization could view the theatrical extravaganza.[56]

Days prior to the opening game at Forbes Field, Bill McKechnie gave a short assessment of his role in Pittsburgh copping the National League flag. "No manager ever won a pennant," stated McKechnie in a very matter of fact manner.[57]

McKechnie was not saying that managers had no influence on a pennant race or the World Series. He simply believed that his players were responsible for the Pirates' success and he fully expected heroes to emerge for them as Pittsburgh battled Washington.

Loyal Pirates fans finally had the chance to see their first World Series contest in 16 years as the festivities commenced on the afternoon of October 7. Prior to the game, several on-field presentations included McKechnie, rival manager Bucky Harris, Washington outfielder Joe Harris and Pittsburgh's Vic Aldridge. Kiki Cuyler also took part in the pre-game adulation, as he received a golden bat and ball from adoring Pittsburgh fans.[58]

Once the game began, it quickly became evident to the fans at Forbes Field that the heroes of the day sat in the visitor's dugout. Veteran hurler Walter Johnson (20–7, 3.07 ERA) locked horns with Pittsburgh staff ace Lee Meadows (19–10, 3.67 ERA) and showed the Pirates why he was considered one of the greatest pitchers in American League history. Johnson held the Pirates' bats easily in check as he cruised to a 4–1 victory. Johnson went the distance and baffled Pittsburgh's hitters as he fanned 10. Joe Harris and Sam Rice supported Johnson's effort. Harris' second-inning home run gave Washington a 1–0 lead and then Rice settled things in the fifth when his single drove home Ossie Bluege and Bucky Harris. Pie Traynor was the only Pirate who touched Johnson as he went 2-for-4 and blasted a home run in the fifth inning.

Kiki Cuyler's World Series debut was disappointing, as he struggled against Johnson throughout the afternoon. Cuyler was fanned by the immortal pitcher in the first inning. He then singled over second base in the fourth inning after Max Carey had struck out to start the frame. Unfortunately, Pittsburgh's resident speedster was picked off first base during a long rundown between first and second base.[59] In the sixth inning, Cuyler made the frame's final out when he was retired on a fly to Joe Harris in right field. The Flint Flash's first World Series appearance ended on a completely negative note when he was called out on strikes in the ninth inning. Cuyler never lifted the bat off his shoulder as he watched Johnson fire three consecutive pitches over the plate.[60]

Bill McKechnie chose Vic Aldridge (15–7, 3.63 ERA) to oppose Washington's Stan Coveleski (20–5, 2.84 ERA) in the second game of the World Series on October 8. It looked as if the Senators would return home to the Nation's Capital with a 2–0 series lead when Joe Judge's second-inning homer made it 1–0. A hero finally stepped forward for Pittsburgh in the fourth inning, when Glenn Wright tied the game by blasting a home run into the left field stands located in front of the scoreboard. Pittsburgh's fans went into a frenzy as they cheered for the first positive development in the series.[61] Aldridge worked out of a critical jam in the fifth inning to keep the score tied, as both pitchers continued to toss zeroes. It was not until the eighth inning that a second Pirate player emerged from the shadows and added his name to the long list of World Series heroes throughout history.

Kiki Cuyler's coming-out party did not materialize throughout the early stages of Game Two. He hit a harmless grounder to Bucky Harris in the first inning. In the third frame, Cuyler failed at the plate with two men on base, as Max Carey was forced at second on a groundball to shortstop Roger Peckinpaugh. In the sixth, Hazen was able to move Carey to second base on a successful sacrifice, but no Pittsburgh teammate could bring Max home. Cuyler received another chance with a runner on base in the eighth inning when Eddie Moore reached first on Peckinpaugh's error and moved to second on Carey's groundout. Hazen quickly gained the upper hand in the crucial at-bat by working the count to two balls and no strikes.[62] Washington's Stan Coveleski felt he could retire Cuyler by pitching him inside, but Coveleski was just as surprised as the 43,364 fans in attendance when Cuyler crushed a high, inside fastball to deep right field.[63] A celebration broke out at Forbes Field as the long drive landed in the right field stands for a home run, giving Pittsburgh a 3–1 lead.[64]

Royal rooters cheered wildly as Cuyler rounded the bases after his epic home run. The two runs in the bottom of the eighth inning proved critical for Pittsburgh, as Washington pushed one run across in the ninth before Aldridge shut the door and closed out the Senators. Pittsburgh's clutch 3–2 victory evened up the series as both teams packed their equipment and made the trip to Washington for the next three games.

As Commissioner Kenesaw Landis was making the decision to postpone the game scheduled for Friday, October 9, Pirate fans were reading Honus Wagner's comments about Game Two of the World Series in *The Pittsburgh Press*.[65] Wagner reasoned in his syndicated column that Cuyler was ready to break loose because of his game-winning home run.[66] "That hit won the game," wrote Wagner, "and I imagine it will do Cuyler a world of good. I believe he was a bit overwrought in the opening contest. He didn't appear to me to be exactly himself, but that wallop in the second game is going to restore his confidence in himself, and he ought to be a mighty dangerous man in the remaining battles."[67]

Prior to the resumption of war on a baseball diamond, the Pirates' entourage visited President Calvin Coolidge at the White House before Game Three on October 10. Barney Dreyfuss, his son Samuel Dreyfuss, Fred Clarke, secretary Sam Watters, Bill McKechnie, mascot Bill McKechnie, Jr., and all Pittsburgh players were permitted to visit with Coolidge in the rear of the executive mansion. Wives and other relatives who made the trip had to wait outside for their loved ones due to the rules that governed this meeting.[68]

When the team finally reached Griffith Stadium after the memorable occasion, Game Three began with Ray Kremer (17–8, 3.69 ERA) facing Washington's Alex Ferguson (9–5, 6.18 ERA). This game proved to be another tight affair as the lead changed hands on three occasions.

Hazen Cuyler received an opportunity to continue his clutch hitting in the first inning after Eddie Moore and Max Carey reached base. But Cuyler failed to come through as he flied out to Goose Goslin in left field. The Pirates then scored a run in the second inning, but Washington matched that in the third stanza. Cuyler scored Pittsburgh's second run of the afternoon when he led off the fourth with a double and tore home on Clyde Barnhart's single to left. Hazen grounded out to third baseman Buddy Myer and left Max Carey on second in the fifth inning, but his teammates made it 3–1 when they pushed another run across in the sixth. This was all Pittsburgh could muster. Goose Goslin cut the lead to 3–2 when he homered in the bottom of the sixth, before the Senators scored two more runs in the seventh inning to secure a 4–3 victory. In the seventh, Cuyler grounded out harmlessly to short, and in the ninth, he died on base along with Moore and Carey, after being hit by a pitch.

Pittsburgh could have been playing extra innings if not for an adverse decision the previous inning. After Washington reliever Firpo Marberry retired Pittsburgh's first two batters in the eighth stanza, catcher Earl Smith strolled to the plate and drilled a long drive to right-center. Right fielder Sam Rice took off quickly and snagged the ball as he fell into temporary bleachers. Umpire Charles "Cy" Rigler, a National League arbiter, ruled that Rice had made the catch. McKechnie and his players believed Rice had not made a legitimate catch. They reasoned that he lost the ball when he tumbled into the crowd. Even though none of the umpires knew for sure exactly what had happened since Rice's back was facing them when he fell into the crowd, Rigler ruled Smith out when Sam emerged from the bleachers with the ball in his glove.[69]

Pittsburgh's bad karma continued the next day as Walter Johnson took the mound for Game Four on October 11. Washington's staff ace pitched even better than he did during Game One in Pittsburgh. Johnson baffled Pittsburgh's hitters and brought the Senators one step closer to claiming the championship as he shut out the Buccaneers, 4–0. Washington scored all the runs they needed in the third inning, when back-to-back home runs by Goose Goslin and Joe Harris against southpaw Emil Yde accounted for all four tallies. The game may have been lost early for Pittsburgh as Yde, who went 17–9 during the regular season, insisted upon warming up on the sidelines well before the game started. Yde wore out his left arm by tossing fastballs for a half-hour. Making matters worse for Pittsburgh's young pitcher were the numerous cameramen who interrupted him. He became nervous and angry at the photographers, finally waving them away and demanding that they stop bothering him.[70]

Kiki Cuyler was stymied like most of his teammates as Johnson gave a commanding performance in Game Four. The Flint Flash went 0-for-4 and fanned on one occasion. The Pirates no longer had any margin for error as they trailed the defending champions, 3–1. Pittsburgh's pitchers had done well during the first four games of the World Series, but the Buccaneers' deadly bats needed to be awakened. Team vice-president Fred Clarke stated that Pittsburgh's troubles revolved around the team's inability to bunch their hits together.[71]

Cuyler concurred with Clarke's assessment as he talked with Pittsburgh writer Ralph S. Davis in the lobby of the Wardham Hotel prior to the fifth game in Washington.[72] "There ought to be a lot of base hits in our bats today," stated Cuyler. "We hit about .308 during the National League season, and we've hit about .150 in the first four games of this series. There's going to be a break, and it's got to come today."[73]

The words of Kiki Cuyler rang true on October 12, as Pittsburgh's hitters broke through and chased starter Stan Coveleski from the mound during a 6–3 victory. The Corsairs slashed out 13 hits as Cuyler went 2-for-4. Cuyler smacked a Texas Leaguer to right in the first, but was stranded along with Max Carey and Pie Traynor when Glenn Wright failed in the clutch. In the third inning, Cuyler walked and then advanced to third base on Clyde Barnhart's RBI single that scored Carey. Barnhart and Cuyler then attempted to pull off a double steal. As Clyde dashed for second, Kiki started home but then reversed his tracks and went back to third. Cuyler scored moments later on Pie Traynor's sacrifice fly.[74]

Cuyler started off the fifth inning by hitting a long fly ball to Sam Rice in center field. In the seventh frame, Cuyler drilled a single off third baseman Ossie Bluege's glove that brought Eddie Moore home and gave Pittsburgh a 3–2 lead. Carey then crossed the plate and Cuyler made it to third on Barnhart's single, giving Pittsburgh a two-run advantage. Barnhart and Cuyler once again attempted a double steal, but on this occasion Hazen was picked off third base.[75] Pittsburgh padded its lead with single runs in the eighth and ninth frames as Cuyler grounded out to first baseman Joe Judge during the final inning. Vic Aldridge emerged as Pittsburgh's star of the day as he battled gamely and won his second game of the 1925 World Series.

A new hero emerged when the World Series resumed on October 13 in

Pittsburgh. Game Three starters Ray Kremer and Alex Ferguson were chosen to face each other once again in the sixth game. Washington quickly jumped out to a 2–0 lead when Goose Goslin homered in the first and Ossie Bluege scored on Roger Peckinpaugh's double in the second. Pittsburgh then rallied to tie the score in the third inning. Eddie Moore walked to start the frame. Roger Peckinpaugh failed to get the force at second after fielding Carey's grounder. Cuyler then laid down a beautiful sacrifice bunt to Bluege at third, moving both runners up a base. Moore scored on Barnhart's groundout while Carey moved over to third. Max then came home, tying the game when Pie Traynor rapped a single to center.[76]

The score remained tied as Moore led off the fifth inning for Pittsburgh. Moore was struggling with a bad hand that he had injured during batting practice. After Moore sustained the injury, he was seen crying under the stands because he feared letting his teammates down during a crucial game. Moore went to the clubhouse for treatment and hurriedly returned to the field to play. Ferguson tried to get Moore to offer at low pitches in his first two at-bats but failed both times, as the second baseman smacked a single and drew a walk. In the fifth, Ferguson started off Moore with another low pitch that he let go for ball one. Alex then threw him a shoulder high, inside curve ball that Moore met squarely and smashed into the scoreboard over the left field fence. Moore joyously rounded the bases amidst a cascade of cheers. When Eddie reached home plate, his teammates took turns shaking his hand and proceeded to carry him to the dugout on their shoulders.[77]

No additional runners crossed home plate the remainder of the afternoon as Pittsburgh forced a deciding seventh game by defeating Washington, 3–2. Cuyler went 0-for-3, but his crucial sacrifice bunt in the third inning helped move up two runners who eventually scored.

Excited fans throughout Pittsburgh and the rest of America were forced to wait an extra day to witness the final World Series game, as rain prevented the marquee matchup from being played on October 14. This meant that Senators ace Walter Johnson would be pitching with an extra day of rest. Bill McKechnie countered with Vic Aldridge, who had pitched only three days earlier.

Rain and muddy field conditions hampered members of both squads once action commenced on October 15. Aldridge was sent to the showers and replaced by Johnny Morrison after Washington scored four runs in the top of the first inning. It seemed like a four-run lead would be enough for Johnson, who had only given up one run in 18 innings of work. Cuyler failed in his first at-bat of the game when he fanned with Carey on second base, but the young outfielder did make a spectacular catch in the third inning as he hauled in Roger Peckinpaugh's drive while tumbling to the ground.[78]

4. The Flint Flash Becomes a World Series Hero

The Pirates finally reached Johnson when they scored three runs in their half of the third and cut the score to 4–3. The sudden surge of hope was tempered a bit when the Senators came back and put two runs on the scoreboard in the top of the fourth. Pittsburgh gained a run back in the fifth inning when two of their best players stepped forward. Max Carey led off the frame by cracking a double to right for his third hit of the afternoon. Kiki Cuyler then drove home his veteran teammate with Pittsburgh's fourth run of the day by smoking a double that landed right on the foul line in left field.[79]

The score remained 6–4 in Washington's favor until the seventh inning. Fog and darkness was now beginning to descend on the field while rain continued to fall. The weather proved disastrous for shortstop Roger Peckinpaugh, who was unable to catch Eddie Moore's popup due to the horrible conditions. Carey doubled down the left line and scored Moore. Cuyler executed another perfect sacrifice bunt, moving Max to third.[80]

After Clyde Barnhart made the inning's second out, Pie Traynor strode to the plate and brought Forbes Field's fans to their feet when he crushed a drive over right fielder Joe Harris' head. Carey scored the tying run as Traynor made a mad dash around the bases in an effort to stretch the long hit into a home run. But Traynor reached the plate a second too late as Muddy Ruel grabbed Bucky Harris' relay toss and tagged out the Pirates' third baseman. The play loomed significantly one inning later when Roger Peckinpaugh lofted a Ray Kremer pitch over the left field wall for a home run to give Washington a 7–6 lead.[81]

Walter Johnson quickly recorded two outs in the bottom of the eighth, as Glenn Wright fouled out and Stuffy McInnis flied out to Rice in center. During breaks in between batters, Johnson asked members of the grounds crew to spread sawdust on the mound.[82] The rain and muddy field conditions seemed to be bothering Johnson as he attempted to bring another championship to Washington. Earl Smith kept Pittsburgh's hopes alive when he scorched a double. Emil Yde came in to run for Smith while veteran Carson Bigbee batted for pitcher Ray Kremer. Bigbee kept the rally going by doubling over Goose Goslin's head in left and driving home Yde with the tying run. Johnson then experienced control trouble as he walked Eddie Moore. The rally then seemed to end when Max Carey bounced a grounder to Peckinpaugh at short, but he was charged with his eighth error of the series when Bucky Harris could not handle his high toss at second base. Johnson then called time again so that groundskeepers could spread more sawdust on the mound with a rake.[83]

Hazen "Kiki" Cuyler now strode to the plate with the bases loaded and two out. A titanic struggle between the veteran pitcher and the young star outfielder lasted several minutes and ultimately produced the final dramatic effort of the 1925 World Series. The count went to two balls and two strikes before Cuyler fouled off some of Johnson's offerings. Walter then fired a fastball that Cuyler took for ball three; Johnson and catcher Muddy Ruel made a few steps to the dugout thinking that it was actually the third strike.[84] Kiki, possibly remembering his credo of never taking a third strike, swung at Johnson's next pitch and sent the ball screaming down the right field line. Cuyler cleared the bases and triumphantly crossed home plate with an apparent grand slam that gave Pittsburgh an 11–7 lead.[85]

The umpires then conferred for a few minutes and eventually ruled that Cuyler was entitled only to a double since the ball had become lodged temporarily under a tarpaulin.[86] The ground rules disallowed a home run. Carey was ordered back to third base, and the inning ended with Pittsburgh leading 9–7 when Barnhart made the final out.

Southpaw Red Oldham was called upon to finish the game by McKechnie. Oldham did so in splendid fashion as he struck out Sam Rice, induced Bucky Harris to line out to Eddie Moore, and fanned Goose Goslin.[87]

After waiting for 16 years, owner Barney Dreyfuss had finally won his second world championship during his tenure as Pittsburgh's owner. Bill McKechnie's bri-

Cuyler's heroic efforts won two games for Pittsburgh during the 1925 World Series against Washington. His two-run homer in Game Two secured Pittsburgh's 3–2 victory on October 8. Cuyler brought the championship to Pittsburgh when his eighth-inning double against Walter Johnson drove home the deciding markers in Game Seven on October 15. The Pirates prevailed by a score of 9–7 (courtesy the National Baseball Hall of Fame Library, Cooperstown, New York).

gade of young guns had done the improbable by rallying to capture the title after trailing Washington, three games to one, in the 1925 World Series.

The celebration began immediately after catcher Johnny Gooch caught Oldham's final pitch of the game. Fans climbed over Forbes Field's short fences and poured onto the field by the thousands. The royal rooters immediately rushed into the Pirate dugout so that they could congratulate the players with a rousing sendoff before they moved to the clubhouse.[88]

After the players participated in a well-deserved celebration in the locker room, Kiki Cuyler showered and left for his Pittsburgh lodgings. When Cuyler emerged from the clubhouse, 5,000 fans were waiting for him. Some of the fans carried Cuyler on their shoulders to his home a half mile away, showering Kiki with hugs and kisses during the festive journey.[89]

After failing to live up to his reputation as a game changer during the early World Series contests, Cuyler played brilliantly as the Fall Classic wound down.[90] Only two years into his National League career, the Flint Flash truly was a World Series hero.

5. Pennant Hopes Crushed by the ABC Affair

Pittsburgh's roster was filled with players who pulled off remarkable feats during the 1925 World Series. Shortstop Glenn Wright starred in the field while pitchers Ray Kremer and Vic Aldridge emerged as the stars of the mounds corps. Most importantly, the all-round play of Pie Traynor, Max Carey and Hazen Cuyler emerged as the most crucial component behind Pittsburgh's come-from-behind victory over Washington. Cuyler hit only .269 for the series, but his six RBIs and his clutch hitting helped Pittsburgh win the second and the seventh games of the World Series. In his syndicated column after the last game, Honus Wagner wrote that Cuyler came through nicely during the crucial contest. Wagner also commended Hazen for his phenomenal third-inning catch and his timely game-winning double in the eighth. Honus believed that Cuyler delivered clutch play when needed at the finish after looking wobbly at the beginning of the World Series.[1]

National League president John A. Heydler also marveled at how well Pittsburgh performed after falling behind in the series. "I have never been more happy since I was married," said Heydler after the final game. "The National League has a great champion and a game champion in the Pittsburgh Pirates. In every game the Pirates won they came from behind and that is the brand of a great ball club. This is a great climax to the golden jubilee of the National League because it is the first time that the National League won the world's series and the Chicago city series in the same year."[2]

Curiously, there was no parade or special celebration for Pittsburgh's players after the World Series concluded. Since the Fall Classic lasted seven games and went two days beyond the original schedule due to weather postponements, most of the Pirate players immediately began to scatter to their winter homesteads. Hazen Cuyler did not waste any time packing up his belongings for the long trip to his winter home in Michigan. Hazen, son Harold and wife Bertha made their getaway from the Smoky City at noon on

October 16. They traveled by car, first to Harrisville and then to Flint, where Hazen once again intended to take up coaching for the industrial athletic association.[3] Hazen Cuyler's career had evolved dramatically since his humble beginnings in Bay City. Just as Hazen's life had seen numerous changes over the past two years, his father had also been involved in new endeavors. After working as Alcona County's Recorder of Deeds for 14 years and then as county clerk for another four years, George Cuyler was now the head of the Michigan State Fish Hatchery in Harrisville.[4]

Once the Cuyler family reached Flint, Hazen immediately immersed himself in his duties at the Industrial Mutual Association. This organization, which was made up exclusively of factory employees from Flint, was the largest institution of its kind in the world. Delegations from all across America came to Flint so that they could study the plan the association used for its 10,500 members. The club was situated in a five-story building that was considered one of the finest in town. Located on the premises were reading and writing rooms, ladies' club rooms, shower baths, two gymnasiums, rooms for playing cards, a bowling alley and a pool, a beautiful dance floor and a dining room. The association's various programs included dancing, a glee club, boxing and wrestling exhibitions, bowling leagues and tournaments, free gym classes, volleyball leagues, basketball leagues for men and girls, and Kiki Cuyler's all-star team.[5]

The Mutual Association's motto was: "Some place to go in Flint." It was a first-rate community center that attracted attention throughout the country. Cuyler enjoyed the work that he did at the club and was extremely popular with the association's members. Kiki was proud of the club and the role he played in making the establishment successful.[6] Cuyler also benefitted from his activities there since they helped keep him in shape during the winter.

Cuyler discussed his work with a writer from a national baseball magazine after the season ended. "It makes me feel," said Cuyler, "that I am really doing something worth-while in the off-season when most players just loaf. I do not find that this work of mine is too intensive. I thoroughly enjoy it and believe it gives me just enough exercise to keep fit. In the last analysis, success in any athletic sport depends upon condition."[7]

Shortly after Cuyler gave out the interview, he discovered some good news in December surrounding the National League's Most Valuable Player Award. Voting by the Baseball Writers' Association placed Cuyler in second place with 61 points, behind St. Louis' Rogers Hornsby, who finished with 73 points.[8] Cuyler also made an All-Star team from *The Sporting News* as its right fielder, along with teammates Max Carey, Pie Traynor and Glenn Wright.[9]

A few weeks after Cuyler received this recognition, he traveled to Pittsburgh near the Christmas holidays with his basketball team in order to play numerous exhibitions throughout the city. Cuyler and his all-stars set up headquarters at the General Forbes Hotel during their stay in Pittsburgh. They scheduled a number of games in the area against teams like Morrys, the Duquesne Lafayettes, the Homestead Rangers, Butler and the Sewickley Y.M.C.A.[10]

Cuyler's team drew large crowds wherever they played in Pittsburgh. The biggest matchup of the exhibition schedule occurred on New Year's Day when Kiki Cuyler's All-Stars played Goldenson Furnitures at the Southside market house. Former Pirate catcher Cliff Knox was a member of Cuyler's squad, along with center Bill Tracey, who was well known to Pittsburghers that followed basketball. Perhaps drawn by these players, several of Cuyler's Pittsburgh teammates came out to watch the game against Goldenson.[11]

Cuyler's I.M.A. team continued its tour by playing games in Ambridge, Braddock and Pittsburgh coach Jack Onslow's hometown of Tarentum. After trips to Uniontown and Erie, Cuyler and his team finished the exhibition tour in which they played 15 games in 14 days against the Claysville Pioneers. Following this final game, they were guests of honor at an exquisite banquet that included fine food and entertainment.[12]

It was rumored that Cuyler discussed salary terms with Pirates owner Barney Dreyfuss while he was in Pittsburgh. No contract was offered or signed, as many fans in Pittsburgh speculated that Cuyler would seek a huge salary increase. Dreyfuss knew that the championship in 1925 would cost him a bit of money meeting salary demands in 1926. This did not mean that Dreyfuss was willing to break the bank since Pittsburgh's owner followed the long running policy of paying his employees according to the value he attached to them.[13] It was not evident at this point if Cuyler was destined to become a holdout, but rumored information in late January painted a different picture. Local newspapers reported that Cuyler had received two contracts in Flint, but returned them to Dreyfuss without attaching his signature. Hazen personally did not consider himself a holdout, but believed his stance was part of the long negotiating process with Pittsburgh management.[14]

"This negotiating on contracts," said Cuyler, "is simply a part of baseball. It is just such a matter as might be engaged in between two business men when trying to put over a deal. It doesn't signify any break between me and the Pittsburgh Club."[15]

Stories from Flint indicated that Cuyler was hoping for a salary in the five-figure range, possibly $10,000 a year. Sam Dreyfuss, chosen by his father to be the club spokesman on this matter, seemed to view the situation in the same vein as Cuyler, since the Pirates did not officially classify him as a holdout.[16]

Cuyler brought his traveling basketball team to Pittsburgh late in 1925 during the Christmas holiday. The marquee matchup of the Smoky City exhibition tour occurred on New Year's Day, when "Kiki Cuyler's All-Stars" played "Goldenson Furnitures" at the Southside Market House (courtesy the *Alcona County Review*).

"The Pittsburgh Club does not care to comment on reports of holdouts in its ranks," stated Sam Dreyfuss. "When the proper time comes, we will discuss such matters. No man is a holdout until he has refused to report when ordered to do so. Inasmuch as reporting time is several weeks away, we do not consider that we have any holdouts at present."[17]

Owner Barney Dreyfuss had a plan of action in mind for signing his ballplayers, as the National League held its birthday party in New York on

February 2, 1926, at the Hotel Astor to officially close out its golden jubilee celebration.[18] Max Carey, Glenn Wright, Pie Traynor, Vic Aldridge, Earl Smith, Clyde Barnhart and Hazen Cuyler were some of Pittsburgh's players who attended the festive occasion. Prior to the dinner, players who had yet to sign contracts for the upcoming season met separately with Dreyfuss in his room at the Waldorf Astoria. When each member of the Pittsburgh squad emerged from Dreyfuss' room, he had a large smile on his face and seemed to be extremely happy.[19]

Hazen Cuyler met with Pittsburgh's owner around noon. It took Dreyfuss only a few minutes to sign the Flint Flash, as both men quickly exited from the meeting. Neither party discussed the terms of the contract, but player and owner both stated that they were completely satisfied with the outcome.[20] People close to the situation suspected that Cuyler received a salary bump to $10,000 a year. A writer from New York claimed that Cuyler was granted a $6,000 increase in his salary from 1925, thereby bringing the total yearly stipend closer to $12,000 per year.[21] Now that Hazen had squared away the matter of signing a contract for the 1926 season, his only remaining concern was to remain in top physical condition. Cuyler also acted as a scout for the Pirates' organization over the winter as Pittsburgh signed two players from Detroit. First baseman Jim Cousins and pitcher Wheeler Wilcox were added to the Middle Atlantic League's Uniontown entry based on Cuyler's recommendation.[22]

Pittsburgh management did not make many changes to its roster prior to the 1926 season. As the World Series was concluding the previous fall, Barney Dreyfuss did add two players through a conditional deal that he brokered with San Francisco of the Pacific Coast League. Infielder Hal Rhyne and outfielder Paul Waner came to Pittsburgh at the cost of $85,000 and a possible multiple player transfer in the future.[23] Pirates management seemed to be more excited about acquiring Rhyne, even though Waner hit .401 for San Francisco in 1925.

Waner discussed the secret to his success as a batter during training camp at Paso Robles and claimed that all moving objects looked twice their size to him.[24] "My eyes magnify and the balls pitched to me seem twice as large as the regulation baseball," said Waner. "Ever since I can remember, things have appeared slightly larger to me than normal, and this seems especially true of a whirling or running object. I believe being able to see the ball so plainly was the secret of my success in the Coast League."[25]

Having an extra outfielder with solid pedigree was beneficial for Pittsburgh prior to the 1926 season because veteran Max Carey was sidelined by illness. Days after the Pirates clinched the championship against Washington, Carey was admitted to Mercy Hospital in Pittsburgh amidst fear that a bad cold could develop into pneumonia. While there, an X-ray revealed that one rib on his right side was cracked and several ligaments were torn loose. Carey had played the final two World Series games with damaged ribs after colliding with Senators second baseman Bucky Harris during Game Five.[26]

While Carey was on the train that took the Pirates to California for spring training, he once again became ill. He was taken to a St. Louis hospital during a scheduled stop in the Mound City, where doctors diagnosed that he was suffering from a severe cold and pneumonia.[27] Carey joined his teammates after lying idly in a hospital bed for one week, but put in very little training work at Paso Robles and was not expected to be ready once the season began.[28]

As uncertainty continued to cloud the outfield situation for manager Bill McKechnie, he could take solace in knowing that Hazen Cuyler would once again take command of right field. Cuyler was the team's leading home run hitter during practice games, and his batting eye seemed as good as ever throughout spring training.[29] Yet, Cuyler's solid spring did not occur without incident as he joined the Pirates' long list of wounded players for two days due to an injured thumb. Hazen suffered the mishap when he was struck while attempting to snag a fly ball after a long run.[30]

On somewhat of a positive note, Smoky City fans were happy that their most revered and loved player planned on making Pittsburgh his full time home in the future. Cuyler purchased an interest in a local real estate firm with the intention of eventually shifting his winter home from Flint to Pittsburgh.[31]

Cuyler continued to pound the ball as Pittsburgh traversed across America during its exhibition tour. On April 10, he smacked two singles and a triple during a 9–3 victory over Louisville in one of the team's final tune-up games before the season opener at St. Louis.[32]

As the Pirates prepared to begin defense of their 1925 championship on April 13, Bill McKechnie lamented the numerous injuries that crippled his squad. Max Carey was definitely out for the opening game. Eddie Moore and Pie Traynor were slated to play despite suffering from sprained ankles. Carson Bigbee was expected to start in the outfield since rookie Paul Waner had missed time due to receiving eight stitches in his upper lip. McKechnie did not want to indoctrinate the San Francisco recruit unless he felt 100 percent.[33]

Pittsburgh's showing during the opener was predictably off-color as the Pirates lost to St. Louis at Sportsman's Park by a score of 7–6. Cuyler launched his third season as a regular by going 1-for-3.

Pittsburgh endured a horrendous season-opening road trip for the second consecutive year by posting a 2–6 record against St. Louis and Cincinnati. During a 2–1 defeat to the Reds on April 19, Kiki Cuyler took it upon himself to shake the Pirates from their early season funk. In the top of the ninth,

Cuyler reached base by working out a walk against pitcher Carl Mays. Cuyler promptly stole second, moved over to third on an out and eventually scored on Pie Traynor's sacrifice.

Unfortunately, Pittsburgh saw another man added to its list of injured players when shortstop Glenn Wright had to leave the field in the eighth inning after being spiked in the hand as Edd Roush slid into second base.[34] Wright remained in the lineup despite the gash and manned his position during Pittsburgh's opening day, 5–3 loss to St. Louis at Forbes Field on April 22. The Pirates' defeat did not dampen the afternoon's festive atmosphere as Senator George Wharton Pepper and National League President John Heydler assisted with the raising of the United States flag and the league pennant. Former Pennsylvania Governor John K. Tener also threw out the game's first ball.[35]

The Pirates continued to play listless baseball throughout the month of April. When fans viewed the National League standings on May 1, they saw that Pittsburgh was in seventh place, three and a half games behind league-leading Brooklyn. The team's hitting was absolutely abysmal as Max Carey (.152), George Grantham (.185), Eddie Moore (.179), Pie Traynor (.267), Glenn Wright (.250) and Clyde Barnhart (.132) all delivered substandard performances. Compounding the issue for Barnhart was the fact that he showed up at training camp out of shape. During a late April series against the Cubs in Chicago, opposing batters purposely drove balls to left because the girth around Clyde's waistline made it difficult for him to stoop down. Windy conditions also tormented Barnhart as he failed to put his hands on a couple of fly balls that easily eluded him.[36] In his place, rookie Paul Waner was given a chance to show what he could do, but the youngster responded with a mere .143 average as April ended.

Kiki Cuyler was one of the few Pittsburgh players achieving positive results at the plate. When May started, his average stood at .302. Cuyler did not hit his first home run of the season until he smacked a prodigious blast at Forbes Field against Boston on May 5, the ball crossing the left field fence four panels from the scoreboard. The home run marked the 12th consecutive game in which Cuyler had recorded a hit.[37] Hazen's fifth-inning smash was the deciding marker as Pittsburgh claimed a 3–2 victory. In the meantime, Lee Meadows' fine pitching kept Pittsburgh's infielders busy throughout the afternoon, as Glenn Wright and Hal Rhyne accepted a total of 23 chances at short and second.[38]

Cuyler ran his streak to 13 games before Boston's George Mogridge and Joe Genewich held him hitless on May 7. Cuyler then returned to the business of torturing opposing pitchers the following day. Even though Pittsburgh succumbed to Boston by a score of 9–5, Cuyler abused pitcher Skinny Graham throughout the afternoon by racking up a single, double and triple.[39] The game started a stretch of phenomenal hitting that had not been witnessed in Pittsburgh for many years. As game box scores reported Pittsburgh victories throughout May, they also told the tale of Cuyler collecting hit after hit. Cuyler used a five-game stretch in which he went 13-for-21 from May 8 through May 14 to raise his average to .352. In a game against Brooklyn on May 14, Cuyler's speed and guile helped Pittsburgh score two runs in the first inning. On the front end of a double steal, he slid into the plate and knocked over catcher Mickey O'Neil. Second baseman Chick Fewster's return throw flew by both men and rolled to the screen behind home plate. Glenn Wright, who had swiped second, came around to score Pittsburgh's second run before the ball was finally retrieved.[40]

Cuyler continued his rampage against Brooklyn the following day. In the first inning, he barely missed swatting a home run when the ball landed foul by a few feet down Forbes Field's right field line. Hazen was rung up on strikes when he allowed Bob McGraw's next offering to sail past him. Undeterred by his early misfortune, Cuyler eventually secured Pittsburgh's 2–0 victory when he crushed a McGraw pitch that landed for a home run well over the left field wall.[41] As Pittsburgh's long homestand at Forbes Field wound down with a series against New York, Smoky City baseball fans were given the chance to see their favorite players away from the diamond. On the morning of May 20, Kiki Cuyler, Max Carey, Pie Traynor, Glenn Wright and Johnny Morrison appeared at the Kaufmann & Baer Co. Store in downtown Pittsburgh. The players' appearance at Sixth Avenue and Smithfield Street coincided with the store's World's Champion Sporting Goods Sale.[42]

Opposing pitchers were unable to keep Cuyler from recording at least one hit during nearly every game during the month of May. Hazen was playing well even though Bill McKechnie had his star performer play all three outfield positions during a ten-day stretch.[43] In a 9–7 victory against Chicago on May 29, Cuyler's fifth-inning double was the hardest hit of the day; it struck the fence in left-center on the fly before caroming into the waiting glove of Floyd Scott.[44] Hazen also legged out an inside-the-park homer that accounted for three RBIs. On May 30, he smoked another home run in the first inning as Pittsburgh eventually vanquished Cincinnati and Dolf Luque, 4–3.[45] When he recorded four hits during a Decoration Day split with Cincinnati on May 31, he lifted his batting average to .373.

Official National League standings on June 1 showed Pittsburgh in third place with a 23–18 record. They trailed first-place Cincinnati by four games. While players like Eddie Moore, Max Carey and Clyde Barnhart continued to struggle at the plate, Pie Traynor and Glenn Wright joined Cuyler on the short list of competitors swinging hot bats. Rookie Paul Waner raised his average to .299 after Bill McKechnie decided to use him more regularly. Waner had the potential to be the Kiki Cuyler of 1926: a rookie that stormed the National League with a vengeance once given the chance. Yet, there were few other similarities between the two players. Waner was a small, slender man who stood five-foot eight-inches, weighed about 150 pounds and batted left-handed. He was a disciplined hitting technician who took his share of pitches. Cuyler was more of a free-swinger who swung the bat harder than Waner.

Cuyler's sweet swinging pushed him to the top of the National League in batting by early June. After Hazen and Pie Traynor rapped out a hit apiece in a 3–2 victory over Chicago on June 3, Cuyler stood at number one in the batting race while his teammate was six points behind in third place.[46] Cuyler also led the league in stolen bases and hits while Glenn Wright topped the circuit in triples.[47] Cuyler continued to be Pittsburgh's catalyst at the plate even though he was suffering from a badly blistered heel on his foot.[48]

On June 8 against Brooklyn, Hazen went 3-for-5 and scored the tying run in a game that Pittsburgh won, 4–3. Cuyler tripled in the eighth inning off Doug McWeeny and came around to score when outfielder Gus Felix threw wildly to the plate. One day later against Philadelphia, Cuyler's two-run single in the tenth inning gave Pittsburgh a 7–5 victory.[49]

When the Pirates defeated Philadelphia on June 9, they leapt into first place as Cincinnati lost to Brooklyn. Pittsburgh moved a mere seven percentage points ahead of the Reds, topping the National League with a 27–19 record. As Pittsburgh rose to the necessary position from which to defend its title, manager Bill McKechnie was suspended for his actions during the Philadelphia series by league president John Heydler. McKechnie was sidelined after he used offensive language while arguing with umpire Bill Klem. In his report to Heydler, Klem complained that McKechnie used profanity during a heated debate. The suspension interrupted a long period of good behavior for which McKechnie was applauded the previous season.[50]

The Pirates continued to roll despite the fact that their manager sat out a few games. The Pirates posted a 7–2 record from June 12 through June 22, as they remained in a fierce battle with Cincinnati for the National League lead. When Hazen Cuyler drilled two singles during a 6–3 win over Boston on June 16, he ran his hitting streak to 22 consecutive games.[51] Pitcher Freddie Fitzsimmons finally kept Cuyler from recording a hit the following day when New York defeated Pittsburgh, 6–5, in 13 innings. Hazen walked and was hit by a pitch, but failed to hit the ball out of the infield in four other plate appearances.

During his hitting streak, Cuyler had smacked 40 hits and scored 19 runs.[52] From May 8 through June 17, Kiki Cuyler hit safely in 30 out of 32 games and raised his average to .372. After the hitless game against Fitzsimmons, Cuyler quickly regained his hitting stride as he connected safely in each contest when Pittsburgh won three straight games over New York. Hazen was the hero on June 20, when his two-run, inside-the-park homer in the third inning proved the game's crucial hit as Vic Aldridge blanked New York, 8–0.[53]

As Bill McKechnie's squad continued its crusade to claim another pennant, it did so without its admiral for the first time since he came to Pittsburgh after the 1899 season. Barney Dreyfuss decided to take a vacation during the season as he took his wife and daughter to Europe. The Dreyfusses' excursion was scheduled to take them to Germany, Switzerland, France and Belgium. Barney planned on returning before the World Series so that he could hopefully watch his Pirates defend their title.[54] When Dreyfuss and his family boarded the Steamer Columbus in New York City on June 10, he handed over the duties of overseeing the Pirates to another party for the first time ever.[55] Pirates vice-president Fred Clarke, team secretary Sam Dreyfuss and manager Bill McKechnie were left in charge during Barney's absence.

Shortly after Barney Dreyfuss left for Europe, the Pirates started playing some of their worst ball of the season as the team lost seven games in a row during the final week of June. Even Kiki Cuyler was not exempt from slumping along with the rest of his teammates. When official batting averages were posted on June 24, Cuyler was still leading the National League with an average of .371. He now saw his average tail off to .346 after he went hitless during the final four games of the month. False rumors surrounding dissension and fights among Pittsburgh's players were prevalent during the team's horrendous losing streak. One phony story claimed that Vic Aldridge and Glenn Wright were involved in a fistfight. Another tale, which seemed more plausible to Pittsburgh's baseball fans, was the accusation that some players were taking an occasional drink.[56]

In reality, many of Pittsburgh's tribulations could be attributed to injuries. Max Carey had not been physically right all season and was struggling to keep his batting average above .200. Pie Traynor eventually sat out with a sprained ankle after playing on the wounded leg for a few weeks. Glenn Wright missed time with a spike wound and illness, Eddie Moore spent time in the hospital with influenza, and Johnny Gooch continued to play despite an infected throat.[57]

Cuyler and his teammates broke out of their funk in July. The Pirates ended their losing streak when they blitzed St. Louis by a score of 7–3 on July 1. Cuyler helped by connecting for a two-run single during Pittsburgh's five-run, seventh inning. Hazen also recorded his 100th hit of the season during a doubleheader split with Chicago at Forbes Field on July 5.[58]

Hazen Cuyler did not record any hits during a 6–3 victory against New

York one week later, but he was a menace to the Giants in left field. Cuyler handled seven chances flawlessly, with his seventh inning catch ranking as the masterpiece. Giants first baseman George Kelly smashed a towering drive to the scoreboard that Cuyler reached with his blazing speed.[59] On July 14, New York swept a doubleheader against Pittsburgh at Forbes Field, dropping the second-place Pirates three and a half games behind league-leading Cincinnati.

The first tangible sign of internal strife on the ballclub became apparent to fans throughout the city who considered previous tales of dissension as groundless rumors. It was announced after the second game that Eddie Moore had been fined $100 and Emil Yde $50 for indifferent play during the day's first game. Both players had been warned in the past that lack of conscientious effort would bring about stiff reprisals.[60]

Moore was benched in favor of veteran second baseman Johnny Rawlings. This decision came on the heels of Moore making no attempt to field a ground ball in a game against New York on July 12. Moore had been in management's doghouse since last October, when he angered owner Barney Dreyfuss.[61]

Eddie had returned to the starting lineup on four different occasions after faltering badly throughout the 1926 season. Despite being given numerous chances to redeem himself, Moore continued to ignore orders on the field and management's warnings regarding other matters.[62] Pittsburgh finally decided to ship Moore and his .227 batting average elsewhere. On July 20, the hero from Game Six of the 1925 World Series was sold on waivers for $4,000 to the Boston Braves.[63] Young infielder Joe Cronin was recalled from New Haven of the Eastern League to replace Moore.[64]

Fines and discipline problems did not stop with Moore's exit from Pittsburgh. Pitcher Vic Aldridge was fined $50 for failing to return to Pittsburgh's dugout after he was lifted from a game. After being knocked out of the box in the first inning of a game against Brooklyn on July 21, Aldridge dressed and remained in the locker room rather than returning to the bench as per team rules. Aldridge claimed that he had a sore arm when he was selected to pitch the game against Brooklyn. Pitcher Johnny Morrison also ran afoul with manager Bill McKechnie for deserting the team without permission and returning to his home in Owensboro, Kentucky. Morrison claimed that he went home since he could not pitch due to an injured arm. McKechnie informed Morrison that he was suspended indefinitely for his actions.[65]

In spite of these disciplinary problems, Pittsburgh held down the National League's top spot with a 55–40 record at the end of July. Kiki Cuyler and rookie Paul Waner were given credit for keeping Pittsburgh's outfield from total collapse, as Max Carey and Clyde Barnhart continued to struggle.[66] Cuyler was hitting .332 while Waner had caught fire and was now batting

.330. Hazen then went 11-for-23 during a six-game stretch on an Eastern trip that saw Pittsburgh go 4–2. The Pirates lost the services of shortstop Glenn Wright during one of those victories when he injured his leg sliding into second base after hitting a seventh-inning double.[67] With one of Pittsburgh's heaviest hitters now on the sidelines, Cuyler went hitless in both games of a doubleheader against Boston on August 7, as the Pirates suffered the humiliation of being shut out by the seventh-place Braves in both games.

It was during a break in between these two games that the fate of Pittsburgh's season was shaped in a profound way. Team vice-president Fred Clarke made a recommendation to manager Bill McKechnie regarding a lineup change for the second game of the doubleheader. Clarke sat on the bench during the first game and watched Max Carey go 0-for-4. Clarke planned on leaving after the first contest so that he could catch a train and arrive in New York ahead of the Pirates' squad. As Fred rose from the bench to leave, he turned to McKechnie and offered some unsolicited advice.[68] "Better get someone out there to play centerfield," bellowed Clarke in a loud voice that could be heard by everyone who remained in the dugout. "Max is having a hard time of it."

"I haven't got anybody," McKechnie replied.

"Put somebody out there, even if it is a pitcher," suggested Clarke as he left the dugout.[69]

Carey was not in the dugout when Clarke offered this radical suggestion to McKechnie. Loyal teammates who heard Clarke's remark quickly informed the veteran outfielder that he had been treated disrespectfully by Pittsburgh's assistant manager. In response, Carey, along with fellow veterans Carson Bigbee and Babe Adams, decided to hold a team meeting to decide whether Clarke should be permitted to remain in the dugout. The players held a secret meeting in their hotel upon arrival in New York. Only six players voted to have Clarke removed from the bench, while 18 favored him continuing as McKechnie's assistant. It was not known who voted against Clarke, other than Carey, Bigbee and Adams. When the press began polling the other players to see where their loyalties stood, each man denied voting against the team vice-president.[70]

When the Pirates arrived in Pittsburgh on August 13, a meeting that included the players, Bill McKechnie, Fred Clarke and Sam Dreyfuss was held at Forbes Field that evening. Those within earshot of a closed door morning meeting between the three members of Pittsburgh's management team could hear loud talking coming from Forbes Field's club office. Many members of the press believed that Clarke would demand that the ringleaders of the uprising be punished severely.[71] That sentiment was echoed when Sam Dreyfuss addressed the media and read a prepared statement. He claimed that the attack on Fred Clarke was absolutely unnecessary and unwarranted. Dreyfuss also stated that the insurrection needed to be stopped quickly, and at the source.[72]

> Clarke, McKechnie and myself are paid to run the ball club, each having his respective duties to perform, whatever they might happen to cover.
>
> We have considered the matter of what should be done in this particular instance, with extreme care, and have reached the firm and unalterable conclusion that for those spokesmen or ring-leaders, of the insurrection, Adams is unconditionally released, effective at once, and Bigbee also is unconditionally released, to take effect immediately. Carey is suspended without pay, pending waivers, which were asked on him today. His services will go to the claimant whose club is the lowest in the standing of the teams, or otherwise he will be sold at the waiver price.[73]

Max Carey's career as a Pirate officially ended on August 18, when the Brooklyn Robins claimed him off waivers. With the matter finally settled, Pittsburgh management had released a veteran outfielder, a pitcher who was the hero of the 1909 World Series victory, and a man who played with broken ribs during the final two games of the 1925 World Series. Sam Dreyfuss still believed that the Pirates would finish on top of the National League standings despite the situation involving Adams, Bigbee and Carey. Clarke and Dreyfuss both thought the insurrection had been nipped successfully. When Dreyfuss was asked why the other three players who voted to have Clarke removed from the bench were not disciplined, he responded that they were young players who had been unduly influenced by the veteran Pirates. Dreyfuss finally closed the door on the whole affair when he announced that Pie Traynor would replace Carey as team captain.[74]

Pittsburgh's management team probably reasoned that the loss of these three players would be minimal since none of them had offered a major contribution to the team's success in 1926. Unfortunately, Dreyfuss and Clarke failed to measure the intangibles these three players possessed. The young baseball executive in waiting failed to realize that the "ABC Affair" (as it was referred to by Pittsburgh newspaper scribes) would prove to be Pittsburgh's downfall in its attempt to repeat as National League champions. After Dreyfuss made his statement to the press, Pittsburgh's players looked funereal as they listlessly filed out of the room.[75]

Rumors immediately began to filter throughout Pittsburgh after Dreyfuss released the three players. There was talk of the players taking part in a sympathy strike during their next ballgame. Another tale claimed that team management planned on requesting 50 extra policemen from the public safety department in case disgruntled fans rushed onto the field.[76]

These concerns turned out to be irrelevant as poor weather prevented the Pirates from playing a game at Forbes Field until August 18. When the Pirates split a doubleheader against Boston, they clung to first place by a mere half-game over St. Louis. Pittsburgh continued to battle gallantly for a few weeks before collapsing badly, going 2–9 during a stretch in late August and early September. The Pirates never recovered and finished the year with an 84–69 record that placed them in third place, four and a half games behind the pennant-winning Cardinals.

The ABC Affair definitely played a significant role in Pittsburgh's disappointing 1926 season. The Pirates posted a mediocre 23–24 record after Adams, Bigbee and Carey were released. Public opinion did not side with team management, as most of Pittsburgh's fans agreed with the three players. The remainder of the Pirate squad was deeply affected by the dismissal of Adams, Bigbee and Carey. Management's goal of achieving team harmony through the release of these men was not realized; displeasure continued to be prevalent throughout the season's final two months. The players were particularly disgruntled over their requirement to play a meaningless exhibition contest in Bridgeport, Connecticut, on September 26 after the season ended. Some of the Pirates were openly hostile about the injustice, while others made sarcastic remarks or laughed off the subject when it was brought up.[77]

The unseemly episode profoundly affected Hazen Cuyler's play during the season's final month and a half. Even though he did not openly show it, Cuyler seemed to be deeply troubled by the dismissal of Carey. Carey had gone to great lengths to teach Cuyler the nuances of baserunning when the Flint Flash came to Pittsburgh. Max had always been the consummate role model for Cuyler and his teammates. Kiki seemed to be detached and distracted at times as the 1926 season mercifully came to an end. In a game against Brooklyn on August 23, he failed to touch home plate after apparently hitting an inside-the-park home run. Umpire Beans Reardon noticed the mistake and catcher Mickey O'Neil trotted over to the Pirates' dugout to tag Cuyler out.[78] On September 15, Cuyler threw the ball wildly to third for no apparent reason in a game against the Giants. The errant toss allowed a New York runner who eventually scored the winning run to move to second base instead of being held at first.[79]

In 1926, Kiki Cuyler appeared in every game for the Pirates and batted .321. He led the National League with 113 runs and 35 stolen bases. He also tied Pie Traynor for the team lead in RBIs with 92. Even though Hazen saw his batting mark drop about 30 points from his final mark of the previous two seasons, he was selected by Babe Ruth as the right fielder on the Bambino's yearly All-Star team. The choice of position seemed odd since Cuyler played only 18 games for Pittsburgh as a right fielder in 1926.[80] Cuyler's season was not subpar compared to other National League players, but it certainly did not measure up to the lofty standards usually placed upon the game's stars. Pittsburgh fans alarmed by Kiki's late-season slump as the season spun out of control also had to be concerned that the Flint Flash might not be happy playing in Pittsburgh. Shortly after Barney Dreyfuss returned from Europe in late August, he was interviewed by Frank Wallace of the *New York Evening Post*. During this interaction between owner and scribe, Dreyfuss denied numerous rumors surrounding Cuyler.[81]

The first point that Dreyfuss refuted was Wallace's contention that Cuyler was the only player who occupied a training table during spring training in Paso Robles. Wallace then made the bizarre claim that Max Carey was jealous of Cuyler and had wanted to get rid of him for the last three years. Dreyfuss replied that Carey never made any such statements to him. Wallace then touched upon the rumor surrounding Cuyler's desire to be traded away from Pittsburgh. Dreyfuss responded by stating that he was not aware of any such request.[82]

After the season ended, Cuyler was also mentioned in connection with the infamous August vote that was taken concerning Fred Clarke's removal from the Pirate bench. Pittsburgh writer Chester L. Smith stated that Eddie Moore, George Grantham and Cuyler had not been fond of Clarke's meddling tendencies from the outset. Smith also claimed that Grantham had possibly joined Adams, Bigbee and Carey in casting a vote against Clarke.[83] Moore was no longer with the team when the vote was taken, and many Pittsburgh baseball fans pondered the possibility that Cuyler had voted to have Clarke removed from the dugout.

Rumors surrounding possible player deals gained traction after the season concluded. It was reported that some players feared they would be disposed of during the winter, while there were others who hoped they would be playing somewhere else in 1927.[84] Pittsburgh rooters hearing these rumors became disturbed at the inclusion of Hazen "Kiki" Cuyler in connection with trade possibilities. Their apprehension was alleviated somewhat when it was reported that Barney Dreyfuss had never intimated that he wanted to trade Cuyler.[85] Other fans, whose fears could not be so easily quelled, wondered if management was still bitter over Cuyler's contract situation at the beginning of the 1926 season. Some rooters speculated that Dreyfuss believed Cuyler's ego had become inflated after hearing about special stationary that the Pittsburgh outfielder ordered following the 1925 season. The letterhead at the top of the paper read: "Hazen S. "Kiki" Cuyler — Star of the 1925 World Series — Flint, Michigan.[86]

Barney Dreyfuss moved swiftly to reshape the Pirate organization for the 1927 campaign. First baseman Stuffy McInnis was released shortly after the season because he had leaked word of the vote to have Fred Clarke removed to the newspapers.[87] Manager Bill McKechnie was the next one to go, as Dreyfuss notified him on October 12 that he would not return as Pittsburgh's

5. Pennant Hopes Crushed by the ABC Affair

One year after winning a championship, manager Bill McKechnie was relieved of his duties following the 1926 season. Fallout from the ABC Affair involving players Babe Adams, Carson Bigbee and Max Carey contributed to the dismissal. In this photograph, McKechnie is shown with his son, Billy Jr. (courtesy the National Baseball Hall of Fame Library, Cooperstown, New York).

manager.[88] Dreyfuss wasted little time in naming a new manager, choosing Donie Bush to be his skipper for the 1927 season. This announcement came as a bit unexpected since Pittsburgh's owner had given every indication that he was going to conduct a long, thorough search for a new manager.[89] The front office restructuring was then completed when Fred Clarke mailed his resignation as vice-president and director to Dreyfuss at the end of October.[90]

Donie Bush had done great work for three years at the Triple-A level as manager of the Indianapolis Indians. Bush also led the Washington Senators to a fourth-place finish in 1923 during his only season as a big league pilot. Donie had played with Ty Cobb in Detroit from 1908 to 1921 before finishing his career with Washington. Molded from the old-school style of baseball, Bush wanted his players to play hard and fight for every advantage on the diamond.[91]

"The fans of Pittsburgh will never be able to accuse me of not hustling," stated Bush upon his introduction as Pittsburgh's new manager. "I will give them my best at all times. If that isn't good enough, then I'll be ready to step out. But as long as I'm in charge, the Pirates will give the fans a run for their money."[92]

Bush also stated that he had heard good things about Glenn Wright, Pie Traynor, George Grantham, Ray Kremer and Kiki Cuyler. He considered each to be a first-class ballplayer and was confident that every Pirate would give him their best efforts. Bush also said that he permitted his players to do their own thinking on the field.[93]

"I encourage them to think," replied Bush, "as long as they exercise their brains, I don't believe in interfering with them. But if they show me that they can't think readily for themselves, I attempt to do it for them."[94]

When Bush went to New York for the league meetings in December, he was unable to broker any player deals to his liking. Bush believed that new personnel could have been brought to Pittsburgh if he was willing to trade something valuable for something insignificant.[95]

Hazen Cuyler's fans and friends felt relieved when no trade involving their favorite player took place. Cuyler believed that he was going to rebound and have a huge season in 1927. Hazen also figured that Donie Bush would make an ideal manager; he was prepared to give the new skipper his utmost cooperation.[96] This type of attitude represented the norm for Cuyler as he prepared for his fourth major league campaign. The previous season had been a turbulent year for every Pirate. Kiki Cuyler would soon find that the situation would worsen in 1927.

6. Manager Donie Bush Banishes Cuyler to the Bench

The arrival of Kiki Cuyler and his industrial basketball team in Pittsburgh early in 1927 did not receive the same intense fanfare that the group was exposed to one year earlier when its most famous player was christened a World Series hero. When he reached Pittsburgh with his basketball troupe in early January, Cuyler immediately called on Barney Dreyfuss. After a very short conference between Cuyler and his boss, it was announced that Pittsburgh's star outfielder had signed a contract for the 1927 season. Salary figures were not leaked to the press, but both sides seemed extremely satisfied when the meeting ended. Cuyler was confident he would bounce back in grand style after a troubling season in 1926. In addition to injuries, Cuyler was affected by the internal strife that resulted from the ABC Affair, which tore apart the team emotionally.[1]

While Cuyler was in Pittsburgh with his basketball team, the star outfielder discussed the state of baseball with a local sports scribe. A dedicated man who approached any endeavor with passion and fortitude, Cuyler continued to be a steadfast supporter of the game of baseball, which supplied a livelihood for him and his family. Kiki was convinced that the vast majority of players who competed on a professional level were honest, honorable men who championed integrity.[2]

"In all my career," said Cuyler, "I can truthfully state that I have not heard anything of a questionable nature said by ball players, and I am convinced that almost every boy who enters the sport is inherently honest. The desire to win is a natural one, which the average player cannot resist."[3]

That natural desire to win was also prevalent when Cuyler performed on a basketball court. The team from Flint, Michigan, was now affectionately known as the "Cuylers"; Pittsburgh patrons who attended games loved watching Kiki and his players. The Cuylers finished off another successful exhibition tour through the Smoky City with a game against St. Michael's at the Lyceum on Pius Street. Before Hazen headed back to Flint, he thanked the people of Pittsburgh for treating his team splendidly during their stay in the Steel City. Cuyler had little else to say about baseball as he departed, other than to assure everyone that he would be ready to begin training camp in Paso Robles at the end of February.[4]

Cuyler also promised Barney Dreyfuss that he would report in the best of physical condition. Cuyler was a workaholic during the winter months who exercised daily and was very careful of his habits.[5] While Cuyler was keeping fit at Flint's Industrial Mutual Association, fellow anti–Fred Clarke faction teammate George Grantham held down an off-season job that indicated a political career was on the horizon after his playing days. Grantham was employed as a doorkeeper at the Senate Chamber of the Arizona Legislature in the state capital. He collected $5 a day performing a cushy job, which allowed him to wear his best clothes in the process. He also relaxed a bit during the off-season by hunting big game in northern Arizona.[6]

As Pittsburgh's players worked over the winter to stay in shape and earn extra money, the team's new manager dodged a bullet when he was falsely accused of throwing games during his playing career. Donie Bush had been implicated by former Black Sox players Swede Risberg and Chick Gandil, as had been a host of other ballplayers. These men were quickly cleared of any wrongdoing by the commissioner's office. Barney Dreyfuss expressed the fullest confidence in Bush's integrity from the outset while the manager vehemently denied the charges. Fans who watched Bush play in Detroit felt the accusation lacked foundation because of his constant hustle.[7]

Shortly after Bush's reputation was restored, he talked about the Pirates' ballclub as spring training loomed. "I have weighed the Pirate boys in my mind," stated Donie Bush, "and I am convinced I will have no club dissension. They appear to be a bunch of good scouts with fine baseball ability and it will be my task to get the best results out of them.

"The fact there are no holdouts is pleasing because it makes me feel everybody is starting the grind satisfied and with minds at rest. With no disturbance in the ranks at the jump-off of spring training, everything is even and throws the burden of responsibility on me, which I accept."[8]

Bush made minimal changes to his roster for the 1927 season. He purchased former World Series opponent Joe Harris of Franklin, Pennsylvania, from Washington for the waiver price in early February. Harris became expendable when Senators owner Clark Griffith signed Tris Speaker for his squad.[9] Paul Waner's younger brother Lloyd was also making the spring trip to Paso Robles so that Bush could get a better assessment of the youngster's capabilities. Lloyd had performed quite proficiently for Columbia of the Sally League in 1926, as he appeared in 121 games and hit .345. Pittsburgh management was anxious to see whether the younger Waner could make the kind of impression that Paul did for the team during his rookie season, when he led the Pirates with a .336 average.

In late February, Harris, Pie Traynor and Clyde Barnhart, in addition to youngsters Herman Layne and Adam Comorosky, boarded a train in Pittsburgh that would transport this second squad of players to Paso Robles for spring training. Kiki Cuyler joined his teammates when the train reached Chicago. Paul Waner, Lloyd Waner and Glenn Wright boarded the special flyer in Kansas City. Players such as George Grantham, Hal Rhyne and rookie Dick Bartell were ordered to join their teammates, along with pitchers and catchers who had already reported, from their homes on the Pacific Coast.[10]

During this trip, Cuyler supposedly made a remark regarding Donie Bush's managerial ability. Hazen's somewhat innocuous comment implied that Donie was just a "busher." Some players who overheard this observation passed the information along to Bush when the team reached California.[11]

The manager quickly laid down his rules of discipline once the full squad arrived at Paso Robles. The players were notified that they had to be in their rooms and ready for bed no later than 11 o'clock every evening, except on Saturday when the curfew was pushed to midnight. They had to report for work in the hotel lobby each morning no later than 7:30.

Bush also banned his players from the consumption of alcohol, since he believed that drinking and playing ball did not mix.[12] Bush vowed that he would search out potential violators rather than incorporating a spy system. He also notified the players that these rules applied only during the training season.[13]

Bush then turned his attention to letting the players know what he expected of them as professionals. "I am always willing to listen to good advice," said Bush, "and I am always open to reasonable suggestions. But when I make up my mind that a certain course is best for the team, I expect to have my orders carried out, and my wishes respected. I am not going to be dictatorial, but I am going to be boss — and there aren't going to be any others. I am interested only in the production of a winning ball team, and I want the perfect cooperation of every man on it."[14]

Kiki Cuyler quickly realized that Bush would be much different from the easy going Bill McKechnie. Shortly after the squad reached California, Bush asked Cuyler to change his technique of leading off from second base. Donie wanted Hazen to face the pitcher rather than having his back to the third baseman. Cuyler had learned this style from Max Carey and used it effectively for the past three seasons, but he complied with Bush's wishes since he conveyed indisputable authority as Pittsburgh's manager.[15] After performing capably for McKechnie, who always utilized his players' ability without much interference regarding individual techniques, Cuyler now faced the prospect of playing for a man who liked to micromanage such things.

As was the case in past spring training sessions, Cuyler hit the ball hard throughout the exhibition season. In a game against the Mission Bells of the Pacific Coast League on March 19, Cuyler accounted for three hits and crossed home plate four times. One of Hazen's safeties was a prodigious three-run home run.[16] Cuyler continued his long ball proficiency on March 24 when he blasted another home run in an 18–11 victory over San Francisco. Paul Waner also banged out three hits against his former team.[17] Not surprisingly, Kiki Cuyler and Paul Waner were pegged by manager Donie Bush to fill two of Pittsburgh's outfield spots. Left field remained a concern for the Pirate skipper since veteran Clyde Barnhart was coming off a horrendous season in which he batted .192.

Barnhart was locked in a battle with Herman Layne and Lloyd Waner for the starter's job in left field. Layne was a good fielder but could not hit much. Waner had played well in spots during the exhibition tour, but it was not yet apparent to Bush that he had the experience or stamina required at the major league level. Barnhart was a streaky hitter whose real problems arose when he had to field a ground ball in the outfield.[18] Bush ultimately benched Barnhart as the exhibition tour wound down, replacing him with Lloyd Waner. For the second year in a row, Barnhart had reported grossly out of shape and was unable to field grounders due to a protruding waistline. In contrast, Lloyd did fairly well defensively except for difficulties with the sun. When this happened, he ran the risk of having the ball hit him in the head.[19]

Prior to the opening game in Cincinnati on April 12, Bush chose Lloyd Waner to start in left field. He planned on playing Waner at ballparks in which left field was not the sun field. Lloyd had done quite well at the plate during the practice season, hitting .320 in sporadic appearances. Brother Paul led the Pittsburgh squad with a .400 average during the training tour, while Kiki Cuyler finished second at .381.[20]

All three of these players had a hand in Pittsburgh claiming a 2–1 victory over Cincinnati in the season opener. Lloyd beat out a bunt with a burst of speed after George Grantham led off the first inning with a single.[21] After Cuyler moved the runners up with a beautiful sacrifice bunt, Paul Waner drove both men home with a blistering single. Besides laying down the crucial first-inning bunt, Cuyler went 2-for-3 at the plate.

Cuyler's hitting sizzled during the first week of the season, as his average stood at .474 after five games.[22] Similarly, the Pirates enjoyed a fantastic start with a record of 7–1 after a 3–1 victory over Cincinnati at Forbes Field on April 22. Praise for Pittsburgh's dynamic duo of Kiki Cuyler and Paul Waner rang throughout the city. The two players were liberally compared to each other during the Pirates' successful start. Writer Lou Wollen remarked that an observer could not always assess a ballplayer on the way he wore his uniform; Cuyler had appealed to scouts when he was young because he was a tidy man, while Paul Waner was rejected by a New York Giants scout due to the fact he did not know how to properly wear his uniform.[23]

Kiki Cuyler's ability was also evident during games when he did not record a hit. During a tight, 3–2 victory over Cincinnati on April 21, Cuyler made a terrific return throw on a long fly holding all runners at their bases. Opponents throughout the league had the utmost respect for Cuyler's cannon arm and were reluctant to challenge him when an opportunity arose.[24] In the same game against the Reds, Lloyd Waner also made a game-saving catch off Curt Walker in the ninth inning. Waner hustled earnestly to make the play after Walker connected against a Ray Kremer offering and drove the ball deep to left. Without ever hesitating, Waner instinctively pursued the ball and grabbed it near the fence. After making the catch, Waner maintained his composure even while crashing into the wall.[25]

Pittsburgh's solid start quickly became a fond memory as Bush's squad played uninspired ball throughout the remainder of April. After losing 7–6 against Chicago on May 1, the Pirates stood in third place with a 9–6 record, which left them a game and a half behind the league-leading New York Giants. Kiki Cuyler had batted exclusively from the number three slot up to that point. Even though the Flint Flash was batting .345, he had only driven home one runner during Pittsburgh's first 15 games. So Manager Donie Bush decided to make some changes to the order in the hope that he could shake some players from their slumber. He switched Cuyler from third in the order to the second spot. Hazen had batted second on numerous occasions while playing for Bill McKechnie the past three seasons and did so without complaining. But things were different in 1927, as Cuyler and Bush's opinions differed for the second time.

After Bush informed Cuyler that he was making the lineup change because the Pirates were not hitting, Hazen responded that he would bat or field in any place the manager desired to help the team. Cuyler told Bush that he had never experienced much luck in the past when batting second, but vowed to do his best. Bad luck seemed to engulf Cuyler immediately after the change was made. He hit the ball as hard as ever, but it seemed that every blistering drive went straight to an opposing fielder or was turned into a double play. Hazen's fellow Pittsburgh players quickly dubbed him "Double O," due to his propensity for grounding into double plays.[26]

Even though Cuyler accepted his plight, it was evident that Pittsburgh's star outfielder was not happy. Cuyler also seemed to lose his confidence a bit as he was razzed by teammates for the first time since joining the Pirates. Hitting second was tough for a free-swinging hitter like Hazen, who was not as adept at slicing the ball behind a runner, as Max Carey had done successfully for many years in Pittsburgh. Still, as time went by, Bush insisted on dictating to his men how they should hit. Pittsburgh's manager asked Cuyler to hit behind his runners, but Hazen insisted on hitting as he saw fit because he either refused to obey orders, or was simply unable to do so. Regardless of what motivated Cuyler in this instance, some within the Pirates' ranks believed that he was more interested in personal goals than in the team's general success.[27]

When Bush first made the lineup switch, he told Cuyler that he would eventually settle into his new role. After a hitless game against St. Louis at Forbes Field on May 5, Bush once again attempted to calm down the irritated player, who was now fuming over his struggles while batting second. Cuyler's frustration boiled over following a particularly humiliating performance against Cincinnati on May 23, when he went 0-for-5. Despite the fact that Pittsburgh won the game, 8–5, Hazen's petulant behavior reached a peak when he slammed his bat into the ground after a difficult plate appearance.

"Take me out of the second slot before I become the worst flop on your team!" Cuyler yelled to Bush in the dugout.

"You'll stay there until I am ready to change you," responded Bush.[28]

Catcher Earl Smith quickly seized upon the opportunity to needle Cuyler. Smith's acid tongue was known to inflict pain on teammates as well as enemy players from an opposing team. Smith decided to inflame the situation by chastising Cuyler in front of Bush.[29]

"Doesn't Kiki like where the manager wants him to bat?" questioned Smith mockingly. "Too bad!"[30]

Nonetheless, Bush's squad played brilliant baseball while Cuyler struggled as the team's number two hitter. Pittsburgh put together a terrific stretch by winning 11 consecutive games and moving into first place. The Pirates raised their record to 22–11 after an 8–7 victory over St. Louis on May 27. They now led the second-place Cubs by a game and a half. Cuyler even rebounded a bit, just as Bush had predicted, after his batting average dropped to .294 on May 23. He went 9-for-17 during the next four contests and pushed his average up to .324. Cuyler also scored over a quarter of the team's runs during that four game stretch. Hazen did good work once again on May 28, when he went 2-for-4 during the Pirates' 6–4 victory over St. Louis.

Cuyler's hustling style actually came back to haunt him late in the game when his star-crossed season took another bad turn. Misfortune once again plagued Cuyler when he injured his ankle making a slide into third base while trying to evade a forceout. Cuyler actually remained in the game for another inning before he was ordered to make a trip to the hospital. When he arrived at the infirmary, Cuyler was reported to have pleaded with attendants to let him return to Forbes Field so that he could watch the remainder of the game. Hazen promised that he would return to his hospital bed after his teammates had secured a Pirate victory.[31] This did not seem like the type of behavior that one would expect from a man who was more interested in personal glory over a team's goal of winning a pennant.

The Pittsburgh organization initially feared that Cuyler had broken a bone in his leg. An X-ray alleviated those concerns but revealed that Cuyler had suffered a torn ligament in his ankle.[32] He was sidelined indefinitely.[33] Clyde Barnhart replaced the Flint Flash in left field and did marvelous work in his place.[34] The Pirates continued to roll while Cuyler rested on the sidelines, as they battled Chicago and St. Louis for the National League lead. They held down the league's top spot on June 15 with a 33–17 record and led second-place Chicago by one game. Barnhart set a torrid pace at the plate with a .440 average. In a negative development, Johnny Morrison, Ray Kremer and Earl Smith quickly joined Cuyler on the disabled list. By June 9, Kremer, Smith and Cuyler were participating in a light exercise regimen while Morrison was hoping to return to uniform that day.[35]

While he was injured, Cuyler warmed up pitchers, threw to batters who wanted to get in some work and took extra batting practice of his own on the sidelines.[36] Just as Cuyler seemed ready to test his ankle in actual game conditions, another Pirate was forced into street clothes even though he was not suffering from an injury. Earl Smith, the man who was lethal with both his quips and his fists, put the latter to good use against an opponent on June 18. In the seventh inning of Pittsburgh's win over Boston, Dave Bancroft drew a walk and strolled down to first base, while Smith whizzed the ball past his ear to first baseman Joe Harris. Bancroft stopped to say something and Smith came right back with a verbal barrage of his own. Bancroft later scored and, without hesitation, approached plate umpire Barry McCormick to complain about Smith's attitude.[37]

Smith quickly responded to Bancroft by tossing away his catcher's mitt and punching the Boston manager in the face with his left hand. Bancroft dropped to the ground, knocked senseless, and was then taken to the clubhouse where a physician revived him and administered several stitches to close a cut on his face. Umpire Barry McCormick quickly threw Smith out of the game. As Pittsburgh's catcher was leaving the field, he attempted to rush Braves coach Dick Rudolph before being restrained.[38] National League president John Heydler took swift action, suspending Smith for 30 days and fining him $500. Heydler also rebuked the catcher in a letter sent both to Smith and the press.[39]

Kiki Cuyler was finally given a chance to appear in a game against Boston the day before the Smith-Bancroft incident. Cuyler pinch-hit for Lloyd Waner in the sixth inning and finished the game in center field, hobbling noticeably. His ankle was not quite ready to withstand the rigors of regular work. Many fans reasoned that it would be good policy on the part of Pittsburgh management to give the injury plenty of time to heal since the present outfield combination was doing such good work.[40]

Cuyler made two appearances as a pinch hitter before finally being put back into the starting lineup on June 22. Hazen was placed in right field while Paul Waner took over at first base. Cuyler also returned to the batting order's second slot, as Pittsburgh defeated Cincinnati, 11–9. Cuyler's ankle seemed to be completely healed as he covered plenty of ground, ran the bases in his usual flashy style and banged out three hits on the day. One of Kiki's safeties carried to the Forbes Field flagpole and brought back memories from the past as he waltzed into third base with a triple.[41]

A few days prior to his triumphant return, Cuyler exhibited the depth of his compassion and caring nature in front of 37,000 fans at Wrigley Field on June 19. While Chicago had been out of town on a road trip, a blackbird had built a nest for her young in the press corps coop. During the afternoon's proceedings between the Cubs and Pirates, the mother took one of her young down on the field in an effort to teach it how to fly. The mother became frantic when the youngster was unable to fly off the grass. Wrigley Field was filled with fans, balls were bounding about, and a foul ball could have killed the little blackbird. Sensing that the youngster would not be flying on this day, Cuyler walked over to where the bird was resting between the catcher and first base. Hazen picked up the bird and placed it in the care of Pittsburgh's batboy. The mother was not completely appeased until the bird was placed in front of the screen directly behind home plate, where it remained until the game was over.[42]

Cuyler wasted little time in doing damage against National League hurlers. During a 6–4 loss against Chicago on June 25, Hazen showed everyone at Forbes Field that he could still hit with power. Cuyler blasted a missile in the third inning that caromed off the top of Forbes Field's left field scoreboard and bounded into nearby Schenley Park.[43] Unfortunately, Cuyler's return to the starting lineup was short-lived as he aggravated his tender ankle during the game. Paul Waner went back to right field and Cuyler once again grabbed a seat on the bench.[44] He played sporadically during the next week and started only one of the games at Sportsman's Park.

Hazen was sitting in the dugout on June 28, when he witnessed a play that nearly had tragic repercussions for a Pittsburgh teammate. In the seventh inning of the game that Pittsburgh won, 9–8, Cardinals pitcher Vic Keen let loose with a pitch that struck Glenn Wright in the head. Wright dropped to the ground upon impact and laid motionless at the plate. Keen, who seemed

6. Manager Donie Bush Banishes Cuyler to the Bench

visibly shaken by what happened, rushed toward home plate. Keen lifted Wright's head, embraced Pittsburgh's shortstop and began hugging and consoling him. Keen was pulled away by several players, but he fought them off and remained kneeling at Wright's side. As it became apparent that Keen was becoming nearly hysterical, St. Louis coaches Bill McKechnie and Alan Sothoron, along with pitcher Grover Alexander, escorted him to the clubhouse. When Vic heard that an ambulance came to take Wright to the hospital, he broke down and wept. Keen was one of the first people to visit Wright at the hospital, and felt relief when he heard that Wright's prognosis was good and the injury was not severe.[45]

Wright was fortunate that he was not killed by Keen's pitch, which struck him just below the left temple. According to medical experts who examined Wright, the blow would have been fatal if it had struck him a fraction of an inch higher. He did not seem to be suffering any ill effects from the beaning other than the large lump where the ball came in contact with his head. Manager Donie Bush informed the press that Wright would immediately leave for Pittsburgh in the company of a teammate after being released from the hospital that afternoon.[46]

The careers of Glenn Wright and Hazen Cuyler had flourished in unison since the two players were part of Pittsburgh's great rookie class in 1924. The two men had been instrumental in transforming the Pirates into a National League powerhouse during the past three years. It seemed fitting that Cuyler returned to the starting lineup and picked up some of the slack while Wright was sidelined for two weeks.

Cuyler finally worked his way back into Pittsburgh's outfield rotation on July 5, as he went 3-for-4 at the plate during the Pirates' 14–2 victory over St. Louis at Forbes Field. Hazen's fans expected Cuyler to perform his usual spectacular feats as Pittsburgh drove to another National League pennant. What most of these fans did not realize was that a deep rift had developed between Cuyler and manager Donie Bush. Cuyler irritated Bush during the Pirates' blowout victory over St. Louis. When Clyde Barnhart smacked a double in the fourth inning, Cuyler set sail for home plate even though Bush, who was coaching from the third base box, instructed him to stop. Cuyler crossed the plate in reckless fashion without giving any thought to his recently mended ankle. After Hazen scored the run, Donie spent several minutes shaking his head as he stood on the sidelines. Bush also picked at the turf with his spikes, apparently as a means to keep his anger in check.[47]

Surprisingly, Bush actually acquiesced to Cuyler's desire to bat anywhere than second in the order by placing him in the fifth spot upon his return. Cuyler continued to bat fifth or sixth as he split time between center and right field and performed adequately as Pittsburgh tried to stay in the National

League race after a mediocre month of June. Hazen kept his average above .300 as he hit safely in eight out of ten games from July 9 to July 20. Cuyler relived past glory when he contributed to Pittsburgh's 3–1 victory over Brooklyn on July 12. In the eighth inning, Pittsburgh tied the game on successive singles by Lloyd Waner, Heine Groh and Paul Waner. The winning run came across in the ninth, when Cuyler walked, stole second base, was sacrificed to third by Joe Harris and then scored on Carmen Hill's grounder to second baseman Jay Partridge.[48]

Cuyler played well until late July, when Bush decided to go with an outfield that consisted of Clyde Barnhart and the Waner brothers.[49] After going 2-for-4 in the second game of a double header against Boston on July 21, Cuyler found himself on the bench once again. But Kiki remained sequestered in the dugout for only three days. He returned to the lineup on July 25, when Barnhart was forced to the sidelines with a damaged leg.[50] Even though Cuyler went 2-for-4 and drove home two runs in Pittsburgh's 6–5 victory over Brooklyn the following day, there was again friction between manager and player after Cuyler begrudgingly played all nine innings in left field. Cuyler wanted to return to his old spot in center field but Bush preferred to keep Lloyd Waner there. Bush explained his decision to Cuyler by saying that Lloyd was doing too well in center field to be shifted back to left.[51]

Both men could make strong arguments that supported their position in this matter. Bush was correct in his belief that Waner was a better center fielder because he could cover more ground, but Cuyler also seemed like a logical choice to hold down the position since he had a cannon like arm. Waner possessed a weaker arm than either brother Paul or Cuyler. Managers usually placed the player with the weakest arm in left field, but it was also possible Bush kept Lloyd out of left field because the sun had caused him problems earlier in the year. No matter what the reason, Cuyler let this situation upset him just as Bush's other changes had caused him to fret and worry earlier in the season.[52]

Cuyler battled onward, playing left field as July ended. Pittsburgh was clinging to a half-game lead over second-place Chicago with a 57–38 record as the season moved into the dog days of August. Cuyler was shifted back to the second slot on August 1 and went 2-for-5 as Boston defeated Pittsburgh at Forbes Field, 4–1. The following day, Cuyler was appeased when Bush moved him back to center and shifted Lloyd Waner to left field. The change seemed to help Kiki as he went 7-for-12 and scored five runs during three consecutive victories over Philadelphia at Forbes Field. Cuyler received massive praise in Pittsburgh newspapers as sports scribes praised his hitting and fielding and marveled at how he had corrected a glaring weakness by hitting well behind baserunners.[53]

Three days after Cuyler was praised for playing stellar ball, he was roasted in the Pittsburgh dailies for making two baserunning gaffes in a game against New York on August 6. A writer for *The Pittsburgh Press* wondered whether more ill-advised baserunning had ever been seen during Forbes Field's short history. Cuyler was criticized for running with his head down on two occasions, both leading to disastrous consequences.[54] In each instance, Cuyler's woozy baserunning prevented the Pirates from eventually adding to their run total as New York crushed Pittsburgh, 9–2.[55]

Rookie Lloyd Waner played in center field during the summer of 1927 with Cuyler shifting to left field (courtesy the National Baseball Hall of Fame Library, Cooperstown, New York).

Cuyler committed his first offense in the fourth inning. After Kiki worked out a walk against Freddie Fitzsimmons, he took off for second when Paul Waner smacked a ground ball to Bill Terry at first base. Terry snagged the ball and threw to second base. Cuyler's speed allowed him to beat the throw, but he overran the bag and was tagged out easily when Travis Jackson made a second stab at him. Pie Traynor then followed with a single that could have scored Cuyler if he still occupied second base. In the sixth, Cuyler again used his speed to good advantage when he beat out a slow tapper along the third base line. Catcher Al Devormer fielded the ball and threw wildly over Terry's head at first base. As the ball caromed off the grandstand, Cuyler kept hustling around the bases. He made an ill-fated attempt to reach third on the wild toss and was gunned down by several yards on George Harper's accurate throw to Jimmy Reese.[56]

Manager Donie Bush had finally reached the breaking point. He plastered a $50 fine on Cuyler. Bush believed that Cuyler would have been safe in the fourth inning if he had not gone into the base standing up and contended that a proper hook slide into the bag would have prevented him from overrunning the keystone sack and being tagged out. When Bush announced the fine, he made it clear that future actions like Cuyler's would be handled in a similar fashion. Bush believed a player deserved to be punished when he was not giving his best effort both physically and mentally.[57]

Some observers believed that Bush was justified in fining Cuyler for his crude and amateurish work on the bases. Others alleged that Bush was not fair since Hazen's style had been considered daring and nervy when it worked in the past. It seemed that Cuyler was being punished for physical mistakes.[58] What fans and writers on both sides of the aisle failed to grasp was the subtle timing of Cuyler's "dressing down." Hazen's daring baserunning exploits occurred almost one year after the ABC Affair that saw its birth when assistant manager Fred Clarke belittled Max Carey within earshot of his teammates. It was feasible that Cuyler may have run the bases so boldly in the game on August 6, 1927, as a tribute to the man who taught him so much.

Pittsburgh's fan base quickly became divided into two camps over Cuyler. There were those who supported Bush's actions and others who argued that Cuyler had been treated unfairly. Those in the second group reasoned that since Cuyler had not been accused of any personal misconduct, slapping a fine on him for merely making a bad play was extreme. Hazen's close friends in Pittsburgh felt the star outfielder was being persecuted because he had been unpopular with Pirate ownership ever since contentious contract negotiations occurred after the 1925 season. Fans that sided with Bush believed that Cuyler had permitted himself to fall into a negative mind set, which kept him from doing his best work on the diamond. Cuyler vehemently believed that he was being mistreated by both Pittsburgh management and the press. Hazen felt that some of the newspaper writers were not giving him as much positive publicity as he deserved, and was not shy about informing them of this fact.[59]

Cuyler believed that he made a smart play going into second base standing up in the game against New York. Cuyler alleged that this action would have prevented the opposition from turning a crucial twin killing. Members of the Giants' team actually backed Cuyler's strategy, stating that the disciplining of a star was incorrect policy on the part of Pirates management. These same players, who spoke anonymously, also said that they would welcome Cuyler on their team if a trade could be worked out between Pittsburgh and New York.[60]

Pirates owner Barney Dreyfuss wasted little time responding to allegations that Pittsburgh management's treatment of Cuyler was unjust and unwarranted.

> I don't know how Bush decided upon the $50 fine for Cuyler and I don't care to ask him about it, all I know is that Cuyler didn't play as he should — that much was evident to anyone who saw Saturday's game from the grandstand. As far as I am concerned, it is a closed incident. It looks like Manager Bush tried his pat-on-the-back methods and, as has often been the case before, found it didn't work and had decided upon a more drastic way of urging him on.

I might also say that it isn't the player who talks the loudest about himself who is the most indispensible. I think by far the majority of ball players who prove of inestimable value to their teams are the ones who do the best they know how on the diamond and after the game, forget all about it.[61]

Dreyfuss also pointed out that the circumstances surrounding Cuyler's fining would have never reached the public if the player had not given out the information.[62] Pittsburgh management's stance seemed to be that Cuyler's persistently moody, temperamental behavior throughout the season was the root of this disciplinary action. Yet, there were those in the press who believed that Cuyler was not the only offender on the team. They reasoned that Bush used this drastic measure in an effort to shake his team out of its doldrums. Some Pittsburgh fans felt Bush tended to play favorites when dealing with his players. Donie's propensity for praising those who struggled while star performers received no encouragement could easily have been misinterpreted by players and fans.[63]

A few days after the incident, Bush offered his views about Cuyler's fine after stating that he held no personal grievance against any member of the Pittsburgh squad.[64] "When a manager is exerting every ounce of energy to win this pennant," said Bush, "and a baserunner fails to slide on such an important play as Cuyler, why they must pay the penalty.

"I had fines plastered against me when I was playing and I was out the next day hustling harder than ever. I am not going to bow and play to the alleged temperament of anybody. I am trying to win this pennant for the Pirates and if I am accused of being too severe, I am afraid I will have to accept such blame, if that is what anybody wants to call it."[65]

Bush's recollection of his playing days was not comparable to the Cuyler situation for one major reason. Cuyler was not going to receive the chance to hustle harder than ever as Bush had done. After the incident against New York on August 6, Bush banished Cuyler to the bench and replaced him with Clyde Barnhart. Hazen saw action as a pinch hitter and defensive replacement throughout August as Pittsburgh continued to trail the league-leading Chicago Cubs. Cuyler did taste glory a final time for Pittsburgh during a game against New York at the Polo Grounds on August 19. During an eight-run seventh inning that aided Pittsburgh's victory, Cuyler blasted a three-run triple while pinch hitting for George Grantham. Hazen's lusty drive swung the game in Pittsburgh's favor.[66]

Donie Bush's assessment that no grievances or misgivings existed between manager and players seemed to be accurate. Cuyler and Bush chatted on the bench throughout a game against St. Louis at Sportsman's Park on August 11. Kiki appeared in uniform, worked out with his fellow players before the game and rooted heartily from the dugout during a ninth-inning rally. Cuyler cheered loudly for his teammates as they came up short against the Cardinals.[67] After all, he was known as a winning ballplayer who always gave his best on a baseball diamond.[68] Contrary to the opinion of some people in Pittsburgh's front office, Cuyler was the consummate team player.

Cuyler finally received an opportunity to start in the second game of a doubleheader against Cincinnati on September 5. Hazen replaced Lloyd Waner in center field after the rookie injured his finger catching a fly ball in the morning game.[69] Cuyler acquitted himself nicely on the day although the Pirates dropped both games against the Reds. Hazen smacked a pinch single in the morning contest and then went 1-for-4 while playing center field in the afternoon affair. Yet, Cuyler was on the bench once again the following day as outfielder Adam Comorosky, recently recalled from Wichita of the Western League, took Lloyd Waner's place in center field for one game.[70] When Bush decided to bench Clyde Barnhart a few days later because of a nagging leg injury, he passed over Cuyler and turned to Comorosky once again.[71] The rookie outfielder appeared in 18 games as the Pirates made a powerful push to claim the National League pennant and rode the wave of a blistering 22–9 record in September to claim their second pennant in the last three years. Pittsburgh won a hard battle over St. Louis and New York that was not decided until October 1, when the Pirates defeated Cincinnati, 9–6.

Pittsburgh topped the National League with a 94–60 record. St. Louis finished second, a game and a half behind with a 92–61 record, while New York came home third, two games behind at 92–62. Kiki Cuyler remained chained to the bench as his teammates made their phenomenal run to the National League pennant. Hazen did not even play in the season finale on October 2, when Donie Bush rested all of his starters except for Lloyd Waner.

Pittsburgh's opponent in the 1927 World Series was the New York Yankees, who waltzed to the American League title with a 110–44 record that placed them 19 games ahead of second-place Philadelphia. The series was viewed as a battle between the power of Babe Ruth and Lou Gehrig and the consistent hitting of the Waner brothers. Ruth had smashed 60 home runs while Gehrig had hit 47. In the meantime, Paul Waner won the National League batting title with a .380 average while brother Lloyd was third at .355.

Hazen Cuyler finished the season with a .309 average in 85 games. Even though the Flint Flash saw limited duty, he still led the Pirate squad with 20 stolen bases. Nonetheless, the final month of the season had been bittersweet for Cuyler. Hazen watched his teammates pull off a remarkable feat by winning the pennant, but he was unable to participate in the effort. Cuyler's roommate and friend, Johnny Gooch, started a petition to have Hazen reinstated as a regular player, but Bush refused.[72] Weeks of sitting on the bench took their toll on Cuyler as the season wound down. During a doubleheader against

New York at Forbes Field on September 22, Cuyler resembled a tragic figure as he sat in the dugout, slumped down and seemingly broken-hearted. After the first game concluded, every Pittsburgh player went to the clubhouse except for Cuyler. He remained sitting there alone on Pittsburgh's bench.[73]

The 1927 World Series between Pittsburgh and New York opened at Forbes Field on October 5. Cuyler participated in fielding and batting practice prior to the game while decked out in a dazzling green practice shirt. A sports writer approached Cuyler and asked him if he believed there was a possibility he would see action in the first game. Hazen grinned wryly. He stated there was no chance of that, as he glanced across the field at Donie Bush. The scribe then approached Bush and posed a similar question, perhaps hoping that the manager would be willing to swallow his pride and permit Cuyler to offer assistance during the World Series. Bush echoed his player's sentiment when he declared that Cuyler would not be in the starting lineup.[74]

The Pirates certainly could have used one of their best clutch players during the first two games at Forbes Field. On October 5 New York claimed a 5–4 victory and followed that up with a 6–2 triumph the following day, when George Pipgras, Cuyler's former minor league teammate at Charleston, stifled Pittsburgh's bats throughout the afternoon.

During the series' first game, a group of fans in the left field bleachers displayed a sign that read: "We Want Kiki." Shouts of "Cuyler, Cuyler" also cascaded throughout Forbes Field when manager Bush sent left-handed hitting youngster Fred Brickell up in the ninth as a pinch hitter for pitcher Johnny Miljus.[75] The shouts of "We Want Cuyler" resounded throughout Game Two, even though Clyde Barnhart banged out two hits and a sacrifice fly. These cries became deafening in the eighth inning as thousands of fans screamed for Cuyler when Bush sent in Earl Smith to pinch hit for pitcher Mike Cvengros.[76] Groans quickly followed as Smith was retired on a ground ball.[77]

While the Pirates were busy playing their final two games of the season at Forbes Field, Hazen Cuyler kept himself occupied taking pictures of his teammates with a portable camera. One of Cuyler's close friends in Pittsburgh claimed the Pirates outfielder was doing this for sentimental reasons. Cuyler wanted something to remember these men by whom he had played with during the past four years. This man, along with Cuyler's other friends in the Smoky City, realized that Hazen would never be permitted to take part in another game as a Pittsburgh Pirate. They firmly believed that Cuyler would be disposed of shortly after the World Series ended.[78]

Pirate executives did a little damage control at the beginning of the series when a story bobbed to the surface that it was the Dreyfusses, rather than Donie Bush, who were keeping Cuyler out of the lineup.[79] Sam Dreyfuss stated after Game One that Cuyler was on the bench because his present playing form was below the standards of the other three regular outfielders. Dreyfuss added that there was no mystery or personal prejudice involved. After Dreyfuss' statements, Bush responded that he would use Cuyler when the need arose.[80]

It is difficult to say how much Cuyler's presence in the starting lineup would have altered Pittsburgh's fortunes during the 1927 World Series. His razzle-dazzle style of play might have injected some enthusiasm into a squad that seemed tired after a long, hard pennant fight.

New York made quick work of the Pirates by claiming Games Three and Four at Yankee Stadium. Pitcher Herb Pennock proved untouchable on October 7, as he carried a no-hitter into the eighth inning and cruised to an easy 8–1 victory. Pittsburgh's season ended the following day, as New York claimed the championship, the winning run scored when Earle Combs scampered home when Johnny Gooch was unable to handle an offering from pitcher Johnny Miljus in the ninth inning. The Yankees' 4–3 victory gave them a four-game sweep over a team that had shown perseverance and spirit against Washington under Bill McKechnie in 1925. Unlike Donie Bush, McKechnie did have a game-breaker named Hazen "Kiki" Cuyler in his lineup.

After the fourth game ended, Cuyler went to the showers with the other players. Hazen showed the depth of his sportsmanship as he struck the proper tone with his depressed teammates. Cuyler never let on that he believed the outcome may have been different if he was permitted to participate in the Fall Classic. He went up to each player individually and commended them on fighting hard, while also claiming that New York won because luck broke on their side.[81] Once he showered and dressed after consoling his teammates, Cuyler gave out a statement to the press that detailed his side of the controversy that led him to be benched by Donie Bush. Much in the same manner that Babe Adams, Carson Bigbee and Max Carey had done the year before, Cuyler waited until the season concluded to unburden himself so that his comments would not create a distraction during the pennant race.

> To tell the downright and whole truth, the whole thing is a mystery to me. There are some things to be told, without doubt, but it is not I who can tell them. In my own heart I have felt some things, and they may or may not be true; but as for what might be called the facts of the case, they will have to come from my employers.
>
> However, I have decided to tell what I know and some of what I feel, and I do it solely because Barney Dreyfuss, the owner of the Pirates, his son, Sam Dreyfuss, and Donie Bush, manager of the team, have each and often told their sides of the case. As long as the Pirates were after the National League pennant, and while they were in the World's Series, I kept still. I have been reported as saying this and that. I said nothing.
>
> Now that is all over. Furthermore, I think I have played for the last time in a Pirate uniform. Not because I don't want to play in that uniform, but because my employers, I have heard, have other plans.

6. Manager Donie Bush Banishes Cuyler to the Bench

Pittsburgh manager Donie Bush feuded with Cuyler throughout the 1927 season, refusing to play him during the regular season's final month and in the World Series against the New York Yankees (courtesy the National Baseball Hall of Fame Library, Cooperstown, New York).

First of all, it should be said that I have no ill feeling for Donie Bush. I am sure that whatever he did, even where he did things that didn't make me feel any too good, he did it for the best; did them because he was convinced that he would help the team. For my part, I was as strong for the team, as Bush, or Dreyfuss, but, perhaps, we did not agree on the best way to help the team.

It has been stated often that the 'Cuyler case' began with my being fined for not sliding into second base. It may have begun there, but I think it began a long time before that. I was fined $50 for not sliding into second base during a game with the Giants. I did go into the bag standing up, and that, in my judgment, was the proper thing to do, for there was an opportunity for a double play at first and second, and by standing up I could interfere with the throw to first and save one out.

However, Travis Jackson dropped the ball. I overran second and was out. Still, there was no double play. Then I was fined. The newspapers got hold of the story of my being fined. Bush said I gave out the story. I had no reason to give it out, and I didn't, still, I saw no reason why it shouldn't have been given out, as was the case with other fines. This led to the belief I was balking, but it was based on the false idea that I had given out the story.

Shortly afterwards, Bush coached me far off third in a game. I protested that it was dangerous but obeyed. The ball was snapped to third and I was caught. Then Bush berated me for being caught. I said I was willing to take the blame for my own lapses, which every player has, but not those of others.

After the fine was imposed, I went to Bush and asked him if I had done anything wrong to let me know, that I was trying to give the best I had and wanted to be told of my wrong plays. He dismissed me with the statement that the whole thing was settled and done.

I had paid for my mistake, whether I thought it right or not, and felt that I should have been permitted to start with a clean slate. But things didn't seem to work out that way. I was being played in left field and batting second. I had what ball players' call a 'yen' against batting in that position, and playing left field is about the worst thing I do. I told Bush about my 'yens' and he told me he needed me in that position, so I could do nothing but bat second. The proof of who was right can be seen in my record as a batter while in second position. And yet I tried as hard there as I ever tried in my life.

I made the mistake, I see now, of speaking about these two things. I should have batted second and played left field without saying anything, but I wanted to help and felt I could be of more help in center and batting in any other position than second.

No doubt I have been guilty of things that might be held against me, but I never loafed, and I was always trying to do my best. I still think Bush is a great fellow, and there is no extreme bitterness in my heart. I, quite naturally, feel that I should have been permitted to play, but who knows that I would have done as well as the man who played my position. Clyde Barnhart played a good game, and he and I are not enemies in any way.

I have heard that the whole matter will be thrashed out soon, and I will be as happy as anyone to find out what is the real trouble. No one feels the team's defeat any more than I do. No one pulled harder for them to win.[82]

Manager Donie Bush did not have much to say in response to Kiki Cuyler's long statement, which explained his behavior during troubled times in 1927. Bush believed that Cuyler's statement spoke for itself in relation to the disciplinary action that Pirates management took against their star player.

"Cuyler's own statement convicts him," said the Buccaneer boss after he arrived back in Pittsburgh. "I would have been foolish to use in the World Series a player who acted the way Cuyler says he acted in his own statement.

"I think the Cuyler statement is its own answer and requires no comment on my part."[83]

In spite of making a limited statement about Cuyler's post–World Series address, Bush planned on saying more during a team meeting at Forbes Field's clubhouse before his players went home for the winter. He was in possession of a letter to the editor of *The Pittsburgh Press* that did not paint the organization in a good light. Critical of Pittsburgh's management team, it was written by one of Kiki Cuyler's friends on the Pirate squad.[84]

7. Joe McCarthy Steals Kiki from Barney Dreyfuss

Pittsburgh manager Donie Bush decided to have one final meeting with his squad before all of the players dispersed to their homes for the winter. Bush spoke during a clubhouse session at 11 o'clock on the morning of October 10. Pittsburgh's manager held the special conference after the humiliation of the World Series in order to find out which player sent a letter to *The Pittsburgh Press* that excoriated Pirates management and supported Kiki Cuyler. The correspondence was not signed by the player who claimed to know the inside story surrounding Cuyler's problems with his manager. Bush read the anonymous letter, which had been sent to a newspaper's sporting editor, out loud to his squad.[1]

> There have been chances to win games thrown away by Bush not using Cuyler, and still Cuyler was silent. In fact, I believe they expected him to pout, and are sorry because he didn't.
> They threatened to send him home from St. Louis because several men were riding Bush for the fine, and they blamed Cuyler for telling it when it was common gossip around town before the papers got it, and the only reason Bush and Dreyfuss didn't want it to get out was because they did not want to be shown up.
> In my opinion Dreyfuss was sore at Cuyler for holding out in 1925, and also sore because someone found out that he gave him a measly $50 raise for getting a regular job in 1924.
> Bush was sore at Cuyler because Cuyler showed him up in a meeting, where he made a wrong play and tried to make Cuyler the goat. But this is what made my blood boil: Cuyler asked if he could be shifted to his regular position out of left, because the sun was hard on his eyes. This was proven by an eye expert in New York, who stated that Cuyler's eyes were strong, but subject to strain when in bright light and suggested Cuyler being away from the sun field as much as possible. Center field didn't get the direct light like left field. This Bush refused, and he made Cuyler play all the sun fields on the Eastern trip, or as much as he was in there.
> I also know that Barney Dreyfuss refused to let men in on Cuyler's passes, etc.,

but what did Cuyler do in return? He took Comorosky out to center field, and showed him how to play different batters and said he would do anything he could to help him.[2]

When Bush finished reading the letter, he asked who wrote the correspondence. There was dead silence in the room; no one took responsibility for being the author of the severe criticism. Bush then turned to Cuyler and asked him if he knew who the author was. Hazen stated that he did, but refused to reveal the player's identity.[3] Cuyler had no intention of outing a teammate and dragging him into the messy situation, and was not going to help Bush make another Pirate walk the plank. Bush had stated that he intended to punish the author of the letter if he could learn the man's identity. Cuyler, who appreciated the support, was glad the letter was not published because it would have created grave problems for its creator.[4]

Fans throughout the Smoky City continued to dissect information about the Cuyler incident, even after the players departed for their homes throughout the country. People wondered if a story that had surfaced during the season's final month was rooted in truth or had only been created to besmirch Cuyler's character. A close friend of a Pittsburgh player claimed that Cuyler was jealous over the success that Paul and Lloyd Waner experienced in 1927. This unknown man stated that Hazen did not like how the Waners were thrust into the limelight by newspapers that previously chronicled the exploits of Cuyler. The man concluded by saying that Cuyler believed he was being treated in a disrespectful manner when Bush did not return him to the starting lineup after his injured ankle healed. The story about Cuyler's alleged jealousy made the rounds even though no one else came forward to corroborate the testimony.[5]

A second story, which seemed plausible, was given out to a New York newspaperman by several Pirates players while the team had finished its season against the Yankees. These players declared that trouble existed between Kiki Cuyler and Barney Dreyfuss even before Donie Bush arrived on the scene. When Bush was named Pittsburgh's manager, he immediately attempted to straighten out the rift between player and owner. Upon meeting Bush for the first time, Cuyler asked the manager who was running the club, him or Dreyfuss.[6] Cuyler's blunt inquiry may have sprung from the previous year's events, when Bill McKechnie's authority was usurped by members of Pittsburgh's front office. Bush tried his best to placate Cuyler, but Pittsburgh's star outfielder insisted on being combative. Bush finally gave up the effort and put the onus on Cuyler to change his attitude.[7] "Well, when you make up your mind what you will do," Bush told Cuyler, "come around and see me."[8]

While these unidentified players were talking to a New York pundit, Bush was busy explaining his side of the story as it related to the Cuyler case. Bush talked to Gene Kessler, sports editor of the *Washington Daily News*. Billy

Smith, a former minor league manager and Bush's friend, was present while Kessler talked to Pittsburgh's manager. Smith related the story as it was told to him during the discussion. According to Bush's version of events, as repeated by Smith, it was Cuyler's decision to remain planted on the bench.[9]

"Cuyler was mumbling to himself and acting dissatisfied early in the season," Bush was quoted by Smith as saying. "I never could understand his action, and apparently he didn't care to understand mine. Then came that incident when he failed to slide into second base and I fined him $50. Naturally I benched him at the time.

"Later I went to Kiki and told him the incident was closed and that he could return to the game and forget about the past. I told him I wanted him to play left field and bat in second place. He said he couldn't do either, as the positions weren't natural to him."

Smith continued to quote Bush. "I told him he'd have to do as I said. I explained to him that Lloyd Waner was too good to be removed from center field and that Paul Waner was hitting so well in third place I couldn't change him.

"'If that's the way you feel about it I'd just as soon not play at all,'" Cuyler replied very sharply. "So I told him I'd keep him on the bench until I was ready to put him in the lineup."

"Remember this," Bush said to Cuyler, "I'm boss of this team. My job means as much to me as yours to you, and I'm not going to let you run me out of it by dictating the way this team should be run."[10]

Cuyler had ample opportunity to reflect upon the ordeal once he reached his home in Michigan. When Cuyler departed from Pittsburgh, the maligned player told his loyal followers that he did not expect to be a member of the Pirates in 1928. Hazen also stated that he planned on giving his new team the same earnest effort he had provided during his four seasons in Pittsburgh.[11] Cuyler found an attentive audience in Flint when he gave out an interview to a local newspaper shortly after reaching his hometown. Hazen rehashed the events that led to his problems with Bush. Cuyler stated that he never refused to take an order from his manager and claimed that Bush never told him why he was kept on the bench during the season's final month. Cuyler mentioned that Bush lacked credibility based on stories alleging Pittsburgh's manager had claimed Kiki was in unfit physical position. Despite their differences, Cuyler concluded the interview by wishing Bush good luck with the Pirates in 1928.[12]

One week after his return to Flint, Cuyler was honored at a huge testimonial dinner in Bay City. Three hundred people were on hand to give accolades to the man whom they still considered to be one of the greatest players in the major leagues. Albert W. Block, toastmaster of the elaborate banquet, presented Cuyler with the gift of a traveling bag on behalf of his friends.

Cuyler's benching at the hands of Donie Bush provided the main topic of discussion throughout the evening. Circuit Judge S.G. Houghton delivered a legal analysis of the Cuyler case and proclaimed that the Pittsburgh player was being persecuted. Colonel A.H. Gansser, a Michigan state senator, concluded that Hazen Cuyler's sterling military record proved he was accustomed to being disciplined in this manner.[13] When the guest of honor was finally called upon to speak, he offered an anecdote that illuminated the differences between him and manager Donie Bush.[14]

"One time when we were on the road," Kiki explained to his audience, "the bench was crowded and I crawled up a little off the bench."

"'Get back in that dugout,' Bush said, 'all your friends know you're here.'"[15]

Talk about the Cuyler case died down eventually. Discussions throughout Pittsburgh and other baseball cities quickly shifted to rumors about Cuyler's eventual destination in a trade. Every National League team seemed to be involved in the bidding. One tale had Cuyler going to St. Louis for either of two pitchers, Flint Rhem or Art Reinhart, along with either Ray Blades or Taylor Douthit. Cincinnati was willing to let the Pirates choose two players from a list that included Hughie Critz, George Kelly, Dolf Luque and Eppa Rixey. The Braves offered Joe Genewich, Dick Burrus and Eddie Brown. Philadelphia told Bush and Dreyfuss that they could have Russ Wrightstone, Fred Leach and a first-rate pitcher in exchange for Cuyler. Word from Brooklyn indicated that the Dodgers offered pitcher Jesse Petty and outfielder Babe Herman.[16]

The Cubs jumped into the Cuyler sweepstakes with a supposed offer of either outfielder Cliff Heathcote or outfielder Earl Webb, and a first-string pitcher.[17] A group of fans from the Windy City were adamant in their belief that Cubs management should pull the trigger on such a deal to acquire Cuyler. Two hundred loyal Chicago rooters organized a "We Want Kiki Cuyler Club" and forwarded a petition to team president William Veeck. These diehard fans believed the addition of Cuyler and a good third baseman would guarantee a pennant in 1928. Cubs officials responded by stating they were unaware that Cuyler was available and had no plans to pursue his acquisition.[18]

The fine line between truth and fiction continued to be stretched as trade scuttlebutt surrounding Cuyler continued. One of the biggest rumors to date had been mentioned in mid–October. The deal was reported to be a three-way transaction that involved Pittsburgh, Philadelphia and New York. Hazen Cuyler, Earl Smith and Johnny Morrison would be shipped to Philadelphia in exchange for outfielder Fred Leach and second baseman Fresco Thompson. Once the Phillies completed that deal, they would then trade Cuyler to the

Giants for third baseman Fred Lindstrom and rookie second baseman Herb Thomas. The proposition had initially been discussed in New York by Sam Dreyfuss, John McGraw, Giants president Charles Stoneham and Phillies president William F. Baker on the day after the final World Series game. When this story made its way into print, denials quickly came in from all sides. Barney Dreyfuss claimed that no member of his family had talked with these representatives. McGraw also vehemently denied that such a swap was going to be considered.[19] "Lindstrom is a great player," said McGraw. "As for Cuyler, it is a question. He hasn't done as well since his weakness was discovered, and besides, he's eccentric."[20]

McGraw claimed that teams throughout the National League discovered Cuyler's Achilles heel as a batter: he had become plate shy.[21] If this perceived shortcoming was so apparent, why was every team in the National League trying to procure Cuyler's services for the 1928 season? Rumors that had flooded the news pipeline after the World Series immediately dried up when New York sportswriter Joe Vila reported that Barney Dreyfuss was thinking about suspending Cuyler for the entire 1928 season. Dreyfuss and his son Samuel claimed that Cuyler grossly insulted both men verbally during a meeting at their Forbes Field office. Dreyfuss had no intention of letting Cuyler off and planned on obtaining approval from Commissioner Landis to ban him for a year. Cuyler was quoted as saying that if Dreyfuss followed this course, he would appeal to the courts.[22]

Once this new development rose to the surface, National League clubs stopped dickering for Cuyler's services.[23] Dreyfuss stated that all of the trade talk had little basis in fact from the beginning. He declared that he had not been overwhelmed with offers from other teams as was reported.[24] Fans were surprised that Dreyfuss seemed to be reducing Cuyler's market value in the name of revenge and vindication. Pittsburgh's baseball magnate quickly answered those critics. "I am not trying to belittle Cuyler," said Dreyfuss. "I would have no object in such a course, for, if he is placed on the market, naturally we want to get as much as possible in return for him. But it is a fact that we have had no offers for him since the season closed."[25]

Diehard fans who wanted Cuyler to remain in Pittsburgh received good news when it was reported that the Pirates might be for sale. Oklahoma millionaire Lou C. Wentz made his yearly pilgrimage to Pittsburgh to meet with Dreyfuss in order to discuss purchasing the Pirates. If Wentz was able to gain control of team ownership, he planned on appointing Fred Clarke to direct the ballclub. It was no secret that Clarke considered Cuyler the most valuable player on Pittsburgh's payroll. Before Wentz and Clarke left for Pittsburgh to make their offer to Dreyfuss, both men stated that, if they gained control of the team, they planned to play Kiki Cuyler in center field. They also planned on placing Lloyd Waner in left field.²⁶ Sadly, all of these hopes on the part of Cuyler's supporters were dashed when Wentz and Clarke left Pittsburgh without reaching a deal to purchase the franchise.

Throughout the taxing ordeal, Cuyler openly claimed that he was a man without a country, as far as baseball was concerned.²⁷ The situation changed completely a few days after Thanksgiving when Pittsburgh and Chicago struck a deal on November 28. Pittsburgh traded Cuyler to the Cubs for infielder Earl "Sparky" Adams and outfielder Floyd "Pete" Scott. The deal was consummated in Pittsburgh, with Cubs president William Veeck and manager Joe McCarthy negotiating the deal with their counterparts, Barney Dreyfuss and Donie Bush.²⁸ The seeds of the deal were planted when Veeck called on Dreyfuss after attending the Army-Navy football game in New York. Barney informed Veeck that he needed a second baseman and proposed a deal involving Cuyler. Pittsburgh's mogul stated that he would not make a trade unless Adams was included. Veeck initially balked at this demand, claiming that Adams was a major part of Chicago's infield. Veeck then telephoned McCarthy to solicit his opinion after Dreyfuss demanded that Scott also be included in the deal. McCarthy offered his opinion that Fred Maguire could replace Adams and the parameters of the deal were eventually finalized.²⁹ Contrary to initial rumors, Chicago did not include any money in the package.³⁰

Negotiations with the Cubs took place secretly, with no reports of a deal until the transaction was announced.³¹ It might have seemed that the Cubs came to the table late in the Kiki Cuyler sweepstakes. Or did they? During a trip to Pittsburgh in the summer of 1927, McCarthy supposedly joined Sam Dreyfuss in his office. McCarthy praised the ability of Sparky Adams and claimed that his team would be well served to have more players like him. Whether McCarthy was sincere in his praise or had simply overinflated Adams' ability as an ulterior motive never came to light. The Cuyler trade, however, was proof that McCarthy's words about Adams carried some weight with the younger Dreyfuss.³²

Baseball experts were split over which team got the best of the deal. New York manager John McGraw believed that Pittsburgh robbed the Cubs. He loved Adams' ability to reach base and set the table for Pittsburgh's heavy hitters. McGraw also questioned whether Cuyler was as good a player as he once was. Manager Bill Clymer of Buffalo's International League entry completely disagreed with McGraw. He reasoned that Pittsburgh got the worst of the deal. Clymer concluded that Dreyfuss and Bush handed the star player to Chicago.³³

During a dinner given in honor of Pennsylvania state senator Frank J. Harris in December, Dreyfuss offered his final word on the whole Cuyler situation.³⁴ "There is no enmity in my heart toward Mr. Cuyler," said Dreyfuss.

"I regard him as a fine young man, and I sincerely hope he makes good with the Cubs. But he made one mistake here — he listened to wrong advice. No ball player is bigger than the game, or than his manager. Only one man can run a ball club, and I am satisfied that I have the best manager I ever had in all my long career in Donie Bush."[35]

Cuyler seemed to have nothing but kind feelings for Dreyfuss and Bush. After the deal was made, Cuyler offered no words of criticism and remained virtually silent.

Philadelphia sports writer Bill Dooly believed that the charges claiming Cuyler was an agitator with a large ego were absolutely false. Dooly felt that Cuyler was grounded and mature and possessed good character. Far from being a detriment to a team or a disruptive element, Cuyler was the type of player who would be welcome in any organization. Dooly felt the Cubs had landed more than a star performer. They had added a good man to their ranks.[36]

Cuyler wasted little time in making a trip to Chicago in order to meet with McCarthy and Veeck. He arrived in town on December 3 and immediately signed a one-year contract. Terms of the agreement were not released, but it was believed to be one of the largest salaries on the team. It was speculated that Cuyler saw a nice increase over the $10,000-plus he earned playing for Pittsburgh in 1927.[37] Cuyler was so impressed with the business-like demeanor Cubs management exhibited that he signed as soon as Veeck placed a contract in front of him. During his trip to Chicago, Cuyler also tried to straighten out some of the false charges that had been made against him during the past six months.[38]

One of those tales involved Cuyler losing his temper after he had visited Dreyfuss in his office to discuss money matters. The visit allegedly concluded with Cuyler making vile and disparaging personal remarks that irritated Dreyfuss. Cuyler told Veeck and McCarthy that he had not lost his temper and could not understand why Dreyfuss would exhibit bitterness toward him.[39] Dreyfuss himself told a group of baseball men that the alleged confrontation never happened. But Cuyler believed that the Pittsburgh owner could kill the rumor once and for all if he would speak up and confirm that his only role in the case was to stand behind manager Donie Bush. As long as Dreyfuss remained silent, the suspicion prevailed that something did happen behind the scenes.[40]

Before McCarthy departed the meeting with Cuyler to make a trip to Dallas, Texas, he reminded Kiki of an exchange the two men had in front of a Pittsburgh hotel last summer. McCarthy had commented that Cuyler would look good in barnstorming games against the White Sox the next October. Hazen responded by asking when the city series started.[41]

Cuyler officially closed the pages on his career in Pittsburgh and started a new chapter as a member of the Cubs. Cuyler returned to his Michigan home after signing his contract in the Windy City. As had been the case during previous winters, Cuyler remained active by participating in basketball. He turned to officiating and supervising games in Flint and the surrounding area. In January, Cuyler was given a standing ovation by Michigan State college students attending a game between the Spartans and Hillsdale.[42] Cuyler also brought his I.M.A. Big Reds team to Chicago for a game against the Chicago Nationals at Loyola University's gymnasium on February 20. Cuyler did not play, instead managing the Big Reds in their contest against Chicago.[43]

Watching Kiki Cuyler play and coach basketball was a nice diversion, but rabid Chicago baseball fans wanted to see the newest Cub perform on a diamond. Prior to the Cubs' departure for spring training at Catalina Island off the California coast, manager Joe McCarthy made a decision on where Cuyler would bat and play. McCarthy planned on utilizing Cuyler's powerful arm by playing him in right field, but he was torn between allowing him to bat third or fourth in the batting order.[44]

While McCarthy was pondering lineup scenarios for the 1928 Cubs, Cuyler received word that a friend on the Pirates had been traded to New York. The Pirates shipped Vic Aldridge to the Giants in exchange for fellow pitcher Burleigh Grimes. There were some observers in Pittsburgh who believed that Aldridge was sacrificed due to his friendship with Cuyler. Aldridge had been outspoken in his defense of Cuyler throughout the 1927 season, making clubhouse speeches supporting Hazen whenever possible. Some Pirate fans felt that Aldridge had also written the infamous letter to the editor.[45]

The time to play ball finally arrived for Kiki Cuyler and his Chicago teammates. Cuyler was afforded a hero's welcome when he arrived in the Windy City to accompany the second squad of players to camp at Avalon on Catalina Island. Many Cubs fans called team headquarters to extend their good wishes to the ex-Pirate.

Cuyler responded to these well-wishers by saying he intended to give Joe McCarthy his best efforts.[46] "I suppose I've got a bad reputation to live down," Cuyler remarked. "If you fellows believe all that has been said about me, I guess I rate right now as a first class anarchist and all that.

"But I'll disprove all that before I am through here. I am going to knuckle down to business. I'll do anything I'm told to do, because I know manager McCarthy will be reasonable, and will not handicap me.

"I'm fit right now for a hard season, and I've got an ambition to have my best year."[47]

Yet, there were some Windy City inhabitants who were not on Cuyler's side. Sparky Adams had attracted a loyal legion of followers who were not happy when Chicago traded him. Chicago newspapers were deluged with letters of protest dubbing Cuyler a born troublemaker.[48] In response, Cuyler quickly took up the task of turning his enemies into followers during the early stages of spring training. Early reports from Catalina Island stated that Cuyler was hitting the ball well during practice games. He batted over .500 during the first four intra-squad games. His all-around form pleased Joe McCarthy. Besides doing stellar work on the field, Cuyler offered valuable tutelage to Chicago's rookie outfielders. Ecstatic to be in Chicago, Cuyler was determined to show the Pirates they had made a mistake in not allowing him to flourish in Pittsburgh.[49]

"I am glad to be with a club where a fellow has a chance to show a little initiative," Cuyler said during a break in spring action. "I am in great shape, and I'm in for a big season. I feel it. Everybody on the Chicago Cubs is treating me white, and I'm glad to treat them the same way.

"My departure from Pittsburgh was one of those things. I always gave the Pirates my best, but I couldn't get along there. That was all there was to it. I'm no trouble maker, and I'm going to prove it this summer. Watch my smoke."[50]

Cuyler's bat was blazing hot during two exhibition series versus a pair of Pacific Coast clubs. Kiki belted seven home runs in six games against Los Angeles and Hollywood.[51] Cuyler and teammate Hack Wilson also decided to have a little fun at the expense of Pittsburgh catcher Earl Smith during a pre-season series against the Pirates. Smith started out by throwing barbs and insults at his ex-teammate and Wilson. Smith gave both men a wicked riding, but the two Cubs enjoyed the last laugh since they were hitting well and Chicago was winning. In one of the games, Wilson seemed to enjoy Smith's comments because he was recording hits in spite of them. In the fourth inning, Hack came to the plate with his team trailing Pittsburgh, 4–0. With two Cubs runners on base and two outs in the inning, the count reached two balls and two strikes.[52]

"It's all over now," remarked Smith.

"The score is now 4 to 0," replied Wilson, "but after this pitch it will be 4 to 3."[53]

Ray Kremer delivered the pitch to Wilson, who took a mighty cut and sent the ball soaring into the bleachers. In the seventh inning of the same game, Wilson turned the tables on Smith and began bragging when he came to the plate with the tying and winning runs on base.[54]

"This game is as good as over right now," vowed Wilson.[55]

He immediately smacked the next offering down the right field line for a double. When Paul Waner mishandled the blistering hit, Cuyler kept running as he bolted from first to home with the winning run.[56]

Cuyler was traded to the Chicago Cubs on November 28, 1927, for infielder Sparky Adams and outfielder Pete Scott. Cuyler was glad for a fresh start in Chicago and seemed determined to disprove those who believed he was a troublemaker (courtesy the National Baseball Hall of Fame Library, Cooperstown, New York).

Spring training went extremely well for Cuyler. He even won an old-fashion waltz dance contest during the training session. Hazen and one of the Catalina Island locals were crowned champions at a dance that was held at the Cubs' hotel.[57]

Cuyler's positive aura was finally punctured a few days before Chicago opened the regular season against Cincinnati. While chasing a fly ball in an exhibition game at Kansas City, Cuyler jammed his hand against a concrete wall in the outfield. The deep bruise on Hazen's hand made it difficult for him to properly grip a bat.[58]

Cuyler did return to the starting lineup and recorded one hit as the Cubs dropped their opener against Cincinnati at Redland Field on April 11, 5–1. Cuyler remained in the starting lineup despite the pain. He collected a hit in all but one game during a season-opening seven-game road trip against Cincinnati and St. Louis that saw the Cubs go 4–3. Cuyler quickly won the hearts of Cubs rooters during the team's home opener against the Reds on April 18. Hazen introduced himself to the 45,000 screaming fans when he smacked a home run into the right field seats to start the eighth inning, sparking a rally that saw Chicago net five runs and take a 6–5 lead. Unfortunately, the heroics of Chicago's players were short lived as Cincinnati came right back with four runs of their own in the ninth and claimed a 9–6 victory.[59]

The Cubs played mediocre ball during the early weeks of the season as they started a big series with the Pirates on April 30, with a record of 9–9 for the year. The series at Forbes Field received special attention from the press due to the high profile trade involving Cuyler. Pittsburgh newspapers that had praised Sparky Adams' every move during the season's early days planned on giving Cuyler careful scrutiny. Cuyler's return to Pittsburgh could not have come at a worse time. He was mired in a horrible batting slump that saw him record one hit in 22 at-bats during a six-game stretch. Hazen's hand injury had not helped, knocking his plate work off stride because of his difficulty gripping a bat properly. Even when the injury healed, Cuyler could not regain his hitting stride because his mechanics at the plate remained out of whack.[60]

Chicago did not fare very well during its trip to the Smoky City as Pittsburgh swept the three-game series. Cuyler received a rousing ovation when he batted in the first inning during the opening contest. Cuyler promptly flied out to Lloyd Waner in center field. Sparky Adams also earned a noisy greeting in the first inning before he grounded into a double play. Later in the game both players received glowing accolades from the fans. In the fifth stanza, Cuyler blasted a safety that drove home two teammates. Hazen eventually came around to score the run that temporarily put Chicago in the lead. Adams became the hero for the day as he drove home three runs, one with a sacrifice fly and two with hits. His single in the eighth inning decided the game in Pittsburgh's favor as the Pirates prevailed, 8–7.[61]

Cuyler inflicted damage against his former mates with his arm the following day during Chicago's 4–1 loss. In the sixth inning, Cuyler made a perfect throw to Woody English after fielding George Grantham's wicked drive off the concrete wall in right field. English then relayed to Johnny Butler, who tagged out Grantham at third when he tried to stretch the hit into a triple. Cuyler struck again in the eighth inning, when he gunned down Pie Traynor after attempting to make it from first to third on Grantham's single to right.[62]

During the series finale on May 2, Cuyler reached base each time he came to the plate as he rapped out two hits, drew a walk and reached on two errors. Pirates second baseman Sparky Adams made three errors on the day and was booed by fans in the grandstand during a particularly wretched fielding performance in the sixth inning.[63] Forbes Field fans were not happy with Adams' play and did not hesitate razzing him for the first time since he came to Pittsburgh.[64]

"What did they ever get you for?" shouted one raucous onlooker.

"Back to Chicago," was another common quip.

"We want Cuyler," roared many a fan.[65]

While Chicago was in Pittsburgh, some of Cuyler's most devout supporters claimed that Pirate hurlers were deliberately throwing the ball at their ex-teammate with the intention of harming or maiming him. It was well known that Pirate pitchers, along with their counterparts throughout the National League, threw the occasional dust-off pitch at Cuyler. Pitchers knew that an inside pitch, followed by a low sweeping curve on the outside of the plate, would cause the Flint Flash severe problems. New York manager John McGraw claimed that Cuyler was particularly vulnerable to that type of pitching strategy.[66]

One member of the Pittsburgh squad declared that Cuyler would not bat more than .200 against Pirate pitchers in 1928.[67] "Our twirlers have Ki's number, and he knows it," said the Pirate player. "In fact, we all know that he has a weakness, and the pitchers are working on it constantly. The information is not confined to any one club, either. The news has been broadcast, as it always is when the opposition discovers a sure weakness on the part of any batter"[68]

Cuyler's other problems at the plate were discussed by another opposing players when his team arrived in Pittsburgh shortly after the Chicago series. The player in question stated that Cuyler was having difficulty fitting into the hitting system employed by manager Joe McCarthy. Cuyler was a first-ball hitter who did not like to take pitches when a runner was on base. When Hazen was flashed the sign that a teammate was going to steal, he struggled with his impatience. Cuyler was still not proficient at hitting behind a baserunner when the hit-and-run sign was given.

Joe McCarthy had stated in the winter that he would not hinder Cuyler with any unreasonable restrictions. This, however, did not mean Chicago's manager would allow Hazen to do as he pleased.[69]

Pittsburgh's pitchers were not the only hurlers keeping Cuyler in check with an average of .200. After a game against Philadelphia on May 6, Cuyler's average stood at .193, which was about 150 points lower than what was expected. Not surprisingly, Cuyler went to the sidelines for a few games so that his hand could be given a chance to properly heal. He returned to the lineup on May 18 after a short hiatus and won a game for the Cubs when he clubbed a third inning homer with Fred Maguire on base to secure Chicago's 3–1 victory over Boston.[70] But games like this were the exception rather than the norm for Cuyler, as he continued to struggle throughout May and June. Cubs' president William Veeck had to shoot down a trade rumor that claimed Chicago would ship Cuyler to New York for Fred Lindstrom.[71]

Kiki Cuyler finally experienced some positive results during a trip through the East in June. Cuyler raised his average from .211 to .261 on an 11-day excursion through Philadelphia, Boston and Brooklyn. Cuyler started to resemble the player he was for Pittsburgh in 1925. In a game against Brooklyn on June 12, he delivered a single in two times at bat. The following day, he smacked two hits in four attempts, including a home run. On June 14, he smashed a double and two singles in five trips to the plate against the Robins. The following day against Boston, Cuyler stroked a double and a single in five trips. On June 16, he went 2-for-2 and then recorded one of Chicago's three hits against Dazzy Vance of Brooklyn the following afternoon.[72] He finished off the fine road trip on June 18 by going 4-for-6 in the second game of a doubleheader against Boston. He blasted two home runs, stroked a double and scored four runs as Chicago ran roughshod over the Braves, 12–0.

Suddenly, Cuyler's batting savvy abandoned him once the Cubs returned home to face St. Louis at Wrigley Field on June 20. He was completely shackled during the four-game series as he went hitless in every contest and saw his average drop to .240. Manager Joe McCarthy decided to bench Cuyler because of his feeble work at the plate.[73]

During a doubleheader against St. Louis on June 21, Hack Wilson supplied some unusual entertainment for the patrons at Wrigley Field. Throughout both games a fan relentlessly heckled the Cubs. Wilson spotted where the man was sitting, but did nothing until the fan began to use foul language. Wilson's patience finally reached a breaking point as the second game ended. Wilson ran over to the stands, climbed the railing, seized the man and forced him to cease and desist. Hack grabbed the man around the neck before Joe Kelly and Gabby Hartnett joined the fray in an effort to separate the combatants. When the noisy patron appeared in police court the following morning, he claimed that all three players had thrown punches at him.[74]

The fighting spirit of the Cubs' players had not translated into positive results on the diamond. When June ended, the Cubs stood in fourth place with a 39–32 record. They were six and a half games behind the league-leading Cardinals and needed to leapfrog both Brooklyn and New York if they wished to move into second place. On July 1, Kiki Cuyler was inserted into the starting lineup for the first time in over a week and went hitless in a 4–1 loss against Cincinnati. The former Pittsburgh star and 1925 World Series hero then began to turn around his season. Cuyler proceeded to go 12 for 27 during the next six contests; injured hands and previous disputes with managers became a distant memory. Cuyler seemed determined to reestablish his credentials as the National League's best outfielder.

Cuyler had experienced a life-changing event on June 22, when he became the father of a baby girl. Hazen and Bertha christened the family's newest member Kelly June. After his hitless performance on July 1, Cuyler celebrated the glorious event of his daughter's birth by smacking three hits and stealing second base standing up in a victory over Cincinnati on July 2. Some of Cuyler's friends in Chicago wondered if worry over his new daughter's arrival had caused some of his early season problems.[75] Windy City scribes who had initially hailed Cuyler as a wonder when the Cubs acquired him then referred to the Flint Flash as an ordinary player. Some National League pitchers still claimed that Cuyler was an abject failure because he was a "water bucket hitter."[76] Those that held membership in both of these clubs would soon find out that Cuyler had returned to prior form.

Cuyler hit the baseball at a .350 clip in early July. During a long home stand at Wrigley Field, Cuyler had a hand in producing runs for the Cubs in practically every game. On July 14, Hazen hit an eighth inning home run that was the decisive blow in Chicago's 3–2 victory over Philadelphia. Cuyler also made a spectacular play in right field that garnered him the largest ovation he had received at Wrigley Field in 1928. Cuyler cut down Fresco Thompson at the plate after he charged near the foul line to snatch a ball in deep right field and tossed a perfect strike to catcher Mike Gonzalez.[77]

Chicago's management never wavered in its support of Cuyler even when criticism ran rampant during his early season slump. Owner William Wrigley believed that he had the best team in the league. Wrigley also considered Cuyler to be a crucial component in the Cubs' machinery. Prior to the season, Wrigley bestowed one glowing compliment after another on Cuyler. He believed that Cuyler was one of the easiest going fellows on the Cubs while scoffing at tales surrounding his temperamental behavior in Pittsburgh. Chicago's owner felt that Cuyler was willing to do anything for the team and would contribute for the Cubs in 1928.[78]

Manager Joe McCarthy also supported Cuyler fervently while he experienced tough times during his first season in Chicago. McCarthy sent Cuyler to the bench on one occasion, but only briefly. McCarthy knew that Cuyler's every move would be scrutinized due to his perceived poor attitude in Pittsburgh. McCarthy's wife had even expressed curiosity about Chicago's newest player after the trade was made. She wanted to know why Pittsburgh was willing to let Cuyler go if he was as good as everyone had said. Joe responded by suggesting that the couple go ice skating; he never talked about baseball with his wife, and this may have been the last time she questioned him about the game.[79]

While McCarthy received vindication as Cuyler's play improved, Pittsburgh manager Donie Bush was being roasted by Smoky City fans who were unhappy with the Pirates' second-division status. The Pirates were the league's biggest disappointment after winning a pennant in 1927. Pittsburgh's fans blamed Bush and showed their displeasure by constantly criticizing Pittsburgh's manager for trading Cuyler to Chicago.[80] The situation became tougher for Bush at the end of July, when one of the players who came to Pittsburgh in exchange for Cuyler was put out of commission. During a game against New York on July 26, Pete Scott was seriously injured when he collided with the concrete stands of the Polo Grounds. Scott, unconscious for a long time, was rushed to the hospital. It was initially feared that he had broken his neck during the collision, but after an examination was made, doctors determined that Scott had suffered a slight dislocation of the vertebra.[81] Scott did return to action in September, but he never played another major league game after the 1928 season.

Cuyler continued to play ball with a renewed fervor as Chicago remained in the thick of the battle to claim a National League pennant. Cuyler was not fazed when McCarthy sat down his star outfielder during a doubleheader against Boston due to a perceived batting slump. He returned to action the following day and cracked a home run and single as the Cubs defeated the Braves, 7–3.[82]

Chicago Cubs manager Joe McCarthy's staunch support of Cuyler was rewarded when the former Pittsburgh Pirate finally caught fire after a slow start in 1928. Cuyler batted .285 on the season, while McCarthy brought the Cubs home in third place with a 91–63 record (courtesy the National Baseball Hall of Fame Library, Cooperstown, New York).

Cuyler did some damage to the slim pennant hopes of his former team one week later when the Cubs defeated Pittsburgh, 3–2, during a Sunday contest at Wrigley Field on September 2. Hazen scored two runs, drilled a single and blasted a home run.[83] The Cubs remained in the hunt during the final weeks of the season. After a 6–2 victory over St. Louis on September 13, Chicago stood in third place, two games behind the league-leading Cardinals. But this was the closest the Cubs could come as St. Louis held on to claim the National League pennant in 1928.

Fans from the Windy City came out in droves to watch their beloved Cubs play at Wrigley Field in 1928. Chicago topped all major league clubs in attendance as more than 1.1 million patrons passed through the turnstiles. Cubs fans were a passionate lot that cheered exuberantly when the team was playing well. Chicago's rooters were also well-educated baseball connoisseurs who could criticize the hometown team with the best of them. Infielder Clyde Beck was the subject of such verbal abuse during a September game at Wrigley Field. He had a particularly tough day as he struck out during a crucial at-bat with men on base. Clyde's wife happened to be sitting in the grandstand of the park near a fan who did not know the woman's true identity. When Beck struck out, the male patron railed at the Chicago infielder.[84]

"Damn that Beck," exploded the irate fan, "I could shoot him for that."[85]

The male fan then spotted Beck's wife looking at him after his verbal barrage. Thinking that she did not appreciate the profanity, the male rooter started to offer an apology.[86]

"Not at all; not at all," said Mrs. Beck. "I echo your sentiments. You see, I happen to be Clyde's wife and believe me, I could shoot him myself!"[87]

The wives of Chicago's players ardently rooted for the team, just like the majority of Chicago's vast North Side population. They cheered on their husbands as Chicago finished the season in third place with a 91–63 record. The Cubs finished four games behind the pennant winners from St. Louis. The Cubs did have the satisfaction of eliminating New York from the pennant race on September 28. Cuyler found himself in the middle of New York's demise when he smacked a two-run triple in the ninth inning and then scored on Charlie Grimm's single. The Giants' rally in the bottom of the ninth fell short as Chicago held on for a 7–5 victory.[88]

Cuyler's late-season surge at the plate pushed his average to a final mark of .285 in 1928. Cuyler also put up great power numbers for the Cubs as his 17 home runs statistic was second on the squad behind team leader Hack Wilson's 31 round-trippers. Cuyler led the Cubs in runs scored with 92 and was tops in the National League with 37 stolen bases.

Cuyler also put on a clutch performance in the popular City Series between the Cubs and White Sox after the regular season. The Cubs claimed the title of best team in Chicago when they defeated the White Sox, four games to three. Cuyler's first-inning double during the initial contest helped clinch the Cubs 5–3 victory. Hazen went 3-for-4 in Game Four as the Cubs squeaked by with a 3–2 win. A crowd of 42,000 fans watched the White Sox stay alive with a 2–0 victory in Game Five.[89] Joe McCarthy's men finally claimed the series when they shellacked the White Sox by a score of 13–2 in Game Seven.

People throughout Chicago were surprised over how high the attendance figures were for the seven-game series. A crowd of 184,061 filed into Wrigley Field and Comiskey Park to view the 1928 Chicago City Series. The attendance total eclipsed the previous high water mark by over 42,000 people. The 44,000 who paid to see a Sunday matinee at Wrigley Field outdrew the attendance for Game Three of the World Series on October 7 between St. Louis and New York at Sportsman's Park.[90]

Shortly after the Cubs finished up their 1928 season, rumors worked their way into Windy City newspapers about a trade involving the legendary Rogers Hornsby. Chicago was loaded with solid performers like Hazen Cuyler, Riggs Stephenson, Hack Wilson, Woody English, Charlie Grimm, Gabby Hartnett, Pat Malone, Guy Bush, Charlie Root and Sheriff Blake. Second base seemed to be one area of weakness borne out of the trade of Sparky Adams to Pittsburgh. Hornsby won the National League batting title in 1928 while playing for the seventh-place Boston Braves. Boston owner Judge Emil Fuchs now seemed eager to move Hornsby after initial reports stated he would remain in Boston.

The first round of hot stove league talk seemed a bit ridiculous as a trade proposition of Hornsby for Gabby Hartnett, Freddie Maguire, Sherriff Blake and Kiki Cuyler was announced by Fuchs.[91] It seemed very unlikely that William Veeck would be willing to part with all of these crucial Cubs performers. There also seemed to be little chance of Cuyler leaving the confines of Wrigley Field anytime soon. As for Hazen Cuyler himself, he was determined to show everyone connected with the game that his early success in Pittsburgh was not a fluke.

8. A Comeback Season and World Series Appearance

For the second straight year, Chicago president William Veeck was front and center attempting a blockbuster deal aimed at pushing the Cubs closer to a National League pennant. Boston owner Judge Emil Fuchs realized that Rogers Hornsby's playing value was limited because the rest of the team was so weak. Many executives throughout the National League believed that Fuchs wanted a large sum of cash along with players in return for Hornsby's services. Chicago was mentioned most frequently in connection with any deal for Hornsby. The Pirates also seemed to be in the running since Barney Dreyfuss wanted to rid himself of numerous athletes. If Dreyfuss was able to entice Fuchs with a solid offer of money and players, Chicago was likely to raise the ante and beat Pittsburgh to Hornsby.[1]

The Cubs were crowned as the winners of the Hornsby lottery when they acquired the star second baseman on November 7. Veeck sent pitchers Socks Seibold, Percy Jones and Bruce Cunningham, second baseman Freddie Maguire, catcher Lou Legett and $200,000 to the Braves for Hornsby. The Cubs now possessed the greatest right-handed power hitter of the 1920s. Hornsby would be playing for his fourth team in the past four years, after wearing out his welcome repeatedly. Hornsby had led the Cardinals to a World Series victory in 1926 as a player-manager before being shipped to New York for Frankie Frisch. Hornsby then lasted only one season in the Big Apple before heading to Boston to ply his trade for a year in 1928.

Chicago now had two players on its squad who were considered the top performers in the National League only four years earlier. Hornsby was named the league's Most Valuable Player in 1925 while Hazen Cuyler finished second in the balloting. Both men were heavy hitting right-handed batters who ranked with the league's best sluggers. Hornsby and Cuyler were also similar in other ways. Both men abstained from drinking while dedicating themselves to a strenuous off-season regimen. During the winter preceding the 1929 season, Hornsby stayed in shape tending to farm chores and hunting on his estate in St. Louis. Cuyler's off-season training included playing and coaching basketball in Flint. Cuyler also did some winter time hunting in Northern Michigan, having shot a buck only hours after deer season had officially opened.[2]

Trade rumors did not die down in the Windy City after the Cubs secured Hornsby from Boston. Reports continued to persist that Chicago was in the running to acquire Glenn Wright from Pittsburgh. Wright, who was benched on numerous occasions in 1928, indicated that he wanted to leave Pittsburgh. He did not seem to be the same player he once was after being beaned by Vic Keen in 1927.[3] Wright also fell out of favor with Pirates management in 1928 when he followed pursuits of pleasure rather than concentrating on work.[4]

Brooklyn ended up being the team that secured Wright from Barney Dreyfuss. The Robins shipped pitcher Jesse Petty and infielder Harry Riconda to Pittsburgh for Cuyler's ex-teammate. Riconda's acquisition created a precarious situation since he was also a star basketball player; Dreyfuss had a rule that prohibited his players from playing basketball during the winter.[5] Wright's departure to Brooklyn left Ray Kremer as the only member of the great rookie class of 1924 to remain with Pittsburgh.

Hornsby's addition to Chicago's lineup meant that Joe McCarthy needed to decide on a batting order that was most beneficial to the team. As spring training dawned, McCarthy still had not given a definitive answer to how his players would line up. He seemed to be leaning toward using Kiki Cuyler as his leadoff man. He could not bat Cuyler second given his past failures there, and it was unlikely that the Flint Flash would be hitting third in 1929.[6] While McCarthy was pondering his strategy for the upcoming season, Cuyler and his basketball team came to Chicago for a game against the Nationals on January 14. The game pitted the Flint Reds against a Nationals team that was undefeated on its home court at St. Philip's Gymnasium, located at Koldzie and Jackson Boulevard. Cuyler's quintet was expected to give its opponents a tough time since former Ohio State star Johnny Miner was a member of the Flint Reds.[7]

Cuyler then put away his basketball equipment for another year and traded it in for baseball gear in anticipation of his training trip to Catalina Island. Cubs players made the journey to Chicago a little early in order to eventually board a special train that would take the team to a special event. Catcher Gabby Hartnett, considered one of the game's most eligible bachelors, would marry Miss Martha Marshall during a grand ceremony in the Windy City. Athletes who were invited to the wedding remained in Chicago as they waited to depart for spring training.[8]

Once the full squad arrived at Avalon under the stewardship of Joe McCarthy, all eyes were on Rogers Hornsby as Chicago began the long, grueling process of capturing a pennant. Some observers wondered how Hornsby and McCarthy would co-exist once the season began. According to Chicago sportswriter Edward Burns, early indications offered proof that Hornsby planned on being the good soldier in 1929.[9]

"Hornsby has been one of the first three players to reach the practice field in practice sessions since he arrived," said Burns.

"He does not kibitz when manager Joe McCarthy is talking, either on the playing field or in the hotel solarium.

"Calls all the rookies by their nicknames, high hatting none.

"Is the chief atta boy shouter in the pepper talk following snappy maneuvers.

"Chums with none of the established stars, but is friendly to all."[10]

Hornsby's new teammates were happy to have him on board. Some experts believed the star second baseman's addition to the roster made Chicago the prohibitive favorite to appear in October's World Series. Hornsby was grabbing all of the attention during camp that had been bestowed on Kiki Cuyler the previous year. Cuyler did not seem bothered at all about falling into the shadows as he weighed in on Hornsby's addition to the Cubs' team.[11]

"We're all mighty glad to have Hornsby," Cuyler said. "He'll win the pennant for us. We lost by only four games last year and we must have lost ten ball games by one run. With Hornsby in there with the other hitters we won't lose many one-run games this year. We're all for him because he's all right and because he's with us."[12]

Hornsby also praised Cuyler as he watched Hazen defend his 1928 Catalina Island waltz championship at the Hotel St. Catherine. Hornsby was amazed at Cuyler's dance floor ability during the competition's final dance, as Ki was awarded the 1929 silver cup. Hornsby was so impressed by the sheer athleticism that he pondered whether Cuyler needed to conserve some of his energy for baseball.[13] But Cuyler did not participate in the event held by the Avalon Boosters Association for social reasons. The National League's top base stealer liked to waltz continuously during spring training in order to keep his ankles strong and nimble. When Cuyler was given a series of blindfold tests during the event, he could not tell whether his female partner was blonde or brunette, and was unable to identify the brand of perfume she wore. Cuyler enjoyed the competition, but he danced to reduce his weight and get into shape during the Catalina Island training jaunt.[14]

Unlike the previous spring when Cuyler injured his hand during an exhibition game, Hazen came through the 1929 training session unscathed. Yet, there was one unsettling event that involved four Chicago players using bad judgment during a trip to El Paso, Texas, for an exhibition game. Cuyler, along with Hack Wilson, Sheriff Blake and Guy Bush, ventured across the border

Chicago acquired second baseman Rogers Hornsby from the Boston Braves on November 7, 1928, for five players and $200,000. Cuyler believed that Hornsby would supply the necessary punch for the Cubs to reverse their bad trend in one-run games during the 1929 season (courtesy the National Baseball Hall of Fame Library, Cooperstown, New York).

into Mexico to visit the camp of some Mexican rebels in Juarez. Cuyler and his mates made the excursion even though Cubs management had ordered all players to remain on the American side of the border. An NEA Service photographer also made the journey and snapped a photo of the players as they posed with rebel officers.[15]

Cuyler, Wilson, Blake and Bush were fortunate that no uprising occurred during their sightseeing tour in Juarez. The loss of any of these players for an extended period of time likely would have crippled Chicago's pennant hopes.

Catcher Gabby Hartnett did not venture into hostile Mexican territory but his status became questionable for the Wrigley Field opener on April 16. Hartnett was sidelined throughout the training and exhibition session with a sore throwing arm. He was not concerned about the condition during the early stages of work at Catalina Island since he always experienced this type of pain during spring training, but Hartnett and Cubs management became alarmed when the pain did not subside. Hartnett was forced to watch Mike Gonzalez and rookies Earl Grace and Tom Angley handle backstop duties while his catching gear remained in a locker for weeks.[16]

Hazen Cuyler launched his 1929 season in robust fashion as the Cubs dropped their opening game against Pittsburgh at Wrigley Field on April 16, 4–3. Cuyler went 3-for-5 stroking a double and scoring one run. Cuyler recorded one hit the following day as Chicago abused four Pirate pitchers on the way to a 13–2 victory. Rogers Hornsby introduced himself to Chicago's fans by crushing a monstrous home run. Hornsby's grand slam came with Pat Malone, Clyde Beck and Kiki Cuyler on base. "The Rajah's" blast represented sweet revenge for the second baseman since pitcher Fred Fussell had fanned him earlier in the game with the bases loaded.[17]

The Cubs jumped out of the gate in solid fashion as they put together a 7–5 record in the month of April. This left them a game and a half behind the surprising Braves, who led the National League with a 7–2 record. Cuyler also started the season well as he hit safely in all but one game during the month. Batting out of his customary third spot in the order, Cuyler was doing lethal damage against opposing National League hurlers.

Heavy hitting by Cuyler, Hornsby and Riggs Stephenson drove Pirates rookie pitcher Steve Swetonic from the mound in the fifth inning at Forbes Field on April 27.[18] Cuyler went 3-for-5, smashing a triple as Chicago prevailed over Pittsburgh, 8–7. While the Cubs were in Pittsburgh, McCarthy took Hartnett to Youngstown, Ohio, to visit Bonesetter Reese during a rained out game. The trip was kept secret until Hartnett returned to Pittsburgh and said that Reese had adjusted the arm trouble. Even though he vowed that he would be catching for Chicago the following day, lingering pain in the star catcher's right shoulder prevented him from keeping that promise.[19]

Chicago's catching corps had become further depleted prior to the team's trip to Pittsburgh. In a game against St. Louis on April 23, Mike Gonzalez was forced to the sidelines in the fifth inning when he injured his finger tagging Bill Sherdel. Earl Grace, a rookie from Little Rock, was then knocked out of the game when the first ball he caught tore a nail off one of his fingers. Third-string rookie catcher Tom Angley was called on to finish the game against St. Louis.[20] On April 24, Joe McCarthy and William Veeck decided to sign former major league catcher Johnny Schulte as extra insurance until Grace and Gonzalez could resume playing. While Chicago management worked hard to piece together a catching unit, players like Riggs Stephenson and Kiki Cuyler acted as catalysts for the team's hitting attack. Official league averages on May 1 showed that Stephenson was first in the league with a .422 average, while Cuyler was giving solid support with a mark of .368.

Injuries began to take their toll as players other than catchers fell out of action with nagging ailments. A game against the New York Giants on May 12 was particularly troublesome for two of Chicago's starting outfielders. Cuyler strained a tendon in his leg while center fielder Hack Wilson was put out of commission due to injuries he suffered during a collision with New York's Andy Cohen.[21] Cuyler remained on the sidelines for only two games. He returned to action against Boston on May 15 and smacked a home run as Chicago defeated the Braves, 7–4. Cuyler was at it again three days later when he led the attack as Chicago demolished Jakie May and Cincinnati, 7–0.[22] Cuyler went 4-for-5 and drove home four Cubs teammates.

Following the Reds' journey into Chicago, Tom Swope of *The Cincinnati Post* talked to St. Louis Cardinals coach Greasy Neale about the recent decline of baserunning in the National League. Neale stated that Frankie Frisch of St. Louis, Lloyd Waner of Pittsburgh and Chicago's Hazen Cuyler were the only players who exhibited proper baserunning technique.[23]

When the month of May ended for the Cubs, they found themselves in third place, a game and a half behind the league-leading Cardinals. St. Louis stood on top at 26–15, Pittsburgh was second with a 23–14 record, and Chicago was close behind at 22–14. Chicago was keeping pace despite the status of Gabby Hartnett. While the team played in the East, Hartnett made a trip to Johns Hopkins Hospital in Baltimore so that he could meet with Dr. Dean Lewis. Hartnett was examined by the renowned surgeon, who informed Chicago's catcher that his arm was sound. Lewis reasoned that Hartnett was having problems because his tonsils were infected and advised him to have them removed once the team returned to Chicago.[24] Hartnett had surgery on his tonsils when Dr. John F. Davis removed the infected tissue at a Chicago hospital on May 14.[25]

Players like Cuyler, Stephenson and Hornsby helped to alleviate the void created by the absence of Hartnett from Chicago's lineup. After some struggles in early May when he only batted .240 over the span of a week, Hornsby went 10-for-25 during a six-game stretch and pushed his mark a few points above .300. Cuyler was not receiving much notice in the press, but he remained near the top of the National League with a .375 average.[26] He had done yeoman's work since the first day of spring training and was having the best season of his career while toiling in anonymity. Cuyler and Hornsby helped push the Cubs into second place on June 15, when they clubbed critical home runs during a ten-inning, 8–7 victory over Philadelphia at Wrigley Field.[27] Cuyler's shot came in the sixth inning with no one on board after the Phillies had taken a 5–0 lead. One inning later, Hornsby delivered his homer with the bases loaded, as Chicago took the lead by putting six runs on the scoreboard.

As Cuyler and his teammates continued to battle for the National League pennant, former colleague Glenn Wright was experiencing an injury problem similar to Gabby Hartnett's. Brooklyn's new shortstop had been of no use all year long due to a crippled shoulder. On June 14, Wright took a break from his disappointing season to make a trip to Fulton, Missouri, for a special ceremony. Wright married Miss Margaret Benn of Harrisonville, Missouri. Mr. and Mrs. Wright quickly left after the ceremony so that Glenn could rejoin his squad during a road trip in the East.[28] Wright played only three games at shortstop and appeared as a pinch hitter on 21 other occasions as his 1929 season came to an end on July 20. Wright's career, which burned brightly alongside Hazen Cuyler's for so many years in Pittsburgh, now seemed to be at a crossroads, just like his former teammate was following the 1927 season.

Excitement continued as a theme at Wrigley Field as Cuyler and his teammates pushed onward. Chicago fans saw some action that did not involve the actual game on June 16, as the Cubs were being slaughtered by Philadelphia, 7–2. The Phillies' Fresco Thompson and Denny Sothern reportedly squirted tobacco juice at a fan who was taunting Philadelphia's starting second baseman throughout the afternoon. When the fan demanded an apology from the players after the game and did not receive one, he was arrested by police for making a scene. Other fans followed officers to the station in order to protest the treatment of the fan who had been humiliated by Sothern and Thompson. After a short demonstration, police released the original perpetrator but then took two more people into custody when they refused to quiet down.[29]

More fireworks resulted when Pittsburgh came to town a few days later. The Cubs suffered three straight defeats at the hands of Donie Bush's Pirates as tempers reached a breaking point. During the game on June 21 between the two heated rivals, Bush and Cubs shortstop Woody English rode each other relentlessly throughout the afternoon. Bush and English almost came to blows after the verbal jousting intensified. Umpires Beans Reardon and Ernest Quigley took control of the situation, averting a round of fisticuffs between both men.[30] The Cubs prevented the four-game series from becoming a total disaster by defeating the Pirates, 4–3, on June 24. Pitcher Charlie Root

Cuyler, with his wife Bertha, daughter Kelly and son Harold (courtesy the *Alcona County Review*).

benefitted from the long ball as Hazen Cuyler, Hack Wilson and Rogers Hornsby delivered the crucial blows that sank the Pirate ship.[31]

The Cubs found themselves clinging to a tight one-half game lead over the second-place Pirates at the close of June. The Cubs' fortunes continued to rest with the bats of Kiki Cuyler (.352), Riggs Stephenson (.351), Rogers

Hornsby (.353) and Hack Wilson (.318). These four players were not only hitting for high average; they also supplied power and plenty of RBIs. The Cubs' fine showing to date had occurred while one of their main power brokers was sidelined with an injury. Gabby Hartnett's shoulder showed no improvement, even after the tonsil operation. Hartnett, who had only been able to appear as a pinch hitter eight times during the first half of the season, made another trip to Bonesetter Reese at the end of June. The veteran muscle and ligament specialist worked on Hartnett's right arm for a while and then recommended that he take a long rest.[32]

Combative rivalries continued to supply entertainment for fans at Wrigley Field. Bad blood existed between members of the Cubs and Reds throughout an early July series. During one particular contest, spikes flew to the level of Ty Cobb. The situation finally boiled over during the afternoon game of a doubleheader on July 4. The ever volatile Hack Wilson became embroiled in a battle with an opposing player when he rambled down to first base after delivering a single. A Cincinnati player baited Wilson as he stood on the bag, claiming that Chicago's stocky outfielder lacked "gameness" and would not dare step into the Reds' dugout. Wilson quickly discovered that pitcher Ray Kolp was his tormentor. Wilson became so angry that he left the bag without considering the fact that he could be tagged out. He raced into the Reds' dugout and made a beeline for Kolp. Some of his teammates attempted to shield Kolp from his enraged opponent, but Wilson was still able to tag Kolp on the jaw several times.[33]

Umpire Cy Rigler ran over to the dugout, picked Wilson up and placed him back on the field. Rigler then sent Wilson to the showers for the remainder of the afternoon. After order was restored on the field, hoodlums that occupied seats behind Cincinnati's dugout told the Cubs' players to go back to their bench. They assured Joe McCarthy's players that Chicago's criminal element would attend to any details if the Reds continued looking for trouble.

Nothing further happened during the game, but Wilson became involved in round two of the battle that evening at the Union Train Station. Wilson was having a friendly discussion with Cincinnati's Jakie May when pitcher Pete Donohue walked by and overheard him say he was going to enter the Reds' car to demand an apology from Kolp for his rude comment. Donohue warned Wilson to change his mind, threatening that he might not come out of the railroad car alive. Wilson replied that there was no need to wait that long, as he landed a hook against Donohue's mouth and dropped him to the ground. Donohue received two stitches to his lip.[34]

Wilson received a three-day suspension from National League President John Heydler and was fined $100 for attacking Ray Kolp.[35] Heydler also heard testimony from Chicago and Cincinnati players concerning the incident at

Union Station. Heydler concluded that Donohue should have been prepared to defend himself since insults were being traded. The league president censured Wilson for instigating the fight and warned him that serious consequences could result unless he learned to control himself.[36]

Wilson's unquenchable fighting spirit seemed to infiltrate the Cubs' team as Chicago tried to put a stranglehold on the National League race. Cuyler was not the type of player who fought with his fists, but he did play hard from March through October. The patrons at Wrigley Field loved his dedication and hustle. Cuyler was now a fan favorite in Chicago just as he had been for Pittsburgh.

Cuyler was Chicago's catalyst against New York on July 10. He rapped out two singles, a walk, a sacrifice fly and stole two bases. Hack Wilson nailed a double and a home run as the Cubs defeated New York, 6–2.[37] Cuyler suffered an injury late in the game and was replaced by Cliff Heathcote, who continued to man the position in New York and Philadelphia while Cuyler was relegated to pinch hitting duty. Heathcote would have remained in the lineup if Brooklyn had not started southpaw Watty Clark against Chicago on July 20. Cuyler played the entire game, but found himself back on the bench one day later.[38] He was forced out of the starting lineup for two weeks due to a nagging charley horse.[39]

Chicago reeled off a nine-game winning streak while Cuyler was sidelined with his injury. He sat out the first game of a doubleheader on July 31, as Boston snapped Chicago's streak by defeating the Cubs, 7–1. Cuyler returned to Chicago's lineup during the nightcap and went 2-for-4 with two RBIs as the Cubs defeated Boston, 6–3. The Cubs went on another tear as they proceeded to go 10–2 during their next twelve games. Cuyler played a huge role in Chicago's success as he thrived during a home series against Brooklyn. He went 9-for-17 as Chicago pulled off a four-game sweep of the Robins in early August. Cuyler did heavy damage before 43,069 fans at Wrigley Field on August 4, as he led Chicago's attack with three hits during a 6–3 victory over Brooklyn.[40] Cuyler was then reduced to the role of pinch hitter for the first two games of a series in Boston before he reemerged in McCarthy's starting lineup and batted fifth during a 4–2 victory on August 13.

Cuyler went 4-for-8 and scored three runs during a doubleheader split with Brooklyn two days later. National League standings on August 15 showed Chicago holding a comfortable lead in the pennant race. The Cubs' recent streak had propelled them eight and a half games ahead of second-place Pittsburgh while pushing their record to 72–34. Joe McCarthy's men pushed their lead to 14 and a half games over the Pirates during the next two weeks before Pittsburgh manager Donie Bush tendered his resignation on August 27. Longtime coach Jewel Ens was selected as Bush's successor.

Pittsburgh sportswriter James J. Long offered his reasons for why Bush decided to sever his relationship with Barney Dreyfuss less than two seasons after leading Pittsburgh to the World Series. "Every fair-minded baseball follower must admit that Bush never had the best chance in the world here to show his ability," stated Long. "He never was given the encouragement of some of the fans to anything like a 100 percent degree, and he never received from other quarters the support and cooperation that he deserved.

"The Cuyler deal appeared to be the starting point of a feeling of resentment toward Bush. That trade was put through with the full sanction of the owners, and those familiar with the existing conditions admitted that Bush could not have taken any other course at the time."[41]

Ens rallied the Pirates spirits somewhat at the end of August, as his club won four out of five games during a series against Chicago at Forbes Field. This proved a minor inconvenience for the Cubs as they proceeded to go on a 9–2 stretch after leaving Pittsburgh, all but giving them the National League pennant. Chicago did not officially clinch the title until September 18, when Boston won the first game of a doubleheader over Pittsburgh as southpaw Carl Hubbell defeated the Cubs, 7–3, at Wrigley Field.[42] The pennant seemed to be anti-climactic since the National League race had become such a one-sided affair. Faint applause came from Chicago's patrons when the Pittsburgh-Boston final was posted on Wrigley Field's scoreboard.[43]

After Chicago clinched the pennant, *St. Louis Times*' writer Sid Keener recalled a short speech that Joe McCarthy gave his troops during the first day of spring training at Catalina Island.[44] "No individual stars on the ball club," said McCarthy. "Everyone is going to play for me and not himself. Everybody's going to get along, too. Ain't they Rajah? Ain't they Hack? And we're going to win this pennant, ain't we boys?"[45]

After they clinched the pennant, the Cubs' players participated in a small celebration with some workers from the city of Chicago on September 20. A crowd of 40,000 men and women listened to speeches and testimonials during a mass assembly at the Hawthorne Plant of the Western Electric Company. When Chicago's National League championship club arrived, every worker was released for the day so that they could assemble in front of a platform. Speeches by Guy Bush and Kiki Cuyler earned the loudest applause from the faithful fans. The two players jokingly told the crowd that Hack Wilson was the man to see if they wanted World Series tickets. All of the players received a hearty reception as each Cub was introduced and took a bow.[46]

McCarthy's team-first concept paid huge dividends as Chicago won its first National League pennant since 1918. The Cubs finished the year with a 98–54 record. The second-place Pirates were ten and a half games back with a record of 88–65, while New York finished in third with a mark of 84–67.

Kiki Cuyler championed McCarthy's initiative throughout the year and hit fiercely during the season's final weeks. Cuyler hit safely in 26 of 29 games from August 31 to the season finale on October 6 and finished the season with the best batting average of his career; he placed third on the squad with a mark of .360. Cuyler also scored 111 runs, smacked 15 homers, recorded 102 RBIs and led the league with 43 stolen bases. He received ample support at the plate from Rogers Hornsby (.380, 39 HRs, 149 RBIs), Riggs Stephenson (.362, 17 HRs, 110 RBIs) and Hack Wilson (.345, 39 HRs, 159 RBIs). Pat Malone was Chicago's top hurler as he went 22–10 and led the National League with 166 strikeouts.

The American League crowned someone other than the Yankees as league champion for the first time since 1925. Connie Mack's Philadelphia Athletics cruised to a relatively easy pennant as they finished with a 104–46 record and topped second-place New York by 18 games. Mack's Athletics were loaded with good hitters like Mickey Cochrane (.331), Jimmy Dykes (.327), Jimmie Foxx (.354), Mule Haas (.313), Bing Miller (.331) and Al Simmons (.365). Twenty-four game winner George Earnshaw emerged as Philadelphia's top winner while southpaws Lefty Grove and Rube Walberg ably complemented the staff ace.

The Cubs would be operating at full strength against the American League powerhouse. First baseman Charlie Grimm had missed over a month of action after colliding with a concrete wall at the Polo Grounds.[47] Grimm played the final week of the regular season and was pronounced healthy for the World Series.

Unfortunately, Gabby Hartnett was not expected to play against the Athletics in the Fall Classic. There seemed to be a slim chance that Hartnett would do anything more than pinch hit during the World Series.[48] Hartnett had caught his first game of the year on September 22, just days after Chicago clinched the pennant.[49] He had tired of listening to critics who claimed the injury was psychosomatic. He caught the entire game in late September and made one throw to third. It was a lame toss which lacked the usual Hartnett velocity. He played a few days later in an exhibition game in order to work out the soreness he had experienced from his previous outing, but after this second attempt, he could barely raise his arm as high as his shoulder.[50]

Hazen "Kiki" Cuyler was considered one of manager Joe McCarthy's valuable assets heading into the World Series against Philadelphia. Over the years, many baseball experts had stated that Cuyler possessed the physical and mental requirements to become another Ty Cobb. He was a natural ball player, and a man who had skills that fellow major league players envied. McCarthy believed that there was no more valuable team player in baseball. When Chicago's manager was reminded that Cuyler was classified as a troublemaker in Pittsburgh, McCarthy responded by stating that Hazen was causing trouble only for opposing pitchers. He concluded by saying the Cubs would like to have more troublemakers like Cuyler.[51]

In the meantime, Chicago's starting right fielder was delighted to be receiving an opportunity to play after Donie Bush had forced him to the bench against New York during the 1927 World Series.[52] "What I didn't get a chance to do in 1927, I hope to do this time," Cuyler admitted. "All season I have felt right and I feel right now. I am going to play to win and this time when the fans yell for me, I'll be swinging."[53]

Over 50,000 Cubs fans squeezed into Wrigley Field to witness the opening clash between the two league titans on Tuesday, October 8. Kiki Cuyler's father, mother and wife were in attendance, sitting behind the Cubs' dugout.[54] The game's starting time was delayed for 15 minutes because of congestion outside of the gates, as ticket holders were unable to push through the turnstiles quickly enough. Chicago owner William Wrigley requested the delay so that fans would not miss any of the action.[55] Those patrons who arrived early had extra time to ponder which pitcher Philadelphia manager Connie Mack would choose to face Chicago in Game One. They wondered if George Earnshaw would receive the nod or if Mack would take a chance using southpaws Lefty Grove or Rube Walberg against the Cubs' heavy-hitting, right-handed lineup. Most everyone who was sitting in Wrigley Field had to be shocked when it was announced that Howard Ehmke would be Philadelphia's starting pitcher for Game One.

Ehmke was a 35-year-old right-hander who appeared in only 11 games for Connie Mack in 1929. It looked as if Mack had two things in mind as he devised his early World Series strategy. He did not want to open with a lefty against Chicago's predominantly right-handed lineup and preferred a junk ball pitcher since the Cubs had tormented hard throwers in 1929. Mack's strategy almost backfired after Chicago's Charlie Root retired Philadelphia with relative ease in the top half of the first inning. Ehmke started the bottom of the frame by retiring Norm McMillan on an easy popup to Cochrane before Woody English beat out an infield roller that caromed off the pitcher's glove. Rogers Hornsby then stepped in, connecting against an Ehmke offering and drilling it deep to right field. Disaster was averted for Philadelphia when Bing Miller hauled in the long drive near the stands. Ehmke then worked out of the inning, retiring Hack Wilson on a shallow fly to right field.[56]

Philadelphia's veteran pitcher settled down after the Cubs nearly took a two-run lead and mesmerized Joe McCarthy's men throughout the afternoon. Cuyler led off the bottom of the second frame and looked horrible as he became Ehmke's first strikeout victim on the day.[57] Ehmke and Root quickly locked into a pitcher's duel as each hurler put zeros on the scoreboard through the first six innings. Cuyler and most of his Chicago teammates continued to struggle with Ehmke's delivery. Hazen led off Chicago's fourth inning by striking out for the second time. Philadelphia finally broke the scoreless logjam in the seventh inning, when Jimmie Foxx crushed a pitch into the center field bleachers. The Cubs tried to respond in the bottom of the seventh; Cuyler singled off shortstop Joe Boley's glove and Riggs Stephenson followed with a single to left. Charlie Grimm then moved both runners up with a sacrifice. But the runners stayed there as pinch hitter Cliff Heathcote flied out to Al Simmons in shallow left and Gabby Hartnett struck out pinch-hitting for Root.[58]

Hartnett was Ehmke's 12th strikeout victim on the day. That tied a record that the White Sox' Ed Walsh had set during the 1906 World Series, when he fanned a dozen Cubs batters. With Ehmke pitching superbly, Philadelphia added two more runs against Guy Bush in the top of the ninth. Chicago finally did some damage to Ehmke in the bottom of the ninth. After Hack Wilson made the inning's first out, Cuyler ended up on second base when third baseman Jimmy Dykes fielded his high chopper and threw the ball into the Athletics' dugout. Cuyler then came around to score Chicago's first run of the series on Stephenson's single to center. It looked as if the Cubs were starting a significant rally against Philadelphia when Grimm followed with a single to right field.[59] But Ehmke composed himself and induced pinch hitter Footsie Blair to force Grimm at second. The 35-year-old veteran pitcher then ended the game, making pinch hitter Chick Tolson his 13th strikeout victim of the day.

Ehmke was the unlikely hero of Game One as the Athletics prevailed over the Cubs, 3–1. Even people who followed the Athletics on a regular basis could not have foreseen Ehmke being the Game One starter since he had made only three pitching appearances after July. Connie Mack did not even take Ehmke with the team during a trip through the West in August. Philadelphia's manager reasoned that Ehmke could get some work in at home during the Western swing. Stories surfaced that Ehmke was left behind because he had fought with some of his teammates, but he put these false rumors to rest when he explained Mack's strategy after Game One.[60]

> I never had any trouble with any of the boys. In fact, several of them told me they hoped I'd be fit for one of the World's Series games. They wanted to see me in there. When the club left, I devoted my time in getting ready for the Series. Then the Cubs came to Philadelphia to play the Phillies. I went out to the Phils' park, bought a ticket each day and sat away by myself. I kept a score card of each game. I watched how every one of the Cubs batted, how they stood in the box, the kind of balls they hit and the kind they looked weak against.
>
> In other words, I watched everything they did while they were in the batting box. I made notations on my score card alongside each player's name and checked them in each game I saw.

> A thing I noticed that interested me was that all the balls used in the game were discolored. This was permitted in the National League to cut down some of the slugging. It gave me an idea.[61]

This final piece of information was crucial since Ehmke believed his delivery style would make it difficult for Chicago's players to pick up the marked ball as it left his hand. The evening before the first Series game, roommate Jimmie Foxx promised Ehmke that he would hit a home run if he pitched the opening contest. On the morning of the first game, Mack called a meeting at the team hotel. After the session broke up, Ehmke remained behind and asked Mack if he had decided who was going to pitch that day. Connie said that he had not. Howard then asked Mack, assuming his arm was sound, if he could receive the assignment. Mack finally ended the suspense by telling Ehmke that he was the choice to pitch.[62]

"It was about 25 minutes," recalled Ehmke, "including our team at bat in the first inning, before I went to the slab. The first inning was the only worrisome one for me in the whole ball game."[63]

Kiki Cuyler, Rogers Hornsby and Hack Wilson each struck out twice during the Series' first contest; the Flint Flash was the only member of Chicago's heavy hitters to record a hit.[64] Fortunes did not get much better for two of these three players as Chicago was crushed by Philadelphia in Game Two of the World Series on October 9. Philadelphia rode homers from Jimmie Foxx and Al Simmons on the way to a 9–3 victory. The Athletics took a 6–0 lead before Chicago did some damage of its own against starter George Earnshaw in the fifth inning. Mack then brought in Lefty Grove to shut the door; his star southpaw pitched four and a third innings of shutout relief.

Hack Wilson rebounded after a tough day at the plate in Game One by going 3-for-3. Cuyler's performance was wretched, as he went 0-for-4, struck out three times and drew a walk. He stranded two runners in the first when he was fanned by Earnshaw. After receiving a base on balls in the third, Cuyler duplicated his previous performance by striking out with Hornsby and Wilson on base in the fifth inning. He also struck out with Wilson on first base in the seventh inning. Cuyler finally made contact with the ball in the ninth, when he reached first on a fielder's choice after Grove fielded his grounder and threw home to retire Hornsby.

Cuyler was writing a syndicated newspaper column detailing the events of the 1929 World Series. The day after Chicago's second defeat at the hands of Connie Mack's troops, Cuyler wrote that the Cubs showed they could hit speedy pitching by knocking Earnshaw out of the box in the fifth inning.[65]

Cuyler also reasoned that the Cubs were finally getting used to Grove's stuff and would be able to hit his type of pitching when they saw the southpaw in future games. He called Al Simmons' Game Two home run "a corker" because it left Wrigley Field in spite of a stiff wind. He also gave credit to Foxx for delivering in the clutch by hitting crucial homers in each game. He knew that the Athletics had outfielded and outhit the Cubs in both games at Wrigley Field, but he also believed the breaks had gone in Philadelphia's favor during the first two contests. Cuyler concluded the article by saying that the Cubs finally might receive some breaks since they were playing on a new and strange field. There was little doubt the squad needed them.[66]

Lucky breaks may not have factored into the equation on Friday, October 11, but solid pitching returned after a one-game hiatus two days earlier. Mack called on Earnshaw to start with only one day rest while Joe McCarthy countered with Guy Bush. Both pitchers did stellar work until Philadelphia broke through with the game's first marker in the fifth inning. Mickey Cochrane started the frame by beating out a grounder to shortstop Woody English for a single. Al Simmons followed with a fly ball to Hack Wilson in center. Cochrane moved up to second on Foxx' grounder to Bush. The Athletics took a 1–0 lead when Bing Miller drove home Cochrane with a single to center. The inning ended when Miller was thrown out by catcher Zack Taylor on an attempted steal.[67]

The Cubs wasted no time obliterating Philadelphia's lead as they quickly assumed control of the game. Earnshaw walked Bush to start the sixth inning. After Norm McMillan was retired on a foul pop to Cochrane, the Cubs added a second runner when Jimmy Dykes fumbled Woody English's grounder. Bush came around to score the game's tying run on Hornsby's single to left field. English and Hornsby each moved up a base when Wilson was thrown out on a grounder to Max Bishop at second. Cuyler then strolled to the plate and brought back memories of his fine work against Washington during the 1925 World Series. Cuyler jumped on an Earnshaw offering and lined the ball into center field for a single, scoring both English and Hornsby as Chicago took a 3–1 lead.[68] Moments before Cuyler delivered his game-winning hit, a frustrated Cubs fan sitting in the upper deck had screamed for the outfielder to change his luck by actually swinging at a pitch.[69] No additional scoring ensued during Game Three as Bush tossed a complete game and gave the Cubs their first win in the World Series.

Momentum seemed to be swinging Chicago's way as McCarthy came back with Charlie Root in Game Four on Saturday, October 12, against veteran right-hander Jack Quinn. It looked like the Cubs would even the series as they started to batter Quinn around after going scoreless in the first three innings. Cuyler banged a one-out single and moved over to third when the ball rolled through Bing Miller's legs. Quinn retired Stephenson on a popup to Boley before Charlie Grimm gave Chicago a 2–0 lead by smacking a home run over the right field fence. The Cubs chased Quinn two innings later when they exploded for five runs in the sixth inning.[70]

Hornsby started the sixth by driving a single to center and moving to second on Wilson's clean safety to right. Cuyler followed with a clutch single that scored Hornsby and moved Wilson to third. Wilson then scored Chicago's fourth run when he scampered home on Riggs Stephenson's infield single to second. Mack then summoned Rube Walberg to replace Quinn. Grimm entered the batter's box and laid down a beautiful bunt to the pitcher. Even though Walberg had no chance of getting Grimm at first, he made an ill-fated toss that Jimmie Foxx could not handle. Cuyler and Stephenson came around to score on the error, while Grimm made it to third. Grimm scored Chicago's seventh run when he crossed home plate on Zack Taylor's sacrifice fly to center.[71] Chicago added another insurance run in the seventh off Eddie Rommel as Hornsby tripled, Wilson worked out a walk and Cuyler drove home the Cubs' eighth run with a single to center.

Chicago seemed to be in control; Root was cruising as Philadelphia came to bat in their half of the seventh. Simmons gave the Athletics' fans some hope when he drove a ball into the stands and cut Chicago's lead to 8–1. Foxx singled to right, Miller singled to center and Dykes singled to left, scoring Foxx. Boley then drove a single to right-center that brought home Miller with Philadelphia's third run. Root finally recorded an out when George Burns pinch hit for Rommel and was retired on a popup to English. But Mack's troops continued their comeback and drove Root from the game on Bishop's single, which scored Dykes and cut Chicago's lead to 8–4. Joe McCarthy decided to bring in veteran southpaw Art Nehf to face two consecutive left-handed batters in Philadelphia's lineup.[72]

The Cubs' nightmarish inning continued when Hack Wilson lost Mule Haas' drive to center field in the sun.[73] Boley and Bishop scored ahead of Haas, who was credited with an inside-the-park home run. After he walked Cochrane, Nehf was then lifted for Sheriff Blake. Simmons greeted Blake by drilling a single to left. Foxx followed with a single to center that drove Cochrane home with the game's tying run. McCarthy called on Pat Malone to replace Blake, and he proceeded to fill the bases by hitting Miller with a pitch. Dykes then won the game for Philadelphia by doubling to left, scoring Simmons and Foxx. Malone finally ended the disastrous inning when he struck out Boley and Burns.[74]

The Cubs had seen a seemingly insurmountable eight-run lead evaporate in one inning, as Philadelphia now held a 10–8 advantage. Chicago succumbed rather meekly in the eighth and ninth, as Lefty Grove retired six straight batters and struck out four Cubs.

Philadelphia now held a 3–1 advantage in the 1929 World Series. The

8. A Comeback Season and World Series Appearance   135

scenario was not something new to Kiki Cuyler, who had experienced the same situation in 1925 before Pittsburgh rallied with three straight victories to capture the championship over Washington. Cuyler had put up respectable numbers in Game Four, as he went 3-for-4, scored two runs and drove home two. While the mood was somber in Chicago's clubhouse after its monumental Game Four collapse, a raucous celebration took place in Philadelphia's quarters. When the game concluded, Connie Mack made an unexpected trip to the Athletics' dressing room. The veteran icon was so filled with emotion that he had difficulty speaking while timidly entering the clubhouse. Mack made a brief remark before he turned and left the wild celebration.[75] "I'd just like to be able to express to you the things I feel," Mack said to his players. "But I can't and I'll have to let it go at that."[76]

Mack decided to come back with Series hero Howard Ehmke to start Game Five against Chicago's Pat Malone on Monday, October 14. President Herbert Hoover attended the game at Shibe Park to potentially watch the Athletics clinch their first world championship since 1913. President Hoover's first demonstration of interest occurred in the top of the second inning. Cuyler reached first when he forced Hack Wilson at second on a slow roller to Ehmke. Cuyler then inexplicably darted for second as Ehmke turned toward the mound to concentrate on the next batter. Ehmke wheeled and ran toward first as Mr. Hoover leaned forward in his seat. As the ball was tossed by Ehmke to Foxx, then to Boley at second, back to Foxx at first, and down to Boley once again, President Hoover smiled as Cuyler continued his efforts to twist out of his trap on the base paths. When catcher Mickey Cochrane finally joined the fray and dove on top of Cuyler to tag him, President Hoover laughed.[77]

Cuyler entertained President Hoover in a different manner during the bottom of the fifth inning. Mr. Hoover clapped vigorously when Cuyler leapt into the air and speared Al Simmons' long drive right in front of Shibe Park's right field fence.[78] Cuyler's catch proved to be critical as the next two Athletics reached base but were unable to score against Pat Malone.

Cuyler also had a hand in the Cubs putting two runs on the board one inning earlier, when they sent Ehmke to the showers after he was replaced by Rube Walberg. Ehmke easily retired Hornsby and Wilson in the fourth inning before Cuyler smacked a two-out double. After a Riggs Stephenson walk, consecutive singles to center by Charlie Grimm and Zack Taylor brought home two runs.[79] Malone and Walberg pitched shutout ball for their respective teams over the next four innings, as Chicago took a 2–0 lead into the bottom of the ninth.

Malone pitched phenomenally for the Cubs through eight innings as he held Philadelphia to two hits. It appeared that the series was headed back to Chicago when Malone recorded the stanza's first out by fanning pinch hitter

Chicago claimed the National League pennant in 1929 by going 98–54 and topping Cuyler's former Pittsburgh team by ten and a half games. After a particularly rough season in 1928, Cuyler re-established himself as a star by batting .360 and leading the circuit with 43 stolen bases. The Cubs were defeated by the Philadelphia Athletics in the 1929 World Series. Cuyler is shown here in the back row, first person standing on the far left (courtesy the National Baseball Hall of Fame Library, Cooperstown, New York).

Walter French. But Max Bishop kept Philadelphia's hopes alive as he lashed a Malone pitch past third baseman Norm McMillan. Anticipation on the part of Philadelphia's fans quickly turned to glee when Mule Haas stepped to the plate and drove a ball over the right field fence to tie the ballgame. Malone then settled down while the crowd of over 29,000 people cheered on the Athletics.[80] Malone recorded the second out when Hornsby easily handled Cochrane's grounder and threw him out at first. But Malone's relief was short-lived as Al Simmons followed with a double to center field. Slugger Jimmie Foxx was passed intentionally so that Malone could pitch to Bing Miller.[81]

Miller battled gamely as Malone tried to send the contest into extra innings. Miller finally gained the upper hand in the struggle when he connected against a pitch and sent it soaring into the right-center gap. The ball landed safely for a double, scoring Simmons with the game's winning run and deciding the 1929 World Series.[82]

For the second consecutive contest, Philadelphia had come from behind to claim a victory against Chicago. The Athletics were crowned as world champions after taking four out of five games from the Cubs.

Kiki Cuyler caught fire as the World Series progressed, in response to his five strikeouts during the first two games. Cuyler batted .300 and tied with Charlie Grimm for the team lead in RBIs with four, while his six runs scored placed him second behind his former Pittsburgh teammate.

Cuyler submitted his final syndicated article after Chicago was defeated in the World Series. He tipped his hat to the Athletics, praising them for their comeback ability. He talked about the helpless feeling he experienced as he watched Miller's game-winning hit bounce between him and Hack Wilson. Cuyler also discussed how he desperately ran toward the wall when Haas' drive soared over his head. He hoped the ball would hit off the top of the wall and bounce back onto the field, but Haas' hit barely cleared the fence for a game-tying home run.

As usual, Cuyler represented the game honorably during this disappointing moment in his career. He claimed that Philadelphia's ninth inning rally once again emphasized the honesty and integrity of baseball. The loss was difficult to accept, but Cuyler felt there was nothing more to do than congratulate the winners and hope for another crack at the Athletics next season.[83]

9. Hazen Cuyler Sets the Table for Hack Wilson

Joe McCarthy's squad was sullen and depressed as it returned to Chicago, even 500 faithful Cubs fans showed up at the train station to cheer on their conquered heroes. The rousing reception did little to relieve the disappointment McCarthy's men were experiencing. Team owner William Wrigley, Jr., was unable to conceal his sadness as he informed the throng of fans that things would be different next year. Kiki Cuyler and Guy Bush were the only players who could find the courage to interact with the devoted fans. Hack Wilson remained inconsolable as he forced his way through the crowd with tears streaming down his face. Wilson asked the fans to leave him alone because he was heartbroken over losing a fly ball in the sun during a crucial moment in Game Four. McCarthy addressed the crowd and proclaimed that he was proud of his team. He concluded by stating that the best team did not win. He believed the best manager had won.[1]

Chicago's World Series defeat became a memory as possible changes to the team's personnel became more prevalent. One rumor that did not seem to make much sense was the claim that Chicago intended to trade Cuyler prior to the 1930 season. Why would the Cubs want to part with a talented player like Cuyler?

Pittsburgh writer Ralph Davis admitted that Cuyler did not play particularly well in the World Series, but the former Pirate did perform better than many of his teammates.[2] "Cuyler didn't find Mackian pitching much to his liking," said Davis, "and yet he batted .300 in the Series. The trouble was that he made few of his hits when they would produce runs. He ran Hornsby a close race for the distinction of striking out oftener in the classic, whiffing seven times to Rogers' eight, but he made six hits, and only Wilson and Grimm made more than that.

"Throughout the National League season, Ki played grand ball, and did his part toward winning the pennant. However, it is claimed that the Cubs want another left-handed hitter in their regular batting order, and that, for this reason, they are willing to dispose of Cuyler, provided they can get as good a man in his stead."[3]

Chicago management was deeply interested in acquiring right-handed hitting third baseman Pinky Whitney from Philadelphia, but Phillies owner William Baker had no intention of turning over his young RBI machine to another club.[4] After being spurned by Philadelphia, William Veeck turned to Boston to fill the team's need at third base. On October 29, 1929, Chicago purchased Les Bell from the Braves. Writers and fans speculated on the purchase price for the veteran third baseman when both parties refused to reveal any specific information. Some scribes estimated that the purchase price was in the range of $35,000. When a writer asked Wrigley if this figure was accurate, he would only say that the amount was larger than what had been reported.[5]

As it turned out, exaggerated stories about Kiki Cuyler being traded were unfounded, as Wrigley and Veeck used cash as their method for upgrading the Cubs.

While the silly rumor about Cuyler leaving the Windy City was proven false, Hazen took it upon himself to kill a story that surfaced following the 1925 season. Prior to the 1929 World Series, the *Chicago Daily Tribune* did a feature story about Cuyler's life and career. Writer Edward Burns brought up the story from a few years earlier when Cuyler supposedly had letterhead that contained the line, "Hazen S. (Kiki) Cuyler — Star of the 1925 World Series."[6] Two days after the story again made its way into print, the newspaper received a package that was mailed from Harrisville, Michigan.[7] Hazen and wife Bertha had recently purchased a house in the town where Cuyler spent part of his childhood.[8] The package contained a collection of stationary that an auto dealership owner had used to advertise Cuyler's appearances at his showroom. It was the car dealer's stationary that actually featured Kiki as the star of the 1925 World Series.[9]

Cuyler also gave the newspaper a minor scolding, but in a polite manner. For years, Cuyler had been deeply embarrassed by the false story that claimed he printed the stationary for personal use. He took great efforts to explain the truth behind the letterhead so that no one would suspect him of being egotistical. Burns graciously accepted Cuyler's explanation and also dismissed any talk of the Cubs' outfielder having an inflated ego. Some people who had been associated with Cuyler throughout his career claimed that he was prone to habitual worrying. This depiction seemed to be more acceptable to Burns than the charge that Cuyler possessed a larger ego than the average major league player.[10]

Cuyler retired to his Michigan sanctuary during the off-season and spent some time at his new home on Church Street in Harrisville.[11] Cuyler's house was only two blocks from Mill Creek, the stream where he first became fanatical about fishing as a child. He used to catch brook trout from Mill Creek by using nothing more than his hands.[12] Cuyler's return to Harrisville gave him the opportunity to be closer to family that lived in Alcona County. Hazen and Bertha's parents both lived in Harrisville, while sister Edna Medor and her husband Peter lived in nearby Gustin Township. Peter, the proprietor of a local garage, and Edna were the parents of eight children ranging from under one year to 17 years of age. The youngest member of the Medor family was a boy named Hazen who was born during the spring of 1929.[13]

Cuyler stayed fit and trim once again during the winter months by playing basketball. Chicago's star outfielder planned on putting in a few weeks of extra work with his hoopsters so that he would not need trainer Andy Lotshaw's liniments after his first day of camp at Catalina Island. So Cuyler and his Pontiac, Michigan, basketball team made a trip to the Windy City to play the Chicago Nationals at St. Philip's Gymnasium on February 8. The game in Chicago came on the heels of an overtime loss on February 6, when Cuyler's team lost to the Majestics by a score of 33–32.

Fans throughout Chicago wondered if contract negotiations would be conducted between Cuyler and Veeck while the Pontiacs were in town. Cuyler had returned a document to Veeck one month earlier, including correspondence that stated it was not satisfactory to the ballplayer.[14]

Veeck was concerned that Cuyler planned on holding out for more money. Nothing could be further from the truth since Cuyler was pleased with the amount of money Chicago management had offered in the original contract. He actually wanted the term of his contract extended from one year to two. This seemed like a reasonable request to a relieved Veeck.[15] When Cuyler came to Chicago with his basketball team, he saw that his new contract had been revised to read two years instead of one, and quickly agreed to the terms offered by Veeck.[16]

While Cuyler was in the Windy City, newspaper writers asked him for his opinion regarding Donie Bush's recent appointment as manager of the White Sox. Cuyler responded that Bush was a smart baseball man who should help the White Sox become a winning team. When asked if Bush might have difficulty controlling "bad boy" Art Shires, Hazen responded by saying that he believed both men would get along just fine.[17]

As usual, the conversation turned to Cuyler's relationship with Bush during the 1927 season. Kiki claimed that he never blamed Bush for his benching during the World Series against New York that year. He always liked and admired Bush. Cuyler suspected that the order came from someone higher up within Pittsburgh's baseball hierarchy. Cuyler reasoned that a previous salary dispute with owner Barney Dreyfuss may have accounted for his placement on the bench throughout that World Series.[18] Cuyler always tried to be accommodating when writers broached him on the subject of Bush, but he preferred to talk about his current team, which was projected to challenge for the National League pennant in 1930. Off-season medical procedures were expected to revitalize two Cubs players so that they could perform at their usual all-star caliber level. Second baseman Rogers Hornsby underwent surgery in a St. Louis hospital to have a growth removed from a bone on his left heel.[19] Gabby Hartnett also had surgery to remove one last bit of infected tonsil that had been missed during his operation the previous year.[20]

The Cubs received a dose of good news when Hartnett began conducting drills with Chicago coach Ray Schalk in January. After a grueling gym workout that basically consisted of throwing, Schalk declared that Hartnett was on his way back to his pre–1929 form. Schalk proclaimed that Hartnett threw without worries about his shoulder, and was not suffering any kind of pain after a series of extensive workouts.[21] Hartnett's arm seemed sound once Joe McCarthy finally had a chance to watch the catcher go through his paces at Catalina Island. McCarthy was confident that Hartnett would be penciled in as his starting catcher for the 1930 season. The position of each player in the batting order was something that McCarthy had not yet decided. It was rumored early during training camp that McCarthy might consider using Cuyler as his leadoff hitter.[22] This idea was quickly scrapped by McCarthy as he toyed with a lineup that had Woody English leading off and Charlie Grimm hitting second. Following Grimm would be Hornsby, Wilson, Cuyler, Stephenson, Bell and the catcher.[23]

Spring training was a time for experiments and surprises. One of the more unexpected events during Chicago's stay at Catalina Island involved the crowning of a new champion during the annual prize dance. Trainer Andy Lotshaw and pitcher Harry Grampp were tied at the conclusion of the waltz event. Lotshaw then won a special showdown and claimed the $10 prize. Pitcher Malcolm Moss won the trophy for the best one-step dance while pitcher Bill McAfee took honors for the fox trotting event.[24] People surprised that Cuyler was not among the winners of the competition showed no such amazement when the Flint Flash was not the Cubs' leadoff hitter during their opener in St. Louis on April 15. Cuyler batted fifth and went 3-for-5 as the Cubs won a slugfest over the Cardinals, 9–8. Hartnett returned to McCarthy's starting lineup, as the Chicago catcher went 2-for-3 and knocked in three runs.

High scoring baseball games quickly became the norm throughout the National League in 1930. League executives had decided to use a more lively baseball so that fan interest would remain strong in spite of the economic problems faced throughout the country. The stock market crash that occurred on October 24, 1929, had thrown America into the early stages of the Great Depression as finding employment and putting food on the table quickly became more important than watching baseball games. Owners in both the National and American leagues hoped that higher averages and more home runs would keep the nation interested in the National Pastime. Not surprisingly, Chicago's heavy-hitting lineup crushed the ball throughout the early weeks of the 1930 season. Despite scoring more than five runs on eight different occasions, Chicago's record stood at only 8–8 when April ended. Cuyler was off to a fairly ordinary start, as his average stood at .306 on April 30.

Injuries to key players kept Chicago from performing beyond expectations during the season's first month. Rogers Hornsby was still bothered by a sore heel. Doctors insisted the irritation was caused because Hornsby favored the foot when he walked. This diagnosis was proven to be inaccurate when an X-ray revealed that Hornsby had two spurs attached to his heel bone. Charlie Grimm also missed a couple of games due to a cracked rib. New third baseman Lester Bell saw his Cubs debut delayed for more than a week due to an injured throwing arm.[25] All of these early season issues were forgotten once the Cubs reeled off an eight-game winning streak from April 30 to May 9, pushing them into first place with a 15–8 record. Excitement was rampant throughout the Windy City, but winning baseball was not the only reason the fans followed the Cubs closely. A special program established by a local newspaper and the organizations of both Chicago teams worked wonders in spurring interest among the area's younger fans.

Kiki Cuyler assumed the role of teacher for the *Chicago Daily Tribune's* baseball school, as members of the Cubs and White Sox assisted in giving advice on how to play the game. Professor Cuyler wrote various detailed articles for the newspaper, instructing youngsters on how to field, bat and run. In his first lesson, Cuyler explained the proper method of catching a fly ball. He stressed that it was crucial to practice in order to develop a proper style. He also presented the basic fundamentals regarding high fly balls and low line drives.[26] He covered the subject of how an outfielder should prepare to make a throw during his second lesson. He reasoned that throwing from the outfield initially depended on the matter of possessing a strong arm. Without a strong arm, positioning was the key in giving a youngster the chance to utilize his arm properly. Cuyler claimed that it was beneficial, whenever possible, for an outfielder to take a step forward as he caught a fly ball so that the power of the player's body equaled the power of his arm.[27]

Cuyler also stated that it was critical to think ahead when an opponent had runners on base. Chicago's star reasoned that quick analysis was vital for an outfielder to prevent him from making a hopeless throw to a base where a runner could not be retired.[28]

Young boys throughout Chicago were finally given some insight into major leaguers' batting secrets when Cuyler and Hack Wilson provided hitting tips in an article that appeared in the *Chicago Daily Tribune* on May 9. Cuyler explained that he enjoyed success at the plate because he stood further back in the batter's box. He did this to offset his weakness as a youngster to hit balls pitched over the inside corner. Cuyler reasoned that he could cover both the inside and outside corners of the plate by standing deep in the box. He also stated it was critical to have proper balance at home plate. Cuyler also cautioned against being overanxious while batting.[29]

Cuyler concluded the lesson by telling his students that not all of them would be natural, free swinging hitters. He reassured them that success could still be achieved by choking up on the bat and using a chopping stroke at the plate.[30]

The newspaper articles were not the only source of knowledge for youngsters who aspired to improve their baseball ability. The *Chicago Daily Tribune's* baseball school also held instructional lessons at Wrigley Field and Comiskey Park. A fourth lesson was held at the Cubs' home ballpark on May 10, with Chicago's own Kiki Cuyler and Hack Wilson providing instruction. These two stars received able assistance from Fred Lindstrom and Mel Ott, whose New York Giants were in town for a series with the Cubs.[31]

A group of 6,000 young men from Chicago and the surrounding area attended the fourth instructional lesson at Wrigley Field. Cuyler, Wilson, Ott and Lindstrom were also joined on the field by Cubs manager Joe McCarthy. The Giants' John McGraw had also promised to address the group of young boys, but was unable to make it due to the early hour of the morning event. McGraw sent coach Dave Bancroft in his place. The lessons for the day involved hitting, throwing a baseball, and baserunning. A special contest was held after each tutoring session to determine which boys were the most proficient in each aspect of the game. Prior to the hitting contest, Hack Wilson slammed three balls into the bleachers while Cuyler followed with blasts to the center field scoreboard. New York's Ott and Lindstrom then showed their own ability to display heavy slugging.[32]

Once the players were finished with their hitting exhibition, Frank Dombrowski of Lindblom High School won the hitting contest by blasting the longest drive of the day at Wrigley Field. Dombrowski, a sophomore at Lindblom, received a ball autographed by Hack Wilson for winning the hitting competition. Robert Kropp, a Milwaukee native who finished second to Dombrowski, had to rise at five A.M. just to make it to Wrigley Field in time to receive tutelage from these great players.

After the hitting competition concluded, Cuyler instructed a group of individuals about the finer points of making accurate throws from the outfield.

When Cuyler was done giving his lesson, the group of boys competed in a throwing contest judged for accuracy and distance. Wilbert Schwingen of 4111 North Lawndale Avenue won an outfielder's glove after he threw a ball the farthest and most accurately from Cuyler's position in right field. Sixteen-year-old Ed Schwartz of 823 Montrose Street was awarded a pair of spikes when he won the last event of the day by running around the bases in 16 seconds.[33]

The three lessons held at Wrigley Field attracted over 17,500 pupils. Other Cubs that provided tutoring besides Cuyler and Wilson included Woody English, Rogers Hornsby, Charlie Grimm, Clyde Beck and Gabby Hartnett.[34] Cuyler's willingness to offer his time and advice to help young boys in the community who hoped to become major leaguers did not surprise anyone who knew him. Kiki personally presented Schwartz with a pair of baseball shoes after he won the baserunning contest. A photographer from the *Chicago Daily Tribune* followed Cuyler throughout the morning as he continued to immerse himself in instruction. One photograph showed Cuyler tutoring some boys on making an accurate throw to home plate. In another photo, Cuyler imparted his wisdom to three-year-old Jackie Boy Johnson as he held the youngster in his arms.[35]

Cuyler and Wilson properly applied their batting techniques that afternoon, when New York slaughtered Chicago, 9–4. Cuyler smacked a double and a triple, while Wilson connected for a home run in the first inning. The two star swatters drove in every Chicago run and also scored three of the team's markers. Chicago's players continued to hit the ball hard throughout the month of May, even as the team struggled to consistently win ballgames. In a game on May 12 against New York, Cliff Heathcote, Clyde Beck, Hack Wilson and Charlie Grimm accounted for six home runs, but the Cubs still found a way to lose, 14–12.[36]

There were other problems. Cuyler had to be shifted to left field from right when Riggs Stephenson injured his shoulder after bumping it against the wall at St. Louis' Sportsman's Park.[37] Pitcher Pat Malone landed in a Chicago court after he refused to pay his bill at a local restaurant. The café's owner alleged that Malone brought a party of friends and then refused to pay the check for $35.40. Malone countered by saying that he was not accustomed to paying for his entertainment.[38]

All of these small problems kept the Cubs from seizing control of the National League race. When May ended, Chicago found itself in third place with a 23–19 record. The Cubs trailed the first-place Brooklyn Robins by three games and second-place St. Louis by one. Cuyler returned to right field and carried a .348 average into the month of June, as he was elevated to the third spot in the order after batting fifth during the season's early stages.

Cuyler assumed the role of baseball teacher during the 1930 season. He wrote a series of instructional articles for the *Chicago Daily Tribune* and participated in the newspaper's baseball clinic with teammate Hack Wilson at Wrigley Field (courtesy the *Alcona County Review*).

Batting averages and positioning in the National League standings took a back seat for Chicago's players when tragedy struck the close-knit team on May 28. Veteran pitcher Hal Carlson died at the age of 38 from a hemorrhage of the stomach.³⁹ Despite the fact that physicians had told Carlson two years ago to retire, the pitcher refused to give up. He battled against the odds and pitched for the Cubs in 1928 and 1929. He had also been one of manager Joe McCarthy's most reliable starting pitchers during the early stages of the 1930 season, and was the only member of the mound staff to go the limit and win a game.[40]

Carlson was in the clubhouse with the rest of his teammates on May 27 as he prepared to make his seventh start of the season, but the game against the Reds at Wrigley Field was postponed due to rain. Carlson went to his hotel room that night and retired at about ten o'clock, reportedly in the best of health and in good spirits. Six hours later, death claimed the man who was both a consummate teammate and a World War I hero. Carlson's untimely death could be directly attributed to the time he spent in France during the war. As a member of the "Suicide Club Machine Gun Corps" that was involved in front line service during the war, Carlson was exposed to waves of German gas that wafted through the trenches. A physical examination during spring training in 1928 showed that the deadly poison was beginning to wreak havoc on Carlson's body.[41] Carlson finally succumbed to the illness when he died from a stomach hemorrhage on the morning of May 28.[42]

Hal had always maintained a philosophical attitude as he fought the malady and continued playing the game he loved. "I prefer to die in the harness, rather than quit the game," Carlson stated on many occasions.[43]

Carlson's body was taken to the family home at Rockford, Illinois, for burial. He was survived by his wife and a four-year-old daughter named Betty Elaine.[44] One day after the tragedy struck the Cubs' family, Joe McCarthy and his players held a meeting in the clubhouse and vowed to win the National League pennant in honor of Carlson.[45]

The determination of Chicago's players suffered another stiff shot during a morning game at Wrigley Field on Decoration Day, when Rogers Hornsby suffered a serious injury. Hornsby doubled home a run for the Cubs and then broke for third on a fly ball that Cuyler hit to right field. He started to make a feet-first slide into the bag before he remembered the status of his damaged heel. Hornsby suddenly changed his mind and tried to come into third standing up. Hornsby's poor judgment proved disastrous as his legs curled up under him, and his left ankle snapped while his lower body was torqued in an awkward manner. Hornsby, who was immediately rushed to the hospital, returned to the ballpark an hour later with a cast on his left foot and crutches under his arms.[46]

The fractured bone in Hornsby's ankle was expected to sideline the star second baseman for at least three months.[47] People outside of the Cubs' locker room believed that Carlson's death and Hornsby's injury created too much adversity for even a great team to overcome. But Joe McCarthy's players were of a different mindset; they had no intention of letting these calamities interfere with their quest for another National League pennant. Gabby Hartnett, Hack Wilson, Woody English and Cuyler kept the squad steered in the right direction as Chicago blitzed through the National League in June. Wilson, English and Cuyler spearheaded a ferocious attack against pitcher Socks Seibold during a contest at Wrigley Field on June 19. Each player smacked a home run during the first three innings, as Chicago defeated Boston, 10–4.[48] Cuyler sent 50,000 Chicago fans home happy a week later, when he blasted a two-run, walk-off homer in the tenth inning, giving the Cubs a 7–5 victory over Brooklyn on June 27.[49]

Prior to the first game of the series against the Robins, Cuyler was told to take a look at a Brooklyn rookie by the name of Neal Finn. When Hazen asked for an explanation, his teammates explained that Finn could easily pass as Cuyler's double. Cuyler decided that he needed further proof and trotted out to where Finn was standing on the diamond to give him a quick look. When Cuyler returned to the Chicago dugout, the Flint Flash was asked if he noticed the striking resemblance.[50] "I'll say I did," grinned Hazen. "I thought I was looking into a mirror. We both had a good laugh."[51]

Young Neal Finn could only hope that his baseball ability mirrored that of his alleged twin from the Cubs. Cuyler continued to do damage against Finn and his Brooklyn teammates as Chicago defeated the Robins, 4–2, on June 28. Cuyler led the Cubs attack with a double and two singles.[52]

The Cubs were practically unbeatable in June as they posted a record of 20–7 for the month. As the Cubs prepared to face New York on July 1, they found themselves in first place with a 43–26 record. Second-place Brooklyn was a game and a half behind the league-leading Cubs, while New York and St. Louis filled out the remainder of the National League's first division spots. A recent spurt at the plate pushed Kiki Cuyler's average up to .350 as the month of June concluded. He continued to abuse opposing pitchers at the beginning of July. He smacked two home runs off New York's Fred Fitzsimmons during the Giants 7–5 win on July 1.[53]

Teams throughout the National League recognized that the Cubs still had some shortcomings despite their strong June showing. McCarthy wanted to upgrade his pitching staff, but was unwilling to accommodate fellow league magnates by succumbing to one-sided trade proposals. McCarthy could only laugh when Cincinnati offered southpaw pitcher Jakie May for Cuyler, and compared the proposed deal to a man trading a telephone booth for a skyscraper.[54] Interest in Cuyler on the part of other clubs was not surprising considering Cuyler was having one of his best seasons. Official averages in mid–July showed that Cuyler was leading the National League in runs scored, triples and stolen bases. Hazen also ranked second to Philadelphia's Chuck Klein in the RBI department.[55] Cuyler continued on his torrid run-scoring pace throughout the summer as he and Woody English became the table-setters during Hack Wilson's assault on the seasonal record for RBIs.

A 15–15 record for the month of July pushed the Cubs into second place behind the league-leading Brooklyn Robins. Cuyler raised his batting average to .355 by hitting safely in 12 straight games. His solid play and overall hustle was a huge reason why Chicago remained in the pennant race.

The Cubs lost a potential victory in Boston on July 13 when the six o'clock Sunday baseball law wiped out a 4–3 Chicago victory. The Cubs trailed Boston, 3–0, when they came up to bat in the ninth inning at 5:34 P.M. Chicago then scored four runs to take a 4–3 lead. Officials gathered in conference after a local cop blew a whistle at six o'clock that signified the end of the day's activities. Cuyler, who had a hit and stole a base, almost fell over when it was announced that Boston was the winner. Since everything that Chicago did after 5:34 P.M. was deemed irrelevant, the score reverted back to the eighth inning.[56]

Cuyler's 1930 season was so remarkable that Chicago's fans started taking his feats for granted. The Windy City faithful had grown so accustomed to watching the Flint Flash burn up the base paths that his dependable hitting, running, fielding and throwing became almost routine. Yet, Cubs followers always pointed to Cuyler as the reason the club did not miss a beat with Hornsby out of the lineup.[57] Joe McCarthy seemed to agree with this assessment and gave credit for most of the Cubs' success to Cuyler and Gabby Hartnett. When given a choice to determine which man was most valuable, McCarthy selected the former Pirate.[58]

"It would be hard to name the most valuable man on our club," said McCarthy. "However, if I had to make a pick, I have an idea I'd name Cuyler. He does everything — hit, field, run — and does them all well."[59]

Cuyler continued to excel as Chicago fought to remain in the race during August. Hack Wilson drove home three runs while Cuyler accounted for two RBIs as Chicago defeated St. Louis, 6–5, on August 7.[60] In the middle of the game, Cuyler had to shift from right to left field because Riggs Stephenson injured his leg.[61] Cuyler made a spectacular catch one week later, aiding an extra-inning victory against Brooklyn at Wrigley Field. In the top of the tenth inning, Cuyler raced from near the right field foul line to Hack Wilson's territory to snare a blistering drive by Brooklyn's Babe Herman.[62] Youngster Danny Taylor secured Chicago's victory in the bottom of the frame by rapping a game-winning double.[63]

Battles with Brooklyn for the National League's top spot during the early weeks of August gave way to tougher matchups with the revitalized Cardinals late in the month. Cuyler participated in the longest game of his major league career on August 28, when St. Louis defeated Chicago, 8–7, during a 20-inning affair at Wrigley Field. He became so exhausted as the game progressed that he began walking in from left field at the end of each inning instead of his customary sprinting to the Chicago dugout.[64]

The Cubs seemed well on their way to another National League pennant as the season moved into September. Chicago held down first place with a 77–51 record. New York stood in second place, five games out, while Brooklyn and St. Louis were within a game and a half of the Giants.

New York Telegram sportswriter Dan Daniel reasoned that Cuyler would be receiving consideration for the league's Most Valuable Player Award if it had not been discontinued after Rogers Hornsby took home the trophy in 1929. Daniel also said that Joe McCarthy and Bill Wrigley owed Pittsburgh owner Barney Dreyfuss a debt of gratitude for giving Cuyler to the Cubs for nothing.[65]

McCarthy's theoretical gratitude quickly became irrelevant as Chicago slumped horribly and St. Louis went on a tear. Rumors of players behaving irresponsibly away from the diamond were quashed when a Chicago newspaper writer reported on the team's nightly itinerary. The writer claimed that all of the players seemed to be following training rules despite gossip to the contrary.[66]

Kiki Cuyler and roommate Clarence "Footsie" Blair could not be accused of bad behavior. They might stay awake until ten o'clock and talk about the end of the season when they could break training by having a vanilla soda or a chocolate éclair.[67] But good intentions and solid play on Cuyler's part could not prevent the surging Cardinals from overtaking the Cubs as September progressed. The Cubs finished an even 13–13 for the month while Gabby Street's Cardinals went 21–4 in September. St. Louis won the National League pennant with a 92–62 record, while Chicago settled for second place with a mark of 90–64. Chicago's September swoon did more than prevent the Cubs from repeating as league champions. It also cost manager Joe McCarthy his job. Owner William Wrigley, who desperately wanted to win a world's championship, came to the conclusion that McCarthy was not capable of achieving that goal. A late-season rumor indicated that Wrigley had already chosen Rogers Hornsby to be his manager in 1931.[68]

McCarthy decided to resign before Chicago played its last series of the season against Cincinnati. He made the decision after rumors were confirmed by a newspaper man who awakened him while the team train traveled from Boston to Buffalo. Wrigley initially declared that McCarthy was dropped because the Cubs had failed in their attempt to repeat as league champions. It was later reported that Wrigley was upset that McCarthy did little to prevent certain Cubs players from indulging in a prolonged celebration after winning the pennant in 1929. It seemed that the players were entertained and worshiped by admirers in Chicago, California, and various road cities throughout the 1930 season. Wrigley believed that McCarthy let the situation fall out of control by not instilling discipline at the outset.[69]

Prior to assuming control of the rein's before Chicago's final series against Cincinnati, Hornsby shot down rumors that he had clashed with teammates during the past two years. He also denied reports that Hack Wilson, Gabby Hartnett, Charlie Grimm and Cuyler viewed his appointment as manager with any animosity.[70]

"Just because a player is a close friend and admirer of McCarthy does not mean that he will be hostile to me," Hornsby said. "One doesn't have to be a bosom pal of all the men on the club, whether he is a player or manager. I don't expect to have trouble with any of the players and think they will give me full cooperation.

"The reports that I have made plans to trade various players are ridiculous. You can't talk of straightening a ball club and of trading Wilson, Cuyler or Hartnett in the same conversation. Cuyler is one of the greatest outfielders in baseball. As for Hack Wilson, there isn't another player like him and his power and color are priceless to the team in my estimation."[71]

Hornsby probably would have been run out of town immediately if he proposed any trade that involved Hartnett, Cuyler or Wilson. Hartnett had rebounded with a spectacular year in 1930 after he was sidelined with a shoulder injury in 1929. Hartnett batted .339, blasted 37 home runs and drove in 122 runs. Cuyler followed up his solid 1929 season with another gem in 1930. He batted .355 and claimed another stolen base title with 37 pilfers. Playing in every game, Cuyler scored 155 runs and smacked 50 doubles, 17 triples, and 13 home runs while recording 134 RBIs. Wilson outperformed both of his teammates as the stocky outfielder from West Virginia had the best slugging season in National League history. Wilson batted .356 and set a league record by clouting 56 homers and driving home 191 runs. Throughout the season, fans who rooted for the Cubs witnessed Wilson driving home Cuyler and Woody English on numerous occasions. In spite of this breakthrough season, it was rumored that Hornsby planned to shift Cuyler to center field and Wilson to right in 1931.[72]

Hornsby quickly endeared himself to the fans in Chicago by sweeping the four-game, season-ending series against Cincinnati and then knocking off the White Sox in the City Series. The Cubs claimed four out of six games against their American League rival as throngs of fans filled Wrigley Field and Comiskey Park.[73] The fifth game at Wrigley Field, which was played on Sunday, October 5, drew over 45,000 fans.[74] Cuyler played the hero in Game Two, when his three-run homer helped pave the way to a 4–2 victory for the Cubs.[75]

Shortly after the Cubs completed the City Series against the White Sox, Cuyler, Hack Wilson, Gabby Hartnett and Cliff Heathcote signed on to do a song-and-dance routine for one of Chicago's loop theaters.[76] Cuyler received

$1,500 a week during a four-week engagement at the theater and three other outlying establishments. Wilson received $2,000 a week, Hartnett earned $1,250 and Heathcote was paid the small stipend of $400.[77]

When these four Chicago players signed on to do four weeks of vaudeville, it was done so under the assumption that each man knew how to sing. The booking agent, after dealing with Charlie Grimm one year earlier and failing to land the veteran first baseman when he changed his mind, figured that all ballplayers could play the banjo, sing and tell jokes like him. When the first rehearsal was conducted two days before the opening, it quickly became apparent to those running the show that these four players had no vaudeville expertise. Cuyler stated that he was capable of carrying the lead if he heard a song a few times and had the opportunity to read the words. Heathcote, who played a ukulele, was the only one from the quartet who could actually read music. Wilson and Hartnett readily admitted that they did not even mumble the "Star Spangled Banner" while attending community events. During the entire four-week engagement, Cuyler and Heathcote sang as Wilson and Hartnett merely moved their lips while two professionals behind a screen did the singing for them. Even though Hack and Gabby did not sing a note, the two men claimed they had never worked so hard to earn money doing a job.[78]

While Cuyler's four weeks of vaudeville work did net him an additional $6,000 in income, it also extended his time working in Chicago an extra month. The desire to reach his home in Harrisville once the show closed explained why Cuyler was tagged by a policeman during his automobile excursion from Chicago to Flint. Cuyler was stopped in Battle Creek, Michigan, for driving 48 miles per hour. The Flint Flash was ordered to pay a local judge $10 before he could continue the trip home.[79]

The winter preceding the 1931 season was a bit peculiar for Cuyler as he added 15 pounds of unexpected girth around his waistline. This was a new experience for the star outfielder, who always possessed the ideal athletic physique. Kiki melted the pounds away through a strict regimen of hunting, ice fishing and a strenuous basketball program.[80]

All of the excess weight vanished by the time Cuyler brought his basketball team to Chicago in January. Cuyler told writer Irving Vaughan that he planned on playing basketball for a couple more weeks so that the extra pounds would not return before spring training. Cuyler also showed interest in rumors surrounding the possible acquisition of first baseman Jim Bottomley from the Cardinals.[81] Talks between Chicago's Bill Veeck and St. Louis' Branch Rickey surrounding a Bottomley deal had failed to net any results. After Rickey and owner Sam Breadon were unable to talk Veeck into parting with some of his regular players, they stated that Chicago could have Bottomley for $150,000. Cubs management countered with an offer of $50,000 before negotiations quickly ceased.[82]

Cuyler was also curious about the purchase of promising outfield prospect Vin Barton, who was rumored as a possible outfield replacement. Once Cuyler was assured by the writer that Hornsby planned on using Barton to spell Riggs Stephenson, Hazen responded that he hoped "Stevie" would not be out of the lineup very often since he was crucial to the team's success. Kiki also stated that he believed Chicago would win the National League pennant in 1931. Cuyler felt that inadequate pitching had prevented the Cubs from claiming the crown in 1930. Chicago's star outfielder also predicted that pitcher Fred "Sheriff" Blake would be a difference maker for the team this year. Cuyler had a gut feeling that Blake was due for a breakout season in 1931.[83]

Two weeks after Vaughan's interview appeared in the *Chicago Daily Tribune*, Cuyler was featured in an article that ran in *The Sporting News*. During the summer of 1930, writer Harry T. Brundidge interviewed Cuyler while the two men were riding to the Polo Grounds one afternoon. Brundidge considered Cuyler one of the nicest men he had met since he began interviewing ballplayers many years ago. It had been nearly ten years since Cuyler made his major league debut with the Pirates in 1921. The September drive up Broadway with Brundidge brought back a flood of memories for Cuyler.[84]

> I always remember my first trip to New York. It was with the Pittsburgh Pirates in 1921. I joined the team late in the season, just in time to see them blow up and lose the pennant to the New York Giants. The team faded just like the Chicago Cubs faded — the pitchers couldn't pitch, the fielders couldn't field and the hitters couldn't hit. What was wrong with the Pirates? The same thing that was wrong with the Cubs — but try and put your finger on it! I was greatly impressed with New York, the city, I mean. I was afraid I would get lost, but I wanted to see the city, so I got up every morning at 5 o'clock and started out.
>
> I rode elevator trains, subways, went up in elevators, stood on roofs, watched the crowds, and did everything you could expect a green boy from the country to do, and I still do it. I never tire of rambling about the town, looking for streets, alleys and buildings I have not previously seen.[85]

Brundidge concluded the interview by asking Cuyler if he had been prudent through the years and saved his money. Cuyler assured the writer that after two or three more years playing baseball, he would have no worries about the future.[86] Cuyler was certainly compensated handsomely for being one of the stars on the Cubs.

Teammate Hack Wilson also cashed in on his record-setting 1930 season as he signed a new contract that was estimated to pay the home run king between $30,000 and $35,000 a year.[87] Whether Wilson would be able to earn that money by posting better numbers in 1931 was doubtful given the rumors that floated out of Catalina Island at spring training. Gossipers revived tales that Wilson did not like Rogers Hornsby and was none too happy when Joe McCarthy engineered his purchase from Boston after the 1928 season. Wilson's bitter feelings were intensified during the 1931 training session when Hornsby stated Wilson might be moved to right or left field so that Cuyler could play center.[88]

Chicago's players quickly found out that Camp Hornsby was going to be different than what they had previously experienced. Hornsby reasoned that he could make his players stronger and more durable by allowing them to eat more during the training season. He vowed to add pounds to pitcher Guy Bush with a special steak treatment. Hornsby ordered three full meals for his men each day. He also set up the buffet table at the private dining room of the Cubs' quarters on Catalina Island in such a way that hungry athletes could eat without inhibition.[89] Rogers also introduced the game of soccer into the training program. Regulation games were not played, but the players strengthened their legs by kicking a soccer ball up and down the practice field.[90] In addition, Hornsby wanted his men to think about nothing but baseball throughout the upcoming 1931 season.[91]

"Before and during games I want nothing discussed but baseball," Hornsby said. "There will be plenty of baseball to discuss and no need of players talking about stocks, automobiles, taxes or girls. We will have meetings during the training season and all during the pennant race, even to the last week of the schedule. I want to get the players' opinions on things that happen during games and I will give them mine."[92]

It was rumored that some of Hornsby's men did not hold a high opinion of their new manager. Two weeks prior to the team's opening game against Pittsburgh at Wrigley Field, a story surfaced alleging dissension and discord in Chicago's ranks. It was reported that Hornsby had been riding Kiki Cuyler, Hack Wilson and Pat Malone relentlessly throughout spring training.[93] Wilson's dissatisfaction over being moved from center field was no secret. Even though he claimed he would be a good soldier if the move happened, it was evident to anyone close to the situation that Wilson wanted to remain in center field.[94] But it was not known why Cuyler was upset with Hornsby. Cuyler accepted the fact that Hornsby wanted to bat him in the leadoff position. Cuyler was fine with this as long as Hornsby did not switch him around the batting order throughout the season.[95]

Cuyler went 1-for-3 and drew a walk batting from the leadoff position as Chicago defeated Pittsburgh, 7–3, during the season opener on April 14. Wilson was now a happy man as he opened the season as Chicago's starting center fielder. Hornsby's Cubs played superbly during the early weeks of the season and finished the month of April with an 8–3 record. That mark put

Chicago in a three-way tie for the National League's top position, along with Boston and St. Louis. Cuyler enjoyed a blistering start before three hitless games at the end of April dropped his average to .278. A stiff neck that forced Cuyler to miss the game against St. Louis on April 20 contributed to his sudden struggles.[96] Chicago president William Veeck was also forced to refute a trade rumor involving Cuyler and the Cardinals. The report had St. Louis trading outfielder Chick Hafey and pitcher Sylvester Johnson to Chicago for Cuyler.[97]

The defending National League champion Cardinals served noticed that they had every intention of repeating as pennant winners in 1931. Chicago traveled to St. Louis for a series at Sportsman's Park in early May and was thrashed by the Cardinals in three straight games. It became apparent to those who rooted feverishly for the Cubs that this squad did not have the spark or energy present in previous units. The situation seemed to be in disarray only one month into the Rogers Hornsby era as players adjusted to the new manager's style.

Hack Wilson had a phenomenal season in 1930 when he smacked 56 home runs and drove home 191 runs. However, Chicago's star outfielder became disgruntled when Rogers Hornsby replaced Joe McCarthy as manager late in the year (courtesy the National Baseball Hall of Fame Library, Cooperstown, New York).

10. Rogers Hornsby, Violet Valli and Another Pennant

When Cuyler found out during spring training that he would likely be Hornsby's leadoff hitter at the beginning of the season, the star outfielder cautioned everyone that he would not be driving home as many runs from that spot. Cuyler also stated that he did not mind batting first as long as Hornsby did not keep switching him around to other spots.[1] Early season statistics showed Cuyler to be accurate about his deficiency at knocking in runs from the leadoff spot. Cuyler recorded only five RBIs during Chicago's first 16 games, but he did flourish in another category by scoring 13 runs. Yet, this level of run-scoring prowess did not seem to matter to Hornsby. Chicago's manager bumped Cuyler down in the order. Footsie Blair was assigned to the top position while Cuyler dropped to fifth in Chicago's batting order.[2]

Hornsby threatened more changes to his squad after Chicago lost two consecutive games against New York at the Polo Grounds in early May. Chicago's manager intimated that Hack Wilson and Gabby Hartnett would be sent to the bench as part of his lineup shake-up, but he did not follow through with these particular threats when Chicago played Brooklyn on May 15.[3] He did make one change that Wilson had feared for months. Wilson shifted over to left field while Johnny Moore assumed his spot in center. Wilson's misfortunes continued in Boston on May 19, when he injured his hand after crashing into the fence attempting to flag down Wally Berger's triple. The injury came one day after third baseman Les Bell was forced to the sidelines when he pulled a muscle in a game against Philadelphia.[4]

Wilson remained on the injured list for a few games. He returned on May 23 and went hitless against Pittsburgh. Rogers Hornsby then sent Wilson back to the bench one day later. Hornsby explained that Wilson was not going to play against the Pirates because he needed a rest. This marked the first time since Wilson joined the Cubs in 1926 that he had been benched for any reason other than an injury.[5] Wilson still remained involved in his team's games while he languished in the dugout. During the second game of a doubleheader against Cincinnati on May 26, Charlie Grimm became angry when he thought Edd Roush had deliberately spiked him while sliding into first base during the third inning. Grimm immediately squared off against Roush. Wilson led a group of five men from Chicago's dugout who rushed out to join in the fracas. Players emptied from Cincinnati's bench in support of Roush. Umpires Bill Klem, Charles Donnelly and Dolly Stark subdued the rebellion and the game resumed without any players being ejected, but Grimm was forced to leave the contest due to his injury.[6]

Wilson finally received a chance to return to action on May 27, when he went in to play right field in the fourth inning after Cuyler complained of a stomach disorder. Wilson shook off the rust and smashed a double as Chicago defeated Cincinnati, 8–4.[7] Cuyler remained inactive for a few days due to his illness, but returned to Chicago's lineup for the first game of a Decoration Day doubleheader, pushing Wilson back to the bench. Cuyler smacked a double and two singles as Chicago downed the Pirates, 9–2.[8] Chicago's star outfielder also hit his first homer of the season in the nightcap, as the Cubs pulled off a holiday sweep by defeating Pittsburgh, 6–5. While the Cubs were busy taking three games from Pittsburgh at Forbes Field, Cuyler was forced to refute a rumor that he had exchanged blows with Rogers Hornsby a week earlier. He denied a report that claimed the two men had engaged in fisticuffs after a dispute.[9]

The Cubs found themselves in third place with a 21–15 record at the end of May. St. Louis held down the National League's top spot with a mark of 23–11, while New York was close behind in second with a 23–13 record. During the off-season, Hornsby had retooled his pitching staff by bringing in veterans Jakie May, Les Sweetland and Bob Smith. These changes had not translated into any improvement in his mound corps. Hornsby did make a deal with the Pirates during the Cubs' stay in the Smoky City; the move upgraded the backstop position immensely. On May 29, Chicago sent catcher Earl Grace to the Pirates for fellow catcher Rollie Hemsley. The deal paid immediate dividends for Chicago when Hornsby benched Gabby Hartnett and placed Hemsley into the starting lineup. Hemsley recorded five hits in 11 trips to the plate during three games against Brooklyn, culminating in a game-winning single in the ninth inning that sunk the Robins, 9–8, on June 3.[10]

Cuyler played the hero role at Wrigley Field one day after Hemsley, as Chicago defeated Brooklyn by a score of 6–4. Cuyler hit a game-winning home run in the ninth, connecting for a two-run walk-off blast against Pea Ridge Day. Cuyler's clutch hit allowed Les Sweetland to secure his fifth consecutive victory.[11]

Cuyler was involved in a bit of a baseball anomaly four days later in a game against New York. In the top of the first inning, Cuyler grabbed Fred Lindstrom's drive to deep right field and made a perfect peg to the plate that retired Hughie Critz, who had tagged up from third base. Lindstrom duplicated this feat in the bottom of the frame when the fleet-footed Cuyler became his victim. Lindstrom gunned down Cuyler at home after he caught Riggs Stephenson's long drive to right and threw a strike to catcher Shanty Hogan.[12]

Rogers Hornsby's decision to move Cuyler back to the leadoff spot did not deter the free-swinging Cubs outfielder a bit. Official National League averages that were posted on June 11 showed Cuyler hitting .353 and tied for fourth in the league with Riggs Stephenson. Cuyler did not seem to be fazed by being moved in the batting order as he hit safely in 24 out of 27 games from June 2 through June 28.

Unfortunately, Cuyler's steadying influence did little to improve the Cubs' prospects as they continued to play mediocre ball throughout the month of June. Hornsby's attempt to inject more speed into the lineup by putting Hemsley behind the plate in place of Hartnett had minimal effect. The Cubs had emerged as the kings of hitting into double plays earlier in the year, largely because Cuyler and Woody English were their only players with speed. Chicago sportswriter Irving Vaughan compared the remainder of the squad's running ability to a child pulling a loaded sled over a concrete sidewalk that had been swept clean of snow by an inconsiderate citizen.[13]

Lack of speed was not the only aspect hampering Hornsby as his team continued to struggle. Wilson was not hitting the ball with the same luster that he did in 1930. Some experts attributed his drop in production to the ball not being as lively in 1931. Wilson also seemed more concerned with having a good time rather than working to reestablish himself as a threat to opposing pitchers. It was rumored that Wilson broke curfew on many occasions, but Hornsby merely reminded him that home run heroes should be in bed by midnight. The situation came to a head on the evening of June 26 in Boston, when Wilson was unable to break away from personal engagements on the same night that Hornsby decided to sit out in front of the hotel. Hornsby said nothing to Wilson when he arrived at the hotel past curfew time. Chicago's manager waited until the following morning to discipline his former star outfielder. Hornsby informed Wilson that he had violated team rules and would be penalized by spending the day on the bench so that he could obtain the necessary rest.[14]

When Hornsby explained this move to newspapermen, he claimed that Wilson was being punished for breaking training rules. On June 27, scribes who covered the Cubs also noticed that catching duties during batting practice were being handled by Rollie Hemsley. This was not usually something that the first-string catcher did. Writers immediately speculated that Hemsley was being punished by Hornsby for some sort of transgression as well.[15] The Pirates had originally decided to move Hemsley after they were forced to deal with his playboy mentality for three years. Hemsley was indeed on the bench while Hartnett handled the catching duties and went 1-for-5 as Chicago beat Boston, 12–3.

Chicago was still mired in third place when June ended. The Cubs stood five and a half games behind the league-leading Cardinals while sporting a 36–29 record. Cuyler's performance during the first three months of the season represented one of the few bright spots as the Flint Flash continued to hold down the fourth spot in the league's hitting race with an average of .351. Cuyler drove home the deciding tally during a 2–1 victory over Philadelphia on July 2, as Charlie Grimm scored on his 11th-inning single.[16] Cuyler was at it again on July 15 as he knocked in the winning run while hitting out of his customary third slot in the batting order for the 13th consecutive game. Cuyler's sharp single in the ninth inning brought home Jakie May with the deciding run as Chicago defeated New York, 5–4.[17]

Cuyler was shifted to center field a few days after his heroics against New York, as Rogers Hornsby took drastic measures to shake his squad from its season-long slumber. After weeks of rumors, pitcher Sheriff Blake was shipped to the Phillies for the waiver price of $7,500. Hornsby also announced that Hack Wilson would be benched for the third time during the season. Cuyler moved to center in place of Wilson, while Danny Taylor went to left and Vince Barton made his debut in right field. These changes, however, did little to stimulate Chicago's attack in its first game with the new lineup. The Cubs banged out only three hits against Brooklyn's Watty Clark on July 20, but still won the game, 1–0, thanks to Taylor's triple and Hemsley's single.[18]

Cuyler showed these two youngsters flanking him in the outfield how a grizzled veteran handled the nuances of his position in center field. Hazen made at least one spectacular catch each day that he roamed the center garden for Chicago.[19] He also continued to be lethal at the plate as he cracked clutch hits that won ballgames. In a game against Boston on July 24, Charlie Root and Ben Cantwell were locked in a pitcher's duel through seven innings, before Chicago finally busted through in the bottom of the eighth inning to win 3–1. Hemsley opened the frame with a double and moved to third on Root's sacrifice. Blair then drove Hemsley home with the game's first run by drilling a single. Billy Jurges walked before Cuyler knocked in the final two tallies with a scintillating double.[20]

St. Louis continued to put distance between itself and the rest of the National League. When July ended, the Cardinals stood on top of the league with a record of 63–37. Chicago was plugging away in second, eight and a half games behind the league leaders with a mark of 53–44. Cuyler continued to play stellar ball even though Chicago's prospects of winning the pennant dimmed each day. The Cubs garnered a crucial 3–2 victory over St. Louis at Wrigley Field on August 1, when consecutive doubles by Blair and English and a hard single by Cuyler brought home the deciding runs in the eighth inning. Chicago was playing without the services of veteran outfielder Riggs Stephenson, who suffered a broken ankle on a close play at first base against Philadelphia on July 27.[21] He was eventually shelved for the remainder of the season when his request to be placed on the voluntary retired list was granted by Commissioner Kenesaw Mountain Landis.[22]

Chicago's management team made a critical acquisition on August 4 with an eye toward improving the Cubs for the 1932 season. The Cubs purchased second baseman Billy Herman from the Louisville Colonels for a large sum of money and two players to be named later. It was reported that Wrigley and Veeck paid between $35,000 and $50,000 to secure Herman's services. The Cubs initially planned on leaving Herman at Louisville for the remainder of the season and bringing him to spring training in 1932, but impatience on the part of Rogers Hornsby prevented him from finishing the season in the minor leagues.[23] Hornsby insisted on seeing his new talent before it was too late.[24] Herman made a rather inauspicious debut at Wrigley Field on August 29 against Cincinnati. He recorded a single in his first major league at-bat, but then had to be removed from the game when his turn to hit came around again. While pulling away from a high, inside pitch during his second trip to the plate, the ball caromed off Herman's bat and smacked him in the head. Herman was knocked unconscious and carried off the field.[25]

Experiments involving young players like Billy Herman served as Hornsby's main goal during the final month of the 1931 season. Chicago now found itself in third place, 14 games behind the league-leading Cardinals as the season moved into September. Hopes of catching New York for second-place money seemed remote given the four-game gap between the Cubs and Giants. During the final month, some of Hornsby's strategy received intense scrutiny from Cubs fans. During a doubleheader against Cincinnati on September 2, Hornsby instructed his outfielders to play close to the infield for every Cincinnati batter. This strategy resulted in the Reds hitting seven doubles and two triples as they emerged victorious in both games.[26] Fans scratched their heads again a few days later when Hornsby made an odd choice to replace Vince Barton, who was called to Toronto due to the death of his brother Jim. Hornsby opted to let Hack Wilson remain on the bench as he placed pitcher Bud Teachout in right field to replace Barton.[27]

This humiliating course taken by Hornsby was done because Wilson once again had been guilty of breaking training rules while Chicago was in New York near the end of August. When Wilson broke the team curfew on this occasion, Hornsby ordered him a ticket back to Chicago, along with a ten-game suspension for the boozing outfielder.[28]

"Wilson thinks I've been picking on him," said Hornsby. "I should have suspended him two months ago for violating club rules, but I felt sorry for him and carried him along."[29]

When Wilson learned what Hornsby planned to do, he begged for a second chance. While standing in front of his teammates in the clubhouse, Wilson apologized for his detrimental behavior and promised to settle down. Wilson's pledge rang hollow as he became involved in another incident after the series in Cincinnati. This one concluded his career in Chicago. Wilson and his frequent drinking companion, Pat Malone, showed up at the train station on the evening of September 5 in jovial spirits. As the train destined for Chicago started moving, Malone bounced through a Pullman door and walked in Wilson's direction while he talked to three reporters.[30]

Malone had fury in his eyes as he made a smart remark to two of the newspapermen and then started to punch them in their faces without any provocation. The incident ended in a few seconds. Wilson could have stopped the messy confrontation before it started, but chose to do nothing. When the two players reached Wrigley Field the following day, front office summons were issued for the perpetrators. Wilson met with president William Veeck, who told him that he was suspended without pay for the remainder of the season on a charge of drunkenness. A frightened Malone also met with Veeck, but the former staff ace of the Cubs' rotation did not receive a punishment as severe as Wilson's. Malone was fined $500 for his display of brutality against the two pundits.[31]

Wilson took some parting shots at Hornsby before he packed up his belongings and departed for his home in Martinsburg, West Virginia.[32]

> Yes, I broke the training rules, but none any more than last year. Hornsby told us we could take a drink as long as we were in bed by midnight, and I didn't violate the rule any more than some of the other players did. When they found out I had broken training this year, Hornsby would tell me to report to the office and President Veeck would fine me. Last year, if I stayed out late, Joe McCarthy would call me off and tell me to lay off that stuff, and I obeyed him.
>
> I took those fines with my chin up, but the two things that hurt me most were when they put a pitcher out in the outfield and made me ride the bench, and then when they promised me box seats for the Cubs–White Sox charity game and gave me seats in the upper tier out in right field.[33]

Rogers Hornsby certainly was not the type of person to keep quiet when a player criticized team management in this way. Hornsby quickly revealed his thoughts in the presence of St. Louis sportswriter Sid Keener. Rogers told Keener that players on his team who insisted on engaging in brawls would soon find themselves not playing while he was manager. Hornsby claimed that he would resign his post as Cubs skipper before he tolerated such behavior. Chicago's manager then told Keener why he was willing to release all of the details surrounding the Wilson-Malone incident.[34]

"I'm not like other managers or magnates who want to keep a mess like this away from the public," explained Hornsby. "Malone socked Wayne Otto of the *Chicago Herald-Examiner* and did some fancy punching at Harold Johnson of the *American*, who attempted to break up the fistic party. Hack batted into it some way, so the club fined Wilson for the remainder of the season and fined Malone $500. That may be their idea of carrying on as ball players, but when you go back to St. Louis tell the fans there Wilson and Malone will not be with my ball club in 1932."[35]

Hack Wilson's statistics plummeted dramatically during his troubled season in 1931. He batted .261, smacked 13 homers and drove in 61 runs one year after he put up the greatest power season in National League history. Wilson may have put up better numbers if he had adhered to Hazen Cuyler's standards of clean living and dedication. Cuyler's .330 average placed him one point behind teammates Rogers Hornsby and Charlie Grimm for club batting honors. Hazen banged out 202 hits, scored 110 runs, and smacked 37 doubles, 12 triples, and nine home runs while knocking in 88 runs. Cuyler's standout season earned him a spot as the starting center fielder on the NEA Service Baseball Board's National League All-Star Team.[36] Cuyler also received recognition from fans who read *The Sporting News*. The publication held its own vote for the game's most valuable player and Cuyler finished in second place behind Lefty Grove of the Philadelphia Athletics. Grove polled 2,350 votes, while Cuyler garnered 840 and squeezed by Al Simmons, who finished in third place with 810 votes.[37]

Umpire George Magerkurth also gave Cuyler accolades during the annual Kewanee City League banquet in Kewanee, Illinois. Magerkurth claimed Cuyler was the National League's Most Valuable Player based solely on his smarts and intelligence.[38] In spite of Cuyler's standout season in 1931, the Cubs could secure nothing better than a third-place finish as they concluded the campaign with an 84–70 record. St. Louis won its second consecutive National League pennant and finished ahead of Hornsby's Cubs by 17 games. This marked the first season since Cuyler broke in with Pittsburgh as a regular in 1924 that his team did not battle into the season's final weeks for the National League pennant. It seemed appropriate that such a disappointing year would end on a sour note as the Cubs lost to the White Sox in Chicago's City Series. Donie Bush's last-place White Sox claimed victory when they defeated the Cubs in the series' seventh game, 7–2. Cuyler could post nothing better than a .174 batting average during the seven-game series, as the disappointing 1931 season mercifully came to an end.[39]

The 1931 season had been bittersweet for Hazen Cuyler. He accomplished great things on the field for the third consecutive year in Chicago, but was unable to bring home a pennant for Cubs fans. Cuyler played the game with honor and dignity and expected those around him to uphold the game's integrity throughout the season. He tried to set a proper example for his teammates and fans that followed the Cubs' exploits. Cuyler never swore and reprimanded his teammates when they cursed in his presence.[40]

The pride of Harrisville conducted his life in accordance with the principles of honesty and decency that George Cuyler had instilled in Hazen as a child. Cuyler's father continued to conduct himself in an honorable manner as one of Harrisville's respected residents. After years of selfless public service, George Cuyler was now a probate judge for Alcona County.[41]

Now 33, Kiki Cuyler immersed himself in off-season activities that were both pleasurable and beneficial to staying in shape. Cuyler and a group of friends bagged eight bucks during a deer hunt in the Michigan woods prior to Christmas.[42] While Cuyler was spending a quiet winter in Michigan, Rogers Hornsby and William Veeck acted swiftly in removing a problem player from their roster. On December 11, Chicago disposed of Hack Wilson by shipping him and pitcher Bud Teachout to St. Louis for veteran hurler Burleigh Grimes. Hornsby believed the Cubs would be much stronger with Grimes in the rotation, but he cautioned observers that this was only one step toward rebuilding a championship team.[43]

Hornsby was confident that Grimes would do well despite puzzling rumors that the two men did not get along while they were teammates with New York in 1927.[44] "One of the many things I admire about Grimes is that he pitches to win for Grimes and his team," said Hornsby, "and doesn't waste time and energy sulking about personal things once he gets on his uniform. Burleigh may show up minus some of his pitching stuff, but he'll never lose his fighting heart and he'll be worth his hire as an example to our young players on that basis, if for no other reason."[45]

Veeck and Hornsby hoped that the Grimes acquisition would be the first of several winter deals. The Cubs still wished to land a star outfielder like Brooklyn's Babe Herman or Pittsburgh's Paul Waner.[46] It was rumored that a three-team deal involving Chicago, Pittsburgh and Boston had been proposed and would bring Waner to the Windy City. The Cubs would also receive pitchers Ed Brandt and Fred Frankhouse from the Braves, but the names of potential Cubs involved in the deal were not revealed. The potential deal slowly died because Pirate owner Barney Dreyfuss refused to complete his phase of the transaction until he had hired a replacement for manager Jewel Ens. Dreyfuss did not want to make any trade until he consulted with the new man who would guide the Pirates in 1932.[47]

10. Rogers Hornsby, Violet Valli and Another Pennant

Hardship slammed the Cubs family once again a month before the start of spring training, when news of owner William Wrigley's unexpected death was wired from Phoenix, Arizona. Chicago's baseball faithful, as well as associates and friends across America, were shocked to hear the news. Wrigley was stricken with an attack of acute indigestion on January 18, but it was not deemed serious since he had been subject to such afflictions on other occasions. The condition affected Wrigley's heart a few hours before his passing on January 26. Wrigley's two children were at his bedside when he died.[48]

The chewing gum mogul was a man known to spend his riches liberally to advance baseball's cause and assure that a winning team resided in Chicago since taking control of the franchise in 1918.[49] A simple funeral service was held for Wrigley in Pasadena, California, on January 28. Wrigley's body was then taken to a vault in Avalon, until a permanent mausoleum was completed at Mount Alda, his favorite Catalina Island retreat.[50]

A will that only covered Wrigley's holdings in Illinois disposed of over $22 million. The bulk of the estate went to immediate family, while annuities were provided for other relatives and business associates. Wrigley's 36-year-old son Philip was bequeathed both the Cubs and the minor league Los Angeles Angels. Philip K. Wrigley immediately stated that he would handle Cubs affairs just as his father did. He planned to spare no expense in bringing a championship to Chicago. Wrigley also said there would be no immediate changes made to the official hierarchy of either the Chicago or Los Angeles clubs.[51] Such an announcement indicated that Wrigley would lean on the expertise of president William Veeck to keep the Cubs competitive. One of Veeck's duties involved signing Chicago's players for the upcoming season. On February 9, the signing of Cuyler for the 1932 season was announced by Veeck in Chicago.[52] Cuyler, along with pitchers Charlie Root and Guy Bush, attached their signatures to documents that covered the next two seasons.[53]

A few weeks before the training trip began at Catalina Island, Cuyler spoke at a father-son banquet in Grand Rapids, Michigan. During his speech, Cuyler claimed that Hack Wilson would have a big season for Brooklyn in 1932. He also pointed out that Wilson played better than the numbers indicated during the previous campaign. On another subject, Cuyler told the crowd that he hoped to become a major league manager once his playing days were over. He also acknowledged that Cubs manager Rogers Hornsby was one of the smartest men in the game today.[54]

Chicago's astute manager planned on making one major change to his team's lineup for the 1932 season. Hornsby intended on managing the Cubs from the dugout so that youngster Billy Herman could hold down the second base position. Hornsby was also banking on infielder Billy Jurges continuing his development now that he had a season of big league ball under his belt.

Chicago's ultimate success in 1932 seemed to rest upon the shoulders of rookie third baseman Stan Hack, who was considered a phenomenal prospect by Cubs management.[55]

Hack, Jurges, Herman and Vince Barton all appeared in the starting lineup on opening day at Redland Field on April 12, as the Reds defeated Chicago, 5–4. Cuyler batted out of the third slot in Hornsby's lineup, went 1-for-4 and scored a run. This marked the first season that Chicago's players wore numbers on the backs of their jerseys. It seemed fitting that Cuyler wore number three since this was the place in the batting order where he believed he could be of optimum value. Cuyler put up consistent numbers during the first few weeks of the season as Chicago jumped out of the gate by winning seven out of ten games. But Cuyler's season was interrupted during a game against Pittsburgh at Wrigley Field on April 24. He suffered a severe injury to his foot, as the Cubs assaulted pitcher Glenn Spencer for three runs in the first inning. It was initially believed that Cuyler injured his left foot while rounding first base on a single.[56] He actually remained in the game until the third frame, before Johnny Moore replaced him in center field.[57]

Cuyler stayed in the game for another inning because trainers initially believed that he had merely twisted his ankle. The diagnosis proved to be faulty as X-rays showed that Cuyler had fractured a bone in his left foot. Chicago's star outfielder was expected to miss about a month.[58] It was also determined that Cuyler had actually cracked the small bone behind the little toe of his left foot while rounding third base before scoring a first-inning tally that fateful day.[59] Cuyler's fractured foot, along with Woody English's absence with a broken finger suffered in an exhibition game against San Francisco, caused Chicago's hitting attack to go into a tailspin.[60] But the slump was short-lived as Hornsby's second-string talent helped Chicago stay competitive against other National League combatants.[61] At the end of April, the Cubs found themselves at the top of the league with an 11–3 record. Boston held down the second-place position with a 10–3 mark.

Despite having an injured leg, Cuyler participated in a baseball school that was conducted at Wrigley Field in conjunction with the *Chicago Daily News* and the *Chicago American*. Cuyler, Stan Hack, Rogers Hornsby and St. Louis' Chick Hafey cooperated with the newspapers in coaching area youngsters on baseball's finer points. Cuyler showed the youngsters in attendance how to shift around the outfield according to where opposing batters were prone to hit. He helped make the experience complete for the boys when a youngster asked the outfielder how he would play Babe Herman. Cuyler ran out to the center field fence and climbed up the screen to the top, much to the delight of the enthusiastic, young fans.[62]

Chicago's club physician replaced the heavy cast around Cuyler's broken toe with a much lighter one in the middle of May. His prognosis seemed to indicate the star outfielder would be missing from Chicago's lineup for another month.[63] Chicago continued to lead the National League race while Cuyler rested on the sidelines. The Cubs were 27–16 and held a two and a half game lead over second-place Boston as the season moved into June. A slight slump in Chicago's hitting proficiency forced Hornsby to leave the dugout and play right field during a doubleheader against Pittsburgh on May 29. In the doubleheader, Hornsby recorded two hits in seven trips to the plate during his baptism under fire in the outfield.[64]

As Cuyler's leg mended and Chicago remained in first place, discussion in Chicago centered around a gag rule that National League president John Heydler had just abolished. Prior to the season, both leagues established a rule that prohibited players from interacting with fans in the stands; any player who responded to a greeting from a fan was fined.[65]

The American League kept this policy in effect even though Heydler eliminated it from the National League's rulebook. Fans in Chicago believed this tenet was put in place due to the fact that a photographer had snapped a picture of Gabby Hartnett signing a ball for gangster Al Capone during the early stages of the 1931 season. Capone was a huge Cubs fan who occupied a field box for many games at Wrigley Field.[66] Fans throughout the Windy City felt the gag rule was established so that players would not fraternize with such unsavory characters. Capone, like most devoted Cubs patrons, anxiously awaited the return of the team's most popular player from the injured list. There seemed to be hope on the horizon as Cuyler was included in the entourage of players that left Chicago on June 5 to begin a trek through the league's four Eastern cities.[67]

Some people feared the injury would slow Cuyler down for the remainder of the season. Hazen's malady had caused him much distress both physically and mentally. There was also concern that it might take Cuyler some time to get back into game shape.[68] On June 15, Cuyler finally took the field at the Polo Grounds against New York after Hornsby convinced his player that there was no risk involved in playing one week sooner than he wished. As an acknowledgment to the fact Cuyler's leg remained weak, Hornsby allowed him to play in right field, where there was less territory to cover.[69] Cuyler went hitless in four trips as Chicago dropped the contest to New York, 6–3.

Hazen Cuyler's return to the lineup did little to help the Cubs as they played pedestrian ball throughout the rest of the month. The Pirates overtook the Cubs and moved into first place by a half game as June concluded. Pittsburgh's record stood at 34–27, while Chicago was only six games above .500 at 36–30. Cuyler's play continued to lack its usual vigor as he battled to put his season back on track. The free-swinging Cub was meeting the ball with less force than fans had come to expect. Kiki also seemed concerned about running into the wall in right field, as balls that he usually caught dropped for hits. A return to center field seemed to be the best remedy for this problem since Cuyler would not have to give much thought to crashing into barriers. At the plate, Kiki's batting average was about 75 points below its usual lofty standards.[70] In Cuyler's first dozen games back, he drove home only four runs. Hornsby was giving strong consideration to sending Cuyler to the bench because he was favoring his injured foot.[71]

Bad luck continued to plague the Cubs as the season moved into July. Rollie Hemsley was sidelined with an eye injury after a firecracker exploded prematurely while the team was in Pittsburgh on July 4.[72] As Cuyler attempted to get back into shape, he became entangled in one of the most bizarre incidents of his long career. On July 6, 1932, teammate Billy Jurges was shot in his room at the Hotel Carlos in Chicago. Jurges was shot twice by a divorcee whom he had dated and supposedly spurned. He was wounded while he attempted to wrestle the weapon from his assailant. While Jurges struggled to gain control of the weapon, one bullet entered his side, glanced off a rib, and exited through his shoulder. The second bullet lacerated the flesh of Jurges' little finger, while the jealous woman was wounded on the hand by a third bullet.[73] Thankfully, neither party was seriously injured. But Cubs physician Dr. John Davis surmised it would be another month before Jurges would return to the Chicago lineup.[74]

Chicago police took control of the incident involving Jurges and his attacker, a pretty brunette by the name of Violet Popovich Valli. The young woman, who was a former chorus girl, insisted that she only intended to shoot herself. This seemed to contradict a letter that Valli wrote, which police had in their possession; she stated it was her intention to murder Jurges and then commit suicide. In the letter, Valli stated that life without Jurges was not worth living. She justified the decision to take Jurges' life by asking herself why she should die alone without Billy joining her in eternal bliss. In an added twist, Valli then blamed Kiki Cuyler for taking their love and dragging it in the mud.[75] She considered Cuyler to be the villain of the sordid matter. She believed that Cuyler deliberately counseled Jurges against continuing their love affair.[76] When the 21-year-old Valli was released under a $7,500 bond a few days later, she continued to blame Cuyler in a newspaper interview.[77]

"Billy and I met at a party a year ago," Miss Valli said. "We were getting along fine until that conceited Kiki Cuyler began putting ideas in Billy's head.

"Cuyler said false things about me. I was afraid Billy was beginning to believe them. I called him last Wednesday and asked to see him.

"I sent Billy out of the room for a glass of water, then took out a revolver, intending to kill myself. Billy saw me and grabbed the gun. We fought for it and the gun went off several times."[78]

Players on the Cubs stated that Cuyler had taken Jurges under his wing in 1931. Jurges was a phenomenal fielder who had severe deficiencies at the plate. Cuyler coached Jurges throughout the 1932 season in an effort to improve his hitting.[79] As far as the affair with Valli, Cuyler admitted that Jurges had come to him seeking advice about his situation with the former chorus girl.[80] "I merely told him he was too young in the game yet," Cuyler said. "I told him he should get established in baseball first and then think of love."[81]

Jurges showed a chivalrous side in the strange incident as he refused to press charges against Valli for shooting him. The whole affair continued to become more peculiar as she passed love notes to him while the two recuperated one floor apart from each other in the same hospital. In spite of the fact that Jurges bore no ill-will against the young woman, police still planned on charging Valli with assault with intent to kill.[82]

A Chicago judge dismissed the case a week after the shooting because Jurges refused to prosecute Valli. Jurges was ordered by subpoena to appear in court but refused to be a prosecuting witness because he was convinced that Valli did not mean to hurt him.[83] Jurges finally returned to Chicago's starting lineup on July 22 against the Pirates.[84] Two days later at Wrigley Field, thousands of handbills alerted Jurges and his teammates to the fact that Valli was seeking solace in burlesque after conferring with her pastor. Additional problems for Valli, Jurges and Cuyler were averted when police arrested Lucius Barnett on the charges of concocting a blackmail plot against the two players.[85]

Barnett was an acquaintance of Valli's who somehow obtained 25 love letters that Jurges had written to Violet. Barnett threatened to have the correspondence published and sold outside of Wrigley Field unless Valli paid him for them. She appealed her case before a Chicago judge and gained peace of mind when the arbiter decided these letters would not appear on newsstands and also ordered Barnett to return them to Valli.[86]

The Valli incident provided a distraction for the Cubs as they trailed the first-place Pirates by five and a half games at the end of July. While Jurges' absence and the ensuing fallout from the shooting contributed to some of the Cubs' problems, another obstacle facing the team involved manager Rogers Hornsby. Differences with his players and president William Veeck made for a precarious situation as the season entered August.

There seemed to be a wide difference of opinion between Hornsby and Veeck regarding the actual strength of Chicago's personnel. Hornsby believed the present roster was not of championship caliber, while Veeck felt the Cubs had the talent to win the National League pennant. Chicago's manager crit-

Billy Jurges was shot by Violet Valli at the Carlos Hotel in Chicago on July 6, 1932. Valli, a former chorus girl who dated Jurges for about a year, claimed that she was attempting to commit suicide when he intervened (courtesy the National Baseball Hall of Fame Library, Cooperstown, New York).

icized his players relentlessly throughout the season and refused to take orders from his boss. Hornsby complained about the team's weaknesses and Veeck countered by questioning his manager's tactics. During a series in July against Pittsburgh, Hornsby criticized Cuyler after he failed to handle a ball hit by Pittsburgh's Earl Grace. Cuyler gave his manager a terse reply when Hornsby called his outfielder on the carpet upon his return to the dugout.[87] Following a long discussion between Hornsby and Veeck on the team train from Brooklyn to Philadelphia on August 2, Chicago's team president fired his uncooperative manager and appointed Charlie Grimm as successor.[88]

Hornsby immediately demanded that Veeck and the Cubs pay the remainder of his contract in one lump sum. Several of Hornsby's former players became upset after Veeck said such a large payout was impossible because the ex-manager owed many Cubs large sums of money. After another short meeting between Veeck, Hornsby and the players involved, a payment schedule was arranged. The story about Hornsby's debts took an ugly turn on August 11, when a Chicago newspaper ran a front page story that stated that Commissioner Landis was investigating a huge betting pool involving the Cubs. On August 13, Landis met with Hornsby, Woody English, Guy Bush, Pat Malone and coach Charley O'Leary while the team was in St. Louis. Landis' investigation revealed that these men were not involved in such a pool. O'Leary and the three players had loaned Hornsby over $10,000 during the past few years. The cash transactions were strictly loans and not part of a gambling pool. For his part, Hornsby stated that he had succumbed to his weakness of betting on horses, but said that he handled all of the bets himself.[89]

The Charlie Grimm management regime started out on an ominous note when he was summoned from his bed at four A.M. on August 6 to bail Rollie Hemsley out of a New Jersey jail.[90] Hemsley was suspended for a week without pay and fined $1,000 by Veeck.[91] Grimm's debut as a skipper on August 4 had gone a bit more smoothly, as Chicago destroyed the Phillies, 12–1. Kiki Cuyler took part in the blowout by drilling a two-run homer in the fourth inning.

Veeck and Grimm made a critical player transaction one day later when the Phillies reversed the result and defeated Chicago, 9–2. The Cubs purchased former New York Yankees star shortstop Mark Koenig from the Mission club of the Pacific Coast League to solidify their infield.[92] Koenig's acquisition proved to be a stroke of genius as he hit .353 while appearing in 33 games for the Cubs. Grimm's hiring as manager also seemed to spark Chicago's players, as they began to relax and have fun playing ball for the first time in nearly two years.

The Cubs' fortunes improved dramatically as the team went 10–4 during Grimm's first 14 games at the helm. The Cubs took over the National League's top spot and dropped Pittsburgh out of the lead for the first time since June 26, as they defeated their rival, 3–2, on August 11. Pirates rookie shortstop Floyd "Arky" Vaughan aided Chicago's cause in the tenth inning, when he threw low to first after fielding Kiki Cuyler's grounder. Cuyler then advanced to third on Stephenson's single and came around to score the game's winning run on Johnny Moore's sacrifice fly.[93] Grimm's solid showing as Chicago's manager prompted Veeck to announce that the managerial change was not a stop-gap measure. He stated that Grimm's performance to date warranted his retention as manager for the 1933 season.[94] Shortly after Veeck made the announcement, Grimm's Cubs reeled off a 14-game winning streak.

When Chicago's phenomenal run began on August 20, the Cubs led second-place Brooklyn by two games. Two weeks later when the streak ended after the Cardinals defeated the Cubs, 3–0, during the second game of a Labor Day doubleheader, Chicago's record stood at 77–52; the Cubs led second-place Pittsburgh by seven games. Cuyler played a huge role during this 14-game stretch as he raised his average from .267 to .278. Cuyler's fifth-inning double brought home Billy Herman with Chicago's second run as the Cubs defeated Philadelphia, 2–0, on August 21.[95] An overflow crowd of 40,000 people at Wrigley Field watched Cuyler provide the driving force behind two Cubs victories on August 27. Cuyler's three-run homer in the first inning of game one sent Burleigh Grimes and the Cubs on their way to a 6–1 victory over New York. Cuyler scored Chicago's first run in the nightcap when he singled in the fourth inning and came home on Riggs Stephenson's home run into the right field bleachers. Pitcher Bob Smith was masterful on the mound, tossing a shutout as the Cubs beat the Giants in the twinbill's nightcap, 5–0.[96]

Cuyler continued his batting onslaught against New York on August 28 by driving home four runs with a single, home run and a sacrifice fly in Chicago's 5–4 victory.[97] Cuyler cracked his homer over the left field bleachers in the eighth and then drove home the winning run one inning later as Marvin Gudat scored on his short fly to Mel Ott in right field.[98] Chicago's star outfielder raised the ante even higher three days later, when he went 5-for-6 against New York and helped Chicago win a ten-inning slugfest, 10–9. Cuyler tied the game in the ninth with an RBI single. He then secured victory in the tenth as a torrential rain turned Wrigley Field into a swampy mess. Cuyler blasted a three-run homer that finished off Chicago's five run rally. Cuyler's bat remained on fire as he drove home 17 out of 38 runs scored by the Cubs in the five-game sweep over New York and a single game against St. Louis on September 2. Cuyler had also crushed five home runs in five playing days.[99]

Cuyler continued to take his spot in right field despite a nagging charley horse. Manager Charlie Grimm wanted Cuyler to rest, but the veteran Cub refused to take himself out of the lineup.[100] He was finally forced to the sidelines for two games against Brooklyn on September 9 and 10. Marvin Gudat took Cuyler's place and performed marvelously in right field. Cuyler then returned to the lineup on September 11 and went 5-for-8 in the final two games of the Brooklyn series. After three consecutive hitless games against New York at the Polo Grounds, Cuyler recaptured some of his heroic past during Chicago's 8–7 victory over the Giants on September 15. Cuyler's 11th-inning homer secured a Cubs victory and helped them maintain a five and a half game lead over the second-place Pirates.[101]

The Cubs' ability to preserve their lead in the National League through September resulted in large part from the team's play immediately after Charlie Grimm's appointment as manager. After St. Louis ended the Cubs' 14-game winning streak on September 3, Chicago played at a 13–12 pace during the remainder of the season. Playing slightly better than .500 baseball was sufficient for the Cubs, who clinched their second National League pennant since Cuyler joined the team in 1928. The clinching provided sweet vindication for Cuyler as it came at the expense of his former team in Pittsburgh. Chicago clinched the pennant when they defeated the Pirates in the first game of a doubleheader at Wrigley Field on September 20.

Cuyler accounted for four of his team's runs. In the third inning, he doubled, took third and scored Chicago's second run on a passed ball. In the seventh inning, with the score tied at 2–2, Cuyler strode to the plate with the bases loaded. The count went full before Hazen took a massive swing.[102] He met the ball squarely and sent a line drive over third base. The ball landed in the farthest left field corner of Wrigley Field; Cuyler cleared the bases with his long triple, which helped Chicago defeat Pittsburgh, 5–2.

Before the contest began, Pittsburgh manager George Gibson had refused to shake Charlie Grimm's hand. Gibson reasoned that no such show of sportsmanship would occur until Chicago beat Pittsburgh. The instant the game ended, Gibson ran across the field and became the first person to congratulate Grimm and wish him good luck in the upcoming World Series.[103]

Chicago closed the 1932 season with a 90–64 record. The Cubs finished four games in front of the second-place Pirates, who finished with a mark of 86–68. Grimm did a terrific job as Chicago's manager, leading the team to a 37–18 record under his steady stewardship. Cuyler also seemed to benefit from the managerial change as he raised his average from .275 to .291. Cuyler appeared in 110 games, scored 58 runs, and drilled 19 doubles, nine triples, and ten home runs, while knocking in 77 runs. Even though injuries had prevented Cuyler from putting up his usual stellar numbers, the veteran outfielder had played his best when his team needed him during the pennant drive. Solid pitching actually outshone the Cubs' hitting prowess for the first time in years as Lon Warneke (22–6, 2.37 ERA), Guy Bush (19–11, 3.21 ERA), Charlie Root (15–10, 3.58 ERA) and Pat Malone (15–17, 3.38 ERA) proved to be vital cogs in Chicago's machinery.

The American League crowned a new champion in 1932 as New York won its first pennant since 1928 and ended Philadelphia's three-year reign as champions. New York went 107–47 as former Chicago manager Joe McCarthy

Cuyler eventually became the catalyst behind Chicago's pennant aspirations after being sidelined early in the 1932 season with a fractured bone in his left foot. Cuyler caught fire during the season's final weeks and carried Chicago on his back, delivering the pennant-clinching hit against Pittsburgh on September 20 which sent the Cubs to the World Series (courtesy the National Baseball Hall of Fame Library, Cooperstown, New York).

guided the Yankees to a pennant during his second season as their skipper. World Series storylines were put into place; McCarthy was not only managing against his former team but the upcoming classic was also viewed as a battle between New York's heavy hitting and Chicago's solid pitching.

A third sidebar to the 1932 World Series could not be overlooked. Cuyler would finally have a chance to play against Babe Ruth and Lou Gehrig in a World Series game. He had ridden the bench during the 1927 Fall Classic and watched the Yankees sweep his Pirates. A chance at redemption was finally at hand.

11. Babe Ruth's Called Shot and Cuyler's Last World Series Appearance

The city of Chicago held a grand parade on September 22 to celebrate their Cubs' second National League pennant in the past four years. Huge crowds stood along the parade route as the Cubs players rode from Wrigley Field to city hall in open automobiles. Charlie Grimm's squad was congratulated by Mayor Anton J. Cermak and a host of city officials. Grimm and president William Veeck gave speeches, and each player was presented with a commemorative bat. Mark Koenig, Burleigh Grimes, Pat Malone and Rollie Hemsley were the only players that did not attend the festivities. Former Cubs catcher Jimmy Archer, White Sox vice-president Harry Grabiner and former White Sox manager Jimmy Callahan were among the notables who cheered the Cubs at the review stand.[1]

Due to the fact that regular season play ended earlier than in past years, the 1932 World Series between the Cubs and Yankees was slated to open at Yankee Stadium on Thursday, September 28. Some miserly deeds by Chicago's squad made national sports headlines before a series game was even played between the two teams. The Cubs were excoriated in some circles for voting to award shortstop Mark Koenig a half share of World Series money, while former manager Rogers Hornsby received nothing. Fans throughout Chicago wrote letters of indignation to local newspapers protesting the fact that Koenig was awarded only a half share. These rooters believed Koenig was the crucial sparkplug who guided Chicago into the World Series. Hornsby decided to take his protest straight to Commissioner Landis, claiming that he deserved to share in the money since he helped develop key performers such as Lon Warneke, Billy Jurges and Billy Herman.[2]

"I feel that as one who handled the club through its major difficulties and had the greatest part in developing it to its present power, I am entitled to share in the distinction of any money the Cubs may gain through World's Series effort," Hornsby declared. "I don't know what the rules on the subject say — I did not even read them. But I do feel that I deserve a share more than some of those who will receive full portions."[3]

Hornsby likely would have been surprised to find that he was deemed irrelevant when the Cubs' players decided how to divvy up their World Series money. One unidentified player stated that Hornsby's name was never even mentioned during the discussion.[4] The stingy policy on the part of Chicago's players ended up being an albatross once the series began. New York's players, particularly upset over ex-teammate Koenig's slight, rode the Cubs unmercifully for their greediness throughout the 1932 Fall Classic.[5] Yet, the perception that his players were cheapskates was the least of Charlie Grimm's worries prior to the World Series opener. Koenig was expected to play even though he was still wearing splints on his left wrist a few days before the first game. Woody English would also remain in the lineup despite his capabilities being limited by a sore hand and a charley horse.[6]

Cuyler was slated to bat third and play right field for Grimm even though he was not physically fit. The fractured bone in Cuyler's foot continued to hamper him to the point that he still worried about it, but he would not permit the injury to keep him out of the lineup.[7] He had missed a chance to face the mighty Yankees in 1927, but planned on being a constant menace to New York's championship hopes in 1932.

The Cubs enjoyed a great start in Game One of the World Series against Red Ruffing, even though Cuyler was not particularly menacing in his first plate appearance. Chicago grabbed a 2–0 lead as Billy Herman and Woody English opened the game with consecutive singles. Herman came around to score after Babe Ruth allowed English's drive to get past him. Cuyler then struck out before Riggs Stephenson drove home English with a single over Ruffing's head into center field.[8]

This proved to be Chicago's one bright moment of the day as New York rallied to score three runs in the fourth inning and five in the sixth. Lou Gehrig's prodigious blast into the right field bleachers drove home Ruth and gave New York a 3–2 lead in the fourth inning. Guy Bush's wildness on the mound contributed directly to New York's five-spot in the sixth inning. Bush walked Joe Sewell, Ruth and Gehrig before he finally retired Tony Lazzeri on a popup to shortstop Mark Koenig. Bill Dickey then drove home two runs with a single, and Gehrig came home on Ben Chapman's fielder's choice. Grimm sent Bush to the showers and summoned Burleigh Grimes from the bullpen after a walk to Frankie Crosetti. Grimes struggled in his effort to subdue New York as two more runners crossed home plate and gave the Yankees an 8–2 lead.[9] The Cubs fought back and scored two runs of their own, but

New York put the game out of reach with three more markers in their half of the seventh. When the dust finally settled, New York emerged victorious in Game One by a score of 12–6.

Cuyler did minimal damage against Red Ruffing as he went 1-for-5. After striking out in the first inning, he was left stranded on base in the third after singling and stealing second. Cuyler struck out once again in the fifth inning before he reached base on an error by Crosetti in the seventh and scored on Stephenson's single. An uneventful day at the plate ended in the eighth when he popped up to second baseman Lazzeri with English on base.

After the game, Bush placed blame for the defeat on his own shoulders. He claimed that he was trying to be too careful with New York's batters. Gabby Hartnett believed the Cubs had beaten themselves, but stated things would have been different if they had received a few breaks. English tried to remain upbeat by pointing out that Chicago outhit the Yankees in Game One. As for Cuyler, he did not have much to say, perhaps because he was still thinking about the ball that Gehrig crushed over his head for a home run.[10]

The Cubs were hopeful that results would be different when the two teams opposed each other for Game Two of the World Series on September 29. Mrs. Charlie Grimm had a dual purpose for staunchly supporting the Cubs during the second game at Yankee Stadium. The day marked the tenth anniversary of her marriage to Chicago's manager; she could think of no better way to commemorate the occasion than to enjoy a Chicago victory over New York.[11]

Charlie Grimm selected young Lon Warneke to work against 24-game winner Lefty Gomez in Game Two. The Cubs seemed to be in great shape for the second consecutive game as they grabbed a quick lead in the first inning. Billy Herman led off the game against Gomez by smacking a double to left field. After Woody English flied to Earle Combs in center, Herman moved to third on Frank Crosetti's muff of Cuyler's grounder. Herman came around to score on Riggs Stephenson's sacrifice fly to Combs in center.[12]

Chicago's lead was fleeting as the Yankees scored two runs in the bottom of the first, thanks largely to some wildness on Warneke's part. Combs and Sewell led off the frame with walks and eventually scored on singles by Gehrig and Dickey, giving New York a 2–1 lead. Chicago rallied and tied the game with two out in the third when Stephenson doubled and scored on Frank Demaree's single to right field. The Yankees quickly reclaimed the lead for good during their half of the third, scoring two tallies that decided Game Two. Warneke retired Sewell before Ruth walked and Gehrig singled. After Lazzeri was retired on a grounder to Billy Jurges, Bill Dickey was passed intentionally so that Warneke could face the right-handed Ben Chapman. The Yankees' left fielder responded by cracking a clean single to right that scored

Ruth and Gehrig.[13] The Yankees added another run in the fifth inning as they defeated the Cubs, 5–2 and took a two-game lead in the World Series.

Cuyler was contained once again by New York pitching. Cuyler went 1-for-4 with a two-out triple in the fifth inning. Lefty Gomez allowed several hits, but maintained his composure during clutch situations. The slender southpaw scattered nine hits and struck out eight bewildered Cubs while using a perplexing mixture of pitches.[14]

Despite the fact that Chicago was in dire straits after dropping the first two games of the 1932 World Series, the widow of former chewing gum mogul William Wrigley expressed pride in her Cubs. Mrs. Wrigley, who was now in her sixties, sat with her son, Philip K. Wrigley, and cheered enthusiastically during both games in New York. Whether the Cubs won or lost, Mrs. Wrigley continued to root for her late husband's team with unflappable exhuberance.[15]

"Our team is a family tradition," Mrs. Wrigley explained. "It doesn't make any difference if they win or lose, they're my boys and I think they're one of the finest collections of men in the world. I know every one of them by their first names."[16]

Chicago fans generally did not agree with Mrs. Wrigley that it did not matter if the Cubs won or lost. Many of the Windy City's rooters believed that their team would turn the tables against Joe McCarthy's Yankees once games began at Wrigley Field. Veteran pitcher Charlie Root was chosen by Charlie Grimm to halt the surging Yankees in Game Three on October 1, as McCarthy countered with George Pipgras. The Yankees wasted no time greeting Root as they scored three runs in the first inning. Earle Combs reached second to start the frame when shortstop Billy Jurges handled his grounder but made a wild throw to first. After Root walked Joe Sewell, Babe Ruth hit a monster home run into the center field bleachers.[17]

Cuyler had a hand in the Cubs getting one run back during the bottom of the first. After Billy Herman walked and Woody English flied out to Ruth in left, Cuyler cracked an RBI double to right field, cutting the Yankees lead to 3–1.[18]

Lou Gehrig restored New York's three-run lead in the third when he launched Root's first pitch, a low curve on the outside corner, into Wrigley Field's right field bleachers. In the bottom of the third, Chicago's fans finally found something to cheer about as Cuyler brought back memories of 1925 by blasting a home run into the right field seats. The roar from the devoted Wrigley Field crowd had barely subsided when Stephenson followed Cuyler by driving a single to right-center and bringing another outburst from the fans.[19] After Johnny Moore forced Stephenson at second on a grounder to Gehrig, he scored Chicago's third run of the afternoon on Charlie Grimm's line drive double to right field. Cubs fans became enthusiastically encouraged in the fourth inning, when their team tied the game, 4–4. Billy Jurges led off the stanza with a double to left field. After Root and Herman were retired by Pipgras, Jurges scored from second base on Tony Lazzeri's bobble of Woody English's groundball.[20]

The fifth inning started out innocently enough for Root as he retired Sewell on a grounder to Jurges at short. Babe Ruth then strode to the plate for the third time in the game. Bench jockeying had been particularly brutal in Game Three of the World Series, as Chicago's players dished out insults just as vociferously as their counterparts from New York. The rancorous verbal jousting reached a crescendo while Ruth batted in the fifth inning. The Babe waved his hands and yelled at Chicago's players after each pitch Root tossed to home plate. When the count reached two balls and two strikes, Ruth made a gesture that has lived in folklore for many decades. According to some observers, the Bambino informed Chicago's dugout that he was going to hit the next pitch out of the park. Ruth wasted no time backing up his boast as Root tossed a low curve on the next pitch that floated right down the alley. The Babe swung and sent the ball soaring more than 450 feet into the deepest corner of the center field bleachers.[21]

It did not take the Yankees long to put another run on the scoreboard after Ruth triumphantly rounded the bases on his second home run of the game. Gehrig stepped into the batter's box and smacked Root's first pitch long and deep down the right field line. Cuyler helplessly watched as Gehrig's drive landed fair by a few feet while traveling over the right field wall. Grimm decided that Root was done for the day and replaced him with Pat Malone. The big right-handed hurler from Altoona, Pennsylvania, came in and promptly loaded the bases with three walks. Malone finally clamped down and retired the Yankees before they could score again.[22] Each team pushed across a single run in the ninth inning, as the Yankees made it three wins in a row by defeating Chicago, 7–5. Ruth and Gehrig were the heroes for New York as each player smacked two home runs while accounting for a total of six RBIs.

Ruth had not been graded favorably when comparisons between Cuyler and him were made prior to the World Series. Ruth seemed to have lost his batting strength as the campaign progressed, while Cuyler was a run-producing machine during the last six weeks of the regular season. Given the fact that Cuyler was far superior to Ruth defensively, baseball experts believed the Cubs outfielders could compete on equal footing with their New York counterparts during the World Series.[23] Yet, such predictions meant little to Ruth once he had an opportunity to perform on the game's biggest stage. The World Series provided great players with the ultimate opportunity to do spectacular things. Ruth relished these moments and delivered superb results. Cuyler, for his part, had also performed heroically for Chicago in Game Three of the 1932 World Series. He went 3-for-4, drilled a double, smacked a home run and drove in two runs.

Guy Bush was once again called upon by manager Grimm for Game Four as Chicago tried to avoid the humility of being swept by New York. Joe McCarthy countered with rookie hurler Johnny Allen at Wrigley Field on October 2. Bush struggled in the first frame and was quickly lifted in favor of Lon Warneke after New York grabbed a 1–0 lead. The Cubs did not allow this to deter their spirits, as they countered for four runs during their half of the first. Rookie outfielder Frank Demaree smacked the crucial blow when he drilled a three-run homer into Wrigley Field's left field seats. The Cubs scored another run before McCarthy sent Allen to the showers and replaced him with veteran Wilcy Moore. But Chicago's 4–1 lead did not last long as New York secured two runs in the third; Gehrig hit a two-out double and then scored ahead of Tony Lazzeri after he launched a home run over the right field screen. The Yankees took a 5–4 lead in the sixth inning, when Gehrig's single off Chicago pitcher Jakie May drove home Earle Combs and Joe Sewell.[24]

The Cubs came back to tie the game in their half of the sixth due to some shoddy fielding by the Yankees before the situation fell to pieces for the Cubs. New York added four runs in the seventh inning, while Grimm rushed Bud Tinning and Burleigh Grimes to the mound in an effort to stymie the Yankees' attack. Grimes was then treated roughly during the final inning of the series, as New York freely connected against the veteran hurler. In the ninth, Earle Combs opened the floodgates by smacking Grimes' first pitch over the right field screen for a homer.[25] By the time that Grimes finally retired the Yankees, four more runs had crossed home plate to give the Yankees a 13–5 lead. The Cubs mounted a weak counter-offensive in the bottom of the ninth. Billy Herman led off the stanza with a single and was permitted to steal second and third base without drawing a throw from Bill Dickey. Herman made it a 13–6 game when he scored on Woody English's bouncer to Tony Lazzeri. Left-hander Herb Pennock finished off Chicago by striking out Cuyler and retiring Riggs Stephenson on a fly ball to Ben Chapman in right field.[26]

The Yankees claimed their first title since they defeated St. Louis in the 1928 World Series. The Yankees made it three sweeps in a row as the 1932 Cubs were added to a group of teams that included the 1927 Pirates and those 1928 Cardinals, all of which had failed to win a single World Series contest against New York. New York obliterated Chicago in the 1932 Fall Classic by scoring 37 runs and hitting .313. Lou Gehrig became the series star as he hit a lusty .529 and clouted three homers. In the meantime, Cuyler put up average numbers for a Cubs squad that pushed across 19 runs in four World Series games. Cuyler did lead Chicago with 11 total bases but hit only .278. For

Cuyler, the sweep by New York was a doubly humiliating experience since he had watched his Pittsburgh teammates fall in similar fashion five years earlier.

There was one footnote to the series. Two weeks after the Fall Classic ended, Commissioner Landis ruled against Rogers Hornsby's appeal to be included in the split of Series money among Chicago's players.[27] As a result, Hornsby received nothing.

Stories about changes to Chicago's roster made their way into newspapers across the country shortly after the World Series concluded. Judge Emil Fuchs of the Boston Braves denied rumors surrounding a possible three-way deal involving his team, the Cubs and the Giants. According to the rumor, New York would deal Fred Lindstrom and Shanty Hogan to Chicago for Pat Malone, Kiki Cuyler and Gabby Hartnett. The Giants in turn would then ship Cuyler and Hartnett to Boston for Wally Berger. New York also planned on

The Chicago Cubs celebrate their clinching the 1932 National League pennant. Cuyler is the player kneeling on the floor, to the right. The celebration was short-lived as the New York Yankees swept Chicago in the World Series (courtesy the National Baseball Hall of Fame Library, Cooperstown, New York).

disposing of Malone by trading him to Cincinnati for Babe Herman.[28] While this particular rumor turned out to be pure fiction, one of the players named in the story did change teams after Thanksgiving. William Veeck struck once again on November 28, when he traded pitcher Bob Smith, catcher Rollie Hemsley, and outfielders Lance Richbourg and Johnny Moore to Cincinnati for outfielder Babe Herman.

Herman was a solid left-handed hitter who came to Chicago with a fine resume as a batter. He had eclipsed the .300 mark in 1928 (.340), 1929 (.381), 1930 (.393), 1931 (.313) and 1932 (.326) while playing for Brooklyn and Cincinnati. During an interview after the trade was made, Herman claimed that he always wanted to play for the Cubs and planned on playing well at Wrigley Field just as he had done in the past. Herman was also confident that he would get along well with his new teammates. Chicago's newest addition concluded by stating that he, Kiki Cuyler and Riggs Stephenson should make an outstanding outfield unit.[29]

While Veeck was once again busy adding personnel to the Cubs that would allow them to be a pennant contender in 1933, Cuyler continued to participate in some of his favorite off-season activities. In November, Cuyler and a few of his friends hunted about 150 miles north of Fora Francis in Canada. His hunting party killed two moose and three deer.[30] Cuyler was responsible for shooting one of the moose, which weighed 1,500 pounds. Hazen then returned to Michigan with the moose head mounted on the front of his car. Once Cuyler reached his home, he paid a visit to sportsman Jimmy Campbell in Flint to discuss every detail of this successful hunting excursion.[31]

Shortly after Cuyler returned from his trip to Canada, he graciously attended the "Sportsmanship Banquet" at Elkton, Michigan, on December 7 as one of the event's keynote speakers.[32] Cuyler was an obvious choice to speak to youths about sportsmanship and fair play since he had followed these principles throughout his career. Youths that attended schools in Bay Port, Elkton, Gagetown, Kinde, Owendale, Pinnebog, Port Austin, Port Hope and Ubly attended the banquet, as Cuyler preached about the virtues of sportsmanship. Detroit motion picture man and sportsman Maurice J. Caplan supplied the rest of the evening's entertainment. He exhibited a number of football films as well as footage of the 1932 Olympic Games.[33]

Cuyler did not have to worry about one key aspect of the off-season as he stayed in shape over the winter. Cuyler, along with manager Charlie Grimm, Charlie Root and Guy Bush were already signed up for the 1933 season.[34] The three players from this group had shown great foresight by agreeing to contracts with terms of two years prior to the 1932 season. Due to the harsh realities of the Depression, many players were willing to choose security over a one-year contract that might supply a higher yearly salary. On two occasions since being shipped to Chicago from Pittsburgh, Cuyler was more than happy to negotiate deals that covered two seasons. Unlike Cuyler, Chicago's newest acquisition preferred a huge payday over the security of having a contract cover more than one year. Babe Herman signed a one-year deal that called for him to make $20,000 in 1933. Herman and president William Veeck both seemed extremely happy with the outcome of these particular contract negotiations.[35]

Grimm made one more roster move prior to spring training that led many observers to believe that he planned on being a bench manager in 1933. Veteran Gink Hendrick was purchased from Columbus a few days after his release from Cincinnati so that he could act as an understudy to Grimm at first base.[36]

Cuyler led a group of players, which included Billy Jurges, Vince Barton, Del Young, Mike Kreevich and Paul McCarren, that left Chicago on February 25 to make the trip to Catalina Island for spring training.[37] Once they reached Avalon, problems began. Grimm was unable to sleep due to the fact that his room was close to a group of sea lions who gathered every night. These creatures, which had grown increasingly friendly on the island's shores during the past few years, played "tag" near the beach under Grimm's window. After being awakened one night by the noisy creatures that had assumed control of the nearby benches, Grimm compared them to a popular American icon.[38] "This is a helluva note," said Grimm, "those things barking and grunting all night. You'd think a lot of Babe Ruths were after you."[39]

Grimm's insomnia quickly became a trivial event once Chicago made a trip to Los Angeles for an exhibition series against the Giants. The series began harmlessly enough on March 10, as New York defeated Lon Warneke and the Cubs, 5–3. After the game, players from both squads returned to their lodgings at the Los Angeles Biltmore to dress for dinner and other evening activities. The routine was interrupted by a violent earthquake that hit Los Angeles at 5:55 P.M. Both clubs' entourages were able to feel the quake's full effects since they occupied the upper floors of the Biltmore Hotel. Even though elevator service was suspended for a few minutes, these level headed athletes, who usually remained cool during a crisis on the diamond, were able to find the stairs and navigate their way down to the hotel lobby. Even those men who paused to calm their upset wives eventually reached the safety of the ground floor.[40]

The lobby of the Biltmore Hotel was packed with people by the time the main earthquake finally subsided. Dozens of players from the Cubs and Giants stood among the frightened guests. Some members of the Cubs were afraid to return to their rooms as minor aftershocks continued throughout the evening.⁴¹ Pat Malone and his wife stood out on the street for hours until the tremors ceased. Malone, who claimed he was not afraid of anything, said the quake taught him a valuable lesson and convinced him to become a Christian.⁴²

The experience was even unsettling to a veteran like Burleigh Grimes, one of the toughest and fiercest competitors to wear a baseball uniform. "It's got me licked," stated Grimes after he attempted to sleep in his room on numerous occasions but then opted for the lobby. "Maybe it's just my imagination, but when I stretch out on the bed I get an all-gone feeling in the pit of my stomach and I see the pictures see-sawing on the wall."⁴³

Although Cuyler emerged from the tragedy unscathed both physically and emotionally, horrible luck on the diamond struck him down three weeks later. Cuyler was having a great camp after an injury-riddled season in 1932. On March 22, he banged out three hits and drove home seven runs as Chicago defeated San Francisco, 17–11.⁴⁴ But optimism surrounding a comeback season by Cuyler came crashing down one week later during an exhibition game against Hollywood. Chicago won the game, 10–8, but lost Cuyler for an extended period of time due to a severe injury. Cuyler fractured his right leg while attempting to steal second base in the fourth inning. He had hesitated for a moment as he approached the keystone sack and then decided to slide at the last second. Cuyler's indecisiveness proved critical as his leg twisted awkwardly while his foot got caught in the bag.⁴⁵

Cuyler was carried from the field and transported to the Cedars of Lebanon Hospital. After an examination, doctors concluded that Cuyler had fractured the lower end of his fibula, or the smaller bone of the leg. Medical experts claimed that a bone three inches in length had been severed from the main bone. Charlie Grimm announced that Cuyler would be out of action for at least eight to ten weeks, depending on how fast the fractured leg healed. Some Cubs fans worried that the injury could handicap Cuyler's fielding and baserunning throughout the 1933 season.⁴⁶ Even though his leg was in a cast, Cuyler departed from Los Angeles and made the trip to Kansas City with his teammates a few days after the accident. He was also accompanied by his wife Bertha, who planned on taking him to their Michigan home while the injured leg healed.⁴⁷

Before Mr. and Mrs. Cuyler returned to Harrisville, Hazen stopped in Chicago so that bone specialist Dr. Edwin W. Ryerson could examine his leg. Ryerson reasoned that Cuyler would be out of Chicago's lineup until July 4. He also speculated that if the injury healed properly, it would be at least two months before Cuyler could resume any kind of baseball activities.⁴⁸

Newspapers throughout the country ran photos of Cuyler lying in a Los Angeles hospital bed with a pair of crutches nearby. When Cuyler and his wife reached Michigan, pictures were taken to document his arrival on crutches. These were not the types of photos that a star National League performer hoped to see as a new season dawned.

Manager Grimm lamented the fact that Cuyler was missing from his lineup, as Chicago went 6–8 during the month of April. Frank Demaree was struggling so badly as Cuyler's replacement that Chicago obtained veteran Taylor Douthit from Cincinnati on April 29 as added insurance for the outfield.[49]

Cuyler's prognosis was upgraded slightly when he returned to Chicago and visited Ryerson at the end of April. An X-ray revealed that Cuyler's broken leg was mending as expected. Ryerson reasoned that Cuyler would remain out of the Cubs' lineup for at least another six weeks. A removable cast was placed on his leg so that he could receive massaging and lamp treatments.[50]

He failed to make a return trip to Chicago a few weeks after being examined by Ryerson. Kiki had previously made known his intentions to attend the pennant raising ceremony at Wrigley Field, but he did not show up and gave no reason for why he broke his promise to attend the festivities.

Cuyler did expect to rejoin the Cubs' squad near the end of May. Cuyler planned on doing easy workouts with the hope of returning to the lineup during the second week of June.[51] Cuyler finally donned a Cubs uniform on May 28, with orders from his physician to take it easy initially before intensifying his workout regimen.[52]

Cuyler eventually joined his teammates on the road when they left for a long trip through the East on June 16. He hoped he would appear in a game before Chicago returned home in July.[53] Cuyler finally appeared in a contest in Boston on June 22, when he batted for Burleigh Grimes in the ninth inning. He still seemed to be hampered, showing little speed on the way to first base. This tentative example of running indicated that Cuyler was not quite ready to perform at his usual proficient level.[54]

Bad luck continued to plague Cuyler in other ways as he attempted to fight his way back into Chicago's regular lineup. One day after he made his 1933 debut, members of the Cuyler family were injured in a car accident. George Cuyler suffered a broken arm when the car he was driving overturned near Lincoln, Michigan. Hazen's mother and niece, 18-year-old Shirley Medor, and several other occupants in the car suffered severe bruises.[55] None of the injuries were considered serious, though, Cuyler's mother and father joined their famous son on the disabled list.

Chicago's season continued to languish with Cuyler on the bench at the end of June. The Cubs stood in fourth place with a 36–35 record, which left them seven games behind league-leading New York as the season moved into July. Charlie Grimm and Bill Veeck were so concerned that the season was slipping away that they criticized Cuyler for remaining on the sidelines. Cubs officials believed that Cuyler's leg had healed sufficiently to allow him to assume his spot in center field. He seemed to be at odds with Grimm and Veeck because of his continued delay in returning to the lineup.[56] He was a proud man who did not want to play at less than 100 percent health.

He appeared to have his own timetable regarding his return to the lineup. "I'll be in there when I feel that the leg is all right and not before," stated Cuyler.[57]

The time for Cuyler to make an appearance in Chicago's outfield came on July 7, when he pinch hit for Babe Herman in the ninth inning and played the bottom of the frame in right field.[58] Grimm then penciled Cuyler in as his starting left fielder for a game against New York on July 9, as the Cubs won, 4–0. Unfortunately, the veteran outfielder did not look good and was given additional time to work the rust from his game. He returned to the lineup for good on July 15 against Boston and seemed to resemble the Cuyler of old as he went 1-for-3 and scored two runs.[59] After spending a few games getting acclimated to National League pitching, Cuyler went on a tear, hitting safely in 13 out of 14 games from July 16 through August 2. Cuyler and Babe Herman were the stars of the day on July 22, as Charlie Root defeated Philadelphia by a score of 4–1. Cuyler smacked a home run and a double and Herman contributed a double and single that accounted for all four of Chicago's runs.[60]

Cuyler's return to Chicago's lineup did little to improve the Cubs' pennant aspirations as the race moved into August. Chicago moved up one spot to third place but still trailed first-place New York by five and a half games.

Fans from Billings, Montana, tried to alter Chicago's luck by sending a bear cub to the Windy City. Members of the Billings Elks Lodge hoped the bruin mascot would help lead the Cubs to another National League championship. President Bill Veeck said that he had enough problems without having to look after a young bear. He turned the animal over to the Chicago Zoo and stated that his team needed hits, not mascots.[61]

Cuyler supplied his fair share of hits as Chicago played out the final two months of the 1933 campaign. Cuyler finished the season with a .317 average, as he appeared in 70 games for the Cubs. Chicago failed to repeat as National League champions, as New York won its first title since 1924. The Cubs finished in third place with an 86–68 record, six games behind the league-leading Giants.

Fans throughout the Windy City placed the blame for Chicago's failure to repeat as league champions on two factors. The first reason was the broken leg that Cuyler suffered during the exhibition season. The fans also blamed Babe Herman's subpar performance at the plate for Chicago's inability to win games during Cuyler's absence.⁶² Cubs fans could not even gloat over the outcome of the Chicago City Series. The crosstown rival White Sox swept the series in four straight games without much resistance from Charlie Grimm's troops. The series' second game on October 5 attracted only 8,367 fans at Wrigley Field due to the fact that many rooters thought the contest would be called off because of another tragic event surrounding the Cubs.⁶³

On October 5, Chicago president William Veeck died from leukemia at the age of 55. Veeck had been confined to his bed in Hinsdale, Illinois, after contracting influenza during a cold and rainy September series between Chicago and New York. When Veeck's illness did not improve after a week, he was taken to a local hospital, where the blood disease was discovered. The end came quickly for the prominent member of Chicago's management team as he died in his sleep.⁶⁴

Cuyler had always enjoyed a good relationship with Veeck ever since the team president had orchestrated the deal that liberated him from Pittsburgh. Like Cuyler, Veeck was also of Dutch descent and had married his childhood sweetheart. Veeck had been one of baseball's most daring innovators since joining the Cubs' staff in 1918. He heartily welcomed radio stations at Wrigley Field, where there were more broadcasting booths than in any other ballpark. Veeck was also responsible for instituting "Ladies Day" and annually refurbished Wrigley Field so that the park looked good every spring.⁶⁵

Philip Wrigley delayed a decision on who would succeed Veeck until January. Initial rumors stated that Wrigley himself would likely be named as the Cubs' new president.⁶⁶ Veeck's vision for the future and his ongoing reconstruction of the Cubs' team was not expected to be altered in any way due to his death.

Trade rumors involving the Cubs and two National League teams rose to the surface near the end of October. One alleged transaction had Chicago sending Mark Koenig, two other players and $65,000 to Philadelphia for star outfielder Chuck Klein. The second deal would bring outfielder Chick Hafey from Cincinnati to the Windy City for Kiki Cuyler, pitcher Pat Malone and outfielder Jimmy Mosolf. President Sidney Weil of Cincinnati and his counterpart from Philadelphia, Gerry Nugent, both claimed that no such deals had been consummated or negotiated. Nugent also denied that he had even been approached by Cubs management regarding player transactions.⁶⁷

One of these rumors was swiftly deflated when Cuyler accepted terms for the 1934 season about two months earlier than usual; he signed his contract in late November.⁶⁸ Stories about Cuyler being traded to Cincinnati for Hafey lost all traction once the league meetings commenced at the Powell Hotel in Chicago in the middle of December. Boston manager Bill McKechnie made a pitch for the star outfielder during the conference, when he offered southpaw pitcher Ed Brandt for Cuyler. When Charlie Grimm was questioned about the validity of such a deal, he stated that Cuyler would remain with Chicago in 1934 unless Boston sweetened the pot considerably.[69]

Rumors surrounding the other deal with Philadelphia turned out to be accurate even though president Nugent had denied any such trade was in the works. On November 21, Chuck Klein came to Chicago for Mark Koenig, Gink Hendrick, Ted Kleinhans and $65,000.

Chicago had once again added another marquee player to its lineup without giving up much more than cash. Klein had put up solid numbers during his five seasons in Philadelphia and had just won the National League's Triple Crown by hitting .368, smacking 28 home runs and driving home 120 runs. Klein did not actually learn about the transfer for several days because he was hunting with Philadelphia pitcher Frank Pearce. After spending days deep in the woods hunting, Klein finally found out about the transaction when he stopped in Louisville to order some hats. His enthusiasm over becoming a member of the Cubs was tempered a bit as Klein refused to say that he was pleased with the transfer, at least until contract figures were discussed.[70] When Klein did sign his 1934 contract a few weeks later, the assessed salary of $23,000 pleased him. The figure was a compromise estimate that seemed feasible, since Wrigley and acting president William Walker had offered $21,000, while Klein wanted $28,000.[71]

Klein's addition to Chicago's roster meant that Riggs Stephenson and Babe Herman would do battle to see who joined the new acquisition in the starting outfield with Cuyler. When the final decision was made, Stephenson or Herman would be playing alongside one of the smartest men in the game. In late December, writer Dick Farrington selected a squad of ten men whom he believed possessed the best minds in all of baseball. Cuyler was on this list, which included Bill Terry, Rogers Hornsby, Frankie Frisch, Dolf Luque, Joe Judge, Jimmy Dykes, Babe Ruth, Pie Traynor and Rabbit Maranville. Farrington reasoned that these ten players were the game's leading thinkers, men who usually did the proper thing at the right time. The writer was not claiming that these men were necessarily brilliant in an intellectual sense like Moe Berg, who spoke eight different languages. He nominated these players because they were effective at making the proper play or innovative in designing new lines of baseball strategy.[72]

A former valedictorian, Cuyler was a man who stood on equal footing intellectually with many of those within his profession. Besides being intelligent, Cuyler's engaging personality made him a hot commodity on the banquet circuit each winter. One of his favorite tales during after-dinner speeches following the 1933 season centered around former Cubs Hack Wilson and Joe McCarthy. One story focused on Wilson's difficulty in fielding ground balls to the outfield one day against Brooklyn. Robins players took an extra base on numerous occasions when they should have been limited to a single. At times, he seemed to stop grounders only by falling in front of them. While Wilson was angered by his poor fielding performance, manager McCarthy was completely enraged by his star outfielder's inadequate defensive capabilities.[73]

Wilson became more embarrassed when McCarthy engaged in conversation with a group of children at the clubhouse door after the game. One of the youths boldly asked McCarthy for a ball. After receiving no answer from the Cubs' manager or any of the players that were nearby, the young fan became even more persistent and inquired about the possibility of the Chicago organization sparing just one ball. After this second request, McCarthy finally looked up and instructed the boy on the proper method for obtaining a baseball at Wrigley Field.[74] "Sonny," said McCarthy, "if you want a ball very bad, go out to the game tomorrow and stand behind Hack Wilson in center field. You'll get plenty of them."[75]

While Cuyler was entertaining baseball enthusiasts over the winter, William Veeck's successor as team president was finally named in Chicago. It certainly did not surprise anyone when Philip K. Wrigley formally installed William M. Walker as the new president of the Cubs. Shortly after the announcement was made, Walker issued a statement that claimed there would be no curtailment of radio broadcasts at Wrigley Field, which had been suspected, and that the current Ladies' Day policy would continue under the new regime.[76] Board chairman Wrigley also announced that all proceeds from an exhibition game on March 26 between Chicago and Los Angeles would go to an equipment fund for high school baseball teams in LA. Wrigley also planned on holding a similar contest in Chicago for the benefit of high school teams there.[77] Just as the Cubs were preparing to leave for another training trip at Catalina Island, Larry MacPhail of Cincinnati's front office claimed that the Reds previously did turn down an offer of Cuyler, Malone, Mosolf and $60,000 for Chick Hafey.[78]

Once Grimm started putting his players through their paces at Avalon, Cuyler's play delighted Cubs management; the front office was relieved that no trade with Cincinnati had occurred. He showed Cubs officials early in the training session that his ankle was fine and that he still possessed plenty of speed. During an exhibition game against Pittsburgh in Los Angeles on March 29, Cuyler raced from center field all the way to right field to stab a long drive by Gus Suhr. Cuyler actually passed right fielder Tuck Stainback as he made the catch.[79] As Cuyler settled down to the business of re-establishing his star credentials during spring training, New York pitcher Carl Hubbell stated during an interview that Cuyler ran second to Spud Davis on a list of players that personally gave him trouble. Hubbell stated that Cuyler was probably on the most dangerous list of every National League pitcher and had been responsible for many pitchers taking that long, slow walk to the showers.[80] Cuyler was slated to be Grimm's main man in center field once again since Chuck "Tiger" Klein had declined to cover that area of the outfield, where he struggled to get good jumps on fly balls hit in that vicinity.[81]

Grimm's plan to have Cuyler in center field for the season opener against Cincinnati on April 17 was scuttled due to a freakish injury. He was scratched from the starting lineup after he injured his hand while giving himself an impromptu manicure with some clubhouse instruments a day before the opener.[82] Cuyler made a trip to Cincinnati's Jewish Hospital, where he was treated for an infected hangnail on his left hand.[83] He was sent home to Chicago, while Gabby Hartnett narrowly missed playing in the opener because his wife was seriously ill.[84] Rookie Tuck Stainback replaced Cuyler in center field and recorded two hits as Chicago won the opener over Cincinnati, 6–0. Stainback was sensational and kept Cuyler on the bench even when the veteran player was healthy enough to return. The young outfielder batted .333 as Chicago won its first seven games of the 1934 season.

Cuyler did not receive a chance to assist in Chicago's strong start until Stainback injured his foot in a game against St. Louis on April 27. Hazen took his spot in center in the 11th inning after Stainback came up lame in the tenth. Cuyler celebrated his debut in the bottom of the 11th by poking Tex Carleton's first pitch to left for a single. Charlie Grimm moved the runner to second with a successful sacrifice bunt before Carleton intentionally passed Billy Jurges. Hartnett then ended an 0-for-12 swoon as he drilled a single to center that drove home Cuyler with the game's winning run.[85] Cuyler wasted little time finding a groove at the plate as he hit safely in 12 out of his first 15 games and pushed his average up to a lusty mark of .411. When the Cubs went to Flint, Michigan, on May 16 to play an exhibition game against a team representing the automobile factory that Cuyler played for in 1920, he smacked two doubles in Chicago's 11–4 victory. He was also presented with a membership card in the Flint Elks Club and received the gift of a new automobile from local admirers.[86]

A minor slump at the plate saw Cuyler's average drop to .368 by May 17. Even though this mark placed him fourth in the National League batting race, Cuyler's play was not viewed as completely satisfactory during the first month of the season. He was not hitting consistently with runners on base while his play in center field could be termed as ragged.[87]

Chuck Klein was also not slugging up to his usual standards; he had two bruised hands that were making it difficult for him to properly catch fly balls or grip a bat.[88] In spite of various issues with the club's composition, Chicago held the National League's second-place spot with a 41–26 record at the conclusion of June. The defending champion Giants led the Cubs by one game with a mark of 42–25.

Any kind of pennant battle between New York and Chicago gave Kiki Cuyler some extra incentive to perform well on the diamond. The Polo Grounds bleacher fans had not liked Cuyler going back to his Pittsburgh days and razzed him heartily when he took his position in the outfield. Cuyler responded to the heckling by doing a little dance whenever he reached base with a hit.[89] The Cardinals were also involved in the pennant fight as they attempted to win their third National League flag of the decade. A doubleheader split between the Cubs and the Cardinals on July 4 left both teams tied for second place. St. Louis' Joe Medwick smacked four singles in the first game and went 2-for-4 in the nightcap. After going hitless during the first contest at Sportsman's Park, Cuyler smacked three doubles and a triple as Chicago won the second game, 6–2.[90]

Even though New York's fans were not very fond of Cuyler, there were fans throughout the country who loved his hustling style of play. A total of 11,184 of these faithful patrons voted to have Cuyler selected to the National League squad for the second edition of the All-Star Game between both leagues. Despite the fact that Cuyler garnered enough votes to be named to the squad, manager Bill Terry planned on selecting outfielder Joe Moore of the Giants for the game at the Polo Grounds on July 10.[91] Terry was forced to add Cuyler to the squad only after Moore was sidelined with an injury one week before the game. Cuyler started in right field and batted in the cleanup spot for the National League stars as they attempted to avenge their defeat at the American League's hands one year earlier. Cuyler went 0-for-2 as the American League prevailed by a score of 9–7. Even though his squad lost, Cuyler was able to witness one of the greatest feats in history from his spot in right field. The Giants' Carl Hubbell did the unimaginable when he struck out Babe Ruth, Lou Gehrig, Jimmie Foxx, Al Simmons and Joe Cronin in succession during the first and second innings.

The experience of playing in the All-Star Game seemed to further inspire Cuyler. People who were critical of Cuyler's play during the first six weeks of the season believed that he deserved the lion's share of credit for Chicago's success as the season moved into the dog days of summer.[92] Cuyler was the hero in the first game of a doubleheader during a sweep over Philadelphia at the Baker Bowl on July 21. With two outs and the score tied 1–1 in the ninth inning, consecutive doubles by Babe Herman and Cuyler produced the winning tally.[93] On July 23, Cuyler smacked two doubles and two singles as Chicago defeated Brooklyn, 8–3, and moved to within two and a half games of first-place New York.[94] He was particularly lethal during a stretch of games in late July and early August. He pounded out a dozen hits in 24 trips to the plate and pushed his average up 11 points to .345. The seven-day hot streak left Cuyler 16 points behind Paul Waner, the National League's leading hitter.⁹⁵

The Cubs continued to hang tough throughout August as they battled New York for the National League lead. The Cubs won three games while losing only one during a crucial late August series against the Giants at Wrigley Field. Cuyler scored the only run of the game on August 27, when he singled in the seventh and scored on Tuck Stainback's double.⁹⁶ Cuyler was the hitting star two days later, when Chicago secured another 1–0 victory against New York and Carl Hubbell on August 29. Stan Hack reached base in the ninth inning after Giants second baseman Hughie Critz fumbled his grounder. Augie Galan forced Hack before Cuyler drove him home with a clutch double. The Cubs' three victories in the series moved them to within four and a half games of the league-leading Giants.⁹⁷

Windy City fans who dreamed of another National League title for their favorite

After a particularly tough year in 1933, when Cuyler missed considerable time due to a broken ankle, he rebounded in phenomenal fashion in 1934. He was also selected to play right field in the second annual All-Star Game against the American League on July 10 at the Polo Grounds (courtesy the National Baseball Hall of Fame Library, Cooperstown, New York).

team were thoroughly frustrated and disappointed by the Cubs' play during crunch time in September. Chicago posted a horrendous record of 12–14 for the month and fell out of pennant contention by going 1–7 from September 16 through September 22. Chicago eventually staggered home in third place with a record of 86–65. The Cardinals surged past the Giants and claimed another title for Frankie Frisch's "Gashouse Gang." St. Louis finished with a 95–58 record while New York ended up two games back at 93–60. During Chicago's disastrous late-season Eastern swing, manager Charlie Grimm blew up in anger while the team was in Philadelphia. Grimm accused some of his players of being lazy and classified them as prima donnas. He also referred to them as whiners who fabricated aliments in order to avoid doing the work required to claim victory. Even though Grimm did not single out any Cubs players specifically, many Chicago fans believed that some of the comments were aimed at Chuck Klein.[98]

Cuyler was not one of the players that Grimm was describing. Cuyler had enjoyed a great comeback season in 1934 as he led Chicago in hitting with a .338 average. He paced the team by scoring 80 runs and led the National League with 42 doubles. Cuyler's average was also good enough to place him third in the league race behind Paul Waner and Bill Terry. Cuyler had proved numerous critics wrong; they believed that his better days were behind him after suffering serious injuries two years in a row. Cuyler had given the fans of Chicago one last glimpse at his superior ability, as 1934 turned out to be his last hurrah in the Windy City.

12. A Great Career in Chicago Comes to an End

Changes involving the Cubs' roster seemed unavoidable as Windy City fans digested all information surrounding Hot Stove League propaganda. One Canadian publication stated that Woody English, Chuck Klein, Pat Malone, Guy Bush, Stan Hack and Cuyler would be disposed of during the off-season.[1] Rumors coming out of Chicago claimed that Klein, English, Hack, Bush, Cuyler, Augie Galan, Charlie Root, Don Hurst and Tuck Stainback were all leading candidates to be involved in any trade discussions.[2] While manager Charlie Grimm remained silent about any potential deals that were in the works, he did speak up in order to clarify statements that he made during his little tirade in Philadelphia. Grimm backtracked on his comments about some of the Cubs being lazy. Chicago's manager claimed that everything was fine with his team and blamed newspaper writers for embellishing the entire episode. Some media denizens believed that Grimm only had a change of heart after being lectured by someone in the front office.[3]

Since there was no Chicago City Series played after the 1934 season, Cubs management enjoyed a head start on making the necessary alterations that would improve the team for 1935. Front office changes were one of the first items on the docket after the World Series concluded. Team president William Walker resigned from that post and sold his stock to Philip Wrigley for somewhere between $150,000 and $200,000. Wrigley assumed the presidency and gave more authority to manager Grimm by creating a vice-president's position for him at the annual stockholder's meeting.[4] Shortly after the announcement was made, Wrigley took care of some difficult business by releasing the ever popular Riggs Stephenson on October 30. Wrigley acted graciously during the difficult meeting, as he presented Stephenson with a $350 engraved watch and told him how much the Cubs appreciated his loyalty and effort during the past nine years.[5]

Stephenson's release came on the heels of Grimm receiving his wish in respect to the removal of Pat Malone from Chicago's roster. On October 26, the Cubs shipped the pitcher to St. Louis for catcher Ken O'Dea. Malone had become entrenched in Grimm's doghouse when he refused to pitch out of his regular turn during a September series in Boston. Grimm had asked Malone to start the first game of a doubleheader on September 9 because Jim Weaver was suffering from a toothache. Malone declined his manager's request and demanded another day of rest.[6] Malone was then used by Grimm as a reliever during the second game of the twinbill but did not appear in another contest for Chicago in 1934. After the season ended, Malone complained that Grimm did not give him a chance as he remained on the bench despite having won seven out of his last eight starts. He also believed that Cubs management prevented him from cashing in on a monetary bonus. Malone, who finished the season with a 14–7 record, was supposed to receive a gratuity of $250 for each game he won above and beyond 15 victories.[7]

The transactions involving Stephenson and Malone seemed to represent only the beginning of a wild trading season, as rumors of additional players leaving Chicago continued to circulate throughout the Windy City. Cuyler's name was prominently mentioned when any piece of information surrounding a potential deal was leaked by the press. Giants manager Bill Terry seemed determined to acquire the star outfielder during the National Association's annual November convention at Louisville. Grimm supposedly offered Cuyler to the Giants, but did not like the exchange terms when Terry responded with an offer of pitchers Joe Bowman and Jack Salveson.[8] Terry then attempted something creative by offering pitcher Carl Hubbell to Pittsburgh for pitcher Larry French and outfielder Fred Lindstrom. If Pirates manager Pie Traynor was willing to swing this particular deal, Terry then planned on shipping Lindstrom to Chicago in exchange for Cuyler.[9]

Grimm beat Terry to the punch when he finalized a deal with Pittsburgh on November 22. The trade brought French and Lindstrom to Chicago in exchange for outfielder Babe Herman and pitchers Guy Bush and Jim Weaver. The Cubs almost pulled off a deal with Boston that would have brought pitcher Fred Frankhouse to the Windy City, but Grimm balked at the proposition when the Braves asked for Cuyler and infielder Woody English in return. The deal officially died after Grimm countered with a proposal of Cuyler and Stan Hack for Frankhouse.[10]

Despite being unable to pry a solid pitcher from Boston, Grimm was ecstatic over the deal that netted French and Lindstrom from Pittsburgh. This deal, coupled with the fact that Chicago acquired pitcher Tex Carleton from St. Louis for pitchers Bud Tinning and Dick Ward on November 21, made the wild trading session in Louisville a rousing success for Chicago.[11] "Our satisfaction with the swaps we made with Pittsburgh and St. Louis in Louisville is based on the 'new faces' and 'change of pastures' idea," said Grimm at the Louisville convention's conclusion.[12]

Cuyler seemed to be one of those players that fell in the "change of pastures" category. Grimm believed that Cuyler was expendable because Chicago was loaded in the outfield, with men like Chuck Klein, Tuck Stainback and Frank Demaree. He also did not believe it would be fair for a man of Cuyler's ability to remain on the bench most of the time.[13] Grimm once again attempted to peddle Cuyler to the Giants during league meetings at New York in December, but he was rebuked by Terry when the Cubs asked for pitcher Hal Schumacher in exchange.[14] When Grimm's house cleaning finally ended two months after the season's conclusion, Cuyler remained on the roster while ten players who played for Chicago in 1934 were no longer Cubs. Cuyler wasted little time securing his signature to a contract for the 1935 season. Cuyler's document arrived at team headquarters on January 25, only two weeks after it had been mailed to him in Michigan.[15]

A connection to one trade rumor after another did not seem to bother Cuyler as he pursued his usual passions while relaxing during the off-season. He made his annual hunting pilgrimage north of the border into Canada and shot

After the 1934 season ended, Cuyler engaged in his usual off-season passions of fishing and hunting. In this photograph, he holds the proper tools needed to insure a successful hunting expedition (courtesy the *Alcona County Review*).

a moose for the fifth straight winter while chronicling the whole event with a movie camera. Cuyler killed only one moose each of those years because Canadian law restricted hunters from shooting more than one animal. Since his camp was based at Lake of the Woods, Ontario, he complied with the edict every hunting season. As for the reason behind Cuyler shooting footage of his hunting exploits, he simply did so to authenticate the event. As an ardent fisherman, Cuyler had been known to stretch the truth when it came to discussing his fishing adventures. As a result of his serious nature, Cuyler filmed these moose hunting excursions so that no one could question the validity of his claims. Those who declared that bellows could be used to make it appear that a long dead moose had just been killed were deemed as "smart alecks" in Cuyler's eyes.[16]

Success in hunting and fishing were not the only sports in which Cuyler showed a strong aptitude for outside of baseball. He had won numerous medals and trophies as the waltz champion during the Cubs' spring training trips to Catalina Island. After winning the cup for four consecutive seasons, Cuyler decided not to defend his title, and the event was cancelled as a result.[17]

Most of the discussion surrounding Cuyler during the spring trip to Avalon centered on Grimm's decision to use him as his leadoff hitter. Grimm's plan called for Cuyler to hit first, Chuck Klein to bat third and newcomer Fred Lindstrom to hit out of the cleanup spot.[18] Klein's spot in the order was contingent on him becoming one of Grimm's starting outfielders. Grimm had decided on Cuyler as his starter in center field, but was still unsure which players from a group featuring Klein, Augie Galan, Tuck Stainback or Frank Demaree would hold down the other two spots.[19] While Grimm was pondering his possible lineup combinations, Yankees manager Joe McCarthy told writers that Cuyler was the smartest baserunner he ever saw.[20]

Klein and Galan flanked Cuyler in the outfield as Chicago defeated St. Louis, 4–3, in the season opener on April 16. Cuyler hit out of the third slot and went 0-for-2. The Cubs and Cuyler struggled together during the first few weeks of the season, as Chicago posted an 8–5 record for April. A few solid games at the plate actually bumped Cuyler's average up to .194 by the end of the month. Cuyler's play was not up to his usual standards due to a lingering illness that had left him well below 100 percent. Grimm might have sent Cuyler to the bench if Frank Demaree was not suffering from a bronchial infection or Tuck Stainback was not mired in an early season funk.[21] Grimm benched himself and installed young Phil Cavarretta at first base after going hitless in 43 trips to the plate during spring training and Chicago's first two regular season games.[22]

As many of Chicago's players continued to put up poor batting figures throughout May, Grimm made changes to the lineup that were aimed at shaking his squad from its lethargy. Klein and Lindstrom were sent to the bench due to protracted hitting slumps. Stan Hack replaced Lindstrom at third and Tuck Stainback took Klein's spot in right field. Cuyler, who was hitting only .232 for the season, was dropped from fifth to seventh place in Grimm's batting order.[23] The new lineup brought home a 6–4 victory against New York at Wrigley Field on May 23, as Cuyler benefited from a lucky break. He broke a 4–4 tie in the eighth inning when the Giants' Hank Leiber misjudged a fly ball as it came off Cuyler's bat. As Leiber hustled to move under the ball, he stumbled and fell. Cuyler circled the bases as the ball rolled to the center field fence.[24]

Grimm's lineup changes failed to achieve the desired results as Chicago hovered around the .500 mark during the early weeks of June. While the Cubs attempted to generate some momentum by winning a few baseball games, members of the squad were asked to weigh in on the Edwin "Alabama" Pitts situation. Pitts was a former convicted felon who was playing minor league baseball after being released from the Sing Sing Correctional Facility in New York. Many people protested the fact that Pitts was permitted to play despite his seedy past. Cuyler was not among this group of people who believed that Pitts could not reform his life. Cuyler stated that he would not mind playing on the same diamond with Pitts. He reasoned that if Pitts was a good player, he should be given the same chance as any other man attempting to carve out a career in the game. Cuyler believed that a man's past made no difference on the field.[25]

Cuyler's appearances on the diamond became more infrequent as the Cubs tried to keep their heads above water during June. Grimm started using an outfield combination that consisted of Augie Galan, Fred Lindstrom and Chuck Klein. Even though Cuyler was able to work his way back into the outfield rotation near the end of the month, it looked as if the veteran's days in Chicago might be numbered. In February, owner Philip Wrigley had announced that his team lost $600,000 over the past three years.[26] Although Cuyler was not the highest paid player on Chicago's roster, he was still making about $14,000 in salary for the 1935 season.[27] Deep cuts to the Cubs' payroll seemed inevitable; Cuyler appeared to be a prime candidate due to his .268 average. Even though Cuyler had been the Cubs' leading hitter in 1934, there were strong hints during the off-season that he would be moved to another team. When the June 15 trade deadline came and went, many Cubs followers now believed that Cuyler would remain in Chicago for at least the remainder of the season.[28]

It was not to be. Cuyler's faithful followers in the Windy City were stunned when the Cubs released the popular player outright on July 3 while Chicago was in Cincinnati for a series against the Reds.[29] The common belief surrounding Cuyler's unconditional release involved the organization's new policy of fiscal prudence, which made it necessary to cut him loose so that a hefty contract could be eliminated from the books. Rival clubs were so certain of Cuyler's imminent release that they all passed on paying Chicago the $6,000 fee when he was placed on waivers. According to Cuyler, the only explanation for the release offered to him by Charlie Grimm was the claim that Chicago's manager had to yield to his bosses.[30] Grimm told the press that the Cubs' organization found it necessary to reduce expenses. He stated that the release of Cuyler, one of the highest salaried players on Chicago's squad, was done with that thought in mind.

Cuyler's initial reaction to this situation was one of unhappiness as he was forced to leave Chicago after seven seasons.[31] "It's a mystery to me," Cuyler said, "why Chicago, of all other National League clubs, should suddenly discover that they can't carry my contract for the rest of the year.

"All the other teams seem to be able to do it."[32]

Cuyler's disappointment was quickly transformed into excitement as the Pirates, Phillies, Reds and White Sox immediately began to bid for his services.[33] The Yankees also threw their hat into the ring when they offered to pay Cuyler $4,000 to finish the season with them while giving him a shot at sharing some World Series money.[34] Pittsburgh manager Pie Traynor made Cuyler a substantial offer when the Pirates rolled into Cincinnati one day after his release. Traynor was confident the veteran outfielder would be returning to the city where his great career had begun. Cuyler confided to a Chicago scribe that he was leaning toward Traynor's offer and figured he would end up signing with Pittsburgh. But Traynor's hopes were dashed at 3 P.M. on July 5, when he received a telegram from Cuyler that informed him the free agent outfielder had signed with Cincinnati.[35] The Reds were able to win the Cuyler sweepstakes by offering to assume his entire Chicago contract while also giving him a $1,000 signing bonus.[36]

Cuyler made his Cincinnati debut against the Brooklyn Dodgers at Crosley Field on July 11. Cuyler batted third, played center field and went 1-for-4 as the Reds came up victorious, 5–4. Cuyler experienced a fairly good start with the Reds before he was forced to the sidelines with a bad leg. His performance during the 62 games in which he appeared for the Reds was very similar to his play as a Cub in 1935. Cuyler batted .251 as a Red and finished up the campaign with a .258 mark, the poorest of his major league career. To make matters worse for him Chicago claimed the 1935 National League pennant while Cincinnati finished in sixth place with a 68–85 record.

In spite of having the most disappointing season of his career, Cuyler was given the opportunity to play in a major league night game for the first time on August 31. Cincinnati management had initiated night baseball in a minor way by scheduling seven such games during the 1935 season. Cuyler had missed a chance to play night ball as a Cub on July 1, when he did not appear in the game. He was also not in Cincinnati's lineup when the Reds played evening games against Brooklyn on July 10, Boston on July 24 and St. Louis a week later. Even though Cuyler did not get into the game on July 31 against the Cardinals, he was able to view the spectacle of 39,000 fans squeezing into Crosley Field, well beyond its normal capacity of 24,000. Spectators were jammed into the ballpark to the point that some spectators sat only a few feet behind the catcher. One fan who was crowding the home plate umpire was actually hit in the teeth with a foul tip. The man momentarily left his spot, went to a nearby water fountain in order to spit out fragments of broken teeth, and then returned to his place behind home plate as if nothing had happened.[37]

This unique baseball enthusiast was not the most interesting fan that took up residence behind home plate. That honor went to night club entertainer Kitty Burke, who spent most of the evening matching wits with the Cardinals' Ducky Medwick.[38] Burke told Medwick that he could not hit the ball with an ironing board. Ducky responded that Miss Burke could not hit a ball with an elephant.[39] This remark galvanized Kitty; the blonde entertainer came onto the field, grabbed Babe Herman's bat and told St. Louis' Paul Dean to pitch to her. Dean performed a few windmill windups and then grinned before he tossed an underhanded pitch to Miss Burke, who tapped a grounder back to Dean and ran part of the way to first base before she turned off into the crowd. Burke became the first woman, or any intruder for that matter, who ever interrupted a regulation big league game by taking a turn at bat.[40]

A little over a month after Cuyler witnessed these added attractions, National League President Ford Frick bestowed a special honor upon him and other members of the Reds' organization. Cuyler, Babe Herman, Jim Bottomley and coach George Kelly were presented with lifetime National League passes by umpire Bill Klem before a game at Crosley Field on September 8. Frick also sent each man a letter stating that he hoped they would remain active in the league for years to come and would not actually have to use the passes.[41]

Cuyler intended to continue pursuing his craft as a baseball artisan in 1936. He was not quite ready to give up the game as an active player just yet, even though he had endured a horrendous year in 1935. Cuyler's off-season routine remained rigid as he once again pulled out his hunting gear and made a trip north of the border. Reds rookie infielder Lew Riggs also accompanied Cuyler on this hunting voyage through the woods of Canada in pursuit of the usual deer and moose.[42]

All members of the Reds were set to engage in an excursion that no other major league team had ever taken during spring training. Cincinnati management accepted the invitation of Governor Blanton Winship, from the U.S. territorial island of Puerto Rico, to hold training camp there in 1936. In early January, Reds general manager Larry MacPhail finalized the plans with Puerto Rican officials in New York. When the first group of Cincinnati players set sail for the tropical island on February 6, it marked the first time that any team had traveled that great a distance over water for spring training. Besides doing training work during their stay, MacPhail also lined up nine exhibition games for his players with native West Indies teams.[43] Cuyler, Lew Riggs and Benny Frey were some of the players who notified MacPhail that they were looking forward to the Puerto Rican invasion.[44]

Reds trainer Dr. Richard Rhode made a practice run to the tropical paradise and gave MacPhail his seal of approval regarding this bold expedition. "There isn't any reason why any of the men should become seasick," said Rhode. "Especially if they eat heavily and that won't be hard for them, as the food on the boat is very excellent.

"I was very much surprised to find the ballpark, known as Escambron Baseball Park, to be such an excellent layout. It compares favorably with anything in the American Association except that it has a skinned infield."[45]

Rhode's glowing report about his trip to Puerto Rico turned out to be a pipedream once Cincinnati's players began the journey to their spring training site. The final group of Reds who made the trek from New York to Puerto Rico on the liner "Coamo" did not have a smooth, enjoyable ocean experience. Most of the players were so sick when they arrived in Puerto Rico that they needed medical attention and could not practice for several days. The rough voyage also forced the writers who were on the ship to visit the infirmary once they reached land.[46] Cuyler was one of the players from the final contingent who felt the grip of sea-sickness during this historic voyage.[47] One Reds player who preferred to remain anonymous claimed that he would never leave the safe confines of America's mainland in the future.

"The voyage—if you care to call it that," said the unnamed Cincinnati player, "was just one series of headaches for me. I didn't eat enough to keep a pigeon alive during the entire trip. I spent the greater part of the time in my stateroom. It was like riding a merry-go-round, grabbing for a brass ring. And you can take it from me, I'll never leave the good old U.S.A. once my tootsies touch terra firma there again."[48]

The boat ride was an easy task compared to what pitchers Si Johnson, Lee Stine, Walter Hilcher, Tony Freitas, Leroy Herrmann and Ray Davis experienced during two separate airplane flights to Puerto Rico. When Johnson, Stine and Hilcher arrived at spring training, they carried with them a harrow-

12. A Great Career in Chicago Comes to an End

ing tale surrounding a stop-over in Haiti. The eight-hour trip from Miami to Puerto Rico was modified to include a layover in Port Au Prince because of horrible weather conditions. All during the night, the three players remained awake in terror, as they heard tom-toms beating in the distance. Three days after this first group arrived in Puerto Rico, Freitas, Herrmann and Davis showed up at training camp telling similar tales of their time spent in Haiti. During these two separate ordeals, all six athletes feared they would become the victims of some voodoo ritual before being given an opportunity to escape the island.[49]

The situation did not get much better for members of Cincinnati's contingent once they hit the diamond. They were exposed to some unexpected drama and danger on February 23, when the San Juan police chief and two of his patrolmen were killed by a Nationalist. Reds manager Chuck Dressen had just started a workout with his squad when detectives and policemen entered the premises looking for the killer. The grandstand and locker rooms in the clubhouse were searched, but the perpetrator had not chosen those locations to hide.[50]

More normal activity on the field involved Cuyler, who once again had taken it upon himself to help a young outfielder improve his game. Cuyler gave Calvin Chapman critical instruction as he taught the rookie how to correctly break for a fly ball at the crack of the bat and where to throw the ball once he made the catch. Cuyler had given Augie Galan similar tutoring during the Cubs' training session in 1935. Even though Cuyler was eventually released after Galan became established, this did not deter him from giving Chapman some much needed coaching.[51]

Solid coaching was not Cuyler's only positive contribution during Cincinnati's training camp. Once the squad finished its work in Puerto Rico and shifted its spring headquarters to Tampa, Florida, Cuyler already seemed to be playing at the top of his game. On March 28 during a 7–3 victory against the Cubs at Tampa, Cuyler and rookie infielder Billy Myers hit two of the longest home runs ever seen at Plant Field. Each drive traveled an estimated 460 feet on the fly over the head of left fielder Johnny Gill.[52] Cuyler had an exceptional spring training both at the plate and defensively, as Cincinnati prepared to open the regular season. He still seemed to possess the speed that made him a successful player during his time in Pittsburgh and Chicago. Cuyler was putting on a splendid display even though he was favoring an ankle that he sprained playing basketball over the winter.[53]

Cuyler also seemed to be meshing quite nicely with his relatively new Cincinnati teammates. During the team's railroad trip north prior to the opener, the train passed through Lew Riggs' hometown of Mebane, North Carolina. Riggs' fellow players, who had heard about Mebane's "redeeming" qualities, gave the young infielder some good-natured ribbing. Cuyler joined the act when he tried to count houses but claimed that he reached only five before the train reached open country once again. Cincinnati's players quit their card games so that they could gaze at the small town before giving Riggs a round of cheers.[54]

All of this team camaraderie did not do the Reds much good once the season began, as they dropped their first two games against Pittsburgh at Crosley Field. Cincinnati finally pulled out a victory on April 16, defeating the Pirates, 7–4. Cuyler went 1-for-5 as he batted from the leadoff spot and played center field.

Cincinnati fans were treated to a barrage of hits on April 17, as Cuyler and Babe Herman did heavy damage against their old mates during a 12–3 victory over Chicago. Cuyler doubled in the fourth after Tex Carleton had retired Cincinnati's first nine batters. He scored a run when he hustled home as Herman beat out an infield single. Herman drove Cuyler home once again in the fifth when he blasted a homer after his teammate drilled a single.[55] Cuyler went 2-for-4 and scored three runs, while Herman went 2-for-5, scored two runs and knocked in three runs. In spite of this great performance against the Cubs, Cuyler struggled during April, as Cincinnati posted a 7–7 record for the month. After going hitless in a 3–1 loss against Boston on April 30, Cuyler's batting average stood at an unimpressive .246.

Even though Cuyler did not look very good on the field during the season's early weeks, writer Robert T. Paul of the *Philadelphia Daily News* still believed that the veteran player looked sharp away from the field. Paul included Cuyler on his list of the ten best dressed ballplayers in major league baseball.[56] Being singled out for wearing fashionable attire was an honor for Cuyler, but results on the field were what drove him. Cuyler finally started to turn his season around in May, as the veteran outfielder seemed to receive an infusion of youth. Kiki pushed his average up 51 points after going 8-for-17 in games against Philadelphia and New York from May 1 through May 4. Cuyler came up heroic on May 4, when he scored the only run of the contest against New York's Carl Hubbell. Cuyler led off the final frame at Crosley Field with a triple. After Hubbell retired Tommy Thevenow and then walked both Babe Herman and Ernie Lombardi, Cuyler scored the winning run on Sammy Byrd's sacrifice fly.[57]

On May 8, Cuyler continued this onslaught against National League opponents during a visit to his old stomping grounds at Forbes Field. He smacked a home run and a triple as Cincinnati defeated Pittsburgh, 9–6. Cuyler roamed Forbes Field's center field pasture like the youngster who had provided so many thrills for Pittsburgh patrons a decade earlier. Besides being lethal with a bat, Cuyler also robbed the Pirates' Bud Hafey and Gus Suhr of sure hits by making great plays in center field. Third baseman Lew Riggs joined Cuyler as Cincinnati's resident thieves when he speared a blistering drive off the bat of Paul Waner.[58] When Waner returned to Pittsburgh's dugout, teammate Jim Weaver offered up two possible courses of action in response to Riggs' spectacular play. "You'd better either get religion or shoot that guy," Weaver remarked to Waner.[59]

Regrettably, Cuyler's resurgent season was halted during late May when he joined Babe Herman and Billy Myers on the injured list and could only be used in emergency situations.[60] After being out of the lineup for a couple of games, Cuyler came back strong and hit safely in 17 out of 18 contests in June, raising his batting average to .324. Cuyler reached a personal milestone on June 16 during a loss against New York, when he doubled off Carl Hubbell for the 2,000th hit of his major league career.[61] That loss to the Giants left Cincinnati with a 27–28 record after the season's first two months. Even though Cuyler was the oldest member of the Reds' squad, he led the team in stolen bases, times at bat, runs scored, hits, doubles and home runs. He was also one of the fastest players on Cincinnati's team as he could outsprint teammates whose average age was 12 years younger than him.[62] Cuyler's play was so inspiring to Cincinnati fans that H.G. Reynolds of Franklin, Ohio, wrote a letter to the editor of *The Sporting News* lobbying for Kiki's inclusion in the 1936 All-Star Game.[63]

"Kiki Cuyler of the Reds is putting on a great comeback this year and it is my opinion that he is one of the best center fielders in the National League," wrote Reynolds. "His work in the field is always spectacular and he can cover acres of ground. I have seen him run far back to the wall in Crosley Field and pull down drives that were labeled for doubles and triples. And he's hitting again, just as he did with the Pirates and Cubs.

"Come on, you Cuyler fans, and let's vote for Kiki when the time comes to ballot on the National League players for the annual All-Star Game."[64]

Cuyler's brigade of faithful followers enjoyed every moment of the star outfielder's comeback season, even though they were unable to put together a voting block powerful enough to send him to the All-Star Game. The year provided pleasant memories for Cuyler as he proved to doubters that his substandard play in 1935 was an aberration. Yet, some harsh realities made the game insignificant at times. During a spring exhibition game in Columbia, South Carolina, between Cincinnati and Detroit, Cuyler had become acquainted with his namesake, a local lad named Kiki Cuyler Atkinson. Young Atkinson, born a few weeks after Cuyler had performed his heroics for Pittsburgh in the 1925 World Series, was named after the star outfielder. Cuyler called on the youngster prior to the exhibition game in Columbia and gave Atkinson an autographed picture and some baseballs. But the feel-good story had a sad ending as the ten-year-old Atkinson lad and two other youths drowned in June after their boat capsized in a river near the boy's home.[65]

Such a gloomy outcome was bound to affect a devoted family man like Cuyler. His daughter Kelly June was only a few years younger than Kiki Cuyler Atkinson, while son Harold, now 16 years of age, was a student at the Western Military Academy in Alton, Ill.[66] Baseball was different from other professions in that it kept father and family apart from each other for long periods.

Cuyler's extended family in Cincinnati was glad that the veteran player was still playing rather than retiring to the tranquility of his Michigan homestead. Cuyler brought back memories of his youth when he put together a phenomenal hitting streak during a doubleheader against Philadelphia on July 30. After being retired and working out a walk during his first two plate appearances of the first game, Cuyler recorded hits in three consecutive at-bats. He banged out five more singles in the nightcap as he went a perfect 5-for-5.[67]

Phillies pitcher Bucky Walters ended Cuyler's string of eight consecutive hits during the first game of a doubleheader on July 31. Cuyler came up two safeties short of tying the record that he jointly shared. He had smacked out ten hits in succession on September 18, 19 and 21 during the championship campaign of 1925.[68] While Cuyler was basking in the praise of another phenomenal achievement, two of his Cincinnati teammates were still feeling the sting of manager Chuck Dressen's reprimand after a game against New York on July 26. Dressen fined outfielder Babe Herman and pitcher Paul Derringer $200 each for committing egregious gaffes in the ninth inning during the first game of a doubleheader at New York's Polo Grounds.[69] Dressen did not mince any words when he talked with reporters about his angst toward Herman and Derringer on this particular occasion.

> I fined Paul Derringer $200 for balking in the ninth inning to score Dick Bartell from third and send Joe Moore to second and I fined Babe Herman $200 for not playing out the string when Hank Leiber singled to left with two out to drive in Moore from second base with the winning run.
> Derringer came to the bench just before he made that balk and I told him I was going to have Scarsella run in, then hustle back to first base while he (Derringer) was pitching to Mel Ott, and that we might be able to catch Moore off the bag. He bluffed a throw to first, but held the ball and this gave the Giants the tying run. I fined him for not throwing the ball.
> Leiber's winning hit went to Herman on the first bounce. He caught it cleanly. He might not have nipped Moore at home had he thrown to the plate, but he might have retired him or caused him to stop at third. Instead he turned and went to the clubhouse and no one can play ball for me like that without paying for it. I want everyone on my team to play out the string. I think they know it now.[70]

12. A Great Career in Chicago Comes to an End

Manager Dressen did not need to be concerned with Cuyler's focus or his dedication to baseball from April through September. If more men on Cincinnati's squad had Cuyler's temperament and played the game in a similar fashion, the Reds might have been contending for a pennant in 1936 rather than battling for a first-division finish. Cincinnati fans who appreciated Cuyler's hustling style were more than happy to give him due recognition when the opportunity presented itself. Prior to a doubleheader against Philadelphia at Crosley Field on August 30, a group of Cincinnati patrons presented Cuyler with a basket of flowers in remembrance of his 38th birthday. Cuyler did not disappoint his fans as he celebrated the special day by hitting two triples and three singles while stealing a base, as Cincinnati swept the twinbill from Philadelphia.[71]

Cuyler's star flashed brightly during the 1936 season. He finished second on the team in hitting behind Ernie Lombardi, as he posted a .326 average in 144 games. Kiki finished tops on the club with 96 runs, 185 hits, 29 doubles, 74 RBIs and 16 stolen bases. He still showed a tendency to be a free-swinger at the age of 38, as he led the Reds with 67 strikeouts. On the upside, Cuyler also paced the team by drawing 47 walks. His solid, all-round play helped bring Cincinnati home in fifth place with a 74–80 record. This marked the Reds' best showing in the National League since they finished fifth in 1928. From 1929 through 1934, the Reds had finished in seventh or eighth place. General manager Larry MacPhail deserved a large amount of credit for giving Cincinnati's fans something to cheer about in 1936.

Diehard rooters who wanted to offer their congratulations to MacPhail for a job well done were forced to do so before November

Chicago released Cuyler on July 3, 1935. He signed with the Cincinnati Reds two days later. Cuyler put up poor numbers as he batted only .258 while playing in the two cities. He proved that he was not quite done when he played solid baseball for Cincinnati in 1936 (courtesy the National Baseball Hall of Fame Library, Cooperstown, New York).

1. Near the end of the 1936 campaign, Leland Stanford (Larry) MacPhail tendered his resignation as vice-president and general manager. Thirty hours after this shocking announcement, Warren Giles was appointed as MacPhail's successor, effective on November 1.[72] Manager Chuck Dressen was also given more power to choose his own coaches while having a louder voice in selecting players and making trades. Dressen did not waste any time offering pitcher Paul Derringer to Pittsburgh. Pirates manager Pie Traynor responded negatively to this overture when Dressen asked for Paul Waner and Arky Vaughan in return. Shortly after Giles officially replaced MacPhail, he stated that Cincinnati owner Powel Crosley, Jr., might be willing to pry Dizzy Dean away from St. Louis for a reasonable amount of cash.[73]

Cuyler rewarded himself for a fine season in 1936 by heading back to his home in Michigan to go pheasant and duck hunting. After Cuyler finished the excursion, teammate Lew Riggs, Cubs infielder Stan Hack and Boston Bees pitcher Bob Smith all joined Cuyler in Canada to go moose hunting.[74] Riggs outdid his older teammate on the trip as he bagged a 225-pound deer and five days later killed a moose that weighed over 1,000 pounds. When Riggs returned to Mebane, North Carolina, after the hunting trip, he recounted glorious tales of his shooting prowess while showing pictures to corroborate the claims. An endless supply of moose steaks for the people of Mebane furnished the final proof regarding Riggs' adventures.[75]

Shortly after Cuyler returned from the hunting expedition, he attended a sports banquet in Saginaw, Michigan, on December 14. He was the featured speaker at the annual American Legion banquet, which was held to discuss plans for the summer of 1937 concerning the national junior baseball program.[76]

General manager Warren Giles received a stack of signed contracts shortly after Christmas that included a document with Cuyler's signature attached to it. The signings of Cuyler, Gene Schott, Gilly Campbell, Johnny Vander Meer, coach Tom Sheehan and manager Chuck Dressen, were announced through "Bulletin No. 21," which was issued by Commissioner Kenesaw Landis.[77] It was reported that Cuyler's contract called for him to make $10,000 in 1937.[78] With the formality of accepting terms completed, Cuyler could now concentrate on preparing for his 14th season as a major league player. After the less-than-favorable experience of training in Puerto Rico in 1936, Reds management was able to obtain a release from a contractual obligation to train there once again in 1937.[79] Two days before the first group of Reds departed for Tampa, Cuyler and a few teammates attended the third annual Citizen's Baseball Dinner, which was held at the Hotel Gibson Roof Garden in Cincinnati on March 1.[80]

On March 3, Cuyler, Gene Schott, Lefty Grissom, Benny Frey, Phil

12. A Great Career in Chicago Comes to an End

Weintraub, Les Scarsella and Floyd Moore departed for Tampa with manager Dressen and coach Sheehan. Before this first aggregation of players left Cincinnati, Dressen told them that the next six weeks would consist of the hardest work they had ever done.[81] Once the team reached Tampa and began going through some of the vigorous workouts that Dressen described, Cuyler showed management that he was serious about being a major contributor in 1937. He was the first Cincinnati player to arrive at the playing field every morning.[82] In spite of rumors that Cuyler's role as a player would be reduced in 1937 due to Cincinnati's youth movement, the veteran player approached spring training as he had throughout his career. He was not quite ready to be relegated to the status of a part-time player who was on the roster merely to act in an advisory role for manager Dressen.[83]

Cuyler's dream of maintaining his status as a regular player was deflated during an exhibition game against Detroit at Lakeland, Florida, on April 1. Cuyler suffered a severe injury when he collided with second baseman Alex Kampouris in the sixth inning. The collision between the players occurred when Cuyler snagged a fly to short center field off the bat of Charlie Gehringer.[84] Cuyler was rushed to a hospital, where it was determined that he had suffered a fractured left cheekbone. Dressen was not pleased with the incident since it was the third such collision between infielders and outfielders during Cincinnati's exhibition tour. Dressen put the onus on Kampouris' shoulders because everyone on the field heard Cuyler clearly call for Gehringer's fly ball.[85] Cuyler was expected to miss at least three weeks while his cheekbone mended.[86]

The veteran outfielder recuperated at his home in Harrisville until he rejoined his teammates two days before the season opener on April 18. Even though Cuyler was unable to chew solid food, he appeared as a pinch hitter in an exhibition tilt against Detroit and delivered a key single with the bases loaded that gave Cincinnati a 5–4 victory. Despite his late-game heroics, manager Dressen realized that Cuyler needed more training in order to withstand the rigors of playing nine innings.[87] He did not play in the opener against St. Louis, but he did appear as a pinch hitter during the fourth inning of a game against the Cardinals on April 22.[88] He finally started a game for Dressen on April 28 as Cincinnati defeated Chicago, 10–3. He turned in several excellent fielding plays while covering ground in center field and also delivered two hits. But he did not play in another game until May 2 due to a severe headache. His face also continued to be a bit tender as he still had difficulty eating solid food.[89]

The game that Cuyler played in on April 28 turned out to be Cincinnati's only victory during the first two weeks of the 1937 season. By May 4, the Reds were firmly entrenched in the National League basement with a 1–9 record. Hope that had been borne out of Cincinnati's strong showing in 1936 quickly turned to despair as it became apparent that 1937 was destined to resemble other horrendous efforts throughout the decade. Cuyler returned to the starting lineup and put forward his usual stellar effort in an attempt to pump some life into the listless Cincinnati squad. He tried to lead by example as he boldly threw around his 38-year-old body. In a game against Chicago on May 16, Cuyler scored the winning tally in the ninth inning on Chick Hafey's sacrifice fly. He crashed into catcher John Bottarini at home plate, scoring the run that gave Cincinnati a 3–2 win as Bottarini had to be carried from Crosley Field.[90]

Rumors surrounding Cuyler plying his craft in new surroundings made their way into the press, as hopes of Cincinnati turning around its season became rooted in fantasy. In the middle of July, a story surfaced alleging that Cincinnati management might purchase the International League's Syracuse Chiefs and install Cuyler as the team's manager.[91] A week after this unlikely scenario was discussed in newspapers, speculation arose that New York manager Bill Terry was possibly interested in acquiring Cuyler, but the theory became moot once Terry secured Wally Berger from the Bees. Fans in Pittsburgh were left to wonder why Pie Traynor did not pursue Cuyler after he had failed in his efforts to bring Berger to the Smoky City.[92]

While Cuyler's future was being discussed by various scribes, writer George Kirksey took time to reveal the nervous habits of major league players. Included in Kirksey's study on players' quirks was Cuyler's habit of continuously touching the visor of his cap while in the outfield or at the plate.[93]

Despite trade rumors regarding Cuyler, he remained with Cincinnati throughout the 1937 season. After being benched for a few games in late July and early August, Cuyler went on a tear as a replacement for the injured Ival Goodman in right field. Cuyler smacked 15 hits in 32 at-bats over a span of seven games, good for an average of .469. His hot streak helped raise his batting average from .258 to .284.[94] Yet, Cuyler's consistent play did little to help Chuck Dressen's fortunes as the manager was relieved of his duties on September 12. Former American League star Bobby Wallace managed the squad for the remainder of the season, but Cincinnati posted only a 5–20 record under his stewardship. The team's wretched play during Wallace's time as skipper guaranteed a cellar finish for Cincinnati in 1937. The Reds posted an overall record of 56–98 that left them 40 games behind the National League's pennant winning Giants.

Shortly after Wallace replaced Dressen, Cuyler made a huge announcement regarding his future. On September 21, 1937, Cuyler informed the sporting world that he was retiring from the game effective at the close of the season. He stated that he would be following the game from newspaper box scores like all other fans in 1938. He also claimed that if an opportunity came along to remain in the game as something other than a player, he might consider it. He may have been referring to the possibility of managing since he was considered as a candidate to replace Dressen on a permanent basis in 1938.[95] He reasoned the time was right to walk away from baseball before he alienated the fans by hanging on too long. "I've been active in the big leagues for 15 years," said Cuyler, "and it's my idea to quit while still retaining the friendship of the fans. If there's a chance for me in baseball other than as a player, I might consider it."[96]

Cuyler finished the 1937 season with a .271 average for the Reds. Cuyler's playing time in the outfield was reduced to 117 games due to injury and the emergence of a collection of younger players. After the campaign concluded on October 3, Cuyler became one of the first veteran players on the Cincinnati squad to draw his release. His playing career seemed to be over and his chances of landing the Reds' managerial position appeared remote since Warren Giles wanted to bring Bill McKechnie into the fold as his pilot for the 1938 season.[97] For the first time in nearly two decades, Hazen Cuyler's future was uncertain, as he pondered the possibility that his time in the game he loved had come to an end.

13. The Dream of Becoming a Big League Manager

Cuyler's options for 1938 were reduced somewhat when Cincinnati general manager Warren Giles immediately turned his attention to Boston Bees pilot Bill McKechnie as a viable replacement for the departed Chuck Dressen.[1] With his opportunity to take over as the Reds' skipper quickly dwindling away, Cuyler began to reassess his decision to walk away from the game as an active player after nearly two decades in Organized Baseball. Rumors concerning Cuyler's intentions for the upcoming season were discussed by scribes and fans. In early December, Cuyler made a trip to Milwaukee in order to discuss the possibility of playing for the minor league Brewers in 1938. Cuyler met with Milwaukee manager Al Sothoron at the Schroeder Hotel during the annual minor league meetings.[2] After a brief, businesslike conference between the two men, Cuyler assured Sothoron that he would accept Milwaukee's offer if he was unable to secure a managerial post elsewhere.[3]

It was believed that Cuyler was definitely in the running for minor league managerial positions with Buffalo and Seattle.[4] Another rumor stated that Cuyler would manage the International League's Syracuse entry in 1938.[5] Stories about potential jobs in Buffalo, Seattle and Syracuse never reached fruition as Cuyler revealed his plans to the Alpena Rotary Club on December 28. He stated that he had signed a major league contract to serve as a coach and utility outfielder. He was unable to divulge the name of the team since the squad in question needed to make other roster moves before the deal could be finalized.[6]

On February 2, Cuyler officially signed on with the Brooklyn Dodgers as a substitute outfielder for the 1938 season.[7] His deal called for him to join the Dodgers for spring training on a tryout basis.[8] He was already familiar with some members of Brooklyn's entourage since ex–Chicago teammate Burleigh Grimes was the Dodgers' manager and former Cincinnati general manager Larry MacPhail had just joined the organization in that capacity.

13. The Dream of Becoming a Big League Manager

Cuyler's job title with Brooklyn for the 1938 season was two-fold. Cuyler hoped to appear in at least 100 games as Brooklyn's center fielder.[9] He would also be responsible for offering veteran leadership and tutoring to some of the squad's younger players. It became apparent during the early stages of spring training that Cuyler had been assigned the task of molding ex-first baseman Buddy Hassett into a full-fledged, top-notch outfielder.[10] Cuyler also helped rookie infielder Pete Coscarart improve his batting eye by taking motion pictures of the youngster while he stood in the batter's box.[11] Throughout Brooklyn's spring training session, Cuyler did good work in instilling team spirit in the Dodgers, as he taught Brooklyn's youngsters the nuances of hitting and fielding.[12] He also hit well enough during Brooklyn's exhibition season to justify his inclusion on Grimes' squad for the 1938 season.[13]

Cuyler saw limited action as a starter during April as problems became prevalent for manager Burleigh Grimes before a regular season had even been played. The major source of consternation surrounding Grimes was his prediction that the Dodgers would finish no better than seventh in the National League race in 1938. The comment received a swift reprisal from MacPhail, who stated that if Brooklyn was actually in seventh place on May 15, he would proceed to make drastic changes to the squad and begin a rebuilding process.[14] MacPhail's response led to rumors that Grimes would not finish the season as Brooklyn's manager, but MacPhail quickly rejected the notion that anybody other than Grimes would manage the Dodgers in 1938.[15] MacPhail was forced to reiterate his prediction to Brooklyn's players after a verbal outburst by pitcher Luke Hamlin, who became upset when Grimes removed him from a game at Forbes Field on May 4. MacPhail traveled to Pittsburgh and held a team meeting aimed at putting a stop to the dissension before it was given an opportunity to fester.[16]

"Grimes is the manager of the Brooklyn club," MacPhail declared, "and he will be manager of the club all year. I'll be supporting him right down to the hilt all the way. He was the Brooklyn manager before I took charge at Ebbets Field and he deserved his chance to continue and that chance includes 100 percent support from me.

"I'll be in Brooklyn for a long while and so far I have seen nothing that makes me think that Burleigh won't be there as long as I will. Meanwhile, I can promise this much. Grimes will handle the Dodgers on the field all season. I never had two managers in one season and I don't intend to begin now."[17]

As it turned out, MacPhail and Grimes were accurate when making their early season prognostications. Grimes did complete the season as Brooklyn's manager and the Dodgers did finish in seventh place in the National League with a record of 69–80. Even though excitement did not develop for patrons at Ebbets Field, Brooklyn did make newspaper headlines during various stages of the 1938 season. On June 15, Cincinnati pitcher Johnny Vander Meer tossed his second consecutive no-hitter and defeated the Dodgers, 6–0, at Ebbets Field. Cuyler batted leadoff for the Dodgers and went 0-for-2. Cuyler also drew two walks as Vander Meer was able to gain immortality despite allowing eight free passes during the contest. Once again, Cuyler was on the field when history was made, as Vander Meer became the only pitcher to toss consecutive no-hitters.

Four days after Brooklyn succumbed to Vander Meer, MacPhail put the Dodgers' franchise in the limelight once again when he announced that he had signed Babe Ruth at a salary of $15,000 to coach for the remainder of the 1938 campaign. Ruth's addition to the Dodgers' coaching staff resurrected rumors that Grimes would be looking for employment elsewhere once the season ended. When it was announced that Ruth would hold down a spot in the first base coaches box, fans throughout Flatbush were left to ponder the possibility that the Bambino was being groomed to take over as team skipper.[18]

MacPhail reasoned that the addition of possibly the greatest player in history could not do any further harm to Brooklyn's fortunes. "I want him around because I think he can help the team," said MacPhail. "He was a star for 20 years and I never heard anyone accuse him of making a dumb play. Younger men on this club respecting his reputation, are bound to listen to him. And they'll hustle because they won't want to look bad before the old master. I can't think of any better reason for hiring a coach."[19]

Brooklyn's young players were privileged to be receiving crucial instruction from two of the game's greatest players from the 1920s and 1930s. Cuyler appeared in 82 games for the Dodgers before he was released as a player on September 16, but then re-signed with the squad as a coach. Cuyler was removed from Brooklyn's active roster to make room for catcher Ray Hayworth, who was acquired from Detroit.[20] On September 14, Cuyler recorded his last hit as a major league player, connecting for a single against Cincinnati. He made his final appearance in a game when he pinch hit for pitcher Lee Rogers during the second game of a doubleheader that same day.

Cuyler posted a respectable .273 average during his last season. For his career, Cuyler cultivated a batting average of .321. The star player from Michigan also used his phenomenal speed to great advantage throughout his career, as he smoked 394 doubles, legged out 157 triples, smacked 128 home runs, garnered 2,299 hits, scored 1,305 runs and drove home 1,065 runs. Considered one of the fastest players of his era, Cuyler led the National League in stolen bases on four occasions and finished with a total of 328 career thefts.

As the 1938 season wound down, word came out of Brooklyn that Burleigh Grimes would likely be replaced as the team's manager for 1939. The

13. The Dream of Becoming a Big League Manager

names of Leo Durocher, Frankie Frisch, Rogers Hornsby, Jimmie Wilson, Billy Herman and Kiki Cuyler were thrown into the ring as possible successors to Grimes.[21] When Grimes finally did get the axe in October, Cuyler's name was quickly separated from a list of prospective candidates; stories out of Brooklyn claimed that he might become a manager in the Dodgers' farm system. More specifically, there was talk of Montreal or Milwaukee becoming Brooklyn's top affiliate in 1939, with Cuyler taking the helm of the chief farm team.[22] Another rumor had Cuyler or former Pittsburgh teammate Johnny Gooch being named to replace Chuck Dressen as the manager of Nashville's Southern Association club.[23]

Cuyler finally reached a decision regarding his plans for the 1939 season during December's minor league meetings in New Orleans. Cuyler signed a one-year deal to be the Chattanooga Lookouts' manager in 1939. He replaced former Chicago teammate and skipper Rogers Hornsby, who had managed Chattanooga in 1938. Cuyler's signing was announced during the preliminary phase of the 37th annual convention of the National Association of Professional Baseball Leagues.[24] Cuyler had decided to return to the league where he once won the award for most

Cuyler signed with Brooklyn on February 2, 1938, to serve as a utility outfielder for the upcoming season. He was released from the active roster on September 16 but re-signed as a coach for the campaign's final weeks (courtesy the National Baseball Hall of Fame Library, Cooperstown, New York).

valuable player while playing for Nashville. Shortly after he signed a contract to be the Lookouts' new pilot, team president Joe Engel offered the former National League star effusive praise and stated that Cuyler had a major league job waiting for him if he made good in Chattanooga.[25]

Engel was a crafty and creative executive who was a cross between William Veeck and P.T. Barnum. Engel was willing to try any public relations stunt that would make the trip to Chattanooga's ballpark more enjoyable for Lookouts baseball fans. Commissioner Kenesaw Landis would thwart Engel's 1939 opening day promotional stunt of staging a bull fight before the game. Landis reasoned that a bull fight was too abhorrent, so he forced Engel to come up with a new strategy to bring fans to the park.[26] Such gimmicks were not really necessary since Cuyler's presence slowly increased fan interest in a Chattanooga squad that finished seventh the previous season. During spring training, Cuyler became an immediate hit with the fans due to his methods of handling the team on and off the field. The Lookouts also seemed to have a group of men who were team players with good attitudes.[27]

Engel and Cuyler meshed quite nicely and the Lookouts quickly showed that they planned on contending for the Southern Association pennant in 1939. Chattanooga's players responded positively to Cuyler's managerial methods from the outset; the big bats of Babe Barna, Bill Nicholson and Cuyler also helped catapult the Lookouts into first place in May.[28] Cuyler capably held down an outfield spot in 58 of Chattanooga's games and batted .270 before being forced to the suspended list with a foot injury in late July.[29] Besides doing excellent work during his first year as a manager, Cuyler was also adept at assisting Engel in his various public relations stunts. On May 15, Cuyler stood by Engel's side at the University of Chattanooga, where a faculty committee of stockholders in the club voted against the team president receiving an honorary degree from the college. Engel was denied an honorary M.S. Degree for master of showmanship on the grounds that he did not meet the educational requirements.[30]

Cuyler and Engel were both adorned in a cap and gown when the Chattanooga team president was denied the special degree. Later that day, Birmingham ended the Lookouts 11-game winning streak with a 5–0 shutout.[31] Besides doing solid work as Chattanooga's manager and acting as a perfect foil for Engel, Cuyler was also dedicated to making sure that star outfielder Bill Nicholson received a much deserved promotion to the major leagues. Nicholson appeared in 105 games for Chattanooga in 1939, batting .334 and crushing 23 home runs. Cuyler quickly went to work finding a home for Nicholson in the big leagues. Cuyler sent a letter to Cubs manager Gabby Hartnett that extolled the virtues of Nicholson's ability as a player. After receiving no response from Hartnett, Cuyler sent a second letter that also went unanswered. Cuyler finally appealed to owner Philip Wrigley on behalf of his star player, and the Cubs' executive immediately became involved in negotiations for Nicholson's services.[32]

Team president Joe Engel used all of his public relations savvy to drive up Nicholson's purchase price. Even though Engel's steep asking price was $60,000, five major league scouts were hot on the trail of Chattanooga's star player. Scout Jack Doyle of the Cubs was one of the emissaries keeping track of Nicholson's exploits. Doyle, who quickly gained the inside track to procure Bill's services, set about to finalize a deal with Engel and Cuyler in the team president's office. While the three men conferred on the various aspects surrounding Nicholson's purchase, a little boy holding a sack full of balls barged into the room and interrupted the important meeting.[33]

"Where'd you get those, boy?" Engel asked sternly.

"I got them outside the park, Mr. Engel, like you told me too," replied the young boy as if he was reciting a school lesson verbatim, "but most of 'em came from over the railroad tracks where Bill Nicholson hit 'em in batting practice."

"Get outta' here, you Engel stool pigeon," Doyle screamed at the child as he jumped from his chair.[34]

Even though Doyle was not happy with Engel's chicanery, he still closed the deal and purchased Nicholson for $35,000.[35] When Nicholson found out that he was headed to the National League as a member of the Cubs, he immediately credited Cuyler for the improvement in his game during the 1939 season. Nicholson explained that it was Cuyler who recommended he widen his batting stance. Nicholson had a bad habit of lunging at pitches as he stood deep in the batter's box, but he altered his stance and was taught by Cuyler to ready himself for pitches before they came to home plate. For his part, Cuyler was confident that Nicholson would flourish in Chicago.[36] He was such a big supporter of his former player that when Chicago attempted to farm Nicholson out to San Diego shortly after purchasing him, he protested so vehemently that the Cubs changed their mind.[37]

Engel figured that Chattanooga would start rebuilding for 1940 once Nicholson joined Chicago on August 1. After losing his top player, Cuyler bucked the odds and brought home a Southern Association pennant as Chattanooga clinched the title on the season's final day.[38] The Lookouts were crowned as regular season champions when they defeated the New Orleans Pelicans by scores of 6–2 and 4–2 during a doubleheader, on September 10, while Memphis was beaten by Nashville, 11–3. Cuyler became the first manager to complete a season running the Lookouts since 1933, as he brought Chattanooga home with an 85–65 record.[39] Cuyler's success as a rookie manager was not diminished a bit when Atlanta upset Chattanooga, three games to none, in the Southern Association playoffs. His ascension as a manager in such a short period of time convinced fans in Chicago that he would be the perfect candidate to lead the Cubs in 1940. Cuyler ranked far ahead of a field of contenders in a Chicago newspaper poll that included Charlie Grimm, Rogers Hornsby and current manager Gabby Hartnett.[40]

Fans who realized that the capable Cuyler would eventually move up the managerial ladder would have to be content with him leading Chattanooga once again in 1940.[41] Besides winning the pennant and receiving numerous gifts from grateful Lookouts fans during the season finale on September 10, Cuyler signed a contract to manage the team next season in front of 10,624 cheering Chattanooga fans.[42] During a break from moose hunting in the north woods in late October, Cuyler penned a letter from his home in Harrisville that stated that he was heavily involved in making preparations for the upcoming season. Cuyler believed his squad had a solid mixture of youngsters and veterans, as well as potential prospects who would be given an opportunity to replace departed players.[43]

"We need some power in the outfield and perhaps a couple of infielders and some pitchers," Cuyler said. "I am glad to get Dick Bass back from Washington, but will miss Dick Lanahan and Charley Letchas more than anyone."[44]

Cuyler was at a bit of a disadvantage when Chattanooga opened training camp at DeLand, Florida, in March. He was handicapped by a cracked rib that he suffered when he slipped on some ice at his home in Harrisville a few weeks prior to spring training.[45] In spite of the injury, Cuyler persevered and prepared the Lookouts for another grueling Southern Association pennant battle. Once the season began, followers of other teams in the league started to refer to Chat-

Cuyler brought the 1939 Southern Association pennant to Chattanooga, as the Lookouts finished with an 85–65 record during his inaugural season at the helm. Cuyler's coaching was also crucial in developing power-hitting Bill Nicholson, who was sold to the Chicago Cubs for $35,000 (courtesy the National Baseball Hall of Fame Library, Cooperstown, New York).

tanooga as the "Cuys" in honor of their popular manager.⁴⁶ While Cuyler worked hard to bring another pennant to Chattanooga, Joe Engel continued to use bizarre methods in efforts to increase attendance. Engel considered including "Bingo Night" as an added attraction on Friday evenings, but had a change of heart after he consulted with some other baseball men within the league.⁴⁷

As his Lookouts flexed their muscles during the season's early stages, a story surfaced that again exhibited the depth of Kiki Cuyler's generosity. Various stars from past and present donated awards to be given to members of the National Youth Administration's junior baseball league in Michigan. Cuyler joined other baseball icons, such as Babe Ruth, Ty Cobb, Charlie Gehringer, Nick Altrock, Clark Griffith, Joe McCarthy and Connie Mack, in donating trophies for high achievement in various categories. Cuyler's award was to be presented to the team that had the boy with the most stolen bases in the NYA Michigan baseball league.⁴⁸ As various young speedsters vied to win an award that was aptly named after the greatest baserunner of his generation, Cuyler managed the Southern Association's top players during the annual All-Star Game in July. Cuyler earned the honor of guiding the team against front running Nashville due to the fact that Chattanooga had won the pennant in 1939. Cuyler exhibited ultimate sportsmanship by making sure that every player selected to the squad by the baseball writers played in the game.⁴⁹

Cuyler was unable to recapture the splendid success that Chattanooga experienced in 1939, as the Lookouts finished the 1940 campaign in fourth place with a 73–79 record. Despite being six games below .500, Chattanooga still qualified for the playoffs and met the pennant winners from Nashville. The Volunteers swept Chattanooga in three straight games as they outscored Cuyler's Crew, 29–9, in the short Southern Association playoff series.

Even though Cuyler was not as successful pushing his squad to the top of the standings, he had developed another player who garnered attention from major league teams. Cuyler's 1940 project was an outfielder named Mike Dejan, who previously had aspirations of becoming a pitcher. During the training session in Deland, Dejan worked tirelessly each day in the outfield shagging fly balls as Cuyler stood by his side.⁵⁰

All of this hard work paid huge dividends, as Dejan batted over .400 and was then traded to the Reds on July 4 for $30,000 and another player. Dejan was unable to maintain the .400 pace in the National League, just as Bill Nicholson did one year earlier, as he only batted .188 before being shipped out to Birmingham in August.⁵¹

Cuyler's solid work during his first two seasons running Chattanooga's squad received rave reviews across the country. Shortly after the Southern

Association season ended, a strong rumor surfaced that Cuyler would likely be managing an American Association team in 1941.[52] Cuyler himself speculated that he could be managing a major league team after receiving two years of training in the Southern Association. Once again, Chicago was mentioned as a possible partner for Cuyler's services.[53] Yet, all of this conjecture regarding Cuyler's career ceased to be a story in December, when it was announced that he would return for a third season as the Lookouts' manager.[54]

Even though Cuyler had signed a contract to manage Chattanooga in 1941, his name was linked to the Seattle job, along with Babe Ruth and Gabby Hartnett, after pilot Jack Lelivelt collapsed and died from a heart attack in January.[55] But Cuyler did not matriculate to the northwest and remained in Tennessee to ply his trade. Managing a team at this lower level of baseball involved more than just strategy and player development for Cuyler. From March through September, he was responsible for every aspect of his squad's behavior. He had to make sure that a rookie player had enough sense to wear a tie in the hotel dining room. He had to advise them about tipping bellboys and always made sure that they wrote letters to family at home. Cuyler had to instruct young players on how to catch a bus at the park and was also responsible for conducting calisthenics once every team member arrived on the diamond. Raw rookies were the norm, as Cuyler often had to work with players who did not know enough to tag up before advancing a base after a fly ball was caught in the outfield.[56]

Changes came Chattanooga's way shortly after the 1941 Southern Association began. The concept of fan ownership was abandoned on May 16, when the organization was returned to the Washington Senators as part of their farm system. Joe Engel was permitted to remain as the team president while Cuyler continued as the Lookouts' manager. Engel was also expected to resume his duties as chief scout and manager of the Senators' farm system just as he did when Chattanooga previously served as a Washington affiliate.[57]

Cuyler's team continued to plod along in the middle of the pack as the Southern Association season moved into the summer. Cuyler and his wife Bertha were treated to a special visit in July from their son Harold, who was stationed at Camp Stuart, Georgia, with the 53rd Quartermaster Corps.[58] Harold had enlisted in the Army only months earlier on March 4, 1941, in Saginaw, Michigan.[59] Harold received a furlough from his basic training activities so that he could relax for a few days and spend some time with his parents.

Harold Cuyler's timing turned out to be impeccable since any journey after July to visit his parents would have required making a trip to Chicago. On August 7, Joe Engel announced that Cuyler had been granted his release as the team's manager so that he could join the Cubs' coaching staff. Engel tabbed third baseman Sparky Olsen to replace Cuyler at the helm for Chattanooga during the remainder of the 1941 season.[60] Lookouts fans who bought tickets to watch the game that evening on "Cuyler Night" went home disappointed when rain washed out the contest. No substitute date could be chosen to honor Cuyler since he was leaving immediately to join manager Jimmie Wilson's staff in Chicago.[61] One week prior to Cuyler receiving his release, Engel heaped mounds of praise upon his manager during an interview on a scouting expedition for Washington. Engel considered Cuyler a rare species because he could take a group of green youngsters and mold them into major league prospects in less than a year.[62]

Cuyler joined the Cubs' staff on August 9 as a replacement for Dizzy Dean, who resigned from his post so that he could begin a career as a radio announcer. Cuyler made it back with the Cubs just in time to see current pitcher and former teammate Charlie Root honored by the fans of Chicago for his years of dedicated service.[63] Cubs fans were also excited to see one of the most revered players in team history return to the Windy City after a six-year absence. While patrons discussed how Cuyler fit into the scheme of things within Chicago's hierarchy, writers followed him around to ask about his past exploits. On one occasion, Cuyler was asked to discuss the greatest thrill of his career. He did not choose playing for National league pennant winners or collecting the deciding hit against Walter Johnson in Game Seven of the 1925 World Series. Instead, he selected the game against Pittsburgh that clinched the pennant for Chicago in 1932.[64]

Chicago's newest coach did not choose that particular game because his triple had secured victory and clinched the pennant for the Cubs. Cuyler claimed it was not the actual hit that stirred his emotions, but what happened afterwards. Cuyler's teammates ran out onto the field, picked him up and hoisted the game's hero on their shoulders. As he was being carried off the field, Cuyler looked into the stands, where his son Harold was sitting.[65] Cuyler was deeply touched by Harold's reaction in viewing his father's game-winning exploits. "The look on my boy's face at that moment is unforgettable," said Cuyler, "and afforded me my greatest thrill and the greatest thrill I ever expect to have."[66]

Pennant memories were all that Chicago fans could retain as Cuyler rejoined the organization late in the 1941 season. The Cubs secured a sixth-place finish in the National League race, as they posted a 70–84 record and finished 30 games behind the pennant-winning Dodgers. The Cubs closed out the 1941 campaign by being swept by the crosstown rival White Sox in the Chicago City Series.[67]

Two months after this annual series was completed, the country as a whole and baseball in particular changed forever when the United States entered into World War II after the Japanese attacked Pearl Harbor on December 7. President Franklin D. Roosevelt demanded that baseball continue in 1942 for the good of the nation, while Commissioner Landis went about the task of making sure that the game persevered during these tough times. Changes to the game's structure were made as needed, as security issues changed the plans of many teams for their upcoming spring sessions.

The Cubs' trip to Catalina Island for spring training was a bit different from past years due to the war. Two water taxis were chartered to take Jimmie Wilson's squad to Catalina because the steamship line was out of operation. Before sailing, each player and member of Chicago's management team was asked to give his birthplace and present documentation that offered proof of his American citizenship.[68] Once the Cubs made it to Catalina, they became the final group of guests that took up lodging at the Hotel St. Catherine, which was closing down along with the local theater and golf course. The island, for which the late William Wrigley, Jr., had turned down an offer of $18 million after converting it into a beautiful resort mecca, was no longer a vacationing destination due to the war and submarine threats.[69]

Shortly after the Cubs concluded their training work on Catalina Island and barnstormed across the country on their exhibition tour, several members of the squad visited an air base hospital in Tucson, Arizona. Army jeeps transported seven members of Chicago's team to the hospital that housed disabled soldiers. Included in this group were team trainer Dr. Andy Lotshaw, Bill Nicholson, Vern Olson, Charlie Gilbert, Stan Hack, Tot Pressnell and coach Cuyler.[70] The exhibition tour degraded into a poor proposition for manager Jimmie Wilson as his Cubs struggled mightily and posted a horrible record. Many fans in Chicago believed Wilson was already on a short lease and faced the prospect of being fired if the Cubs struggled coming out of the gate during the 1942 campaign. Some observers claimed that Cuyler had been brought in as a stern warning to Wilson; if the team did not improve, Chicago's ownership would find a pilot who could change the franchise's fortunes.[71] Others believed that Cuyler was hired strictly to work with Nicholson after he slumped terribly during the last 97 games of the 1941 season.[72]

Cuyler's work with Nicholson's batting stance and approach at the plate provided immediate results, as he pushed his batting average up 40 points from the previous year, to .294. Nicholson also smacked 21 home runs and drove in 78 runs. In the meantime, Wilson's work as the Cubs' manager once again produced another sixth-place finish as the Cubs crafted a poor 68–86 record that left them 38 games behind first-place St. Louis. Despite all of the threats that Wilson would be dismissed if the Chicago squad did not improve noticeably, he was brought back to lead Philip Wrigley's troops in 1943. When the 1942 Chicago City Series concluded on the night of October 6, Wilson ended up on the losing end against the White Sox for the second consecutive season, as their rivals clinched the series, four games to two.[73]

Chicago's roster was not overflowing with quality players during Cuyler's first full season as a Cubs coach. Stan Hack and Phil Cavarretta, two performers who played for Chicago when Cuyler left in 1935, still had some pop in their bat seven years later. Youngster Lou Novikoff had a solid sophomore season, while veteran Jimmie Foxx batted only .205 after being claimed off waivers from the Red Sox. Claude Passeau was the pitching staff's ace; he went 19–14 and posted a 2.68 ERA in 1942.

On November 30, Passeau joined Cuyler and former star pitcher Mordecai "Miner" Brown as honored guests at a Bradley Tech banquet in Peoria, Illinois.[74] Patrons who attended the festive dinner were treated to the opportunity of a lifetime as they met three Cubs players whose careers spanned five decades. Several weeks after these men enjoyed an evening with the public, Cubs management announced that the team would hold spring training at French Lick, Indiana, due to travel restrictions brought on by World War II.[75]

A few weeks before Cuyler was scheduled to leave for spring training with the Cubs' contingent, his father George A. Cuyler died on February 3, 1943, at the age of 79. For years, George Cuyler was a revered inhabitant of Harrisville who held numerous public offices in Alcona County.[76] When Hazen Cuyler was a child, George spent countless hours hitting balls to him as he helped his son begin the process of becoming a major league ball player. Hazen had always kept a promise to his father to never drink or smoke and continued to do so even after George Cuyler died. A few weeks after his father was buried, Cuyler left for spring training and prepared to participate in his 24th year in Organized Baseball.

Snow and poor weather wreaked havoc on the Cubs' training plans as they experienced life away from Catalina Island for the first time in many years. When wretched field conditions forced the Cubs to postpone their April 13 exhibition game against Detroit in Vincennes, Indiana, the contest was transferred to George Field, an Army training field located ten miles across the Wabash River in Illinois. Both teams played the game during a snowstorm because more than 5,000 soldiers and civilians had purchased tickets to watch the two teams clash. Chicago and Detroit participated in a five-inning exhibition so that the soldiers could keep thousands of dollars for their recreation fund. The game had special meaning for Kiki Cuyler since his son Harold had graduated from Army training at George Field.[77]

Once the regular season began, Chicago's play had a chilling effect on Windy City baseball fans as the Cubs found themselves in last place with a 12–23 record on May 31. Things were not going particularly well for slugging outfielder Bill Nicholson. Cuyler began to work with Nicholson on his batting deficiencies after he failed to hit a home run during the season's first five weeks. Noticing that Nicholson was holding the bat too close to his body, he worked with the Cubs' star to correct the problem. Bill experienced immediate positive results as he went on a 13-for-31 tear and blasted four homers.[78] Such good work seemed to raise Cuyler's managerial stock in the eyes of Chicago's faithful patrons, who were becoming disgusted with Jimmie Wilson's numerous deficiencies. Fans made life particularly difficult for Wilson during a 10–6 loss to Cincinnati in the first game of a doubleheader at Wrigley Field on June 13. According to *Chicago Sun* writer Edgar Munzel, Wilson was booed relentlessly during the first game before Chicago claimed the nightcap, 4–1.[79] "Wilson stuck it out in the opener," said Munzel, "but when the second game began, he stayed in the shelter of the dugout and Kiki Cuyler appeared on the third-base coaching line."[80]

Chicago fans continued to demand that Wilson be removed as the Cubs' manager when the team embarked on a swing through the East in late June. Some of the rooters were screaming for Pepper Martin to succeed Wilson, while a group of newsboys displayed "Novikoff for Manager" signs. Cuyler, Stan Hack and Bill Terry were also mentioned as possibilities to replace Wilson.[81] On July 13 during an exhibition game at Camp Campbell, coach Cuyler showed that he had not lost his batting eye when he came up as a pinch hitter and delivered a single during the Cubs' 11–0 rout.[82] Some fans pondered whether Cuyler, at the age of 44, would be the perfect complement for Bill Nicholson in Chicago's everyday lineup. Nicholson experienced a breakout season for Chicago in 1943 as he batted .309 and led the National League with 29 home runs and 128 RBIs. Manager Jimmie Wilson experienced some minor success in comparison to past seasons, as Chicago moved up one spot to fifth place and finished the season with a 74–79 record.

Five Cubs fans were vociferous in their support of Cuyler for manager during the season's late stages. The boisterous supporters of Cuyler were arrested during a doubleheader at Wrigley Field on September 26 on charges of disorderly conduct. The pro-Cuyler faction supporters were eventually discharged by Judge Mason S. Sullivan in Town Hall Court. These five enthusiasts were freed but had to promise that they would not be so passionate in the future while campaigning for the appointment of their favorite former player as Chicago's skipper.[83] But Cuyler figured to have stiff competition. A few weeks after the season ended, Bill Sweeney, Bill Terry, Bill Jurges, Larry Gilbert, Charlie Grimm, Jimmy Dykes, Leo Durocher, Wilson and Cuyler were all named as candidates to lead the Cubs in 1944.[84]

It's difficult to say whether Cuyler was ever given serious consideration to manage Chicago in 1944. When he finally announced his intentions for the following season, many fans believed that Chicago's ownership probably told Kiki his chances were slim.[85] On the evening of October 23, Atlanta Crackers president Earl Mann announced that Cuyler had signed a two-year contract to manage the Southern Association team in both 1944 and 1945. Mann was ecstatic that he was able to secure a man of Cuyler's pedigree and ability to manage the Crackers in 1944. Mann also stated that the Cuyler signing indicated that Atlanta planned on winning a pennant during the upcoming season.[86] Cuyler replaced Al Leitz and Harry Hughes, who split the season managing Atlanta in 1943. Leitz finished fourth in the season's first half and Hughes brought the Crackers home in last place during the campaign's second phase.[87]

Cuyler returned to managing at the minor league level during a time when teams had to scramble to fill their rosters due to youngsters replacing war bound major league players.

Atlanta's aggregation suffered crucial losses prior to the 1944 campaign when news reached Cuyler that Marshall Mauldin and Mickey Haslin were joining the Army while Dewey Adkins had decided to remain on his farm in Nebraska.[88] Crackers team president Earl Mann attempted to fill some of these roster voids by taking a scouting trip to Cuba in late January. The excursion was aptly named a "Mann Hunt," as Atlanta's president claimed the brand of ball played in Cuba's professional leagues was just as good as that of any American semi-professional team. Mann's trip was a huge success from a numbers standpoint, as he added 10 players to Atlanta's depleted roster.[89]

"I saw all kinds of players and we signed 10," Mann said. "We have hopes all will report. One of them is a big six-foot, 200-pound right-handed pitcher, who looks as if he can win in the Southern Association. They are all draft exempt for six months, so we'll be sure of having them for the entire season. Two are professionals and the rest are amateurs."[90]

As Mann accomplished his goal of restocking the Crackers' roster, manager Cuyler went about the task of raising fan interest throughout Atlanta prior to the season opener. Cuyler took to the pulpit at Atlanta's Cascade Methodist Church, where he talked about baseball and the human race. Cuyler reasoned that the human race was made up of a diverse group of people. For this reason, there were as many different kinds of ballplayers as there were performers on a diamond. Cuyler also believed that these dissimilar baseball players were all religious, even if they did not wear their religion on their sleeves.[91] On April 11, Cuyler spoke during an event held by the Optimists Club of Atlanta. He entertained the members with anecdotes about the game and also showed his own home movies of a previous spring training trip to Catalina Island with the Cubs.[92]

Cuyler did great work as Atlanta's manager in 1944. Despite being forced to use 41 different players, Cuyler brought the Crackers home in second place during both halves of the Southern Association season. Unfortunately, this performance did not translate into a playoff appearance since only the pennant winners under the split-season format appeared in the post-season. Nashville and Memphis were afforded that honor as Cuyler's former Volunteers squad, for whom he played over two decades ago, claimed the Southern Association title by defeating the Chicks, four games to three. As had been the case during his previous managerial stint with Chattanooga, Cuyler worked tirelessly developing a young player who possessed the ability to become a major league ballplayer. Eighteen-year-old Billy Goodman absorbed Cuyler's teaching and batted .336 while playing his first season of professional ball. Cuyler also received recognition for his solid work in December, when he finished second behind Albany's Jimmy "Rip" Collins in voting by *The Sporting News* for top manager among the smaller minor circuits.[93]

The Southern Association's decision to eliminate the split-season concept would be beneficial for upper tier franchises like Atlanta, which were expected to contend for a title in 1945. It quickly became obvious to fans throughout the Southern Association that Cuyler's squad was poised to take control of the pennant race from the outset. On many occasions, Cuyler was forced to deal with circumstances that no major league manager would ever allow in his job description. Prior to a doubleheader against Little Rock on May 13, the Crackers were forced to borrow uniforms and other equipment from their opponent because Atlanta's equipment trunks failed to arrive with the team. Atlanta had only four borrowed bats to use during the twinbill, while southpaw relievers John Burrows and Darwin Cobb were forced to wear right-handed gloves. Manager Cuyler was also forced to coach his squad from the box at third base in dress shoes.[94]

Cuyler also did not have teenage superstar Billy Goodman on his squad in 1945 due to the young man's entry into the military. Atlanta's manager did not let this inconvenience prevent him from fielding a team that competed passionately in every game. Cuyler was blessed to have two stalwart performers who pushed their way to the forefront with breakthrough seasons in 1945. Veteran minor league pitcher Lew Carpenter had a phenomenal season for Cuyler in his final year playing Organized Baseball. Carpenter went 22–2 on the year and posted an ERA of 1.82. On the offensive side of the ledger, Cuban shortstop Tony Ordenana had a breakout season after several uninspiring campaigns in minor league baseball at various levels. Ordenana batted .303 for Atlanta in 1945, as Cuyler praised his star shortstop and rated him as the best at that position in the Southern Association.[95] "If we had him last year we would have won the pennant — and by ten games," proclaimed Cuyler.[96]

Cuyler's 1945 Atlanta Crackers had little trouble winning the Southern

Association pennant as they led the race throughout the summer and finished on top at season's end with a 94–46 record. Fans who cheered their favorite players throughout the season at Ponce de Leon Park received a jolt of disappointment when New Orleans upset Atlanta in the first round of the playoffs, four games to one. Some experts believed the Crackers' defeat could be directly attributed to the fact that slugging outfielder Connie Creedon quit the club during the season's final week.[97]

Despite their surprising defeat at the hands of New Orleans, the 1945 season was a rousing success for the Crackers. Cuyler was immediately rewarded for his good work; in mid–October, president Earl Mann secured Kiki's signature on a contract to manage Atlanta for the next three seasons.[98] Cuyler and his fellow Southern Association managers would be embarking into new territory since the league would be playing under a new AA classification after a unanimous vote by club owners in August of 1945.[99]

The Crackers convened on March 3, 1946, for spring training in Gainsville, Florida, to begin the long journey of defending their title from the previous season. Once again, manager Cuyler was handicapped by the fact that many members of his 1945 pennant-winning squad were no longer on the roster. Pitchers John Burrows, Lew Carpenter and Dick Mauney all departed as Cuyler looked for new arms to stabilize his mound corps.[100] Shortstop Tony Ordenana was not in Atlanta's camp either, as he opted to play for Puebla of the Mexican League in 1946.[101]

Prior to the Crackers' season opener, Commissioner Happy Chandler visited Atlanta and spoke to a group of fans. During the gathering, Chandler sang "My Old Kentucky Home," Governor Ellis Arnall belted out a version of "As Time Goes By" and Kiki Cuyler beautifully soloed on "Can't Begin To Tell You." All three men insisted there was no significance to their choice of tunes.[102]

Cuyler's prowess as a singer was indisputable, but it was his ability as Atlanta's manager that truly shined in 1946. The Crackers barreled through the competition in the Southern Association race and made a spirited effort at winning 100 games. Things went so well for Atlanta that they were able to pull off unbelievable plays even when an opposing batter received a walk. In an August game against Little Rock, the Crackers pulled off a double play after the Travelers' Butch Nieman drew a walk. With Bill Burgo on first base and Bob Mavis on second, Nieman reached first after a close pitch on a three-and-two count was called ball four. Atlanta catcher Les McGarity, thinking the pitch was a strike, threw to second in an effort to retire Burgo. After seeing the toss go to second, Mavis broke for the plate but was thrown out at home. Burgo, who then strayed too far off second base after reaching it safely, was likewise caught in a rundown and tagged out. Nieman ended up on second base after drawing the walk that started the double play.[103]

The Crackers fell a few games short of hitting the 100-win mark, but they still copped the Southern Association pennant with a 96–58 record. Cuyler's men then pulled off the goal that every team in the league strived to achieve when they won the Association's playoff championship. The Crackers had to battle every step of the way as New Orleans and Memphis extended each series the full seven games. The Crackers did not seem to have much energy left for the Dixie Classic battle; Dallas swept Atlanta in four straight games. Nonetheless, Cuyler's managerial style was being hailed throughout the game as the former star outfielder achieved tangible results in his first three seasons as Atlanta's manager. Cuyler was not considered a strict disciplinarian, as he gave his players a free hand as long as the team was winning. Whenever a player started to exhibit a chronic, lackluster effort on the field, Cuyler quietly investigated the man's off-field behavior and doled out discipline if he found conditions were not right.[104]

"A bunch of grown men should have enough common sense to keep themselves in condition at all times to play winning baseball," stated Cuyler. "If they don't, it's my firm belief that's where the manager should step in and take a hand."[105]

Cuyler also did not feel that a bench manager should remain in the dugout while navigating his team. He insisted upon being in the coaching box during every inning so that he could guide and encourage his players from the third base line.[106] As it turned out, Cuyler's players needed all the inspiration they could handle during the 1947 season; the Crackers took a step backwards after winning two consecutive pennants. Atlanta finished in fifth place and failed to make the playoffs, going 73–78 in the process. Despite the disappointing showing in the league standings, Cuyler had once again molded a young man into a bonafide star. Cuyler's project in 1947 was Charley Trippi, a football player who had just received All-American honors as a halfback for the University of Georgia. One month into the season, as Trippi made the jump from a college campus to Class-AA baseball with Atlanta, Cuyler praised the solid work ethic of the rookie player who had previously enjoyed immense success on the gridiron.[107]

> He knows his weaknesses and he works on them. He has the pitchers throw to certain spots in batting practice, which is a little unusual for a rookie, who usually likes them where they can knock them over the fence.
>
> Charley is definitely showing improvement. He knows his way around as far as athletic competition is concerned and the riding he takes from opposing benches and some of the fans doesn't bother him in the least.
>
> He's a fine boy and his teammates are pulling for him. He's no pop-off and has the knack of saying the right thing at the right time, something you don't always find in a boy who has had as much publicity and made as much money out of football as he has.[108]

Cuyler's confidence in Trippi's ability was well founded, as the star football player appeared in 106 games for Atlanta in 1947 and batted .334. His season receiving instruction and guidance from a baseball icon ended up being Trippi's lone foray into playing professional ball, as he opted to concentrate exclusively on playing football for the Chicago Cardinals. Cuyler probably wished that Trippi had continued in his endeavor as a two-sport athlete for one more year. In 1948, the Crackers slid one spot in the final standings to sixth place, as Cuyler's squad could muster nothing better than a 69–85 record. Amid losing games during a tough season, Cuyler continued to work hard to develop his players so that they could better their careers. In June, Cuyler even offered batting advice to Nashville's Carmen Mauro. Mauro listened intently to the sage counsel and expertly applied Cuyler's tip to loosen his grip on the bat, going 4-for-9 in two games against Atlanta.[109]

Rumors that circulated throughout Atlanta indicated that Cuyler would not be returning as the Crackers' pilot in 1949. In Kiki's home state of Michigan, faithful fans started circulating a petition in late July that urged the appointment of Cuyler as manager of the Tigers in place of current skipper Steve O'Neill. George Killmaster, Chesaning High School's athletic director, circulated these petitions throughout Harrisville, Chesaning and Flint.[110] When the Crackers reached Chattanooga on September 1 for a series against the Lookouts, Cuyler announced that he would not return to the club for the 1949 season. This seemed to be news to president Earl Mann, who stated that Cuyler had not discussed any such decision with him. Mann also thought it strange that his manager would make this announcement without consulting him.[111]

Another announcement regarding Cuyler's status as Atlanta's manager quickly found its way into sports page headlines when he resigned from that post with two weeks left in the season.[112] The rumor mill immediately went into overdrive as pundits pondered whether Cuyler was finally going to receive a chance to manage a major league team. A story that suggested that Cuyler would be chosen to lead Detroit in 1949 continued to pop up at the conclusion of the season.[113]

As it turned out, this prediction became irrelevant when the management of the Red Sox made an announcement in October. After Boston manager Joe McCarthy announced the resignation of coach Del Baker, he immediately called up the Fenway Park offices to notify officials that Cuyler had been signed to replace him.[114] After being apart for almost 20 years since their glory days in Chicago from 1928 to 1930, McCarthy and Cuyler were coming together once again with the goal of bringing an American League pennant to the city of Boston.

14. An Enduring Legacy and Baseball's Highest Honor

Joe McCarthy was not the only person connected to the Red Sox' franchise with whom Kiki Cuyler had a past relationship. The Red Sox were run by former star shortstop Joe Cronin, who acted as the team's general manager. Cuyler and Cronin were teammates on the Pirates for parts of two campaigns before both players were jettisoned after the 1927 season. Cuyler had played briefly with fellow coach Johnny Schulte while both men were members of the Cubs in 1929. Cuyler was also well acquainted with Billy Goodman, who had played for him in Atlanta until Boston purchased the youngster for $75,000 in 1947. Shortly after Cuyler was chosen to be a member of the Red Sox' coaching staff, the former major league outfielder stated that he was returning to the big leagues to work for the best manager he had ever had. Cuyler also revealed that Goodman was the greatest player he had ever developed while managing at the minor league level.[1]

Boston was considered a legitimate pennant contender following its strong season in 1948. The Red Sox battled Cleveland and New York down to the wire as two games separated all three teams when the American League schedule was completed. When the season concluded on October 3, Boston and Cleveland stood on top of the league with identical records of 96–58. Boston's successful campaign came to a bittersweet ending on October 4, when the Indians earned a spot in the World Series by defeating the Red Sox, 8–3, in a playoff game at Fenway Park. Cuyler was joining a squad loaded with star talent that was one of the favorites to win it all in 1949. Besides Goodman, the superior aggregation of Red Sox consisted of Ted Williams, Bobby Doerr, Dom DiMaggio, Johnny Pesky, Vern Stephens and Mel Parnell.

Shortly after Boston began spring training at Sarasota, Florida, Cuyler and others connected with the organization were treated to vintage sarcasm on the part of manager Joe McCarthy. During an exhibition game against the

Phillies in Clearwater, McCarthy and Philadelphia president Robert Carpenter engaged in a heated argument over Boston's decision not to bring Williams, Doerr, Stephens and DiMaggio along for the trip. McCarthy claimed that since Phillies management had never called up the Red Sox to find out who would be making the trip, Carpenter had no one but himself to blame for advertising the fact that these men would be playing.[2] McCarthy's comments to reporters following this confrontation brought back great memories for Cuyler of their days together in Chicago, when Joe's comments made good newspaper copy. "I brought Williams over here last year and the Philly pitchers walked him three times," said McCarthy. "If the Clearwater folks want to see Ted walk, they can come over to Sarasota and see him for nothing any evening when he goes for a stroll with the baby."[3]

Cuyler's excitement and enthusiasm over the upcoming season became somewhat tempered when his mother, Anna R. Cuyler, died at the age of 82 on April 13, 1949.[4] As had been the case when his father died six years ago, the game became a secondary matter for Hazen while he spent time grieving with his family.

After his mother's funeral, Cuyler returned to the Red Sox ready to help the team in any way that he could. Early returns surrounding Joe McCarthy's squad indicated that the Red Sox needed all of the help they could muster. The Red Sox finally pushed their record above .500 on May 23, when they shut out Detroit, 4–0. When they reached the unofficial halfway point of the season on July 4, the Red Sox stood in fifth place with a 35–34 record.

The Red Sox' fortunes did not seem destined to get much better when they lost the first contest of an Independence Day doubleheader against the league-leading Yankees in a most bizarre way. New York was holding on to a tight 3–2 lead as the game entered the top of the ninth. After Vic Raschi struck out Dom DiMaggio, Johnny Pesky and Ted Williams followed with back-to-back singles that left runners on first and third. Boston then loaded the bases when Vern Stephens worked out a walk against Raschi. As Al Zarilla strode to the plate, a gale force wind suddenly started a small dust storm at Yankee Stadium. Zarilla connected for a single to Cliff Mapes in right field, but third base coach Cuyler held up Pesky at third because the dust prevented him from seeing the play clearly. Charging in from his deep position in right field, Mapes fielded the sharply hit drive and threw a perfect strike to Yogi Berra that forced Pesky, who got a late start running, at the plate.[5] Raschi finally recorded the game's final out when Mapes corralled Bobby Doerr's liner to right.

When New York claimed the second game of the holiday twinbill, the Red Sox found themselves trailing the first-place Yankees by 12 games. After hitting their nadir on the season and looking like a major flop, the Sox went on a relentless streak, tearing through the American League at a 61–22 pace for the remainder of the campaign. The Red Sox finally supplanted New York from first place when they completed a two-game sweep at Fenway Park and then won a single contest at Yankee Stadium on September 26.

The next day, McCarthy, along with Cuyler and Johnny Schulte, made a trip to Martinsburg, West Virginia, to attend a special ceremony at the Rosedale Cemetery.[6] McCarthy was asked to dedicate a monument that honored former major leaguer Hack Wilson, who had died in 1948. The stone monument over Wilson's grave, which was made of tapered granite, stood ten feet high and 30 inches wide at the square of the base. The monument featured an etching of crossed baseball bats with the inscription: "One of baseball's immortals, Lewis R. (Hack) Wilson, rests here.[7]

After the unveiling, McCarthy gave a brief speech about Wilson's achievements. "To me, along with the sorrow I experience in thinking of Hack," said McCarthy, "comes the pleasant memory of happy days with him. This monument we unveil to his memory recalls great accomplishments in baseball. His record of 56 home runs in 1930 speaks for itself."[8]

When McCarthy made the trip with Cuyler and Schulte to Martinsburg to honor Wilson, his team looked to be in great shape thanks to three straight victories against New York's powerhouse squad. The Red Sox held a tight one-game edge after they knocked New York from the top spot for the first time in months. When Casey Stengel's Yankees rolled into Boston for a season-ending two-game set at the beginning of October, the Red Sox still held the lead and needed only one win in order to claim the American League pennant. The job became tougher for McCarthy's team after New York claimed the series opener on October 1, 5–4. Red Sox fans at Fenway Park watched a potential World Series trip slip through their fingers as the Yankees also defeated Boston, 5–3, on October 2, to win the pennant. New York finished on top of the American League standings with a 97–57 record, while Boston fell one game short with a mark of 96–58.

After being involved in the kind of frenzied pennant race that he had become accustomed to during his long career as a player, Cuyler decided to sign a contract to come back as Joe McCarthy's third base coach in 1950. While he was making this decision about his baseball future, son Harold resigned as the business manager of the Gainesville team in the Florida State League.[9] Harold had taken over the team's business affairs after giving it a shot as a player for Gainesville in 1948 and 1949. He had minimal success making a comeback since he last played minor league ball at the lower level many years earlier. Harold returned to his home in Harrisville, where his father once again would spend another off-season doing what he loved before the season began in late February.

14. An Enduring Legacy and Baseball's Highest Honor

Cuyler was engaged in one of those activities when he suffered a heart attack while ice fishing in Glennie, Michigan, on February 2.[10] Cuyler was rushed to Alpena General Hospital for treatment.[11] He was placed under the care of Dr. Roy A. Marshall, who stated that Cuyler was in good spirits and doing well after doctors attempted to dissolve a blood clot in his leg on Feb-

When Cuyler was a youngster, the pursuits of swimming and fishing were the only two sports he loved more than playing baseball. In this photograph, Cuyler shows off the rewards from a highly successful day of trout fishing (courtesy the *Alcona County Review*).

ruary 4. Marshall told Cuyler that he might be forced to delay his departure for spring training, which was scheduled to begin on February 20 in Florida. Marshall ordered Cuyler to stay in bed for ten days and see no visitors.[12] His condition improved considerably to the point that he was permitted to leave the hospital and return to his home in Harrisville.[13]

Cuyler seemed to be on the road to recovery while resting at his home when he suffered a relapse on the afternoon of February 11. His condition became so serious that he was placed in an ambulance and rushed to the University of Michigan Hospital at Ann Arbor. As the ambulance transported him to the hospital in Ann Arbor, Cuyler died.[14] Varicose veins, from which Cuyler suffered during the latter stages of his career, formed the blood clot in his leg that contributed to a fatal heart attack.[15] Dr. James Ludwig, a University Hospital physician, stated that Cuyler likely died about ten minutes outside of Ann Arbor.[16]

The northern Michigan town of Harrisville paid one final tribute to its favorite son at his funeral on Tuesday, February 14. Services were held at St. Anne's Catholic Church at 10 o'clock in the morning, before the body was taken to St. Anne's Cemetery for burial.[17]

Stirring tributes poured in from the world of baseball after Cuyler's untimely death. Longtime Cubs scout Jack Doyle gave Cuyler one of the highest compliments imaginable when he referred to him as a right-handed Ty Cobb. Doyle also rated Cuyler as the most graceful player of all time. He believed that Cuyler could do more things with a glove than Cobb, could throw better than the "Georgia Peach," and could pick up ground balls in the outfield like an infielder. The only criticism that Doyle leveled at Cuyler was that he was too gentlemanly. Doyle reasoned that Cuyler lacked Cobb's drive and aggressiveness since he was so soft spoken, polite and polished both on the field and off.[18] "Cobb was ornery and fierce," recalled Doyle, "and that's where Cuyler didn't match him. But he was virtually a carbon copy in other respects."[19]

Doyle was not holding Cuyler's lack of ruthlessness against him in making this comparison to Cobb. Most men who had played the game during the first five decades of the 20th century were destined to fall short when compared to Cobb regarding this particular character trait. Doyle concluded his comparison by acknowledging that Cobb had a bit more speed than Cuyler, plus an uncanny ability for breaking for the ball at the proper time and garnering an extra base when he saw fit.[20]

"He had that, plus aggressiveness that was unmatched," declared the veteran scout, "but it isn't right to say that the mold was broken after Cobb came along. There was another Cobb—a right-handed Ty Cobb—and that was Cuyler."[21]

Cuyler died of a heart attack at the age of 51 on February 11, 1950. This photograph shows his casket being carried from the Cuyler home on Church Street in Harrisville (courtesy the *Alcona County Review*).

Red Sox general manager Joe Cronin's praise for his former teammate in Pittsburgh and most recently, as a coach on the Red Sox staff, fell in line with Doyle's comments. Cronin described Cuyler as gentlemanly and kind, both in baseball and other aspects of his life. Cronin's remarks revealed the depth of Cuyler's willingness to help a rookie player when he needed instruction. "He was one of the finest and cleanest living fellows I ever met in baseball," said Cronin. "Cuyler was an established star when I joined the Pirates in 1925 but he was always willing to help. He'd answer questions and show you how to solve your problems."[22]

When the Red Sox reached Sarasota for the start of spring training, Cronin and Joe McCarthy announced that former American League manager Steve O'Neill would replace Cuyler as the team's third base coach. In a bit of a sad, ironic twist, O'Neill was named to assume the reins as Boston's pilot in June, when McCarthy resigned and officially retired as a big league skipper. Pirates scout Claude Dietrich believed that Cuyler always had aspirations of being a major league manager. He reasoned that Cuyler would have been named as McCarthy's replacement if he were still alive, since Kiki had joined the coaching staff in 1949 to be groomed for that purpose.[23]

There was no disputing the list of Hazen "Kiki" Cuyler's accomplishments in baseball. He was repeatedly praised for his gentlemanly demeanor and willingness to offer assistance to fellow players. Outside of baseball, Cuyler conducted himself as a valuable member of society. In this respect, Cuyler followed in his father's footsteps as a revered member of the Harrisville community who offered tireless service to his fellow man.

In the 1930s, Cuyler started the "Bick Club," which eventually morphed into a group known as the "Harrisville Goodfellows." Cuyler and other members of the club collected money from people on Main Street every December and then used the donations to help underprivileged local children enjoy a traditional Christmas. He was also the founding member of the Harrisville Lions Club and acted as the driving force behind the Lions Club Minstrel Show, which was a rousing success for eight straight years before his death. He was a charter member of the Alcona County Sportsmen's Club, had an association with the Alpena Council, Knights of Columbus, and also belonged to the St. Anne Holy Name Society in Harrisville. He also utilized his passion for singing as a member of the St. Anne Catholic Church choir and always attended Sunday Mass, even during some of Harrisville's more brutal winter days.[24]

Cuyler was a family oriented man who believed in hard work. He liked to fix things around the house and always looked after matters for both his parents and his wife Bertha.[25] Cuyler's legacy was defined by his caring, giving nature. In 1951, during a reunion of the 1925 World Champion Pirates, Cuyler was honored posthumously along with other deceased team members, which included team president Barney Dreyfuss, vice-president Sam Dreyfuss, coaches Chick Fraser and Jewel Ens, secretary Sam Watters and assistant trainer George Asten.[26] Current Pirates executive Branch Rickey held a moment of silence for all of these men at a special luncheon in the team's honor, before former Pirates Bill McKechnie, Fred Clarke and Pie Traynor addressed the crowd.[27]

Stories surrounding Cuyler's playing career continued to arise. In 1958, Ralph McGill, sports editor for the *Atlanta Constitution,* reminisced about his days as a Vanderbilt law student, when Cuyler played for Nashville in 1923. McGill claimed that Cuyler was responsible for his decision to give up the law profession and become a sportswriter. While at Vanderbilt, Ralph sat in classes and daydreamed about the game when he should have been learning about torts and contracts. Visions of Cuyler on a diamond consumed McGill, as teachers like Judge Ed Seay and Judge John Bell Keeble struggled to keep the young man's attention.[28] After weeks of this nonproductive routine, McGill reasoned that it made more sense to go watch Cuyler in person, as he decided to trade in writing legal briefs for keeping a box score.[29]

Circumstances surrounding Cuyler's final season as a player in Pittsburgh continued to be debated long after his death; the true, inside story about his disagreement with manager Donie Bush never rose to the surface. Cuyler, for his part, never seemed interested in discussing the controversy once he re-established his credentials as a great player in Chicago. Cuyler remained modest to a fault when he was questioned on the subject by writer Frederick Lieb a few years prior to his death. Cuyler refused to lash out at Bush, as Lieb gathered information for a book he was writing that focused on the Pittsburgh franchise's history. "You know, Barnhart was a real good hitter," said Cuyler, "but not too good in the field. It was really a case of one player getting hurt and another getting in there and going so good that he stayed.

"While I was in the lineup I played between the two Waners, the greatest fielding outfield I ever had the good fortune to be with. We weren't together long, but I believe if I hadn't been released to Chicago there is no telling what records this trio could have compiled had we held together for a span of years."[30]

Donie Bush's approach to repeated questioning about this dispute ran in stark contrast to Cuyler's. Whereas Cuyler wanted to close this chapter on his life, Bush seemed more willing to offer new insights about their dispute. In 1947, Bush sat down with Pittsburgh sportswriter Les Biederman to chat about his new role as president of the Pirates' Indianapolis farm team. When the discussion turned to Bush's feud with Cuyler in 1927, the former Pittsburgh manager willingly gave his opinion of Cuyler and also explained why he resigned as the team skipper in 1929.[31]

> You know. I wanted to resign right after that 1927 season. I wasn't too happy, but Barney Dreyfuss talked me into staying. The Cuyler incident was one of those things. I didn't think he was a good player at the time and I thought he was trying to run things, so I didn't use him.
> The fans thought I was mistreating him and they came to Forbes Field with banners shrieking "We Want Cuyler," and they certainly made life miserable.
> Barney was a great baseball man, one of the best that ever lived, but somehow we didn't hit it off too good. Barney often came into the clubhouse and I didn't think he should have.
> He didn't like it when I told him that. Once his son, Sam, told me I had offended his father and I told Sam I was sorry if I hurt his feelings, but that's the way I felt about the clubhouse.
> This undercurrent went on for two more years and finally, in August of 1929, even though the Pirates were up in the race, I told Barney I was quitting at the end of the season.

"Why not now?" he asked.
I said NOW, and that's how it was.³²

Bush elaborated further on Cuyler when Nashville writer Fred Russell cornered him 11 years later during the spring of 1958, while Indianapolis was conducting spring training in Hollywood, Florida. Russell wanted to hear Bush's side of the story since Cuyler had never cleared up the issue when pressed by the writer during his time as a Southern Association manager.³³ Bush claimed that he benched Cuyler during the 1927 season in order to maintain team discipline. He insisted that he had great respect for Cuyler as a player, admiring his ability to stay in great shape. He claimed that Kiki's main problem that year was his bullheadedness. His combative nature led to his benching after a confrontation between player and manager over Cuyler's bad habit of making high throws from his outfield position, which often eluded the cutoff man and allowed runners to take an extra base.³⁴

"One day in early August," said Bush, "in a close game, the opposing club had runners on first and third, with one out. The batter flied to Cuyler. He threw toward the plate, too high for a cutoff, and the runner on first advanced to second. From there he scored on a single. That run beat us.

"When Cuyler came in to the bench, I said to him: 'Won't you ever learn to throw the ball low?'

"He said: 'If you don't like the way I play, get somebody else.'

"I said: 'I will.' And I did."³⁵

Two years after Bush divulged this information to Russell, former Pirate Paul Waner corroborated his former manager's story. Waner was interviewed by writer Nick Robertson at his Florida home on the eve of the first game of the 1960 World Series between the Pirates and the Yankees. The Pirates were making their first trip to a Fall Classic since Waner's squad was swept by Ruth and Gehrig in 1927. Waner confirmed the course of events surrounding the confrontation between Cuyler and Bush over his habit of missing the cut off man. Waner also discussed how Cuyler fumed as Bush moved his players around in the batting order early in the season. Waner remembered one particular exchange, when Bush reminded Cuyler that the team was winning games and that it was the goal of everyone involved to win a pennant. Waner mused that his former teammate was likely annoyed over moving all over the outfield because of the presence of the Waners. Paul's opinion regarding the outfield trio was similar to Cuyler's, since he too considered it a fairly solid unit.³⁶

Paul Waner was the first member of this stellar outfield corps, which performed for only a few months together in Pittsburgh, to gain induction into baseball's most exclusive club. Waner was inducted into the Baseball Hall of Fame in 1952. Eleven years later, Cuyler was honored in his home state of Michigan for his athletic accomplishments. Cuyler, along with former Tigers pitcher Tommy Bridges and Guy Houston, Northern Flint High School's legendary football coach, were all inducted into Michigan's Sports Hall of Fame during a testimonial dinner on May 23, 1963.[37] Five years later, Cuyler finally received baseball's highest honor as the final member of Pittsburgh's great 1927 outfield to gain immortality in Baseball's Hall of Fame. Cuyler was selected to join the game's greatest players one year after Lloyd Waner gained entry in 1967.

On January 23, 1968, Joe "Ducky" Medwick was the only player who received enough support from the Baseball Writers' Association to be inducted at Cooperstown's shrine in July. On January 28, the Veterans' Committee held its vote and added Cuyler and 1925 World Series foe Goose Goslin as members of the class of 1968. After the vote was taken, former commissioner and current committee chairman Ford Frick announced that both Cuyler and Goslin had been unanimous choices of his caucus. Goslin and Cuyler became the 109th and 110th players to receive the highest honor bestowed on a major league ball player.[38]

Following the announcement that Cuyler was joining fellow greats in the Hall of Fame, Les Biederman of *The Pittsburgh Press* stated that Cuyler's election was richly deserved. Former teammate Pie Traynor remembered Cuyler as a complete player, a four-letterman who could hit, run, throw and field.[39]

A crowd of 3,500 baseball fans showed up at Cooperstown on July 22 to see Medwick, Goslin and Cuyler gain induction into the Hall of Fame. Previous inductees Frankie Frisch, Lefty Grove, Pie Traynor, Charlie Gehringer, Ray Schalk, Joe Cronin, Zach Wheat, Max Carey, Edd Roush, Sam Rice, Heinie Manush, Casey Stengel, Lloyd Waner and Red Ruffing were all on hand to watch Commissioner William "Spike" Eckert greet and welcome the new members. Members of Cuyler's family who witnessed the grand ceremony included his widow Bertha, son Harold, daughter Kelly Kruttlin, son-in-law Ted Kruttlin, Sr. and two grandchildren.

When Bertha Cuyler was handed the plaque on behalf of her deceased husband, she made a stirring remark in describing the man who had been a fan favorite in Pittsburgh and Chicago during his illustrious career.[40] "I know my husband would be very proud today," said Bertha Cuyler. "Baseball was his life and it was a good life."[41]

In addition to Kiki Cuyler's inclusion in the Hall of Fame, the former star player's legacy has endured and remained vital in other ways. Since 1929, the player deemed to be the most valuable in the Michigan American Legion State Tournament has received an award named after Cuyler. Hal Newhouser,

Cuyler was inducted into the Baseball Hall of Fame on July 22, 1968. In this photograph, Cuyler's widow Bertha is flanked by fellow inductees Ducky Medwick, to the left, and Goose Goslin, to the right. Hall of Fame executive Ed Stack is standing to the far left (courtesy the *Alcona County Review*).

Milt Pappas, Merv Rettenmund and Steve Avery were all past winners who went on to play major league baseball.[42] In 2008, a section of Highway M-72 in Alcona County was renamed the "Hazen Shirley 'Kiki' Cuyler Memorial Highway" in his honor.[43] The bar that son Harold opened in Harrisville after his father's death remains in business, although the family ended its affiliation with the establishment. "Ki Cuyler's Sports Bar and Grill" remains a destination for locals and visitors interested in visiting the building that once was Hazen's childhood home.

Baseball historians and youths alike can still learn Cuyler's tips on base stealing if they are willing to do the research. In the 1930s, he provided expert instruction in *Kiki Cuyler's Rules for Base Stealing*, a book that was put out by the Sears, Roebuck Company. Cuyler was as thorough a baserunning tactician as men like Ty Cobb and Max Carey as well as more modern players like Lou Brock and Rickey Henderson.

14. An Enduring Legacy and Baseball's Highest Honor

Cuyler also had an impact on popular culture. Those who are aficionados of television Americana might know that Cuyler was mentioned as "Ward Cleaver's" favorite childhood player in an episode of *Leave It to Beaver*.

Cuyler's legacy may have reached its high point in 1982, when his name came up in a discussion within the most hallowed walls of justice in the United States. The question of which outfield position Cuyler played for the Cubs in 1933 entered the debate during proceedings of the United States Supreme Court on December 1. As the court was concluding its day on the bench, its members listened to a lawyer explain how its 1980 decision in a case called Cuyler vs. Sullivan helped aid his client's cause. Justice William H. Rehnquist interrupted the lawyer to ask a poignant question. Ignoring the attorney's response, Justice Rehnquist made a comment that Cuyler played center field for the Chicago Cubs in 1933. Justice John Paul Stevens offered his opinion from the other side of the bench that Cuyler actually played right field that season. The court finally turned to other matters after Justice Rehnquist seemed to concur with Justice Stevens.[44]

When the justices retired to discuss the particular case that cited Cuyler vs. Sullivan, Justice Rehnquist returned to the issue of what position Cuyler played in 1933. He was positive that Cuyler played center field, but Justice Stevens, who was a 13-year-old baseball fan living in Chicago at the time, insisted that it was right field. Both judges decided that research would be needed to solve the matter. Law clerk Ronald Blunt called the *Chicago Tribune* and received irrefutable testimony confirming that Justice Stephens was correct in his assertion that Cuyler played right field for the Cubs in 1933.[45] Of course, official records show that Cuyler played all three outfield positions in 1933.

The question surrounding Cuyler's problems with Donie Bush and Barney Dreyfuss in 1927 continues to be debated. Since all of the principle characters involved in the incident are no longer alive, the actual truth will likely never be sorted out. After Cuyler was shipped to Chicago, Dreyfuss told sportswriter John Sikes that he did not let Kiki play in the 1927 World Series because his player could not look him "straight in the eye."[46] The true story behind the rift may have involved Dreyfuss not wanting Cuyler to play basketball during the off-season. When Dreyfuss acquired Harry Riconda and Jesse Petty from Brooklyn in December of 1928 for Glenn Wright, Pittsburgh's owner quickly informed his new player that playing basketball during the winter was prohibited.[47]

Hazen "Kiki" Cuyler's baseball career cannot be judged solely on a unique disagreement with Pittsburgh management in 1927. Pirates fans have often pondered how great Pittsburgh's team could have been if Cuyler had been permitted to remain there alongside Paul and Lloyd Waner. Their counterparts in the Windy City did not want to consider this scenario since Cuyler became Chicago's catalyst during two pennant-winning seasons in 1929 and 1932.

Misunderstood by some and adored by many, Cuyler always had a positive personality, a broad smile and the determination to excel. Even though hard work and dedication encompassed Cuyler's mantra throughout his career, he assessed the game philosophically on more than one occasion. "What a game," Cuyler was known to chuckle at times, "when a thousandth of an inch where the ball and bat come together can mean the difference between a hit and just another out."[48]

Simple physics and mathematics did not form the real story behind Kiki Cuyler's success. He was an honest man, whose faith and perseverance guided him throughout his life. He was willing to help those who needed it whether he was on a baseball diamond or in his hometown of Harrisville. Known as the Flint Flash when he entered the big leagues, Hazen "Kiki" Cuyler developed into one of the best players of his era. He was truly a Hall of Famer to fans who cheered for him across America and a genuine hero to those from the small community of Harrisville who knew him personally.

Appendix: Statistics

Career Statistics

	G	AB	R	H	2B	3B	HR	RBI	SB	AVG	OBP	SLG
1921 PIT-NL	1	3	0	0	0	0	0	0	0	.000	.000	.000
1922 PIT-NL	1	0	0	0	0	0	0	0	0	.000	.000	.000
1923 PIT-NL	11	40	4	10	1	1	0	2	2	.250	.348	.325
1924 PIT-NL	117	466	94	165	27	16	9	85	32	.354	.402	.539
1925 PIT-NL	153	617	144	220	43	26	18	102	41	.357	.423	.598
1926 PIT-NL	157	614	113	197	31	15	8	92	35	.321	.380	.459
1927 PIT-NL	85	285	60	88	13	7	3	31	20	.309	.394	.435
1928 CHI-NL	133	499	92	142	25	9	17	79	37	.285	.359	.473
1929 CHI-NL	139	509	111	183	29	7	15	102	43	.360	.438	.532
1930 CHI-NL	156	642	155	228	50	17	13	134	37	.355	.428	.547
1931 CHI-NL	154	613	110	202	37	12	9	88	13	.330	.404	.473
1932 CHI-NL	110	446	58	130	19	9	10	77	9	.291	.340	.442
1933 CHI-NL	70	262	37	83	13	3	5	35	4	.317	.376	.447
1934 CHI-NL	142	559	80	189	42	8	6	69	15	.338	.377	.474
1935 CHI-NL	45	157	22	42	5	1	4	18	3	.268	.331	.389
1935 CIN-NL	62	223	36	56	8	3	2	22	5	.251	.337	.341
1935 TOT-NL	107	380	58	98	13	4	6	40	8	.258	.335	.361
1936 CIN-NL	144	567	96	185	29	11	7	74	16	.326	.380	.453
1937 CIN-NL	117	406	48	110	12	4	0	32	10	.271	.333	.320
1938 BRO-NL	82	253	45	69	10	8	2	23	6	.273	.363	.399
TOTALS	1879	7161	1305	2299	394	157	128	1065	328	.321	.386	.474

World Series Statistics

	G	AB	R	H	2B	3B	HR	RBI	SB	AVG	OBP	SLG
1925 PIT-NL	7	26	3	7	3	0	1	6	0	.269	.321	.500
1927 PIT-NL				Did Not Play								
1929 CHI-NL	5	20	4	6	1	0	0	4	0	.300	.333	.350
1932 CHI-NL	4	18	2	5	1	1	1	2	1	.278	.278	.611
TOTALS	16	64	9	18	5	1	2	12	1	.281	.313	.484

Accomplishments

National League Leader in Games Played — 1925, 1926, 1930

National League Leader in Runs Scored — 1925, 1926

National League Leader in Doubles — 1934

National League Leader in Triples — 1925

National League Leader in Stolen Bases — 1926, 1928, 1929, 1930

Single Season Record for Total Bases in Pittsburgh Pirates Franchise History — 369 Total Bases in 1925

Second in Pittsburgh Pirates Franchise History for Most Extra Base Hits in a Single Season — 87 in 1925 (Willie Stargell set the record with 90 in 1973)

Second in Chicago Cubs Franchise History for Most Hits in a Single Season — 228 in 1930 (Rogers Hornsby set the record with 229 in 1929)

Second in Chicago Cubs Franchise History for Most Runs Scored in a Single Season — 155 in 1930 (Rogers Hornsby set the record with 156 in 1929)

Third Highest Career Batting Average in Pittsburgh Pirates Franchise History — .336 (Jake Stenzel is first with an average of .360)

Sixth Highest Career Batting Average in Chicago Cubs Franchise History — .325 (Bill Madlock and Riggs Stephenson are tied for first with an average of .336)

Inducted Into the Baseball Hall of Fame in 1968

Chapter Notes

Chapter 1

1. Perry Francis Powers and Harry Gardner Cutler, *A History of Northern Michigan and Its People*, vol. 2 (Chicago: Lewis Publishing, 1912), p. 835.
2. *Alcona County: A Pictorial History*, vol. I (Harrisville: The Alcona County Review, 2007, reprinted by Cheryl L. Peterson and John D. Boufford, 2009), p. 153.
3. Public Members Tree, The Harrisville Byces, www.ancestry.com.
4. Powers and Cutler, *A History of Northern Michigan and Its People*, vol. 2, p. 835.
5. David L. Fleitz, *More Ghosts in the Gallery: Another Sixteen Little-Known Greats at Cooperstown* (Jefferson, NC: McFarland, 2007), p. 108.
6. *Alcona County: A Pictorial History*, vol. I, p. 153.
7. Edward Burns, "It Takes a Moose to Bring Out the Tiger in Cuyler!" *Chicago Daily Tribune*, June 2, 1935, p. B2.
8. *History of the Lake Huron Shore* (Chicago: H.R. Page, 1883; reissued through Ann Arbor: University of Michigan Library, 2005), p. 269.
9. Fleitz, *More Ghosts in the Gallery*, p. 108.
10. Powers and Cutler, *A History of Northern Michigan and Its People*, vol. 2, p. 835.
11. *Alcona County: A Pictorial History*, vol. I, p. 153.
12. Powers and Cutler, *A History of Northern Michigan and Its People*, vol. 2, p. 835.
13. *Alcona County: A Pictorial History*, vol. I, p. 153.
14. Public Members Tree, The Harrisville Byces, www.ancestry.com.
15. *Alcona County: A Pictorial History*, vol. I, p. 154.
16. *Ibid.*, p. 153.
17. "Sturgeon Point Lighthouse and Museum," Alcona Historical Society, www.alconahistoricalsociety.com.
18. *Ibid.*
19. "Sturgeon Point Lighthouse: Michigan's Official Travel and Tourism Site," www.michigan.org.
20. Public Members Tree, The Harrisville Byces, www.ancestry.com.
21. 1920 United States Census, www.ancestry.com.
22. *Alcona County: A Pictorial History*, vol. I, p. 151.
23. *Ibid.*
24. *Ibid.*
25. Harry T. Brundidge, "Cuyler, Leading Base Stealer, Was Traded for Not Sliding: Star Gives Own Version of Why He Was Benched and Shipped to Cubs by Pirates," *The Sporting News*, February 5, 1931, p. 5.
26. Powers and Cutler, *A History of Northern Michigan and Its People*, vol. 2, p. 835.
27. *Alcona County: A Pictorial History*, vol. I, p. 153.
28. Brundidge, "Cuyler, Leading Base Stealer, Was Traded for Not Sliding," p. 5.
29. *Alcona County: A Pictorial History*, vol. I, p. 154.
30. Powers and Cutler, *A History of Northern Michigan and Its People*, vol. 2, p. 501.
31. *History of the Lake Huron Shore*, p. 272.
32. Powers and Cutler, *A History of Northern Michigan and Its People*, vol. 2, p. 504.
33. *Ibid.*, p. 835.
34. David L. Porter, ed., *Biographical Dictionary of American Sports: Baseball Revised and Expanded Edition A–F* (Westport, CT: Greenwood Press, 2000), p. 335.
35. *Alcona County: A Pictorial History*, vol. I, p. 151.
36. Burns, "It Takes a Moose to Bring Out the Tiger in Cuyler!" p. B2.
37. Public Member Trees, The Harrisville Byces, www.ancestry.com.
38. 1910 United States Census, www.ancestry.com.
39. Burns, "It Takes a Moose to Bring Out the Tiger in Cuyler!" p. B2.
40. Edward Burns, "Clubhouse Confessions of Our Cubs," *Chicago Daily Tribune*, June 23, 1929, p. A2.
41. *Ibid.*

42. *Ibid.*
43. Fleitz, *More Ghosts in the Gallery*, pp. 108–109.
44. *Alcona County: A Pictorial History*, vol. I, p. 151.
45. Brundidge, "Cuyler, Leading Base Stealer, Was Traded for Not Sliding," p. 5.
46. "Pirates' Great Young Hitter: Hazen Cuyler," *The Sporting News*, August 21, 1924, p. 1.
47. Burns, "Clubhouse Confessions of Our Cubs," p. A2.
48. John J. McGrath, *The Brigade: A History: Its Organization and Employment in the U.S. Army* (Fort Leavenworth: Combat Studies Institute Press, 2004), p. 167.
49. "Pirates' Great Young Hitter: Hazen Cuyler," p. 1.
50. Burns, "Clubhouse Confessions of Our Cubs," p. A2.
51. "Pirates' Great Young Hitter: Hazen Cuyler," p. 1.
52. Fleitz, *More Ghosts in the Gallery*, p. 109.
53. "Necrology: Kiki Cuyler, Outfield Star for Pirates and Cubs, Dies," *The Sporting News*, February 22, 1950, p. 20.
54. "Pirates' Great Young Hitter: Hazen Cuyler," p. 1.
55. Public Members Tree, The Harrisville Byces, www.ancestry.com.
56. 1900 United States Federal Census, www.ancestry.com.
57. Fleitz, *More Ghosts in the Gallery*, p. 109.
58. *Alcona County: A Pictorial History*, vol. I, p. 151.
59. Fleitz, *More Ghosts in the Gallery*, p. 110.
60. Brundidge, "Cuyler, Leading Base Stealer, Was Traded for Not Sliding," p. 5.
61. Fleitz, *More Ghosts in the Gallery*, p. 110.
62. *Ibid.*
63. Public Tree Members, The Harrisville Byces, www.ancestry.com.

Chapter 2

1. William A. Berridge, *The Review of Economic Statistics and Supplements*, vol. 4 (Cambridge, MA: Harvard University Press, 1922), p. 19.
2. *Ibid.*
3. Irving Vaughan, "How I Got My Start in Baseball by Hazen (Kiki) Cuyler," *Chicago Daily Tribune*, April 29, 1932, p. 27.
4. *Ibid.*
5. Harry T. Brundidge, "Cuyler, Leading Base Stealer, Was Traded for Not Sliding: Star Gives Own Version of Why He Was Benched and Shipped to Cubs by Pirates," *The Sporting News*, February 5, 1931, p. 5.
6. Vaughan, "How I Got My Start in Baseball by Hazen (Kiki) Cuyler," p. 27.
7. Cullen Cain, "Maine's Top Baseball Fan: Developed Three Big Stars," *Miami Daily News*, April 17, 1954, p. 2B.
8. Stein, "Michigan Cities Vote to Continue Circuit," *The Sporting News*, January 8, 1920, p. 3.
9. Vaughan, "How I Got My Start in Baseball by Hazen (Kiki) Cuyler," p. 27.
10. Cain, "Maine's Top Baseball Fan," p. 2B.
11. Harry Dayton, "Minters Agree to Use Three Rookies," *The Sporting News*, February 10, 1921, p. 3.
12. "Michigan-Ontario League Standing on Saturday Morning," *The Sporting News*, June 17, 1920, p. 6.
13. "Michigan-Ontario League Standing on Saturday Morning," *The Sporting News*, June 24, 1920, p. 7.
14. "Michigan-Ontario League Standing on Saturday Morning," *The Sporting News*, July 15, 1920, p. 6.
15. "Caught on the Fly," *The Sporting News*, September 9, 1920, p. 4.
16. "Michigan-Ontario League Standing at Close of Season, Sept.12," *The Sporting News*, September 23, 1920, p. 7.
17. "Twenty-One Minor Leagues Reserve Players for 1921," *The Sporting News*, November 11, 1920, p. 7.
18. "Santy Brings Minters No New Team Leaders," *The Sporting News*, December 30, 1920, p. 3.
19. "News Notes from the Minors," *The Sporting News*, February 3, 1921, p. 8.
20. Dayton, "Minters Agree to Use Three Rookies," p. 3.
21. Rhodes, "Sarnia and Port Huron Share," *The Sporting News*, April 21, 1921, p. 5.
22. Al Graham, "Flint Club Builds Portable Ball Park," *The Sporting News*, April 14, 1921, p. 5.
23. Vaughan, "How I Got My Start in Baseball by Hazen (Kiki) Cuyler," p. 27.
24. Cain, "Maine's Top Baseball Fan," p. 2B.
25. Vaughan, "How I Got My Start in Baseball by Hazen (Kiki) Cuyler," p. 27.
26. *Ibid.*
27. Chester L. Smith, "The Village Smithy: Bigbee, Carey, Then Cuyler!" *The Pittsburgh Press*, July 29, 1951, p. 34.
28. Vaughan, "How I Got My Start in Baseball by Hazen (Kiki) Cuyler," p. 27.
29. "Mint Splits to Save Itself," *The Sporting News*, July 7, 1921, p. 1.
30. "Michigan-Ontario League Standing on Saturday Morning," *The Sporting News*, August 25, 1921, p. 7.
31. "Caught on the Fly," *The Sporting News*, September 15, 1921, p. 4.
32. "Michigan-Ontario League Standing on Saturday Morning," *The Sporting News*, September 1, 1921, p. 8.
33. Cain, "Maine's Top Baseball Fan," p. 2B.
34. "Caught on the Fly," *The Sporting News*, September 22, 1921, p. 4.

35. L.H. Wollen, "Buccaneers Must Play Improved Ball to Defeat Giants: Rivals Open Series Today," *The Pittsburgh Press*, September 16, 1921, p. 30.
36. Ralph S. Davis, "Pittsburg in Rage as Pirates Falter," *The Sporting News*, September 8, 1921, p. 1.
37. Ralph Davis, "Ralph Davis Column: A Suspicious Lot," *The Pittsburgh Press*, September 17, 1921, p. 10.
38. Davis, "Pittsburg in Rage as Pirates Falter," p. 1.
39. Ralph S. Davis, "Buccaneers Left to Their Dismal Fate: Fans Desert Them and No More Cheers Are Heard," *The Sporting News*, September 29, 1921, p. 2.
40. "Defeat Makes Bucs Morose," *The Pittsburgh Press*, September 30, 1921, p. 32.
41. "Sun and Wind Dry West Baden Diamond for First Real Workout: Big Squad Is Divided," *The Pittsburgh Press*, March 6, 1922, p. 22.
42. *Ibid.*
43. "Pirate Players Show Great Form in First Practice Contest: Second Game Carded Today," *The Pittsburgh Press*, March 16, 1922, p. 24.
44. "Two Hard Sessions Are Planned for Buccaneers Today: Gibson to Push Men," *The Pittsburgh Press*, March 21, 1922, p. 24.
45. "Only One Practice Period Slated for Pirates Today: Play Intra-Club Game in Morning," *The Pittsburgh Press*, March 22, 1922, p. 22.
46. "Hot Weather Sends Buccaneers Into More Strenuous Training: Corsairs Active at Ozark Camp," *The Pittsburgh Press*, March 23, 1922, p. 24.
47. "Pirates and Red Sox Resume Series Today: Pair of Players on Hospital List," *The Pittsburgh Press*, March 25, 1922, p. 10.
48. "Pirates' 1922 Pennant Quest Begins at St. Louis Today: Youngsters Are in Bucco Lineup," *The Pittsburgh Press*, April 12, 1922, p. 26.
49. "Gibson Lectures Pirates Before Second Game with Cardinals: Glazner Likely to Twirl Today," *The Pittsburgh Press*, April 13, 1922, p. 30.
50. Ralph Davis, "Ralph Davis Column: Whitted Getting It Wrong," *The Pittsburgh Press*, April 22, 1922, p. 12.
51. Ralph Davis, "Ralph Davis Column: What Dreyfuss Says," *The Pittsburgh Press*, April 22, 1922, p. 12.
52. "Stewart Is Given Release: Returned to Birmingham Under Option—Blake, Cuyler and Wilson Also Turned Loose," *The Pittsburgh Press*, April 23, 1922, p. 2.
53. Ralph S. Davis, "Gibson Figures to Gain in Home Stand: Pirates Will Be Given Drilling Early and Late," *The Sporting News*, May 4, 1922, p. 3.
54. "South Atlantic League Standing on Monday Morning," *The Sporting News*, May 4, 1922, p. 7.
55. Charles Lasemann, "Hazen Cuyler, Former Major League Star and Now Chattanooga Manager, Got Start with the Charleston Pals," *The News and Courier*, May 28, 1939, p. 1.
56. *Ibid.*
57. "Makes Columbia Eat Dust," *The Sporting News*, June 15, 1922, p. 2.
58. Ralph S. Davis, "It's Plain M'Kechnie Has Big Job on Hand: Easy Going Gibson Left Pirates Badly Demoralized," *The Sporting News*, July 13, 1922, p. 3.
59. Lasemann, "Hazen Cuyler, Former Major League Star and Now Chattanooga Manager, Got Start with the Charleston Pals," p. 1.
60. *Ibid.*
61. "Buccaneers Win and Lose," *The Pittsburgh Press*, September 17, 1922, p. 1.
62. "Pirates Take Twin Wallop," *The Pittsburgh Press*, September 24, 1922, p. 1.
63. *Ibid.*
64. Ralph S. Davis, "Pirates' Campaign Is All Mapped Out: And No Laggards Looked for When Call Sounds," *The Sporting News*, February 1, 1923, p. 3.
65. "Reb Russell Can't Call Job All His Own," *The Sporting News*, March 1, 1923, p. 8.
66. James M. McAfee, "Loose Play Brings Double Session for Pirates Today: Outfield Trio Gets Day Off," *The Pittsburgh Press*, March 27, 1923, p. 24.
67. James M. McAfee, "Pirates Defeat Red Sox," *The Pittsburgh Press*, March 25, 1923, p. 1.
68. "Play By Play Story of Pirates' Victory," *The Pittsburgh Press*, March 25, 1923, p. 2.
69. James M. McAfee, "Clyde Barnhart Arrives at Hot Springs: Squad of Buccos Is Now Complete," *The Pittsburgh Press*, March 26, 1923, p. 24.
70. McAfee, "Loose Play Brings Double Session for Pirates Today: Outfield Trio Gets Day Off," p. 24.
71. James M. McAfee, "Pirates Carry 9 Hurlers," *The Pittsburgh Press*, April 1, 1923, p. 2.
72. Ralph S. Davis, "M'Kechnie Not So Sure of Pitchers: Pirate Twirlers Haven't Had Sort of Work They Need," *The Sporting News*, April 19, 1923, p. 3.
73. James M. McAfee, "Cuyler, Wright and Michaels Farmed Out to Nashville: Bucs Squad Is Cut Again," *The Pittsburgh Press*, April 11, 1923, p. 28.
74. Davis, "M'Kechnie Not So Sure of Pitchers," p. 3.
75. Nolly J. Sams, "Charleston Gets an Added Bit of Glory: Hamilton's Sally Champions Put It Over on Wilson," *The Sporting News*, September 28, 1922, p. 3.
76. "Southern League Standing on Monday Morning," *The Sporting News*, May 24, 1923, p. 8.
77. Ralph McGill, "Dying? Not Baseball!" *Baseball Digest*, May 1958, p. 56.
78. "Elect Cuyler to Hall of Fame: Ex-Cub

Star Picked Along with Goslin," *Chicago Tribune*, January 29, 1968, p. C4.
  79. L.H. Addington, "In the Bull Pen," *The Sporting News*, December 8, 1927, p. 8.
  80. "Elect Cuyler to Hall of Fame," p. C4.
  81. "Southern League Standing on Monday Morning," *The Sporting News*, August 23, 1923, p. 8.
  82. Ralph S. Davis, "Dreyfuss Willing to Call It a Season: Efforts of Pittsburg Magnate Center on Next Year," *The Sporting News*, September 20, 1923, p. 3.
  83. "Veteran Emil Huhn Shows 'Em How to Swat Dixie Pitching," *The Sporting News*, November 29, 1923, p. 7.
  84. David L. Fleitz, *More Ghosts in the Gallery: Another Sixteen Little-Known Greats at Cooperstown* (Jefferson, NC: McFarland, 2007), p. 110.
  85. Lasemann, "Hazen Cuyler, Former Major League Star and Now Chattanooga Manager, Got Start with the Charleston Pals," p. 1.
  86. "Buccaneers Begin Last Home Stand of Season: Dodgers Opening Foemen," *The Pittsburgh Press*, September 13, 1923, p. 29.
  87. L.H. Wollen, "Boston Braves Here for Three Contests: Second Place Is Lost by Pirates," *The Pittsburgh Press*, September 17, 1923, p. 24.

Chapter 3

  1. L.H. Wollen, "Giants Open Farewell Series with Buccaneers Today: Redlegs Not Out of Pennant Fight," *The Pittsburgh Press*, September 20, 1923, p. 26.
  2. L.H. Wollen, "Braves Face Pirates in Farewell Combat: Hazen Cuyler to Break Into Game," *The Pittsburgh Press*, September 19, 1923, p. 24.
  3. Wollen, "Giants Open Farewell Series with Buccaneers Today," p. 26.
  4. L.H. Wollen, "Double-Header Opens Giants' Series at Forbes Field: Star Mound Trio Ready for Work," *The Pittsburgh Press*, September 21, 1923, p. 30.
  5. L.H. Wollen, "Johnny Morrison Opposes Giants in Farewell Contest: Reds Draw Away From Buccaneers," *The Pittsburgh Press*, September 22, 1923, p. 13.
  6. *Ibid.*
  7. L.H. Wollen, "Phillies Open Farewell Series Here with Twin Bill: Giants and Reds Continue Battle," *The Pittsburgh Press*, September 24, 1923, p. 22.
  8. L.H. Wollen, "Bucs Say Farewell with Today's Contest: Quakers Foes in Last Home Game," *The Pittsburgh Press*, September 26, 1923, p. 26.
  9. "Pirates in Chicago for Series with Cubs: Four Tilts Scheduled," *The Pittsburgh Press*, September 27, 1923, p. 27.
  10. Ralph S. Davis, "Pirates Have More Grudges Than One: While Settling Those Abroad They Might Work Within," *The Sporting News*, August 16, 1923, p. 3.
  11. Ralph S. Davis, "Only One Part of It In Minds of Pirates: No Member of Pittsburg at World's Series," *The Sporting News*, October 25, 1923, p. 3.
  12. "Glenn Wright Hailed as Star," *The Sporting News*, November 22, 1923, p. 7.
  13. Ralph S. Davis, "Sam Dreyfuss All Het Up Over Coast: Finest Training Place Ever, Says Pittsburg Club Official," *The Sporting News*, November 15, 1923, p. 3.
  14. *Ibid.*
  15. Davis, "Only One Part of It in Minds of Pirates," p. 3.
  16. Frederick G. Leib, *The Pittsburgh Pirates* (1948; reprint, Carbondale: Southern Illinois University Press, 2003), p. 199.
  17. L.H. Wollen, "Buccaneer Training Party Speeds Through Kansas: Glenn Wright Boards Train," *The Pittsburgh Press*, February 25, 1924, p. 22.
  18. William F. McNeil, *The California Winter League: America's First Integrated Professional Baseball League* (Jefferson, NC: McFarland, 2002), p. 76.
  19. Ralph S. Davis, "Pirates Can Count on Their Outfield: No Team in Big Time Boasts Such Garden Class," *The Sporting News*, February 7, 1924, p. 3.
  20. *Ibid.*
  21. L.H. Wollen, "Pirates Tackle Sacramento Team Today: Regulars Quit Training Camp," *The Pittsburgh Press*, March 20, 1924, p. 30.
  22. L.H. Wollen, "No More Aerial Trips for Pirates: Bucco Skipper Bans Sky Rides," *The Pittsburgh Press*, March 11, 1924, p. 29.
  23. *Ibid.*
  24. L.H. Wollen, "Cooper Likely to Pitch Opener: Southpaw in Best of Trim," *The Pittsburgh Press*, April 10, 1924, p. 36.
  25. Ralph Davis, "Sport Chat: Opening Day Statements," *The Pittsburgh Press*, April 15, 1924, p. 26.
  26. Ralph S. Davis, "Pirates Could Use Several Kremers: One Recruit Who Has Cheering Effect Upon M'Kechnie," *The Sporting News*, May 15, 1924, p. 3.
  27. L.H. Wollen, "Pirates and Braves Meet in Second Contest of Series: Drop in Race Is Faced By Buccos," *The Pittsburgh Press*, May 10, 1924, p. 13.
  28. Ralph S. Davis, "Pirates Kick About Umpires Retort: Davis Says Players Believe Bad Example Is Thus Set," *The Sporting News*, May 22, 1924, p. 3.
  29. "National League Standing on Tuesday Morning," *The Sporting News*, May 22, 1924, p. 9.
  30. Davis, "Pirates Kick About Umpires Retort," p. 3.
  31. Ralph S. Davis, "M'Kechnie Rumor Nailed By Dreyfuss: Club Fully Satisfied with

Manager's Efforts," *The Sporting News*, May 29, 1924, p. 2.

32. L.H. Wollen, "Buccaneers Seek to Make Clean Sweep of Series Today: Kremer to Face New York Outfit," *The Pittsburgh Press*, May 21, 1924, p. 27.

33. L. H. Wollen, "Even Split with East Still Possible for Buccaneers: Morrison Faces Brooklyn Today," *The Pittsburgh Press*, May 23, 1924, p. 37.

34. Ralph S. Davis, "Pirates Must Show More Hitting Power: Bill M'Kechnie's Men Air Tight in Fielding Department," *The Sporting News*, June 12, 1924, p. 3.

35. L.H. Wollen, "M'Kechnie Admits He's Puzzled: Blames Lack of Basehits," *The Pittsburgh Press*, June 10, 1924, p. 32.

36. Ibid.

37. Ibid.

38. "National League Standing on Tuesday Morning," *The Sporting News*, June 12, 1924, p. 9.

39. L.H. Wollen, "Cooper Or Kremer to Face Cincinnati Today: Another Winning Streak Desired," *The Pittsburgh Press*, June 23, 1924, p. 20.

40. "National League Standing on Tuesday Morning," *The Sporting News*, June 26, 1924, p. 9.

41. Wollen, "Cooper or Kremer to Face Cincinnati Today: Another Winning Streak Desired," p. 20.

42. L.H. Wollen, "League-Leading Giants Open Series Here Tomorrow: Quakers Face Bucs in Last Game Today," *The Pittsburgh Press*, July 15, 1924, p. 24.

43. Ralph Davis, "Sport Chat: Beware of Pirates, Says Klugman," *The Pittsburgh Press*, July 16, 1924, p. 24.

44. Ibid.

45. "National League Standing on Tuesday Morning," *The Sporting News*, July 17, 1924, p. 9.

46. Ralph S. Davis, "Bucs Show to Best Advantage of Year: Cuyler Has Had Much to Do with Success of Pirates," *The Sporting News*, July 24, 1924, p. 2.

47. Ibid.

48. "National League Standing on Tuesday Morning," *The Sporting News*, July 24, 1924, p. 9.

49. Ibid.

50. L.H. Wollen, "Pirates Strive to Repeat Victory Over Giants Today: Emil Yde to Face League Leaders," *The Pittsburgh Press*, July 18, 1924, p. 24.

51. "National League Standing on Tuesday Morning," *The Sporting News*, July 24, 1924, p. 9.

52. L.H. Wollen, "Last Pirate-Giant Battle Draws Huge Crowd of Fans: Yde Or Meadows to Face Leaders," *The Pittsburgh Press*, July 19, 1924, p. 9.

53. Ralph Davis, "Sport Chat: Pirates and Giants," *The Pittsburgh Press*, July 17, 1924, p. 27.

54. Ibid.

55. L.H. Wollen, "Hurling Jinxes Gone, Pirates Look for More Victories Over Dodgers: Johnny Morrison to Twirl for Bucs," *The Pittsburgh Press*, July 22, 1924, p. 24.

56. L.H. Wollen, "Pirates After Clean Sweep at Boston: Poor Work on Bases Shown," *The Pittsburgh Press*, July 29, 1924, p. 20.

57. L.H. Wollen, "Giants Desperate as Buccaneers Win: Morrison to Pitch Today," *The Pittsburgh Press*, August 1, 1924, p. 24.

58. Ralph S. Davis, "Bucs Not Conceding Pennant to M'Graw: McKechnie's Speedsters Make Great Record on Road," *The Sporting News*, August 14, 1924, p. 1.

59. L.H. Wollen, "Pirates Open with Phils Today: Six Games on Series List," *The Pittsburgh Press*, August 8, 1924, p. 25.

60. "National League Standing on Tuesday Morning," *The Sporting News*, August 14, 1924, p. 9.

61. L.H. Wollen, "Buccos Win Dual Bill: Capture Two from Phils," *The Pittsburgh Press*, August 10, 1924, p. 1.

62. L.H. Wollen, "Buccaneers Seek to Further Diminish Advantage of Giants: Kremer to Face Premiers Today," *The Pittsburgh Press*, August 15, 1924, p. 24.

63. "National League Standing on Tuesday Morning," *The Sporting News*, August 21, 1924, p. 9.

64. L.H. Wollen, "Buccaneers Sweep Series; Win Final in the Twelfth," *The Pittsburgh Press*, August 17, 1924, p. 1.

65. "Baseball By-Plays," *The Sporting News*, September 25, 1924, p. 4.

66. Ibid.

67. Ralph Davis, "Sport Chat: Hazen Cuyler, Hero," *The Pittsburgh Press*, August 18, 1924, p. 18.

68. Ibid.

69. "Pirates Great Young Hitter: Hazen Cuyler," *The Sporting News*, August 21, 1924, p. 1.

70. Ralph Davis, "Sport Chat: Cuyler on Stealing Bases," *The Pittsburgh Press*, August 25, 1924, p. 18.

71. Ibid.

72. Ralph Davis, "Sport Chat: Cuyler Saves the Umps Trouble," *The Pittsburgh Press*, August 28, 1924, p. 27.

73. Ibid.

74. "National League Standing on Tuesday Morning," *The Sporting News*, August 28, 1924, p. 9.

75. L. H. Wollen, "Play of Pirates Lacking Enthusiasm: Little Pep Is Being Shown," *The Pittsburgh Press*, September 13, 1924, p. 11.

76. L.H. Wollen, "Buccaneers Close Series in Boston Today: Adams Will Face Braves," *The Pittsburgh Press*, September 15, 1924, p. 20.

77. L.H. Wollen, "Buccaneers Close Giants Series Today: Pirates' Pennant Chances Are Gone," *The Pittsburgh Press*, September 25, 1924, p. 26.

78. "National League Standing on Tuesday

Morning," *The Sporting News*, October 2, 1924, p. 6.
79. Ralph Davis, "Sport Chat: Tipping Off the Pirate Owner," *The Pittsburgh Press*, October 9, 1924, p. 31.
80. Ralph Davis, "Sport Chat: And Another Tip," *The Pittsburgh Press*, October 9, 1924, p. 31.
81. Ralph S. Davis, "M'Kechnie Hears Shouting of Mob: Dreyfuss Says He's Satisfied with Bill's Work, However," *The Sporting News*, October 9, 1924, p. 1.
82. "Believes His Team Stronger: Bill McKechnie Confident Improvement Has Been Made by Changes Decided on in Lineup," *The Pittsburgh Press*, December 15, 1924, p. 28.
83. *Ibid.*

Chapter 4

1. Ralph Davis, "Sport Chat: Fans Still Discuss Big Deal," *The Pittsburgh Press*, October 29, 1924, p. 26.
2. Ralph Davis, "Sport Chat: Says Pirates Got Best of Deal," *The Pittsburgh Press*, November 7, 1924, p. 38.
3. "Caught on the Fly," *The Sporting News*, November 27, 1924, p. 8.
4. *Ibid.*
5. "Maranville Auto Victim Given $700," *The Pittsburgh Press*, January 14, 1925, p. 22.
6. "Baseball By-Plays," *The Sporting News*, December 3, 1925, p. 4.
7. "Caught on the Fly," *The Sporting News*, January 29, 1925, p. 8.
8. *Ibid.*
9. Lou Wollen, "M'Kechnie Now Heads Big Party: Don Songer Is Delayed," *The Pittsburgh Press*, February 26, 1925, p. 28.
10. Lou Wollen, "M'Kechnie Lays Down Law to Team: New Policy Decided On," *The Pittsburgh Press*, March 2, 1925, p. 20.
11. "Training Camp Notes," *The Sporting News*, March 19, 1925, p. 8.
12. Lou Wollen, "McKechnie Continues Pruning Squad: Royce Williams Latest to Depart," *The Pittsburgh Press*, March 26, 1925, p. 30.
13. *Ibid.*
14. Lou Wollen, "Both Pirate Teams in Action Today: Rookies to Play Contest," *The Pittsburgh Press*, March 27, 1925, p. 38.
15. Lou Wollen, "Pirates Meet Little Rock Today: Yde Or Kremer to Work in Opener," *The Pittsburgh Press*, April 10, 1925, p. 38.
16. Lou Wollen, "Lee Meadows Will Oppose Cubs Today: Pirate Lineup to Be the Same," *The Pittsburgh Press*, April 15, 1925, p. 26.
17. "National League Standing on Tuesday Morning," *The Sporting News*, April 23, 1925, p. 7.
18. Wollen, "Lee Meadows Will Oppose Cubs Today: Pirate Lineup to Be the Same," p. 26.
19. "National League Standing on Tuesday Morning," *The Sporting News*, April 23, 1925, p. 7.
20. Ralph Davis, "Sport Chat: Let the Band Play On," *The Pittsburgh Press*, February 10, 1925, p. 28.
21. *Ibid.*
22. Lou Wollen, "Sullen Pirates Crew Starts Eastern Trip: Open Series with Phillies Today," *The Pittsburgh Press*, May 8, 1925, p. 38.
23. "National League Standing on Tuesday Morning," *The Sporting News*, May 21, 1925, p. 9.
24. "Caught on the Fly," *The Sporting News*, May 21, 1925, p. 9.
25. "National League Standing on Tuesday Morning," *The Sporting News*, May 21, 1925, p. 9.
26. "Caught on the Fly," *The Sporting News*, May 21, 1925, p. 9.
27. *Ibid.*
28. Lou Wollen, "Rain Prevents Third Game of Corsair-Brave Series: Earl Smith Is Set Down by Heydler," *The Pittsburgh Press*, May 15, 1925, p. 38.
29. Lou. Wollen, "M'Kechnie to Bench Niehaus: Grantham to Cover First," *The Pittsburgh Press*, May 13, 1925, p. 28.
30. "National. League Standing on Tuesday Morning," *The Sporting News*, May 21, 1925, p. 9.
31. Ralph. S. Davis, "Pittsburgh Fans Not in Insurrection: Expect Pirates to Rise in East," *The Pittsburgh Press*, May 17, 1925, p. 4.
32. Lou. Wollen, "Buccos Out to Even Up New York Series: Lee Meadows Will Pitch," *The Pittsburgh Press*, May 22, 1925, p. 38.
33. Lou. Wollen, "Pirates Press Dodgers in Battle for Runner-Up Place: Only Half Game Separates Clubs," *The Pittsburgh Press*, June 5, 1925, p. 38.
34. "National. League Standing on Tuesday Morning," *The Sporting News*, June 11, 1925, p. 7.
35. Ralph. S. Davis, "Clarke Goes Back with His Old Team: Former Manager to Serve as an Assistant to Dreyfuss," *The Sporting News*, June 18, 1925, p. 3.
36. Ralph S. Davis, "There's Something to Those Pirates: They Have Beaten Back Gamely and Are Dangerous," *The Sporting News*, June 25, 1925, p. 1.
37. Ralph Davis, "Sport Chat: Dusting Off Ball Players," *The Pittsburgh Press*, June 12, 1925, p. 38.
38. "National League Standing on Tuesday Morning," *The Sporting News*, June 25, 1925, p. 7.
39. Lou Wollen, "Buccaneers Overwhelm Brooklyn Robins, 21 to 5: Superbas Trounced," *The Pittsburgh Press*, June 21, 1925, p. 1.
40. Ralph Davis, "Sport Chat: Homewood and the Grays," *The Pittsburgh Press*, June 22, 1925, p. 20.
41. "National League Standing on Tuesday Morning," *The Sporting News*, July 9, 1925, p. 7.
42. Ralph S. Davis, "Ten Pirates Batting Over

.300: And Pitching Has Been Showing Some Improvement," *The Sporting News*, July 23, 1925, p. 1.

43. Ralph S. Davis, "Bucs Try to Prove They Are Fighters: Gooch and Cuyler Tangle When One Resents Criticism," *The Sporting News*, August 6, 1925, p. 1.

44. *Ibid*.

45. "National League Standing on Tuesday Morning," *The Sporting News*, July 30, 1925, p. 7.

46. Davis, "Bucs Try to Prove They Are Fighters," p. 1.

47. "National League Standing on Tuesday Morning," *The Sporting News*, August 6, 1925, p. 7.

48. "Ralph Davis, "Sport Chat: Rooters in Alaska," *The Pittsburgh Press*, August 19, 1925, p. 22.

49. Lou Wollen, "Hazen Cuyler Shines," *The Pittsburgh Press*, August 21, 1925, p. 24.

50. "National League Standing on Tuesday Morning," *The Sporting News*, September 24, 1925, p. 9.

51. *Ibid*.

52. "Baseball Gossip," *The Pittsburgh Press*, September 23, 1925, p. 26.

53. Ralph Davis, "Sport Chat: The Pennant Is Clinched," *The Pittsburgh Press*, September 24, 1925, p. 30.

54. Ralph S. Davis, "M'Kechnie Deserves Full Credit for Pirate Achievements: His Judgment Proved Sound," *The Pittsburgh Press*, August 30, 1925, p. 2.

55. Ralph Davis, "Sport Chat: An Unspoiled Hero," *The Pittsburgh Press*, September 24, 1925, p. 30.

56. "Bleacher Seats and Standing Room Only to Be Placed on Sale," *The Pittsburgh Press*, October 4, 1925, p. 2.

57. Ralph Davis, "Sport Chat: Bill McKechnie's Policy," *The Pittsburgh Press*, October 6, 1925, p. 28.

58. "Gossip of First Game," *The Sporting News*, October 15, 1925, p. 3.

59. "First Game in Detail," *The Sporting News*, October 15, 1925, p. 3.

60. "Gossip of First Game," *The Sporting News*, October 15, 1925, p. 3.

61. "Second Game in Detail," *The Sporting News*, October 15, 1925, p. 3.

62. "Cuyler's Homer Following Peck's Error Decides Second," *The Sporting News*, October 15, 1925, p. 3.

63. Ralph Davis, "Sport Chat: Rivals Are Even Up Now," *The Pittsburgh Press*, October 9, 1925, p. 38.

64. "Second Game in Detail," *The Sporting News*, October 15, 1925, p. 3.

65. Henry L. Farrell, "Third World's Series Game Postponed: Shower's Prevent Today's Contest," *The Pittsburgh Press*, October 9, 1925, p. 1.

66. Honus Wagner, "Aldridge Exhibits Courage," *The Pittsburgh Press*, October 9, 1925, p. 38.

67. *Ibid*.

68. Ralph S. Davis, "Pirates Meet President and Have a Big Day — Everywhere Except in Baseball Arena," *The Pittsburgh Press*, October 11, 1925, p. 1.

69. Ralph S. Davis, "No Protest to Be Made by Pirates," *The Pittsburgh Press*, October 11, 1925, p. 1.

70. Ernest A. Phillips, "The Passing Show: What a Former Player Saw at the Series," *The Sporting News*, October 22, 1925, p. 7.

71. Ralph Davis, "Sport Chat: Clarke Also Hopeful," *The Pittsburgh Press*, October 12, 1925, p. 24.

72. Ralph Davis, "Sport Chat: A New Lease on Life," *The Pittsburgh Press*, October 13, 1925, p. 30.

73. *Ibid*.

74. "Fifth Game in Detail," *The Sporting News*, October 15, 1925, p. 5.

75. *Ibid*.

76. "Sixth Game in Detail," *The Sporting News*, October 22, 1925, p. 3.

77. Ralph Davis, "Sport Chat: Game Little Eddie Moore," *The Pittsburgh Press*, October 14, 1925, p. 24.

78. "Seventh Game in Detail," *The Sporting News*, October 22, 1925, p. 6.

79. *Ibid*.

80. *Ibid*.

81. *Ibid*.

82. *Ibid*.

83. *Ibid*.

84. Jeff Carroll, *Sam Rice: A Biography of the Washington Senators Hall of Famer* (Jefferson, NC: McFarland, 2008), p. 140.

85. "Seventh Game in Detail," *The Sporting News*, October 22, 1925, p. 6.

86. Carroll, *Sam Rice*, p. 140.

87. "Seventh Game in Detail," *The Sporting News*, October 22, 1925, p. 6.

88. "Gossip of Seventh Game," *The Sporting News*, October 22, 1925, p. 6.

89. "Peckinpaugh Sets Record for Errors in World Series Play," *Chicago Daily Tribune*," October 16, 1925, p. 27.

90. "Baseball Gossip of the Major Leagues," *The Pittsburgh Press*, October 16, 1925, p. 39.

Chapter 5

1. Honus Wagner, "Pirate Speed Was Too Much for Senators," *The Pittsburgh Press*, October 16, 1925, p. 38.

2. "Baseball Gossip of the Major Leagues," *The Pittsburgh Press*, October 16, 1925, p. 39.

3. Lou Wollen, "Exodus of World Champs Begins: Bucs Leave for Homes," *The Pittsburgh Press*, October 17, 1925, p. 9.

4. Edward Burns, "It Takes a Moose to Bring Out the Tiger in Cuyler!" *Chicago Daily Tribune*, June 2, 1935, p. B2.

Notes. Chapter 5

5. Ralph Davis, "Sport Chat: Cuyler's Winter Job," *The Pittsburgh Press*, January 2, 1926, p. 11.
6. *Ibid.*
7. "A Word on the Proper Batting Stance," *Baseball Magazine*, November 1925, p. 542.
8. Henry L. Farrell, "Pirates Place Three on National All-Star Lineup: Cuyler Gets High Rating," *The Pittsburgh Press*, December 7, 1925, p. 28.
9. "Big League Writers Select All-Star Team for The Sporting News," *The Sporting News*, November 19, 1925, p. 3.
10. "Cuyler's Passers Due Tomorrow," *The Pittsburgh Press*, December 26, 1925, p. 11.
11. "Cuyler's Team at Southside Market House Tomorrow," *The Pittsburgh Press*, December 31, 1925, p. 13.
12. "Cuyler's I.M.A. Five Faces Braddock K. of C. Tonight," *The Pittsburgh Press*, January 7, 1926, p. 23.
13. Ralph S. Davis, "Pennant Pleasures Generally Run High: So Barney Dreyfuss Is Prepared to Do Some Spending," *The Sporting News*, January 7, 1926, p. 1.
14. Ralph Davis, "Sport Chat: Cuyler and Dreyfuss," *The Pittsburgh Press*, January 28, 1926, p. 24.
15. Ralph S. Davis, "Cuyler Is Hep to Business Methods: Pittsburgh's Star Twice Returns Contract Proffered Him," *The Sporting News*, February 4, 1926, p. 5.
16. *Ibid.*
17. *Ibid.*
18. "Jubilee Function Attended by More Than 1,000 Persons," *The Sporting News*, February 11, 1926, p. 3.
19. Ralph S. Davis, "B. Dreyfuss Holds Jubilee of His Own: Gets Pittsburg Stars in Festive Mood, Then Signs 'Em," *The Sporting News*, February 11, 1926, p. 1.
20. Ralph S. Davis, "Tribute Paid Pirates at National League Banquet: Carey Makes Fine Address," *The Pittsburgh Press*, February 3, 1926, p. 22.
21. Davis, "B. Dreyfuss Holds Jubilee of His Own," p. 1.
22. "Caught on the Fly," *The Sporting News*, March 4, 1926, p. 8.
23. Ralph S. Davis, "Winter Fiction, Says Dreyfuss of Report On Moore and Bigbee: Club Has Year to Pay for Rhyne, Waner," *The Sporting News*, November 5, 1925, p. 1.
24. "Scribbled By Scribes," *The Sporting News*, March 18, 1926, p. 4.
25. *Ibid.*
26. Davis, "Winter Fiction, Says Dreyfuss of Report On Moore and Bigbee," p. 1.
27. "Carey Resting in St. Louis Hospital," *The Pittsburgh Press*, March 3, 1926, p. 26.
28. Ralph Davis, "Sport Chat: Will Captain Max Be Fit?" *The Pittsburgh Press*, March 4, 1926, p. 27.
29. Ralph S. Davis, "Carey Only Pirate Uncertain Starter: But Captain Max Is Gradually Getting Strength Back," *The Sporting News*, April 1, 1926, p. 2.
30. Lou Wollen, "M'Kechnie Calls Off Pirate Game Scheduled Today: More Cripples Added to List," *The Pittsburgh Press*, March 24, 1926, p. 28.
31. "Caught on the Fly," *The Sporting News*, March 18, 1926, p. 6.
32. Lou Wollen, "Bucs Easy Victor Over Colonels: Vicious Attack Brings Triumph," *The Pittsburgh Press*, April 11, 1926, p. 1.
33. Lou Wollen, "Champs and Cards to Lift Lid Today," *The Pittsburgh Press*, April 13, 1926, p. 32.
34. "National League Standing on Tuesday Morning," *The Sporting News*, April 22, 1926, p. 7.
35. Lou Wollen, "Pirates and Cardinals Clash in Opener Here: Big Crowd to See Inaugural," *The Pittsburgh Press*, April 22, 1926, p. 37.
36. "Playing the Game with the Pirates," *The Pittsburgh Press*, April 28, 1926, p. 28.
37. "Playing the Game with the Pirates," *The Pittsburgh Press*, May 6, 1926, p. 36.
38. "National League Standing on Tuesday Morning," *The Sporting News*, May 13, 1926, p. 7.
39. *Ibid.*
40. "Playing the Game with the Pirates," *The Pittsburgh Press*, May 15, 1926, p. 9.
41. "Playing the Game with the Pirates," *The Pittsburgh Press*, May 16, 1926, p. 2.
42. "Kaufmann & Baer, Co. Store Advertisement," *The Pittsburgh Press*, May 19, 1926, p. 32.
43. "Playing the Game with the Pirates," *The Pittsburgh Press*, May 20, 1926, p. 38.
44. "Playing the Game with the Pirates," *The Pittsburgh Press*, May 30, 1926, p. 2.
45. "National League Standing on Tuesday Morning," *The Sporting News*, June 3, 1926, p. 7.
46. "Playing the Game with the Pirates," *The Pittsburgh Press*, June 4, 1926, p. 39.
47. Ralph S. Davis, "Pirates Move Into Strategic Position: M'Kechnie's Men Make Strides with Consistent Ball," *The Sporting News*, June 10, 1926, p. 1.
48. Lou Wollen, "Braves, Recent League Sensations, Encountered by Buccaneers Today: Bancroft Outfit Setting Hot Pace," *The Pittsburgh Press*, June 14, 1926, p. 24.
49. "National League Standing on Tuesday Morning," *The Sporting News*, June 17, 1926, p. 7.
50. *Ibid.*
51. "National League Standing on Tuesday Morning," *The Sporting News*, June 24, 1926, p. 7.
52. Lou Wollen, "Playing the Game with the Pirates," *The Pittsburgh Press*, June 18, 1926, p. 38.
53. "National League Standing on Tuesday Morning," *The Sporting News*, June 24, 1926, p. 7.
54. "Caught on the Fly," *The Sporting News*, June 10, 1926, p. 10.
55. Ralph S. Davis, "Dreyfuss Goes on His

Way Rejoicing: Pirates' Bon Voyage to Their Boss Carries Fine Sentiment," *The Sporting News*, June 17, 1926, p. 1.
56. Ralph Davis, "Ralph Davis Says: The Why of the Pirate Slump," *The Pittsburgh Press*, June 30, 1926, p. 33.
57. Ralph S. Davis, "All Isn't Well in Pirate Menage: Truth Is, Some of 'Em Have Been Cutting Up a Little," *The Sporting News*, July 8, 1926, p. 1.
58. "National League Standing on Tuesday Morning," *The Sporting News*, July 8, 1926, p. 7.
59. Lou Wollen, "Playing the Game with the Pirates," *The Pittsburgh Press*, July 13, 1926, p. 26.
60. Lou Wollen, "Playing the Game with the Pirates," *The Pittsburgh Press*, July 15, 1926, p. 30.
61. Ralph S. Davis, "They'll Be Careful Now, If Not Serious: But Why Must Big Leaguers Be Driven and Disciplined?" *The Sporting News*, July 22, 1926, p. 1.
62. "Scribbled by Scribes," *The Sporting News*, July 29, 1926, p. 4.
63. Lou Wollen, "Playing the Game with the Pirates," *The Pittsburgh Press*, July 21, 1926, p. 26.
64. "National League Standing on Tuesday Morning," *The Sporting News*, July 22, 1926, p. 7.
65. Ralph S. Davis, "M'Kechnie Wields an Iron Fist to Restore Champions to Order: Rigid Disciplinary Rule Being Followed," *The Sporting News*, July 29, 1926, p. 1.
66. The Observer, "Casual Comment," *The Sporting News*, July 29, 1926, p. 4.
67. "National League Standing on Tuesday Morning," *The Sporting News*, August 12, 1926, p. 7.
68. "Carey Wages Fight in Rebellion Ouster," *The Sporting News*, August 19, 1926, p. 1.
69. *Ibid.*
70. *Ibid.*
71. Ralph S. Davis, "Showdown Near in Pirate Controversy: No Team Can Serve Two Managers, Says Captain Max Carey," *The Pittsburgh Press*, August 13, 1926, p. 1.
72. Ralph S. Davis, "Guillotine Quickly Puts Down Pirate Anti-Clarke Rebellion: Carey's Head Falls with Two Other Vets," *The Sporting News*, August 19, 1926, p. 1.
73. *Ibid.*
74. *Ibid.*
75. Ralph S. Davis, "Carey, Bigbee and Adams Expected to Tell Real Story," *The Pittsburgh Press*, August 14, 1926, p. 2.
76. "Wild Rumors in Wake of Big Pittsburgh Team Shakeup," *The Pittsburgh Press*, August 15, 1926, p. 1.
77. Lou Wollen, "Playing the Game with the Pirates," *The Pittsburgh Press*, September 25, 1926, p. 9.
78. Lou Wollen, "Playing the Game with the Pirates," *The Pittsburgh Press*, August 24, 1926, p. 23.
79. Lou Wollen, "Playing the Game with the Pirates," *The Pittsburgh Press*, September 16, 1926, p. 34.
80. Lou Wollen, "Playing the Game with the Pirates," *The Pittsburgh Press*, September 13, 1926, p. 24.
81. Ralph Davis, "Ralph Davis Says: Mr. Barney Dreyfuss Grants an Interview," *The Pittsburgh Press*, September 14, 1926, p. 28.
82. *Ibid.*
83. "Scribbled by Scribes," *The Sporting News*, October 7, 1926, p. 4.
84. Ralph S. Davis, "Murder Will Out, Even with Pirates: Misplaced Zeal Trio Does Some Talking for Press," *The Sporting News*, October 7, 1926, p. 1.
85. Ralph S. Davis, "Donie Bush at Work On Personal Staff: Release of Onslow First Move in Reorganization of Coaches," *The Sporting News*, November 25, 1926, p. 7.
86. Edward Burns, "Wanted for Larceny! Man Named Cuyler," *Chicago Daily Tribune*, September 25, 1929, p. 21.
87. Davis, "Murder Will Out, Even with Pirates," p. 1.
88. "McKechnie Let Out as Pirate Manager," *The Sporting News*, October 21, 1926, p. 1.
89. Ralph S. Davis, "Donie Bush Named to Pacify Pirates: M'Kechnie's Successor Has Fine Record in Indianapolis," *The Sporting News*, October 28, 1926, p. 1.
90. "New Pirate Manager Assured Free Rein as Fred Clarke Quits: Fans Win Fight for One-Man Leadership," *The Pittsburgh Press*, October 27, 1926, p. 26.
91. Ralph S. Davis, "Ralph Davis Says: Bush Wants Them to Fight," *The Pittsburgh Press*, November 29, 1926, p. 24.
92. Ralph S. Davis, "I Will Hustle All the Time, Says New Buccaneer Manager: Bush Promises to Give Best Efforts," *The Pittsburgh Press*, November 4, 1926, p. 38.
93. Ralph S. Davis, "Dreyfuss Renews an Acquaintance: It Was 16 Years Ago Barney Saw Bush and He Was a Foe," *The Sporting News*, November 11, 1926, p. 3.
94. *Ibid.*
95. Ralph S. Davis, "Donie Bush Learns There Isn't a Santa: Majors Willing to Trade, But Not on Satisfactory Basis," *The Sporting News*, December 23, 1926, p. 1.
96. Ralph S. Davis, "Dreyfuss Washes Hands of Schedule: Pittsburgh Veteran Got Enough of It Last Winter," *The Sporting News*, January 20, 1927, p. 1.

Chapter 6

1. Ralph S. Davis, "Dreyfuss Washes Hands of Schedule: Pittsburgh Veteran Got Enough of It Last Winter," *The Sporting News*, January 20, 1927, p. 1.

2. *Ibid.*
3. *Ibid.*
4. "Cuyler and Team Leave for Flint," *The Pittsburgh Press*, January 21, 1927, p. 38.
5. Ralph S. Davis, "Dreyfuss Backs Up Anti-Betting Rules: Thinks Landis' Four Points Will Be Good for the Game," *The Sporting News*, January 27, 1927, p. 2.
6. "Caught on the Fly," *The Sporting News*, January 13, 1927, p. 8.
7. Davis, "Dreyfuss Washes Hands of Schedule: Pittsburgh Veteran Got Enough of It Last Winter," p. 1.
8. "Bush Expects Successful Season If Pirate Twirlers Come Through," *The Pittsburgh Press*, February 19, 1927, p. 12.
9. Lou Wollen, "Joe Harris' Acquisition Enhances Pirate Punch," *The Pittsburgh Press*, February 5, 1927, p. 9.
10. Ralph S. Davis, "Bush Lets Bucs Know Who Is Boss: And It Goes for Club Officials as Well as Athletes," *The Sporting News*, March 3, 1927, p. 3.
11. Irving Vaughan, "Yanks Escaped Cuyler Menace Once, Not Twice," *Chicago Daily Tribune*, September 21, 1932, p. 19.
12. Davis, "Bush Lets Bucs Know Who Is Boss," p. 3.
13. Lou Wollen, "Donie Bush Puts Absolute Ban on Liquor Drinking by Pirates: Pilot Asserts His Authority," *The Pittsburgh Press*, February 25, 1927, p. 37.
14. Davis, "Bush Lets Bucs Know Who Is Boss," p. 3.
15. "Kiki Cuyler Tells Home-Town Fans About His Troubles: Explains He Has No Ill Feelings," *The Toledo News-Bee*, October 13, 1927, p. 17.
16. Lou Wollen, "Buccaneers Give Mission Tossers Real Lacing: Lee Meadows and Johnny Morrison Show Great Form," *The Pittsburgh Press*, March 20, 1927, p. 1.
17. Lou Wollen, "Vic Aldridge's Pitching Arm Is Bothering Him Again: Goes to Los Angeles to Visit Osteopath," *The Pittsburgh Press*, March 25, 1927, p. 45.
18. Lou Wollen, "Sicking Reports to Pirate Manager with Lame Arm: Bush's Problems Still Unsolved," *The Pittsburgh Press*, April 8, 1927, p. 52.
19. Lou Wollen, "Bush to Name Pirates' Opening Game Hurler Tonight: Rhyne Will Start at Keystone Sack," *The Pittsburgh Press*, April 9, 1927, p. 13.
20. Lou Wollen, "Pirates in Cincinnati Await Opening of Campaign: Dick Bartell Is Sent to New Haven," *The Pittsburgh Press*, April 11, 1927, p. 22.
21. Ralph S. Davis, "Bush Gets Pirates Off Impressively: Mopping Up of Cincy Indicates Team Will Carry Far," *The Sporting News*, April 21, 1927, p. 2.
22. "Playing the Game with the Pirates," *The Pittsburgh Press*, April 18, 1927, p. 24.
23. Lou Wollen, "Playing the Game with Lou Wollen," *The Pittsburgh Press*, April 15, 1927, p. 48.
24. Ralph Davis, "Ralph Davis Says: Some Brilliant Bits of Defensive Play," *The Pittsburgh Press*, April 22, 1927, p. 45.
25. Lou Wollen, "Playing the Game with Lou Wollen," *The Pittsburgh Press*, April 22, 1927, p. 45.
26. "Kiki Cuyler Tells Home-Town Fans About His Troubles: Explains He Has No Ill Feelings," p. 17.
27. Ralph S. Davis, "Bush's Judgment on Cuyler Is Being Vindicated: Hazen Fails to Set Swift Pace," *The Pittsburgh Press*, May 13, 1928, p. 2.
28. Frederick G. Lieb, *The Pittsburgh Pirates* (1948; reprint, Carbondale: Southern Illinois University Press, 2003), p. 227.
29. *Ibid.*
30. *Ibid.*
31. Ralph Davis, "Ralph Davis Says: Cuyler Proponent Unburdens Himself," *The Pittsburgh Press*, August 15, 1927, p. 23.
32. Ralph S. Davis, "Pirates' Gameness Shows in Results: Donie Bush's Crew Fights Hardest When Odds Pile Up," *The Sporting News*, June 9, 1927, p. 1.
33. "National League Standing on Tuesday Morning," *The Sporting News*, June 2, 1927, p. 7.
34. Davis, "Pirates' Gameness Shows in Results," p. 1.
35. Lou Wollen, "Pirates Meet Giants Again, Then Await Coming of Dodgers: Carmen Hill Hurls Today," *The Pittsburgh Press*, June 10, 1927, p. 43.
36. Davis, "Ralph Davis Says: Cuyler Proponent Unburdens Himself," p. 23.
37. "Catcher Smith's Act Hits Pittsburg Team," *The Sporting News*, June 23, 1927, p. 1.
38. *Ibid.*
39. The Observer, "Casual Comment," *The Sporting News*, July 7, 1927, p. 4.
40. Lou Wollen, "Playing the Game with Lou Wollen," *The Pittsburgh Press*, June 18, 1927, p. 15.
41. Lou Wollen, "Ray Kremer Not Yet in Shape for Regular Work: Pirate Mound Ace Needs More Rest," *The Pittsburgh Press*, June 23, 1927, p. 28.
42. "Fans Pass Up Game for Birds," *The Youngstown Daily Vindicator*, June 20, 1927, p. 11.
43. Lou Wollen, "Chicago Cubs Defeat Buccaneers: Homers Best Bush Outfit," *The Pittsburgh Press*, June 26, 1927, p. 1.
44. "Cardinals' Trail Similar to That of Buccaneers: Difficulties Fail to Stop Champs," *The Pittsburgh Press*, June 27, 1927, p. 26.
45. "Wright's Injury Another Hazard for Buccaneers: Troubles Continue to Heckle Corsairs," *The Pittsburgh Press*, June 29, 1927, p. 24.
46. *Ibid.*

47. Lou Wollen, "Barnhart's Comeback as Slugger Without Parallel: Hitting Features Pirate Offensive," *The Pittsburgh Press*, July 6, 1927, p. 26.
48. "National League Standing on Tuesday Morning," *The Sporting News*, July 21, 1927, p. 7.
49. Ralph S. Davis, "Tension Increases in National Joust: Pirates Ready for Fight to Finish with Three Leaders," *The Sporting News*, August 4, 1927, p. 1.
50. *Ibid*.
51. "Bush Tells Why Cuyler Was Lifted," *The Pittsburgh Press*, October 11, 1927, p. 29.
52. Vaughan, "Yanks Escaped Cuyler Menace Once, Not Twice," p. 19.
53. Lou Wollen, "Comeback of Hazen Cuyler Features Play of Buccaneers: Flint Flash Stars in Field and at Bat," *The Pittsburgh Press*, August 5, 1927, p. 30.
54. Lou Wollen, "Buccaneers Stagger as Midsummer Pace Becomes Torrid: Mound Aces Wilt Before Enemy Fire," *The Pittsburgh Press*, August 8, 1927, p. 29.
55. "Giants Score 9 to 2 Victory Over Pirates: Fourth Inning Attack Sends Hill to Cover," *The Pittsburgh Press*, August 7, 1927, p. 1.
56. *Ibid*.
57. Lou Wollen, "Hazen Cuyler Fined $50 by Manager Bush," *The Pittsburgh Press*, August 8, 1927, p. 29.
58. Lou Wollen, "Indifferent Play by Buccaneers Arouses Manager: Mailed Fist Policy Is Inaugurated by Pilot," *The Pittsburgh Press*, August 9, 1927, p. 28.
59. Ralph S. Davis, "Pittsburg Divided on Cuyler Incident: In Meantime, Bush Has Backing of Boss Barney Dreyfuss," *The Sporting News*, August 18, 1927, p. 1.
60. *Ibid*.
61. Lou Wollen, "Pirate Owner Backs Manager in Disciplining Cuyler: Bush Is Given Free Rein, Says Barney Dreyfuss," *The Pittsburgh Press*, August 10, 1927, p. 24.
62. "National League Standing on Tuesday Morning," *The Sporting News*, August 18, 1927, p. 7.
63. "Scribbled by Scribes," *The Sporting News*, August 18, 1927, p. 4.
64. "Pirates Must Win Two Out of Three to Stay in Second: Cardinals Threaten Buccaneer Position," *The Pittsburgh Press*, August 12, 1927, p. 28.
65. *Ibid*.
66. Lou Wollen, "First Lap of Pirates' Eastern Trip Is Unproductive: Buccaneers Unable to Gain on Leaders," *The Pittsburgh Press*, August 20, 1927, p. 13.
67. "Pirates Must Win Two Out of Three to Stay in Second," p. 28.
68. Max E. Bannum, "Pirates Troubles Loom as Football Seeks Limelight," *The Pittsburgh Press*, August 13, 1927, p. 11.
69. "National League Standing on Tuesday Morning," *The Sporting News*, September 8, 1927, p. 7.
70. "Comorosky Will Oppose Cincinnati," *The Pittsburgh Press*, September 6, 1927, p. 28.
71. Lou Wollen, "Bush Likes Work of Comorosky In Pirates' Outfield: Manager Confident Recruit Will Shine," *The Pittsburgh Press*, September 10, 1927, p. 13.
72. Fred Russell, "Why Cuyler Was Benched: Here's New Light on 40-Year-Old Mystery," *Baseball Digest*, May 1968, p. 48.
73. Ralph Davis, "Ralph Davis Says: Donie Bush Will Be Glad When Flag Is Cinched," *The Pittsburgh Press*, September 27, 1927, p. 23.
74. "Cuyler Will Not Be Used," *Providence News*, October 5, 1927, p. 8.
75. "Gossip of First Game," *The Sporting News*, October 13, 1925, p. 3.
76. "Gossip of Second Game," *The Sporting News*, October 13, 1925, p. 5.
77. Lou Wollen, "Pirates Must Improve General Play to Defeat Yankees: Buccos Feeble in All Departments," *The Pittsburgh Press*, October 7, 1927, p. 38.
78. "Something to Remember Him By," *The Pittsburgh Press*, October 7, 1927, p. 40.
79. "Cuyler Is Out of World Series Because of Slump: Buc Fielder Off His Game, Claims Bush," *Miami Daily News and Metropolis*, October 5, 1927, p. 8.
80. "Cuyler Out of Game Because Below Form," *The Ottawa Evening Citizen*, October 6, 1927, p. 1.
81. "Bucs May Trade Off Kiki Cuyler," *The Toledo News-Bee*, October 11, 1927, p. 17.
82. "Cuyler Discusses Banishment Case: Admits He Differed with Bush on Where He Should Play," *The Sporting News*, October 13, 1927, p. 6.
83. "Cuyler Convicts Self, Says Bush: Manager Tells Why He Did Not Use Ki in Series," *The Pittsburgh Press*, October 10, 1927, p. 1.
84. *Ibid*.

Chapter 7

1. "Cuyler Convicts Self, Says Bush: Manager Tells Why He Did Not Use Ki in Series," *The Pittsburgh Press*, October 10, 1927, p. 1.
2. *Ibid*.
3. *Ibid*.
4. Ralph Davis, "Ralph Davis Says: Aldridge Was Friend of Hazen Cuyler," *The Pittsburgh Press*, February 15, 1928, p. 28.
5. Ralph Davis, "Ralph Davis Says: Jealousy May Have Figured in Cuyler Case," *The Pittsburgh Press*, September 10, 1927, p. 13.
6. Ralph Davis, "Ralph Davis Says: Many Alleged Angles to Case," *The Pittsburgh Press*, October 11, 1927, p. 29.
7. *Ibid*.
8. *Ibid*.

9. "Bush Tells Why Cuyler Was Lifted," *The Pittsburgh Press*, October 11, 1927, p. 29.
10. *Ibid.*
11. Ralph S. Davis, "Bush Keeps Cuyler Load for Himself: Reply to Kiki's Statement Is That He Did the Best for Team," *The Sporting News*, October 20, 1927, p. 1.
12. "Kiki Cuyler Tells Home-Town Fans About His Troubles: Explains He Has No Ill Feelings," *The Toledo News-Bee*, October 13, 1927, p. 17.
13. "Cuyler Is Feted at Home at Bay City," *The Border Cities Star*, October 19, 1927, p. 3.
14. "Caught on the Fly," *The Sporting News*, November 3, 1927, p. 8.
15. *Ibid.*
16. Ralph Davis, "Ralph Davis Says: Plenty of Guessing as to Where Cuyler Goes," *The Pittsburgh Press*, October 14, 1927, p. 40.
17. *Ibid.*
18. "World Series Yell Easily Vetoes This," *The Pittsburgh Press*, October 13, 1927, p. 30.
19. "Big Three-Cornered Player Deal Said to Be Under Way: May Land Cuyler in New York," *The Pittsburgh Press*, October 14, 1927, p. 42.
20. Ralph Davis, "Ralph Davis Says: The Society of the Mentioned," *The Pittsburgh Press*, October 22, 1927, p. 14.
21. Ralph Davis, "Ralph Davis Says: Much Guessing as to National's Most Valuable Man," *The Pittsburgh Press*, November 3, 1927, p. 32.
22. "Scribbled by Scribes," *The Sporting News*, November 17, 1927, p. 4.
23. *Ibid.*
24. Ralph S. Davis, "Wherein Dreyfuss Feels a Sickness: Pirate Owner Tires of Ceaseless Talk About His Ball Team," *The Sporting News*, November 24, 1927, p. 5.
25. *Ibid.*
26. Frank Getty, "Sale of Pirates Would Put Cuyler Back in Buc Lineup," *The Independent*, October 14, 1927, p. 5A.
27. "Man Without a Baseball Country," *Telegraph-Herald and Times-Journal*, October 28, 1927, p. 12.
28. Irving Vaughan, "Cubs Land Cuyler from Pirate Club: Pittsburg Storm Center Traded for Two Chicago Players," *The Sporting News*, December 1, 1927, p. 1.
29. John B. Foster, "Joe McCarthy Is Strong for Fred Maguire," *The Leader*, December 7, 1927, p. 14.
30. Vaughan, "Cubs Land Cuyler from Pirate Club," p. 1.
31. Ralph S. Davis, "Fans Approve Trading Judgment of Manager Bush: More Deals May Be Made by Pirates," *The Pittsburgh Press*, December 4, 1927, p. 2.
32. Joe Williams, "Joe Williams Says: McCarthy Denies the Story, But It Is True, Just the Same," *The Pittsburgh Press*, October 31, 1930, p. 53.
33. "Cuyler Trade Gives Pirates Best of Deal," *Miami Daily News and Metropolis*, November 30, 1927, p. 14.
34. Ralph S. Davis, "Trade Week Meant Little to Pittsburg: Only Real Deal Offered Was One Bush Couldn't See," *The Sporting News*, December 22, 1927, p. 5.
35. *Ibid.*
36. "Scribbled by Scribes," *The Sporting News*, December 15, 1927, p. 4.
37. "Kiki Cuyler Signed," *The Gazette*, December 5, 1927, p. 21.
38. Irving Vaughan, "Kiki Cuyler Signs His 1928 Contract with Cub Bosses," *Chicago Daily Tribune*, December 4, 1927, p. A1.
39. *Ibid.*
40. Irving Vaughan, "Cuyler's First Act as Cub Peaceful: Outfield Star Quickly Signs Up and Says He's Happy," *The Sporting News*, December 8, 1927, p. 1.
41. Vaughan, "Kiki Cuyler Signs His 1928 Contract with Cub Bosses," p. A1.
42. "Kiki Cuyler Turns Basketball Official," *The Toledo News-Bee*, January 16, 1928, p. 12.
43. "Cuyler's Cagers Meet Nationals Here Tomorrow," *Chicago Daily Tribune*, February 19, 1928, p. A2.
44. Ralph Davis, "Ralph Davis Says: Cuyler May Be Cubs' Cleanup Clouter," *The Pittsburgh Press*, February 13, 1928, p. 26.
45. Davis, "Ralph Davis Says: Aldridge Was Friend of Hazen Cuyler,*"* p. 28.
46. Ralph Davis, "Ralph Davis Says: Chicago Gives Hazen Cuyler Big Welcome," *The Pittsburgh Press*, February 25, 1928, p. 11.
47. *Ibid.*
48. "Scribbled by Scribes," *The Sporting News*, January 5, 1928, p. 4.
49. Ralph Davis, "Ralph Davis Says: Hazen Cuyler Is Off to Great Start," *The Pittsburgh Press*, March 23, 1928, p. 41.
50. *Ibid.*
51. Lou Wollen, "Smith Will Be Valuable to Pirates This Season: Earl Was Slated to Be Discarded," *The Pittsburgh Press*, March 30, 1928, p. 50.
52. Ralph Davis, "Ralph Davis Says: Cuyler and Wilson Had Laugh on Smith," *The Pittsburgh Press*, April 10, 1928, p. 28.
53. *Ibid.*
54. *Ibid.*
55. *Ibid.*
56. *Ibid.*
57. "Training Camp Notes," *The Sporting News*, March 22, 1928, p. 8.
58. Irving Vaughan, "Cubs Not Alone in Failure to Go Over: Nobody Running Away with John Heydler's Flag to Date," *The Sporting News*, May 10, 1928, p. 1.
59. Irving Vaughan, "Cubs Doing All Any Sane Fan Could Ask: Only Those Looking for Miracles Are Disappointed," *The Sporting News*, April 26, 1928, p. 1.

60. Irving Vaughan, "Cubs Held Down by Failure of Hitters: Kiki Cuyler Biggest Flop So Far, but Has an Alibi," *The Sporting News*, May 3, 1928, p. 1.

61. Lou Wollen, "Burleigh Grimes Demonstrates Defensive Ability: Pirate Pitcher Stars in Field," *The Pittsburgh Press*, May 1, 1928, p. 37.

62. "You Won't See This Often," *The Pittsburgh Press*, May 2, 1928, p. 37.

63. Lou Wollen, "Sparky Adams, Booed for Errors, Stages Comeback: Wins Game with Sacrifice Blow," *The Pittsburgh Press*, May 3, 1928, p. 34.

64. Ralph Davis, "Ralph Davis Says: What Does Baseball Fan Loyalty Mean?" *The Pittsburgh Press*, May 4, 1928, p. 46.

65. *Ibid.*

66. Lou Wollen, "Cubs Make First Appearance at Forbes Field Today: Cuyler, Former Buc, in Lineup," *The Pittsburgh Press*, April 30, 1928, p. 33.

67. Ralph S. Davis, "Bush's Judgment on Cuyler Is Being Vindicated: Hazen Fails to Set Swift Pace," *The Pittsburgh Press*, May 13, 1928, p. 2.

68. *Ibid.*

69. *Ibid.*

70. "National League Standing on Tuesday Morning," *The Sporting News*, May 24, 1928, p. 7.

71. *Ibid.*

72. Irving Vaughan, "Cub Fans Rejoice in Cuyler's Comeback: It Raises Their Hopes of Better Things in Future," *The Sporting News*, June 21, 1928, p. 1.

73. Lou Wollen, "Pirates Notes," *The Pittsburgh Press*, June 25, 1928, p. 26.

74. Irving Vaughan, "An Extra Act by Hack Wilson in Which There Is a Lesson," *The Sporting News*, June 28, 1928, p. 1.

75. Ralph Davis, "Ralph Davis Says: Stork Pays Visit to Cuyler Family," *The Pittsburgh Press*, July 11, 1928, p. 27.

76. *Ibid.*

77. Irving Vaughan, "Root and Cuyler Cross Crabby Fans: Both Come Through Just as They Were Counted Out," *The Sporting News*, July 19, 1928, p. 1.

78. "Wrigley Sure Cubs Pennant Winners After Sweep in Pirate Series," *The Independent*, April 3, 1928, p. 4.

79. "Mrs. Joe Knows by Knocks How Goes It," *The Eugene Guard*, April 13, 1928, p. 4.

80. Arthur Markey "Between Ourselves Intimate Sport Chat: Bush on the Pan," *Providence News*, July 14, 1928, p. 9.

81. Ralph S. Davis, "Jinx Hands Pirates Another Hard Blow: Injury of Floyd Scott in Line with Team's Bad Luck," *The Sporting News*, August 2, 1928, p. 3.

82. Irving Vaughan, "Give Cubs a Record on This One Anyway: Probably No Team Ever Has Won So Many Home Games," *The Sporting News*, August 30, 1928, p. 1.

83. "National League Standing on Tuesday Morning," *The Sporting News*, September 6, 1928, p. 7.

84. "Baseball By-Plays," *The Sporting News*, September 20, 1928, p. 4.

85. *Ibid.*

86. *Ibid.*

87. *Ibid.*

88. "National League Standing at Close of Season," *The Sporting News*, October 4, 1928, p. 6.

89. Irving Vaughan, "Chicago City Series Pulls a Comeback: Fans Turn Out in Droves to See Cubs and White Sox," *The Sporting News*, October 11, 1928, p. 1.

90. Irving Vaughan, "Cubs Learn About Rolling in Wealth: Enjoy Experience of Sharing in Two Fall Purses," *The Sporting News*, October 18, 1928, p. 1.

91. "Cuyler May Be Traded to Boston," *The Pittsburgh Press*, October 18, 1928, p. 33.

Chapter 8

1. Irving Vaughan, "Hornsby's Price Is Only Question Now: No Doubt About His Going to Chicago Cubs," *The Sporting News*, October 25, 1928, p. 1.

2. Irving Vaughan, "Hornsby and Cuyler Keep Eyesight Sharp by Hunting," *Chicago Daily Tribune*, November 29, 1928, p. 31.

3. "Caught on the Fly," *The Sporting News*, November 8, 1928, p. 8.

4. Ralph S. Davis, "Pirates Win and So Bush Regains Favor: Fortune Turns When Smith and Miljus Are Discarded," *The Sporting News*, July 26, 1928, p. 3.

5. Thomas S. Rice, "Petty Stuff Turns Out to Be Big Stuff: Jess Says He'll Not Join Bucs Till Robby Remits $1,000," *The Sporting News*, December 27, 1928, p. 1.

6. Ralph Davis, "Cuyler to Lead Off for Cubs," *The Pittsburgh Press*, December 12, 1928, p. 37.

7. "Kiki Cuyler's Quintet to Meet Nationals Tomorrow," *Chicago Daily Tribune*, January 13, 1929, p. A4.

8. Irving Vaughan, "Hartnett Gives Up to His Eligibility: Cubs' Noted Bachelor Quits Life of Single Blessedness," *The Sporting News*, January 31, 1929, p. 8.

9. "Scribbled by Scribes," *The Sporting News*, March 14, 1929, p. 4.

10. *Ibid.*

11. Dan Thomas, "Chicago Cubs, with Hornsby, Look Very Powerful: Up to Hurlers, Says McCarthy," *The Pittsburgh Press*, March 28, 1929, p. 32.

12. *Ibid.*

13. Edward Burns, "Clubhouse Confessions of Our Cubs," *Chicago Daily Tribune*, June 23, 1929, p. A2.

14. Edward Burns, "Wanted for Larceny! Man Named Cuyler," *Chicago Daily Tribune*, September 25, 1929, p. 23.
15. "The Cubs Visit the Mexican Rebels," *The Meriden Daily Journal*, April 6, 1929, p. 4.
16. Irving Vaughan, "Cubs Manager Lets His Feelings Slip: M'Carthy Admits Cubs Are Good and Looks for Pennant," *The Sporting News*, April 18, 1929, p. 1.
17. "National League Standing on Tuesday Morning," *The Sporting News*, April 25, 1929, p. 9.
18. "National League Standing on Tuesday Morning," *The Sporting News*, May 2, 1929, p. 7.
19. Irving Vaughan, "Yes, It's Catching, If You Should Ask: Injuries Hit Three Cub Receivers, Including New Addition," *The Sporting News*, May 2, 1929, p. 3.
20. "National League Standing on Tuesday Morning," *The Sporting News*, May 2, 1929, p. 7.
21. "Wilson-Cuyler Return to Lineup of Bruins Today," *The Pittsburgh Press*, May 15, 1929, p. 35.
22. "National League Standing on Tuesday Morning," *The Sporting News*, May 23, 1929, p. 7.
23. "Scribbled by Scribes," *The Sporting News*, May 16, 1929, p. 4.
24. Irving Vaughan, "Cubs Shake Habit of Losing On Road: At Least, Current Trip Has Found Team Able to Win," *The Sporting News*, May 16, 1929, p. 1.
25. "National League Standing on Tuesday Morning," *The Sporting News*, May 23, 1929, p. 7.
26. Irving Vaughan, "Cubs Keep Right on Winning, Though Rajah's Batting Sags," *The Sporting News*, May 30, 1929, p. 1.
27. "National League Standing on Tuesday Morning," *The Sporting News*, June 20, 1929, p. 7.
28. *Ibid.*
29. *Ibid.*
30. "National League Standing on Tuesday Morning," *The Sporting News*, June 27, 1929, p. 7.
31. *Ibid.*
32. Irving Vaughan, "M'Carthy's Cubs Find Nicest Kind of Cousins in Cardinals," *The Sporting News*, July 4, 1929, p. 1.
33. Irving Vaughan, "Wilson Gives Boys Touch of Old Days: Outfielder Invades Reds' Bench, Later Wallops Donohue," *The Sporting News*, July 11, 1929, p. 1.
34. *Ibid.*
35. *Ibid.*
36. Irving Vaughan, "Chicago Applauds Heydler's Decision: Hint Passed Cincinnati Sought to Weaken Chicago Team," *The Sporting News*, July 18, 1929, p. 1.
37. "National League Standing on Tuesday Morning," *The Sporting News*, July 18, 1929, p. 7.
38. Irving Vaughan, "Cubs Must Hustle to Shake Off Bucs: Successful Eastern Trip Keys Up Team for Home Stand," *The Sporting News*, July 25, 1929, p. 1.
39. Irving Vaughan, "Chicago Cubs Make Turnstiles Click: Everything Pointing to Another Mark for Wrigley," *The Sporting News*, August 1, 1929, p. 1.
40. "National League Standing on Tuesday Morning," *The Sporting News*, August 8, 1929, p. 7.
41. "Scribbled by Scribes," *The Sporting News*, September 5, 1929, p. 4.
42. "National League Standing on Tuesday Morning," *The Sporting News*, September 26, 1929, p. 7.
43. Irving Vaughan, "Commy to Emerge from Retirement: Shires Influences Veteran's Plan to Again Run Club," *The Sporting News*, September 26, 1929, p. 1.
44. "Scribbled by Scribes," *The Sporting News*, September 26, 1929, p. 4.
45. *Ibid.*
46. "40,000 Workers Honor Cubs at Mass-meeting," *Chicago Daily Tribune*, September 21, 1929, p. 22.
47. Irving Vaughan, "Chicago Fans Begin Figuring Things Out: One Series Disappointment Ahead Seems to Be in Tickets," *The Sporting News*, September 12, 1929, p. 1.
48. Irving Vaughan, "Bush Has Two-Year Contract with Sox: Former Pirate Leader Succeeds Blackburne as Chief," *The Sporting News*, October 3, 1929, p. 1.
49. "National League Standing on Tuesday Morning," *The Sporting News*, September 26, 1929, p. 7.
50. Vaughan, "Bush Has Two-Year Contract with Sox: Former Pirate Leader Succeeds Blackburne as Chief," p. 1.
51. Werner Laufer, "Kiki Cuyler Is Valuable: Despite Long List of Injuries Chicago Star Has Proved His Worth," *Providence News*, September 24, 1929, p. 7.
52. Paul R. Mickelson, "Much Expected of Kiki Cuyler," *The Free Lance-Star*, September 30, 1929, p. 2.
53. *Ibid.*
54. Paul Mickelson, "World Series Sidelights," *Sarasota Herald*, October 9, 1929, p. 6.
55. "Gossip of First Game," *The Sporting News*, October 17, 1929, p. 3.
56. "First Game in Detail," *The Sporting News*, October 17, 1929, p. 3.
57. "Gossip of First Game," *The Sporting News*, October 17, 1929, p. 3.
58. "First Game in Detail," *The Sporting News*, October 17, 1929, p. 3.
59. "Ehmke Real Hero of Opener: Fanning 13 Chicago Batters," *The Sporting News*, October 17, 1929, p. 3.
60. Bill Dooly, "It's a Secret No Longer! Ehmke Turns Witness in Expose of Late World's Series, and Relates How He Clipped Cubs' Claws," *The Sporting News*, January 2, 1930, p. 3.
61. *Ibid.*

62. *Ibid.*
63. *Ibid.*
64. "Gossip of First Game," *The Sporting News*, October 17, 1929, p. 3.
65. Hazen (Kiki) Cuyler—Chicago Cubs Outfielder, Spectacular Hitter and Base Stealer, "Cubs Showed They Can Hit Fast Pitching," *The Milwaukee Journal*, October 10, 1929, p. 7.
66. *Ibid.*
67. "Third Game in Detail," *The Sporting News*, October 17, 1929, p. 6.
68. *Ibid.*
69. Damon Runyan, "Advice Heeded By Kiki Cuyler," *Milwaukee Sentinel*, October 12, 1929, p. 12.
70. "Fourth Game in Detail," *The Sporting News*, October 17, 1929, p. 6.
71. *Ibid.*
72. *Ibid.*
73. "Gossip of Fourth Game," *The Sporting News*, October 17, 1929, p. 8.
74. "Fourth Game in Detail," *The Sporting News*, October 17, 1929, p. 6.
75. "Gossip of Fourth Game," *The Sporting News*, October 17, 1929, p. 8.
76. *Ibid.*
77. "Hoover Neutral Fan; Knows His Baseball," *The Milwaukee Journal*, October 15, 1929, p. 6.
78. *Ibid.*
79. "Fifth Game in Detail," *The Sporting News*, October 17, 1929, p. 8.
80. *Ibid.*
81. *Ibid.*
82. "Haas' Homer and Miller's Hit Put Over Deciding Wallop," *The Sporting News*, October 17, 1929, p. 8.
83. Hazen (Kiki) Cuyler—Chicago Cubs Outfielder, "Rally in Ninth Proved Game Is on the Level," *The Milwaukee Journal*, October 15, 1929, p. 6.

Chapter 9

1. "Cubs Homecoming Is Like Funeral," *The Telegraph Herald and Times-Journal*, October 16, 1929, p. 11.
2. "Scribbled by Scribes," *The Sporting News*, October 31, 1929, p. 4.
3. *Ibid.*
4. *Ibid.*
5. Irving Vaughan, "Chicago Fans Give Wrigley Big Order: Impression Prevails Bell Is Not Only Addition Needed," *The Sporting News*, November 7, 1929, p. 1.
6. Edward Burns, "Wanted for Larceny! Man Named Cuyler," *Chicago Daily Tribune*, September 25, 1929, p. 21.
7. Edward Burns, "It Takes a Moose to Bring Out the Tiger in Cuyler!" *Chicago Daily Tribune*, June 2, 1935, p. B2.
8. *Alcona County: A Pictorial History*, vol. I (Harrisville: The Alcona County Review, 2007; reprinted by Cheryl L. Peterson and John D. Boufford, 2009), p. 152.
9. Burns, "It Takes a Moose to Bring Out the Tiger in Cuyler!" p. B2.
10. *Ibid.*
11. 1930 United States Census, www.ancestry.com.
12. Burns, "It Takes a Moose to Bring Out the Tiger in Cuyler!" p. B2.
13. 1930 United States Census, www.ancestry.com.
14. Irving Vaughan, "Kiki Cuyler Accepts Terms; All Cubs in Fold," *Chicago Daily Tribune*, February 7, 1930, p. 17.
15. *Ibid.*
16. "Kiki Cuyler Given Two Years' Contract," *Sarasota Herald*, February 7, 1930, p. 5.
17. "Cuyler Lauds Bush as Pilot," *The Milwaukee Sentinel*, February 9, 1930, p. 4.
18. *Ibid.*
19. "Caught on the Fly with the Sports Writers," *The Sporting News*, November 28, 1929, p. 8.
20. Irving Vaughan, "Those Pestiferous Hartnett Tonsils: They're Out Again, Though Gabby Thought He Was Cured," *The Sporting News*, November 28, 1929, p. 1.
21. Irving Vaughan, "Landis Outpoints Shires in Oratory: Commissioner Tells Chicago Lad to Quit Ring—He Does," *The Sporting News*, January 23, 1930, p. 1.
22. "Training Camp Notes," *The Sporting News*, March 13, 1930, p. 8.
23. Irving Vaughan, "M'Carthy Judges Cub Batting Order: English and Cuyler Considered as 1930 Leadoff Men," *The Sporting News*, March 20, 1930, p. 1.
24. "Training Camp Notes," *The Sporting News*, March 13, 1930, p. 8.
25. Irving Vaughan, "Cubs Team Crippled, with Stars Injured: Grimm Recovers, but Hornsby and Bell Sit on Bench," *The Sporting News*, April 24, 1930, p. 1.
26. Kiki Cuyler, "Cuyler Tells Boys How to Catch Flies," *Chicago Daily Tribune*, May 5, 1930, p. 25.
27. Kiki Cuyler, "Cuyler Tells Boy Outfielders How to Prepare for Throw," *Chicago Daily Tribune*, May 6, 1930, p. 30.
28. *Ibid.*
29. Hack Wilson and Kiki Cuyler, "Be Comfortable at Plate—Hack; Kiki Tells How He Meets Ball," *Chicago Daily Tribune*, May 9, 1930, p. 27.
30. *Ibid.*
31. Arch Ward, "Giants to Help Kiki and Hack in Baseball Class," *Chicago Daily Tribune*, May 9, 1930, p. 25.
32. Arch Ward, "6,000 Attend Baseball Class; Lindblom Boy Is Best Hitter," *Chicago Daily Tribune*, May 11, 1930, p. A1.

33. *Ibid.*
34. *Ibid.*
35. *Ibid.*
36. "One for the Book," *The Sporting News*, May 15, 1930, p. 5.
37. Irving Vaughan, "Hornsby in Line-up Only on His Nerve: Pitchers' Disappointing Showing Now Worries M'Carthy," *The Sporting News*, May 8, 1930, p. 1.
38. "Caught on the Fly," *The Sporting News*, May 15, 1930, p. 5.
39. "National League Standing on Tuesday Morning," *The Sporting News*, June 5, 1930, p. 7.
40. Gene Kessler, "Casual Comment," *The Sporting News*, June 5, 1930, p. 4.
41. Irving Vaughan, "Chicago Cubs, Stricken by Grief, Battle with Vengeance to Win: Tragedies Fire Players with Determination," *The Sporting News*, June 5, 1930, p. 1.
42. Kessler, "Casual Comment," p. 4.
43. *Ibid.*
44. "National League Standing on Tuesday Morning," *The Sporting News*, June 5, 1930, p. 7.
45. Vaughan, "Chicago Cubs, Stricken by Grief, Battle with Vengeance to Win: Tragedies Fire Players with Determination," p. 1.
46. *Ibid.*
47. "National League Standing on Tuesday Morning," *The Sporting News*, June 5, 1930, p. 7.
48. "National League Standing on Tuesday Morning," *The Sporting News*, June 26, 1930, p. 7.
49. "National League Standing on Tuesday Morning," *The Sporting News*, July 3, 1930 p. 7.
50. "Baseball By-Plays: Cuyler and Finn Twins," *The Sporting News*, July 10, 1930, p. 4.
51. *Ibid.*
52. "National League Standing on Tuesday Morning," *The Sporting News*, July 3, 1930, p. 7.
53. "National League Standing on Tuesday Morning," *The Sporting News*, July 10, 1930, p. 7.
54. Irving Vaughan, "Blair Filling Hornsby's Shoes While Cubs Claw Robins' Wings," *The Sporting News*, June 26, 1930, p. 1.
55. "O'Doul Shows Way to Nat. League Sluggers," *The Meriden Daily Journal*, July 12, 1930, p. 4.
56. Copeland C. Burg, "Four Runs in Ninth Are Wasted," *Rochester Evening Journal*, July 14, 1930, p. 14.
57. "Cubs' Accelerator for Pennant Drive: Outfielder Kiki Cuyler," *The Sporting News*, July 24, 1930, p. 3.
58. "Bruins Begin Stretch Drive with Two Wins," *Pittsburgh-Post Gazette*, July 29, 1930, p. 16.
59. *Ibid.*
60. "National League Standing on Tuesday Morning," *The Sporting News*, August 14, 1930, p. 7.
61. Irving Vaughan, "Chicago Cubs Must Amble Along Without Hornsby for Some Time: Uncertain When Rogers Will Return to Game," *The Sporting News*, August 7, 1930, p. 1.
62. "Cubs Down Robins in Tense 10-Inning Struggle: Danny Taylor's Hit Scores Winning Run," *Schenectady Gazette*, August 15, 1930, p. 12.
63. "National League Standing on Tuesday Morning," *The Sporting News*, August 21, 1930, p. 7.
64. "Cards Defeat Cubs, 8 to 7, in 20 Innings: Single by High, Scoring Douthit, Wins Long Battle," *The Milwaukee Sentinel*, August 29, 1930, p. 11.
65. "Scribbled by Scribes," *The Sporting News*, September 11, 1930, p. 4.
66. Edward Burns, "No, Fans, It Isn't Lack of Sleep That Slows Cubs," *Chicago Daily Tribune*, September 7, 1930, p. A2.
67. *Ibid.*
68. Irving Vaughan, "M'Carthy Through at Chicago, Hornsby in Line as Successor," *The Sporting News*, September 25, 1930, p. 1.
69. Irving Vaughan, "Several Bruins Due to Change Addresses: Hornsby Plans Numerous Deals Which May Include Bell," *The Sporting News*, October 2, 1930, p. 1.
70. "Hornsby Says He Will Not Trade Off Stars of Club," *The Pittsburgh Press*, September 24, 1930, p. 29.
71. *Ibid.*
72. Vaughan, "Several Bruins Due to Change Addresses: Hornsby Plans Numerous Deals Which May Include Bell," p. 1.
73. "Cubs Win Chicago Series, Retaining City Crown: Pitching of Blake and Malone Gives National Leaguers Edge," *The Sporting News*, October 9, 1930, p. 2.
74. Irving Vaughan, "Cub Partisans Quick to Forget M'Carthy: Take Their City Series Seriously in Supporting Cubs," *The Sporting News*, October 9, 1930, p. 1.
75. "Cubs Win Chicago Series, Retaining City Crown: Pitching of Blake and Malone Gives National Leaguers Edge," p. 2.
76. "Hack Wilson Puts on Vaudeville Act," *Sarasota Herald*, October 9, 1930, p. 1.
77. Burns, "It Takes a Moose to Bring Out the Tiger in Cuyler!" p. B2.
78. *Ibid.*
79. "Caught on the Fly," *The Sporting News*, November 13, 1930, p. 8.
80. Irving Vaughan, "Cuyler Enrolls in Cubs' 1931 Optimist Club," *Chicago Daily Tribune*, January 16, 1931, p. 29.
81. *Ibid.*
82. Irving Vaughan, "Tag On Bottomley Stops Deal by Cubs: Breadon Asks $150,000 For Star, Causing Wrigley to Gasp," *The Sporting News*, December 18, 1930, p. 1.
83. Vaughan, "Cuyler Enrolls in Cubs' 1931 Optimist Club," p. 29.
84. Harry T. Brundidge, "Cuyler, Leading Base Stealer, Was Traded for Not Sliding: Star

Gives Own Version of Why He Was Benched and Shipped to Cubs by Pirates," *The Sporting News*, February 5, 1931, p. 5.
85. *Ibid.*
86. *Ibid.*
87. Irving Vaughan, "Hack Wilson Signs, Given Boost In Pay: Cub's Home Run Slugger to Draw Approximately $35,000," *The Sporting News*, February 5, 1931, p. 1.
88. Ronald McIntyre, "Between You and Me," *The Milwaukee Sentinel*, February 28, 1931, pp. 23–24.
89. "Caught on the Fly," *The Sporting News*, February 19, 1931, p. 8.
90. Irving Vaughan, "Hornsby Lays Down Laws for Cub Camp: Demand Men Think, Eat, Sleep Baseball While Training," *The Sporting News*, February 26, 1931, p. 1.
91. Francis J. Powers, "Current Comment," *The Sporting News*, March 5, 1931, p. 4.
92. *Ibid.*
93. Les Conklin, "Dissension Crops Out Among Big League Baseball Clubs: Report Discord in Coast Den of Chicago Bruins," *The Telegraph-Herald and Times-Journal*, April 2, 1931, p. 11.
94. "Hack Wilson Wants to Play His Old Position in Center," *The Telegraph-Herald and Times-Journal*, February 22, 1931, p. 13.
95. "Training Camp Notes," *The Sporting News*, March 5, 1931, p. 5.
96. "Homer by Bottomley Beats Cubs and Puts Cards in First Place," *Milwaukee Sentinel*, April 21, 1931, p. 14.
97. "Behind the Scene with Scoop," *The Telegraph-Herald and Times-Journal*, April 24, 1931, p. 11.

Chapter 10

1. "Training Camp Notes," *The Sporting News*, March 5, 1931, p. 5.
2. "National League Standing on Tuesday Morning," *The Sporting News*, May 14, 1931, p. 7.
3. *Ibid.*
4. "National League Standing on Tuesday Morning," *The Sporting News*, May 28, 1931, p. 7.
5. *Ibid.*
6. "National League Standing on Tuesday Morning," *The Sporting News*, June 4, 1931, p. 7.
7. "Chicago Cubs Make It Three Straight Over Cincy Reds: Hack Wilson Gets Into Game, Hits 2-Bagger," *The Telegraph-Herald and Times-Journal*, May 28, 1931, p. 13.
8. "National League Standing on Tuesday Morning," *The Sporting News*, June 4, 1931, p. 7.
9. *Ibid.*
10. Irving Vaughan, "Hemsley Quickens Pace of Cubs, Helps Them Into Second Place: Pirate Backstop Replaces Hartnett," *The Sporting News*, June 11, 1931, p. 1.

11. "Cuyler's Homer Gives Cubs Win Over Brooklyn," *The Telegraph-Herald and Times-Journal*, June 5, 1931, p. 11.
12. "Rare Feat at Chicago," *The Reading Eagle*, June 9, 1931, p. 12.
13. Irving Vaughan, "Cubs' Slow Machine Slips Into Low Gear: Charlie Grimm Replaced by Blair to Inject Speed in Team," *The Sporting News*, May 14, 1931, p. 1.
14. Irving Vaughan, "Cubs' Play Boys Feel Iron Hand of Hornsby for Breaking Rules: Wilson, Hemsley Rouse Ire of Manager," *The Sporting News*, July 2, 1931, p. 1.
15. *Ibid.*
16. "National League Standing on Tuesday Morning," *The Sporting News*, July 9, 1931, p. 9.
17. "National League Standing on Tuesday Morning," *The Sporting News*, July 23, 1931, p. 9.
18. "Cubs Seeking Art Shires to Brace for Strong Pennant Drive," *Rochester Evening Journal and The Post Express*, July 21, 1931, p. 18.
19. Irving Vaughan, "Rajah Still Juggles to Get Winner: Many Combinations Are Tried to Muster Full Strength," *The Sporting News*, July 30, 1931, p. 1.
20. "National League Standing on Tuesday Morning," *The Sporting News*, July 30, 1931, p. 9.
21. "National League Standing on Tuesday Morning," *The Sporting News*, August 6, 1931, p. 9.
22. "National League Standing on Tuesday Morning," *The Sporting News*, September 3, 1931, p. 9.
23. Irving Vaughan, "Wholesale Shaking Up of Cubs Presaged by Moves of Wrigley: Four Scouts Scour All Minors for Talent," *The Sporting News*, August 13, 1931, p. 1.
24. Irving Vaughan, "Cubs to Experiment with Young Players: Ignore Fight for Second Place Coin to Build for '32," *The Sporting News*, September 3, 1931, p. 1.
25. *Ibid.*
26. "National League Standing on Tuesday Morning," *The Sporting News*, September 10, 1931, p. 9.
27. Irving Vaughan, "Cubs Stage Spring Try-Outs This Fall: Hornsby to Test All New Talent Regardless of Standing," *The Sporting News*, September 10, 1931, p. 3.
28. Irving Vaughan, "Wilson and Malone Break Their Slates: Pitcher and Outfielder Playboys Scheduled to Leave Cubs," *The Sporting News*, September 17, 1931, p. 3.
29. Sid Keener, "Sid Keener's Column," *The Sporting News*, September 17, 1931, p. 4.
30. Vaughan, "Wilson and Malone Break Their Slates: Pitcher and Outfielder Playboys Scheduled to Leave Cubs," p. 3.
31. *Ibid.*
32. "Hack Wilson Puts Blame for Troubles on Hornsby," *The Sporting News*, September 17, 1931, p. 1.

Notes. Chapter 10

33. *Ibid.*
34. Sid Keener, "Sid Keener's Column," *The Sporting News*, September 17, 1931, p. 4.
35. *Ibid.*
36. William Braucher, "All-Star Nine in Nat Named," *The Florence* (AL) *Times-News*, September 19, 1931, p. 5.
37. "Fans Vote Lefty Grove Most Valuable Player in Majors," *The Sporting News*, October 15, 1931, p. 2.
38. "Caught on the Fly," *The Sporting News*, October 29, 1931, p. 8.
39. "White Sox Outplay Cubs and Win Chicago City Series in 7 Games," *The Sporting News*, October 15, 1931, p. 5.
40. Edgar G. Brands, "Between Innings," *The Sporting News*, December 31, 1931, p. 4.
41. Edward Burns, "It Takes a Moose to Bring Out the Tiger in Cuyler!" *Chicago Daily Tribune*, June 2, 1935, p. B2.
42. "Caught on the Fly," *The Sporting News*, December 24, 1931, p. 7.
43. "Rajah Molding Speedy Club," *Rochester Evening Journal and The Post Express*, December 22, 1931, p. 20.
44. Edward Burns, "Hornsby Is Banking on Grimes as Big Aid: Rajah Denies That He Anticipates Trouble with Burleigh," *The Sporting News*, December 24, 1931, p. 1.
45. *Ibid.*
46. "Rajah Molding Speedy Squad," p. 20.
47. "Brief Bits of Winter Diamond Gossip," *The Sporting News*, November 26, 1931, p. 2.
48. Irving Vaughan, "Passing of Wrigley Is Shock to Nation: Owner of Chicago Cubs Succumbs at Phoenix, Arizona," *The Sporting News*, January 28, 1932, p. 1.
49. "William Wrigley Jr.," *The Sporting News*, January 28, 1932, p. 1.
50. Angel, "Catalina Final Resting Place for Wm. Wrigley," *The Sporting News*, February 4, 1932, p. 2.
51. *Ibid.*
52. "Kiki Cuyler Signs," *The Washington, Pennsylvania, Daily Reporter*, February 9, 1932, p. 8.
53. "Caught on the Fly," *The Sporting News*, April 7, 1932, p. 6.
54. "Caught on the Fly," *The Sporting News*, February 18, 1932, p. 6.
55. Irving Vaughan, "Cubs and Pale Hose Face Unusual Tests: Bruins Count on Rookie, with Hornsby on Bench," *The Sporting News*, April 14, 1932, p. 6.
56. "Cuyler Lost to Cubs," *Rochester Evening Journal and The Post Express*, April 25, 1932, p. 13.
57. "National League Standing on Tuesday Morning," *The Sporting News*, April 28, 1932, p. 7.
58. Irving Vaughan, "Tribe Aids Fonseca in Darning His Hose: Hodapp and Seeds Are Expected to Bolster Sox' Attack," *The Sporting News*, April 28, 1932, p. 1.
59. Irving Vaughan, "Trades by Sox and Cubs' Spurt Keep Chicago Fandom Keyed Up: Rajah Has Team in High with Stars on Shelf," *The Sporting News*, May 5, 1932, p. 1.
60. Vaughan, "Tribe Aids Fonseca in Darning His Hose: Hodapp and Seeds Are Expected to Bolster Sox' Attack," p. 1.
61. Vaughan, "Trades by Sox and Cubs' Spurt Keep Chicago Fandom Keyed Up: Rajah Has Team in High with Stars on Shelf," p. 1.
62. J.G. Taylor Spink, "Casual Comment," *The Sporting News*, May 5, 1932, p. 4.
63. "Kiki Cuyler Will Be Out for Another Month," *Cape Girardeau Southeast Missourian*, May 18, 1932, p. 3.
64. Irving Vaughan, "Hornsby Takes Post in Outfield to Add Power to Bruins' Punch: Leaves Infield Intact While it Clicks," *The Sporting News*, June 2, 1932, p. 1.
65. "The Cause of the Gag Rule," *The Sporting News*, June 2, 1932, p. 3.
66. *Ibid.*
67. Irving Vaughan, "Presence of Cuyler to Strengthen Club: Star Outfielder Ready to Return After Six Weeks' Absence," *The Sporting News*, June 9, 1932, p. 1.
68. Irving Vaughan, "Cubs Cling to Top, Despite Light Hitting and Road Jinx Complex: Airtight Pitching Saves Hornsby's Outfit," *The Sporting News*, June 16, 1932, p. 1.
69. Irving Vaughan, "Cuyler's Return to Game Gives Cubs Full Fighting Strength," *The Sporting News*, June 23, 1932, p. 1.
70. Irving Vaughan, "Rajah Again Frisks Barton for Bingles: Recalls Outfielder from Reading to Produce Base Hits," *The Sporting News*, July 7, 1932, p. 1.
71. "Practice Ordered by Disappointed Hornsby," *The Tuscaloosa News*, June 30, 1932, p. 8.
72. "National League Standing on Tuesday Morning," *The Sporting News*, July 14, 1932, p. 8.
73. *Ibid.*
74. "Girl Who Shot Cub Shortstop Planned Murder and Suicide; Kiki Cuyler Looms as Villain," *The Herald-Telegraph and Times-Journal*, July 7, 1932, p. 1.
75. *Ibid.*
76. "National League Standing on Tuesday Morning," *The Sporting News*, July 14, 1932, p. 8.
77. "Conceited Kiki Angers Violet," *The Pittsburgh Press*, July 10, 1932, p. 4.
78. *Ibid.*
79. *Ibid.*
80. "National League Standing on Tuesday Morning," *The Sporting News*, July 14, 1932, p. 8.
81. "Girl Who Shot Cub Shortstop Planned Murder and Suicide; Kiki Cuyler Looms as Villain," p. 1.
82. *Ibid.*
83. "National League Standing on Tuesday Morning," *The Sporting News*, July 21, 1932, p. 8.

84. "National League Standing on Tuesday Morning," *The Sporting News*, July 28, 1932, p. 8.
85. Edward Burns, "Five Wild Weeks Give the Cubs a Succession of Varied Thrills: Climax Comes in Probe by Judge Landis," *The Sporting News*, August 18, 1932, p. 1.
86. "National League Standing on Tuesday Morning," *The Sporting News*, August 18, 1932, p. 8.
87. "Wrangles with Players, Refusal to Take Orders Hurt Hornsby: Believed Paramount Factor in Rajah's Dismissal," *Pittsburgh Post-Gazette*, August 4, 1932, p. 14.
88. Burns, "Five Wild Weeks Give the Cubs A Succession of Varied Thrills: Climax Comes in Probe by Judge Landis," p. 1.
89. *Ibid.*
90. *Ibid.*
91. "National League Standing on Tuesday Morning," *The Sporting News*, August 18, 1932, p. 8.
92. "National League Standing on Tuesday Morning," *The Sporting News*, August 11, 1932, p. 8.
93. "National League Standing on Tuesday Morning," *The Sporting News*, August 18, 1932, p. 8.
94. *Ibid.*
95. "National League Standing on Tuesday Morning," *The Sporting News*, August 25, 1932, p. 8.
96. "National League Standing on Tuesday Morning," *The Sporting News*, September 1, 1932, p. 8.
97. "Cubs Continue Mad Dash Toward National Loop Flag: Little Bears Take Tenth in a Row," *Rochester Evening Journal and the Post Express*, August 29, 1932, p. 12.
98. "National League Standing on Tuesday Morning," *The Sporting News*, September 1, 1932, p. 8.
99. Irving Vaughan, "Cubs Omit Nothing in Taking 14 in Row: Thrills Abound as Grimm's Men Pull Games Out of Fire," *The Sporting News*, September 8, 1932, p. 1.
100. "Malone to Pitch for Cubs Today in Brooklyn Opener," *Chicago Daily Tribune*, September 10, 1932, p. 19.
101. "National League Standings on Tuesday Morning," *The Sporting News*, September 22, 1932, p. 7.
102. "Cuyler Expected to Star in World Series," *The Telegraph-Herald and Times-Journal*, September 21, 1932, p. 11.
103. "National League Standing at Close of Season," *The Sporting News*, September 29, 1932, p. 8.

Chapter 11

1. "Caught on the Fly," *The Sporting News*, September 29, 1932, p. 5.
2. Irving Vaughan, "Cubs' Slicing of Melon Proves Old Sores Are Still Unhealed: Slight to Former Pilot Resented by Fans," *The Sporting News*, September 29, 1932, p. 1.
3. *Ibid.*
4. Dick Farrington, "Fanning with Farrington," *The Sporting News*, September 29, 1932, p. 4.
5. Irving Vaughan, "Snubbing of Rajah Likely to Backfire: Landis' Ruling Opens Way for All Eligibles to Full Share," *The Sporting News*, October 20, 1932, p. 5.
6. Vaughan, "Cubs' Slicing of Melon Proves Old Sores Are Still Unhealed," p. 1.
7. Irving Vaughan, "Yanks Escaped Cuyler Menace Once, Not Twice," *Chicago Daily Tribune*, September 21, 1932, p. 19.
8. "First Game in Detail," *The Sporting News*, October 6, 1932, p. 3.
9. *Ibid.*
10. Jimmy Corcoran, "Cork Tips Hat from World Series," *The Telegraph-Herald and Times-Journal*, September 29, 1932, p. 11.
11. "Gossip of Second Game," *The Sporting News*, October 6, 1932, p. 6.
12. "Second Game in Detail," *The Sporting News*, October 6, 1932, p. 6.
13. *Ibid.*
14. "Two-Game Lead in Series Taken by New Yorkers," *The Palm Beach Post*, September 30, 1932, p. 2.
15. "Gossip of Second Game," *The Sporting News*, October 6, 1932, p. 6.
16. *Ibid.*
17. "Third Game in Detail," *The Sporting News*, October 6, 1932, p. 6.
18. *Ibid.*
19. "Homers by Ruth and Gehrig Spill Chicago in Third Battle," *The Sporting News*, October 6, 1932, p. 6.
20. "Third Game in Detail," *The Sporting News*, October 6, 1932, p. 6.
21. George Kirksey, "Yanks Take Third from Cubs, 7 to 5: Ruth, Gehrig Each Hit Pair of Homers, Scoring Six Runs," *The Pittsburgh Press*, October 2, 1932, p. 3.
22. *Ibid.*
23. "Babe Ruth May Be Just Passenger in this World Series," *The Vancouver Sun*, September 23, 1932, p. 18.
24. "Fourth Game in Detail," *The Sporting News*, October 6, 1932, p. 6.
25. *Ibid.*, p. 8.
26. *Ibid.*
27. Vaughan, "Snubbing of Rajah Likely to Backfire: Landis' Ruling Opens Way for All Eligibles to Full Share," p. 5.
28. Jack Cuddy, "Trade Winds Blow Through Major League," *San Jose Evening News*, October 18, 1932, p. 8.
29. George H. Beale, "Babe Herman Makes a Splash," *The Border Cities Star*, December 16, 1932, p. 4.

30. "Caught on the Fly," *The Sporting News*, November 24, 1932, p. 6.
31. "Ki! Yi! Kiki Gets His Big Moose," *The Telegraph-Herald and Times-Journal*, November 14, 1932, p. 8.
32. "Caught on the Fly: Cuyler on Sportsmanship," *The Sporting News*, December 8, 1932, p. 6.
33. *Ibid.*
34. Edward Burns, "No Holdouts Among Cubs, Sox Expected: Grimm, Cuyler, Bush, Root Lined Up Already for 1933," *The Sporting News*, December 29, 1932, p. 1.
35. Edward Burns, "Babe Herman Play Staged by the Cubs: Herman the Great's Preview Satisfactory to All," *The Sporting News*, January 26, 1933, p. 1.
36. Edward Burns, "Cubs Get Hendrick as Sub for Grimm: Veteran Bought from Columbus After Release from Reds," *The Sporting News*, January 19, 1933, p. 1.
37. "Bill Jurges Leaves for Cubs' Training Camp," *The Reading Eagle*, February 26, 1933, p. 7.
38. "Training Camp Notes: Sea Lions Keep Grimm Awake," *The Sporting News*, March 9, 1933, p. 5.
39. *Ibid.*
40. Edward Burns, "Cubs Shock Grimm, Then Get Real Jolt: Players Have Experience of Lives as Quake Cleans Hotel," *The Sporting News*, March 16, 1933, p. 3.
41. *Ibid.*
42. "Quakes," *The Sporting News*, March 16, 1933, p. 5.
43. *Ibid.*
44. "Cubs Win Loose Game with Seals," *Berkeley Daily Gazette*, March 22, 1933, p. 10.
45. "Kiki Cuyler Breaks His Leg," *Lewiston Morning Tribune*, March 30, 1933, p. 7.
46. *Ibid.*
47. "Kiki Cuyler Comes to Michigan to Rest," *The Ludington Daily News*, April 3, 1933, p. 6.
48. "Cuyler Will Be Out of Lineup Until Around July 4," *Saskatoon Star-Phoenix*, April 6, 1933, p. 10.
49. Irving Vaughan, "White Sox' Worries Over at Shortstop: Appling Begins to Pay Dividends on Faith in His Ability," *The Sporting News*, May 4, 1933, p. 1.
50. "Kiki Cuyler Out for Six More Weeks," *The Pittsburgh Press*, April 27, 1933, p. 28.
51. "Cub Outfield Is Brand New Since Pennant Clinching," *Chicago Daily Tribune*, May 19, 1933, p. 29.
52. "National League Standing on Tuesday Morning," *The Sporting News*, June 1, 1933, p. 8.
53. "Kiki Cuyler Back to Form," *The Middlesboro Daily News*, June 17, 1933, p. 4.
54. "National League Standing on Tuesday Morning," *The Sporting News*, June 29, 1933, p. 8.
55. "Kiki Cuyler's Father Injured in Auto Crash," *Chicago Daily Tribune*, June 24, 1933, p. 17.
56. "National League Standing on Tuesday Morning," *The Sporting News*, July 6, 1933, p. 8.
57. *Ibid.*
58. "National League Standing on Tuesday Morning," *The Sporting News*, July 13, 1933, p. 8.
59. Irving Vaughan, "Haid Makes Sox Staff Winner Without Putting in an Inning," *The Sporting News*, July 20, 1933, p. 1.
60. "National League Standing on Tuesday Morning," *The Sporting News*, July 27, 1933, p. 8.
61. "National League Standing on Tuesday Morning," *The Sporting News*, August 3, 1933, p. 8.
62. Irving Vaughan, "Cubs' Failure to Land Traced to Two Causes," *The Sporting News*, September 21, 1933, p. 3.
63. "White Sox Drub Cubs, Win Four Straight Games in City Series," *The Sporting News*, October 12, 1933, p. 2.
64. "William Veeck: He Made the Cubs Popular," *The Sporting News*, October 12, 1933, p. 4.
65. *Ibid.*
66. "Report Cubs in Big Deal," *The Sporting News*, November 2, 1933, p. 8.
67. "Trade Rumors Fly as Stove Leaguers Start," *Painesville Telegraph*, October 30, 1933, p. 6.
68. Edward Burns, "Cubs' Early Signing of Cuyler Ends Talk of Transfer to Reds: Kiki Due to Flank Klein in Garden Patrol," *The Sporting News*, November 30, 1933, p. 1.
69. "Hafey Appears Doomed to Stay with Cincinnati," *The Telegraph-Herald and News-Journal*, December 12, 1933, p. 9.
70. "Caught on the Fly," *The Sporting News*, November 30, 1933, p. 2.
71. Edward Burns, "Klein's Pay as Cub to Be About $23,000: Outfield Star at First Had Asked $28,000 of New Bosses," *The Sporting News*, December 21, 1933, p. 2.
72. Dick Farrington, "Fanning with Farrington," *The Sporting News*, January 4, 1934.
73. Edgar G. Brands, "Between Innings: When Hack Needed a Backstop," *The Sporting News*, February 22, 1934, p. 4.
74. *Ibid.*
75. *Ibid.*
76. Edward Burns, "New Cub President Keeps Veeck Policy: Radio and Ladies' Days Remain as Wrigley Field Fixtures," *The Sporting News*, January 18, 1934, p. 1
77. "Caught on the Fly," *The Sporting News*, February 8, 1934, p. 2.
78. Dick Farrington, "Fanning with Farrington," *The Sporting News*, February 15, 1934, p. 4.
79. "Flashes from Spring Training Camps: Cuyler Still Has Speed," *Reading Eagle*, March 30, 1934, p. 24.
80. Carl Hubbell, "Lindstrom, Paul Waner,

Cuyler, Davis Rate Carl Hubbell's Respect When They're at Bat," *The Pittsburgh Press*, March 9, 1934, p. 46.

81. Irving Vaughan, "Klein Declines Job of Covering Center: From Left to Right Field, It'll Be Chuck, Cuyler, Herman," *The Sporting News*, March 22, 1934, p. 1.

82. Irving Vaughan, "Cub Pitchers Share Spotlight with Stainback in Early Tilts," *The Sporting News*, April 26, 1934, p. 1.

83. "Cuyler on Shelf as Cubs Launch Baseball Season," *The Independent*, April 17, 1934, p. 10.

84. Irving Vaughan, "Cub Staff Delivers, But Sox' Is Gamble: Grimm's Lineup, However, Must Recover Batting Punch," *The Sporting News*, April 19, 1934, p. 1.

85. "Cubs Win in 11 Innings," *The Border Cities Star*, April 28, 1934, p. 2.

86. "National League Standing on Tuesday Morning," *The Sporting News*, May 24, 1934, p. 8.

87. Irving Vaughan, "Cubs, at Home, Expect to Shake Dust of Rivals," *The Sporting News*, May 31, 1934, p. 2.

88. "National League Standing on Tuesday Morning," *The Sporting News*, June 14, 1934, p. 8.

89. George Kirksey, "Dots and Dashes," *The Telegraph-Herald and Times-Journal*, July 18, 1934, p. 8.

90. "Cardinals and Cubs Split Up Two," *The Spartanburg Herald*, July 5, 1934, p. 8.

91. "Cronin and Terry Studying Lineups for All-Star Game," *The Washington, Pennsylvania, Daily Reporter*, July 3, 1934, p. 8.

92. Irving Vaughan, "Cubs' Flag Chances Hinge on Trip East: Improved Play on Foreign Fields Vital to Pennant Hopes," *The Sporting News*, July 12, 1934, p. 3.

93. "National League Standing on Tuesday Morning," *The Sporting News*, July 26, 1934, p. 8.

94. "Cubs Gain as Leaders Lose," *The Milwaukee Journal*, July 24, 1934, p. 3.

95. "Kiki Cuyler Is Batting Leader," *Sarasota Herald*, August 5, 1934, p. 8.

96. "National League Standing on Tuesday Morning," *The Sporting News*, August 30, 1934, p. 8.

97. "National League Standing on Tuesday Morning," *The Sporting News*, September 6, 1934, p. 8.

98. Irving Vaughan, "Grimm Rides Reds on the Cubs and They May Be Real Reds in '35: Charges Some of Stars Are Soldiering," *The Sporting News*, September 27, 1934, p. 1.

Chapter 12

1. "Baseball Trade Winds Blowing! Chicago Cubs to Dispose of Stars," *The Border Cities Star*, September 5, 1934, p. 3.

2. Irving Vaughan, "Wheeling Out Trading Block for the Cubs: Gossip Has Majority Wearing New Uniforms Next Season," *The Sporting News*, September 13, 1934, p. 2.

3. Irving Vaughan, "Twas All Mistake — Grimm Isn't Angry: Higher-Ups Suspected of Causing Cubs' Pilot to Pipe Down," *The Sporting News*, October 4, 1934, p. 6.

4. Irving Vaughan, "Grimm, as Manager, Goes Front Office: Election of Pilot as Vice-Prexy Gives Him New Authority," *The Sporting News*, November 1, 1934, p. 5.

5. Edward Burns, "New Wrigley Policy in Stephenson Gift: Cub Prexy Eases Vet's Release by Giving Him a Watch," *The Sporting News*, November 8, 1934, p. 2.

6. Irving Vaughan, "Soft-Pedal Placed on Cub Trade Talk: Walker Steps in with Denial as Gossip Becomes Too Hot," *The Sporting News*, October 18, 1934, p. 6.

7. "New Trail Opens for This Cub: Perce (Pat) Malone," *The Sporting News*, October 25, 1934, p. 1.

8. George Kirksey, "Most of Other Clubs Unable to Make Up Minds," *The Telegraph-Herald and Times-Journal*, November 22, 1934, p. 13.

9. "Chicago Cubs Happy as They Beat Bill Terry," *The Vancouver Sun*, November 23, 1934, p. 16.

10. *Ibid*.

11. "Grimm Seeks Ace Chucker for His Cubs," *The Telegraph-Herald and Times-Journal*, December 2, 1934, p. 18.

12. Edward Burns, "Grimm Lists Deals as New Face Drive: Cub Pilot Regrets Loss of Some Players in Transfer," *The Sporting News*, November 29, 1934, p. 5.

13. "Grimm Seeks Ace Chucker for His Cubs," p. 18.

14. "How Trade Winds Are Blowing," *The Pittsburgh Press*, December 13, 1934, p. 34.

15. Ed Burns, "Bonura's Job Safe If Left to Sox Fans: Hint of Side-Tracking Big Zeke Brings Wide Protest," *The Sporting News*, January 31, 1935, p. 5.

16. Edward Burns, "It Takes a Moose to Bring Out the Tiger in Cuyler!" *Chicago Daily Tribune*, June 2, 1935, p. B2.

17. *Ibid*.

18. "Kiki Cuyler Put in Lead-Off Spot," *Rochester Evening Journal and the Post Express*, March 2, 1935, p. 2.

19. "Training Camp News," *Sarasota Herald*, April 1, 1935.

20. Samuel B. Cohen, "Sayings of the Spectator," *The Meriden Daily Journal*, April 13, 1935, p. 4.

21. Irving Vaughan, "Cubs Exhibit Punch Though Not at Bat: Pirate Ruction, However, Gives Team's Spirit Real Test," *The Sporting News*, May 9, 1935, p. 1.

22. "National League Standing on Tuesday Morning," *The Sporting News*, April 25, 1935, p. 7.

Notes. Chapter 12

23. "Klein and Lindstrom Benched as Grimm Revamps Cub Line-Up: Hack, Stainback to Get Chance Against Giants," *The Milwaukee Journal*, May 23, 1935, p. 8.
24. "National League Standing on Tuesday Morning," *The Sporting News*, May 30, 1935, p. 8.
25. "Cubs Would Not Bar Sing Singer," *The Spartanburg Herald*, June 14, 1935, p. 6.
26. Irving Vaughan, "Cubs Learn to Like Wrigley's Medicine: P.K.'s Ultimatum Swings Both Klein and Herman in Line," *The Sporting News*, February 21, 1935, p. 1.
27. Dick Farrington, "Fanning with Farrington," *The Sporting News*, July 11, 1935, p. 4.
28. Ed Burns, "Grimm on Hot Seat, Cuyler Case Shows: 'I've Got Bosses, Too,' Charlie's Only Explanation to Kiki," *The Sporting News*, July 11, 1935, p. 7.
29. Tom Swope, "Cincy Sees Cuyler as Balance Wheel: Veteran Hawk Expected to Help Stabilize Young Outfit," *The Sporting News*, July 11, 1935, p. 1.
30. Burns, "Grimm on Hot Seat, Cuyler Case Shows," p. 7.
31. "Kiki Cuyler Will Play with Redlegs," *The Pittsburgh Press*, July 5, 1935, p. 30.
32. *Ibid*.
33. *Ibid*.
34. "Sports Stew—Served Hot," *The Pittsburgh Press*, July 13, 1935, p. 7.
35. Volney Walsh, "Pirates, Chasing Jinx Pitcher, See New Hope: Bucs Finally Best Lefty for 4-0 Win," *The Pittsburgh Press*, July 6, 1935, p. 8.
36. "Sports Stew—Served Hot," *The Pittsburgh Press*, July 13, 1935, p. 7.
37. J.G. Taylor Spink, "Three and One: Looking Them Over with J.G. Taylor Spink—Things We Could Have Done Without in 1935," *The Sporting News*, January 2, 1936, p. 4.
38. Tom Swope, "Cincy's Night Mob Gives Club Lesson: Disgraceful Scene Due to Lack of Official Vigilance," *The Sporting News*, August 8, 1935, p. 2.
39. Spink, "Three and One," p. 4.
40. Swope, "Cincy's Night Mob Gives Club Lesson," p. 2.
41. Tom Swope, "Cincy Boots Chance with Infield Boots: Reds Make 10 Errors in Twin Bill with Dodgers, Before 15,000," *The Sporting News*, September 12, 1935, p. 2.
42. Edgar G. Brands, "Between Innings: Caught in the Bull Pen," *The Sporting News*, October 31, 1935, p. 4.
43. Tom Swope, "M'Phail Defying Logic in Sending Reds to Puerto Rico," *The Sporting News*, January 16, 1936, p. 1.
44. Tom Swope, "Reds to Sail Feb. 6, Puerto Rico Bound," *The Sporting News*, January 23, 1936, p. 1.
45. Tom Swope, "Reds' Trainer Finds Rainbow End in Rico: It Looks Like Treasure Island to Cincy Advance Man," *The Sporting News*, February 6, 1936, p. 3.
46. "Major League Notes: Rough Voyage for Reds," *The Sporting News*, February 27, 1936, p. 2.
47. "Reds Card More Exhibition Games," *The Milwaukee Journal*, February 19, 1936, p. 3.
48. "Major League Notes: Rough Voyage for Reds," p. 2.
49. "Major League Notes: Voodoo Ritual for the Reds?" *The Sporting News*, February 27, 1936, p. 2.
50. "Training Camp Notes," *The Sporting News*, March 5, 1936, p. 2.
51. Tom Swope, "Red Rookie Trying to Emulate Galan: Given Chance in Garden, Chapman Looks Like Sensation," *The Sporting News*, March 5, 1936, p. 6.
52. Tom Swope, "Razor-Edge Reds Hope to Give First-Division Foes Close Shave," *The Sporting News*, April 2, 1936, p. 1.
53. Tom Swope, "Dressen Stressing Rhineland Defense: Reds, as a Result, Look Better Than Team of Last Year," *The Sporting News*, April 9, 1936, p. 8.
54. "Caught on the Fly," *The Sporting News*, April 16, 1936, p. 2.
55. "Cold Welcome Given Champs in Open Stand with Redlegs," *The Palm Beach Post*, April 18, 1936, p. 7.
56. "Scribbled by Scribes," *The Sporting News*, April 30, 1936, p. 4.
57. "National League Standing on Tuesday Morning," *The Sporting News*, May 7, 1936, p. 8.
58. "Wingo Comes Back—So Reds Should Have Hope," *The Pittsburgh Press*, May 9, 1936, p. 7.
59. *Ibid*.
60. Tom Swope, "Red Outlook Fades in Mound Washout: Hollingsworth Only Consistent Member of Hurling Staff," *The Sporting News*, June 4, 1936, p. 6.
61. "National League Standing on Tuesday Morning," *The Sporting News*, June 25, 1936, p. 8.
62. "Kiki Cuyler Sets Hot Pace for Young Cincinnati Reds," *The News and Courier*, June 27, 1936, p. 6.
63. "Voice of the Fan: On the Cuyler Bandwagon," *The Sporting News*, June 4, 1936, p. 4.
64. *Ibid*.
65. "National League Standing on Tuesday Morning," *The Sporting News*, June 18, 1936, p. 8.
66. "Kiki Cuyler Sets Hot Pace for Young Cincinnati Reds," p. 6.
67. "National League Standing on Tuesday Morning," *The Sporting News*, August 6, 1936, p. 8.
68. *Ibid*.
69. Tom Swope, "Dressen Opens Red Eyes; Fines Herman and Derringer $200," *The Sporting News*, July 30, 1936, p. 1.
70. *Ibid*.

71. Tom Swope, "Reds All Pepped Up with a Place to Go: Fourth Rung Not Beyond Reach as Spurt Buoys Team," *The Sporting News*, September 3, 1936, p. 2.
72. Tom Swope, "M'Phail After Browns; Rajah's Job Totters: Cincy Still Trying to Get Low Down," *The Sporting News*, September 24, 1936, p. 1.
73. Tom Swope, "Dressen Ace's High in New Deal at Cincy: Reds' Little Pilot Is Given Hoist in Pay by Warren Giles," *The Sporting News*, October 22, 1936, p. 3.
74. Edgar G. Brands, "Between Innings," *The Sporting News*, November 19, 1936, p. 4.
75. "Caught on the Fly," *The Sporting News*, December 3, 1936, p. 6.
76. "Two Banquets," *The Windsor Daily Star*, December 14, 1936, p. 4.
77. Tom Swope, "Reds Have Running Starts on Contracts: Landis' Bulletin Reveals Cuyler, Campbell, Schott Signed," *The Sporting News*, January 14, 1937, p. 7.
78. "1937 Big League Salaries Total Over $3,200,000, Record Figure," *The Meriden Daily Journal*, March 24, 1937, p. 6.
79. Tom Swope, "Reds Finish in Black with $105,000 Profit," *The Sporting News*, November 26, 1936, p. 2.
80. Tom Swope, "Giles Sees Red Over Hafey's Comeback: Veteran Doesn't Want Any Ifs Inserted Into Contract," *The Sporting News*, February 25, 1937, p. 3.
81. "Cincinnati Reds Are Off for Training Camp," *The Portsmouth Times*, March 3, 1937, p. 10.
82. Pete Minego, "Sport Gossip," *The Portsmouth Times*, March 14, 1937, p. 20.
83. "Cincinnati Reds Revel in Catchers," *The Bend Bulletin*, March 9, 1937, p. 10.
84. "Cuyler Injured in Collision," *Pittsburgh Post-Gazette*, April 2, 1937, p. 18.
85. "Training Camp Notes: Kiki and Campy Collide," *The Sporting News*, April 8, 1937, p. 6.
86. "Ill Luck Still Pursues Cuyler," *The Pittsburgh Press*, April 2, 1937, p. 18.
87. Tom Swope, "Reds Present a New Inaugural-Day Cast: Lombardi, Myers, Goodman Only 1936 Starters Repeating," *The Sporting News*, April 22, 1937, p. 5.
88. "National League Standing on Tuesday Morning," *The Sporting News*, April 29, 1937, p. 8.
89. "National League Standing on Tuesday Morning," *The Sporting News*, May 6, 1937, p. 8.
90. Tom Swope, "Cincy's Hopes Soar as Chick Flies Back: Hafey's First Time at Bat Since '35 Produces Winning Run," *The Sporting News*, May 20, 1937, p. 3.
91. Sid Feder, "Bob Feller Will Face Yankees Sunday: Iowan Will Try Out His Curve Against Rivals," *The Telegraph-Herald and Times-Journal*, July 18, 1937, p. 16.
92. George Chadwick, "Berger Hits Ball Hard for Terry," *Miami Daily News*, July 25, 1937, p. 3.
93. George Kirksey, "Studies Habits of Ball Players," *The Bend Bulletin*, May 25, 1937, p. 2.
94. Tom Swope, "Reds Build Up Fine Defensive Record: Only 1.75 Earned Runs Per Game for Foes in 14 Contests," *The Sporting News*, August 12, 1937, p. 6.
95. "Kiki Cuyler Announces He Will Quit Baseball," *The News-Sentinel*, September 22, 1937, p. 4.
96. "National League Standing on Tuesday Morning," *The Sporting News*, September 30, 1937, p. 8.
97. Tom Swope, "Pilot Hunt by Reds Veers to M'Kechnie: Giles Won't Sacrifice Man-Power to Get Playing Manager," *The Sporting News*, October 7, 1937, p. 2.

Chapter 13

1. Tom Swope, "Pilot Hunt by Reds Veers to M'Kechnie: Giles Won't Sacrifice Man-Power to Get Playing Manager," *The Sporting News*, October 7, 1937, p. 2.
2. "Sothoron and Cuyler Talk Terms: Final Huddle May Send Kiki to Milwaukee," *The Milwaukee Journal*, December 2, 1937, p. 1.
3. Red Thisted, "Brewers Seek Cuyler for Garden Patrol: Kiki Willing to Talk Contract If Pilot Post Fails," *Milwaukee Sentinel*, December 3, 1937, p. 21.
4. *Ibid.*
5. "Cuyler Slated for Syracuse Manager," *The Clinton County Times*, December 2, 1937, p. 9.
6. "Kiki Cuyler to Be Coach," *The Pittsburgh Press*, December 28, 1937, p. 18.
7. "Brief Bits of Gossip," *The Sporting News*, February 10, 1938, p. 6.
8. George Kirksey, "Mancuso Put on Block for Giant Trade," *The Pittsburgh Press*, February 2, 1938, p. 26.
9. Harvey Boyle, "Mirrors of Sport: Dodgers Counting on Cuyler," *Pittsburgh Post-Gazette*, March 19, 1938, p. 66.
10. "Cuyler Comeback Prospects Bright," *The Independent*, March 9, 1938, p. 3.
11. "Major League Notes," *The Sporting News*, April 7, 1938, p. 6.
12. Sid Feder, "Tony's Shoes Too Big for Joey Gordon," *The Telegraph Herald*, April 6, 1938, p. 9.
13. Tommy Holmes, "Injury to Blimp Phelps Deflates Flatbushers," *The Sporting News*, March 31, 1938, p. 1.
14. "Major League Notes: Dodgers Will Climb—Or Else," *The Sporting News*, April 21, 1938, p. 7.
15. "National League Standing on Tuesday Morning," *The Sporting News*, May 5, 1938, p. 8.
16. Tommy Holmes, "Dodger Dissension

Brings Fast Action by Larry MacPhail: Brooklyn Boss Reads Riot Act, Backing Up Grimes," *The Sporting News*, May 12, 1938, p. 1.
17. *Ibid.*
18. Tommy Holmes, "MacPhail Denies Bambino Will Get Grimes' Job: But —: Reports Persist Brooklyn Chief Plans to Install Babe," *The Sporting News*, June 23, 1938, p. 1.
19. *Ibid.*
20. "Cuyler Made Dodger Coach," *Milwaukee Sentinel*, September 17, 1938, p. 17.
21. Tommy Holmes, "Dodgers Made Good — On Grimes' Prediction," *The Sporting News*, September 29, 1938, p. 2.
22. Tommy Holmes, "Grimes Gets Gong as Brooklyn Pilot: But Incoming Manager Is Still Kept Under Whiskers," *The Sporting News*, October 13, 1938, p. 9.
23. "Caught on the Fly," *The Sporting News*, October 27, 1938, p. 8.
24. "Chattanooga Club Picks Kiki Cuyler as New Manager," *The Milwaukee Journal*, December 6, 1938, p. 1.
25. W. Gammon, "Fruit Instead of Dividend," *The Sporting News*, January 19, 1939, p. 10.
26. "Caught on the Fly," *The Sporting News*, March 9, 1939, p. 9.
27. Wirt Gammon, "Engel Builds Lookouts to Fit Proved Pitching," *The Sporting News*, April 6, 1939, p. 1.
28. "Lookouts' Bats Keep Ringing," *The Miami Daily News*, May 18, 1939, p. 2.
29. "Southern Association Class A-1 Standing on Tuesday Morning," *The Sporting News*, July 27, 1939, p. 11.
30. "Southern Association Class A-1 Standing on Tuesday Morning," *The Sporting News*, May 25, 1939, p. 11.
31. *Ibid.*
32. "Baseball: Brewers Had Chance to Buy Jim Nicholson, New Cub Star, for $1,000," *The Milwaukee Journal*, August 8, 1939, p. 9.
33. Fred Russell, "Sales Talk," *Baseball Digest*, June 1950, p. 8.
34. *Ibid.*
35. "Baseball: Brewers Had Chance to Buy Jim Nicholson, New Cub Star, for $1,000," p. 9.
36. "Cubs Paid $35,000 for Prize Recruit," *Reading Eagle*, August 4, 1939, p. 18.
37. Red Thisted, "The Second Guess," *Milwaukee Sentinel*, September 3, 1939, p. 2B.
38. "Dixie Miracle Man: Hazen (Kiki) Cuyler," *The Sporting News*, September 14, 1939, p. 2.
39. "Southern Association Class A-1 Standing at Close of Season, September 10," *The Sporting News*, September 14, 1939, p. 12.
40. Eddie Brietz, "Sports Roundup: Election Dope," *Reading Eagle*, November 3, 1939, p. 24.
41. "Dixie Miracle Man: Hazen (Kiki) Cuyler," p. 2.
42. "Southern Association Class A-1 Standing at Close of Season, September 10," p. 12.

43. Wirt Gammon, "Nimrod Cuyler Sets Sights on Another Lookout Winner," *The Sporting News*, November 2, 1939, p. 6.
44. *Ibid.*
45. "Caught on the Fly," *The Sporting News*, March 14, 1940, p. 10.
46. "Southern Association Class A-1 Standing on Tuesday Morning," *The Sporting News*, April 25, 1940, p. 12.
47. "Southern Association Class A-1 Standing on Tuesday Morning," *The Sporting News*, May 16, 1940, p. 14.
48. "Caught on the Fly," *The Sporting News*, May 23, 1940, p. 10.
49. "Southern All-Stars Will Play Monday," *The Palm Beach Post*, July 7, 1940, p. 11.
50. Buss Walker, "Mike Dejan, Reds $30,000 Rookie Outfielder, Like Bambino, Batted Himself Off Mound," *The Sporting News*, July 11, 1940, p. 5.
51. "Southern Association Class A-1 Standing on Tuesday Morning," *The Sporting News*, August 29, 1940, p. 13.
52. Val J. Flanagan, "Gilbert, Richards Only Pilots Certain to Be Back in S.A.," *The Sporting News*, October 3, 1940, p. 12.
53. Bob French, "Mirrors of Sport: Tom Sheehan Is Cautious," *Toledo Blade*, October 12, 1940, p. 10.
54. Val J. Flanagan, "Southern Siftings," *The Sporting News*, December 19, 1940, p. 8.
55. "Babe Ruth Mentioned in Seattle Baseball," *Eugene Register-Guard*, January 23, 1941, p. 12.
56. Henry McLemore, "Minor League Pilots on Spot," *The Milwaukee Journal*, March 11, 1941, p. 2.
57. Noogan, "Lookouts Returned to Griffith; Engel Remaining as President," *The Sporting News*, May 15, 1941, p. 3.
58. "Southern Association Class A-1 Standing on Tuesday Morning," *The Sporting News*, July 17, 1941, p. 8.
59. U.S. World War II Army Enlistment Records 1938–1946, www.ancestry.com.
60. Buss Walker, "Olson Assumes Lookout Post Vacated by Cuyler," *The Sporting News*, August 14, 1941, p. 2.
61. "Southern Association Class A-1 Standing on Tuesday Morning," *The Sporting News*, August 14, 1941, p. 12.
62. Sam Levy, "Engel: Calls Grimm and Cuyler Ideal Minor League Club Managers," *The Milwaukee Journal*, July 31, 1941, p. 10.
63. Ed Burns, "Fans Root for Root — and Paul Erickson: Recruit's First Victory of Year Is Shutout of Pirates," *The Sporting News*, August 14, 1941, p. 5.
64. "National League Standing on Tuesday Morning," *The Sporting News*, August 21, 1941, p. 10.
65. *Ibid.*

66. *Ibid.*
67. "It's Same Old Story—Sox Strangle Cubs: Pale Hose Win Seventh Straight Series from N.L. Rivals," *The Sporting News*, October 16, 1941, p. 7.
68. "Major League Notes," *The Sporting News*, February 26, 1942, p. 9.
69. "Training Camp Notes," *The Sporting News*, March 5, 1942, p. 6.
70. "Training Camp Notes," *The Sporting News*, April 9, 1942, p. 8.
71. "Manager Wilson Must Bring Cubs Into Running for Chicago Fans," *Painesville Telegraph*, April 7, 1942, p. 7.
72. "Williams Only Sox Not in Camp as DiMaggio and Finney Arrive," *Sarasota Herald-Tribune*, March 6, 1942, p. 6.
73. Ed Burns, "Shy Crowds at Chi Danger Tip to Sox: Dykes Must Become Miracle Man Again Or Build Up Team," *The Sporting News*, October 15, 1942, p. 9.
74. "Caught on the Fly," *The Sporting News*, December 10, 1942, p. 9.
75. Ed Burns, "Cubs-Sox Camp Stay to Be Short, Snappy: They'll Put in Only Three Weeks Drilling at French Lick," *The Sporting News*, January 7, 1943, p. 3.
76. "Necrology: George A. Cuyler," *The Sporting News*, February 11, 1943, p. 6.
77. Ed Burns, "Chi's Interest High with Mercury Low: Sunday City Series Game Attracts 8,281 Cash Crowd in Chill," *The Sporting News*, April 22, 1943, p. 14.
78. "Nicholson Hitting Hard Since Novikoff Arrived," *The Milwaukee Journal*, June 3, 1943, p. 2.
79. "National League Standing on Tuesday Morning, June 15," *The Sporting News*, June 17, 1943, p. 10.
80. *Ibid.*
81. Ed Burns, "Bruins Expect No Feast East, Nor a Famine," *The Sporting News*, July 1, 1943, p. 2.
82. "Major League Flashes," *The Sporting News*, July 22, 1943, p. 13.
83. "Cuyler for Pilot Rooters Promise to Muffle Shouts," *The Sporting News*, October 7, 1943, p. 7.
84. Ed Burns, "Bouncing Around: For Cub Manager—No-Flaw Lotshaw!" *The Sporting News*, October 21, 1943, p. 10.
85. Ed Burns, "Cub Grapevine Gets Twisted in Pilots' Story," *The Sporting News*, November 4, 1943, p. 6.
86. "Kiki Cuyler Signs 2-Year Contract as Atlanta Pilot," *The Pittsburgh Press*, October 24, 1943, p. 13.
87. Ernie Harwell, "Cuyler Named Cracker Chief," *The Sporting News*, October 28, 1943, p. 3.
88. "Southern Association: Crackers Lose Four Players," *The Sporting News*, April 6, 1944, p. 19.
89. "Cuba Combed for Players," *The Pittsburgh Press*, January 21, 1944, p. 31.
90. *Ibid.*
91. "Cuyler in Pulpit, Tells How Players Show Faith," *The Sporting News*, April 13, 1944, p. 23.
92. "Training with Minors: Flashes from AA and A-1 Camps," *The Sporting News*, April 20, 1944, p. 22.
93. Stan Mockler, "DeWitt, Sewell Marion Get Top Sporting News Awards," *Youngstown Vindicator*, December 27, 1944, p. 6.
94. "Atlanta's Streak Ended in Little Rock Uniforms," *The Sporting News*, May 24, 1945, p. 20.
95. Fred Russell, "Southern Association Class 1-A Standing on Monday Morning, June 25," *The Sporting News*, June 28, 1945, p. 18.
96. *Ibid.*
97. Fred Russell, "Crackers Crack Before Pelicans," *The Sporting News*, September 20, 1945, p. 21.
98. Guy Butler, "Topics of the Tropics: Sportpourri," *Miami Daily News*, October 17, 1945, p. 8A.
99. Fred Russell, "Southern Association Class A-1 Standing on Monday Morning, August 13," *The Sporting News*, August 16, 1945, p. 18.
100. Ernie Harwell, "Few Holdovers Due at Atlanta," *The Sporting News*, February 21, 1946, p. 12.
101. "Training with Minors: Flashes from AAA, AA and A Camps," *The Sporting News*, April 11, 1946, p. 19.
102. Hugh Fullerton, Jr., "Last Fling," *The Milwaukee Journal*, April 18, 1946, p. 2.
103. Ernie Harwell, "Crax Real Crackerjacks; Turn Walk Into Twin Out," *The Sporting News*, August 14, 1946, p. 28.
104. "Necrology: Kiki Cuyler, Outfield Star for Pirates and Cubs, Dies," *The Sporting News*, February 22, 1950, p. 20.
105. *Ibid.*
106. *Ibid.*
107. John Bradbery, "Trippi Pulls Up Batting Mark, Turns on Speed as Base-Runner," *The Sporting News*, May 21, 1947, p. 15.
108. *Ibid.*
109. "Mauro Gets Tip Off Kiki, Then Tees Off on Crackers," *The Sporting News*, July 7, 1948, p. 26.
110. "Cuyler Boomed for Tiger Job," *St. Petersburg Times*, July 30, 1948, p. 20.
111. "Kiki Cuyler Will Retire as Crax Pilot This Year," *The Sporting News*, September 8, 1948, p. 25.
112. George K. Leonard, "Rumors Wash Out Dixie Pilot Setup," *The Sporting News*, September 15, 1948, p. 27.
113. Hugh Fullerton, Jr., "Sports Roundup," *The Nevada, Missouri, Daily Mail*, September 20, 1948, p. 6.
114. John Drohan, "Baker Falls in Bosox Axe-Swinging, Replaced by Cuyler, McCarthy

Chapter 14

1. Oscar Ruhl, "From the Ruhl Book," *The Sporting News*, November 3, 1948, p. 20.
2. John Drohan, "'I'll Do It My Way,' Declares McCarthy," *The Sporting News*, March 30, 1949, p. 10.
3. *Ibid.*
4. "Obituary: Mrs. Anna R. Cuyler," *The Sporting News*, April 27, 1949, p. 39.
5. Harry Grayson, "Boston Finds New Methods to Lose," *Wilmington Morning Star*, July 10, 1949, p. 12A.
6. "Hack Wilson's Monument to Be Dedicated, Sept. 26," *The Sporting News*, September 21, 1949, p. 38.
7. "McCarthy Unveils Wilson Monument at Martinsburg," *The Sporting News*, October 5, 1949, p. 22.
8. *Ibid.*
9. "Caught on the Fly," *The Sporting News*, November 23, 1949, p. 26.
10. "Major League Flashes," *The Sporting News*, February 15, 1950, p. 24.
11. "Hazen (Kiki) Cuyler, Former Big League Ball Player, Dies," *The News and Courier*, February 12, 1950, p. 2A.
12. "Kiki Cuyler Doing Well," *The Pittsburgh Press*, February 4, 1950, p. 6.
13. "Hazen (Kiki) Cuyler, Former Big League Ball Player, Dies," p. 2A.
14. "Heart Ailment Fatal to Kiki Cuyler, Ex-Buc Star: Red Sox Coach Dies En Route to Hospital," *The Pittsburgh Press*, February 12, 1950, p. 37.
15. "Necrology: Kiki Cuyler, Outfield Star for Pirates and Cubs, Dies," *The Sporting News*, February 22, 1950, p. 20.
16. "Kiki Cuyler Dies at 50," *St. Joseph News-Press*, February 12, 1950, p. 2D.
17. "Kiki Cuyler, Bosox Coach, Heart Victim," *Sarasota Herald-Tribune*, February 13, 1950, p. 7.
18. "Kiki A Righthanded Cobb, Says Veteran Scout Doyle," *The Sporting News*, February 22, 1950, p. 20.
19. *Ibid.*
20. *Ibid.*
21. *Ibid.*
22. Les Biederman, "The Scoreboard," *The Pittsburgh Press*, February 21, 1950, p. 27.
23. Guy Butler, "Topic of the Tropics: Cuyler Might Have Managed Red Sox," *Miami Sunday News*, July 2, 1950, p. 1C.
24. *Alcona County: A Pictorial History*, vol. I (Harrisville: The Alcona County Review, 2007; reprinted by Cheryl L. Peterson and John D. Boufford, 2009), p. 152.
25. *Ibid.*
26. "Pirates to Bring 1925 Champs Back This Month," *The Pittsburgh Press*, July 8, 1951, p. 40.
27. "1925 Bucs Did It Before, Rickey Will Do It Again," *Pittsburgh-Post Gazette*, August 1, 1951, p. 14.
28. Ralph McGill, "Dying? Not Baseball!" *Baseball Digest*, May 1958, pp. 56.
29. *Ibid.*, p. 57.
30. Frederick G. Lieb, *The Pittsburgh Pirates* (1948; reprint, Carbondale: Southern Illinois University Press, 2003), p. 228.
31. Les Biederman, "Once a Pirate, Always a Pirate, Says Bush, Sending Help to Bucs," *The Sporting News*, December 24, 1947, p. 6.
32. *Ibid.*
33. Fred Russell, "Why Cuyler Was Benched: Here's New Light on 40-Year-Old Mystery," *Baseball Digest*, May 1968, p. 47.
34. *Ibid.*, p. 48.
35. *Ibid.*
36. Nick Robertson, "Hall of Famer Paul Waner Recalls 1927 Series," *Sarasota Herald-Tribune*, October 4, 1960, p. 11.
37. "Three Inducted in Hall of Fame," *The Owosso (MI) Argus Press*, May 23, 1963, p. 16.
38. Jack Lang, "Goose and Kiki Join Diamond Immortals: Old-Timers' Group Picks Ex-Flyhawks," *The Sporting News*, February 10, 1968, p. 18.
39. Lester J. Biederman, "The Scoreboard: A Four-Letter Man," *The Pittsburgh Press*, February 1, 1968, p. 32.
40. Dick Connors, "Medwick, Goslin, Cuyler Enter Hall of Fame," *The Sporting News*, August 3, 1968, p. 5.
41. *Ibid.*
42. "Kiki Cuyler Award," www.michiganlegion.org.
43. "Kiki Cuyler Memorial Highway," www.legislature.mi.gov.
44. "Kiki Cuyler...in Right Field," *Beaver County (PA) Times*, February 18, 1983, p. A4.
45. *Ibid.*
46. John Sikes, "One of the Good Guys," *Wilmington Morning Star*, March 25, 1972, p. 6A.
47. Thomas S. Rice, "Petty Stuff Turns Out to Be Big Stuff: Jess Says He'll Not Join Bucs Till Robby Remits $1,000," *The Sporting News*, December 27, 1928, p. 1.
48. "Hundred Thousand Dollar Knothole," *The Buckingham Post and Papineau County Echo*, July 1, 1955, p. 12.

Bibliography

Books

Alcona County: A Pictorial History. Volume I. Harrisville: The Alcona County Review, 2007. Reprint by Cheryl L. Peterson and John D. Boufford, 2009.
Berridge, William A. *The Review of Economical Statistics and Supplements.* Volume 4. Cambridge, MA: Harvard University Press, 1922.
Carroll, Jeff. *Sam Rice: A Biography of the Washington Senators Hall of Famer.* Jefferson, NC: McFarland, 2008.
Finoli, David, and Bill Ranier. *The Pittsburgh Pirates Encyclopedia.* Urbana, IL: Sports Publishing L.L.C., 2003.
Fleitz, David L. *More Ghosts in the Gallery: Another Sixteen Little-Known Greats at Cooperstown.* Jefferson, NC: McFarland, 2007.
History of the Lake Huron Shore. Chicago: H.R. Page, 1883. Reissue, Ann Arbor: University of Michigan Library, 2005.
Lieb, Frederick G. *The Pittsburgh Pirates.* New York: Putnam's, 1948. Reprint, Carbondale: Southern Illinois University Press, 2003.
McGrath, John J. *The Brigade: A History: Its Organization and Employment in the U.S. Army.* Fort Leavenworth: Combat Studies Institute Press, 2004.
McNeil, William F. *The California Winter League: America's First Integrated Professional Baseball League.* Jefferson, NC: McFarland, 2002.
_____. *Gabby Hartnett: The Life and Times of the Cubs' Greatest Catcher.* Jefferson, NC: McFarland, 2004.
Parker, Clifton Blue. *Big and Little Poison: Paul and Lloyd Waner, Baseball Brothers.* Jefferson, NC: McFarland, 2003.
_____. *Fouled Away: The Baseball Tragedy of Hack Wilson.* Jefferson, NC: McFarland, 2000.
Peterson, Richard, ed. *The Pirates Reader.* Pittsburgh: University of Pittsburgh Press, 2003.
Porter, David L., ed. *Biographical Dictionary of American Sports: Baseball.* Revised and Expanded edition. Volume A–F. Westport, CT: Greenwood Press, 2000.
Powers, Perry Francis, and Harry Gardener Cutler. *A History of Northern Michigan and Its People.* Volume 2. Chicago: Lewis Publishing, 1912.

Newspapers and Magazines

Baseball Digest
Baseball Magazine
Beaver County (PA) *Times*
The Bend (OR) *Bulletin*
Berkeley Daily Gazette
The Border Cities Star (Windsor, Ontario)
The Buckingham (Quebec) *Post and Papineau County Echo*
Cape Girardeau Southeast Missourian
Eugene Register-Guard
The Florence (AL) *Times-News*
The Free Lance Star (Fredericksburg, Virginia)
The Gazette (Montreal, Quebec)
The Independent (St. Petersburg, Florida)
The Leader (Regina, Saskatchewan)
Lewiston (ME) *Morning Tribune*
The Ludington (MI) *Daily News*
The Meriden (CT) *Daily Journal*

Chicago Daily Tribune
The Clinton County Times (Lock Haven, Pennsylvania)
Miami Sunday News
Miami Daily News and Metropolis
The Middlesboro (KY) *Daily News*
The Milwaukee Journal
Milwaukee Sentinel
The Nevada, Missouri Daily Mail
The News and Courier (Charleston, South Carolina)
The News-Sentinel (Rochester, Indiana)
The Ottawa Evening Citizen
The Owosso (MI) *Argus Press*
The Palm Beach Post
Pittsburgh-Post Gazette
The Pittsburgh Press
The Portsmouth (OH) *Times*
Providence News
The Reading Eagle
Rochester Evening Journal and the Post Express
St. Joseph (MO) *News-Press*
St. Petersburg Times
San Jose Evening News
Sarasota Herald Tribune
Saskatoon Star-Phoenix
Schenectady Gazette
The Spartanburg (SC) *Herald*
The Sporting News
Telegraph-Herald and Times-Journal (Dubuque, Iowa)
Painesville (OH) *Telegraph*
Toledo Blade
The Toledo News-Bee
The Tuscaloosa News
The Vancouver Sun
The Washington (PA) *Daily Reporter*
The Windsor Daily Star
Wilmington (NC) *Morning Star*
The Youngstown Daily Vindicator

Websites

books.google.com
news.google.com
pqasb.pqarchiver.com
www.alconahistoricalsociety.com
www.ancestry.com
www.baseball-alamanac.com
www.baseballhall.org
www.baseball-reference.com
www.legislature.mi.gov
www.michigan.org
www.michiganlegion.org
www.paperofrecord.com
www.retrosheet.org
www.sabr.org
www.southernassociationbaseball.com

Index

Numbers in ***bold italics*** indicate pages with photographs.

Adams, Charles "Babe" 77–80, 98
Adams, Earl "Sparky" 106, 108, 111–112, 117
Adkins, Dewey 223
Alcona County, Michigan 6, 8–10, 140, 162, 221, 238
Aldridge, Vic 46–49, 51, 58–59, 61–62, 66, 70, 75–76, 108
Alexander, Grover "Pete" 91
Alger, General R.A. 6
Allen, Johnny 179
Altrock, Nick 217
Angley, Tom 122–123
Ann Arbor, Michigan 232
Anson, Adrian "Cap" 5
Archer, Jimmy 174
Arnall, Gov. Ellis 225
Asten, George 234
Atkinson, Kiki Cuyler 203–204
Atlanta Crackers 31, 215, 223–227
Augusta Tygers 22
Au Sable, Michigan 7, 12
Avery, Steve 228

Baker, Del 227
Baker, William F. 105, 139
Baker Bowl 190
Baltimore Orioles 1, 32
Bancroft, Dave 54, 89, 143
Barna, Babe 214
Barnes, Everett 28
Barnes, Jesse 54
Barnett, Lucious 167
Barnhart, Clyde 21, 25–26, 32, 36, 38, 40, 46, 53–54, 57, 60–64, 70, 72–73, 76, 85–86, 89, 91–92, 95–97, 100, 235
Barnum, P.T. 214
Bartell, Dick 85, 204
Barton, Vince 152, 158–159, 164, 182
Bass, Dick 216

Battle Creek Custers 14, 16
Bay City, Michigan 15, 27, 67, 103, 151
Bay City Wolves 14–18, 21, 33
Bay Port, Michigan 181
Beck, Clyde 116, 122, 144
Bell, Les 139, 141–142, 155
Benn, Margaret 124
Berg, Moe 187
Berger, Wally 155, 180, 208
Berra, Yogi 229
Biederman, Les 235, 237
Bigbee, Carson "Skeeter" 20, 25, 34, 36, 44, 49, 63, 71, 77–80, 98
Birmingham Barons 21, 26, 214, 217
Bishop, Max 133–134, 136
Black River, Michigan 5–7
Blades, Ray 104
Blair, Footsie 131, 149, 155, 158–159
Blake, Fred "Sheriff" 18, 22, 117, 120, 122, 134, 152, 158
Block, Albert W. 103
Bluege, Ossie 58, 61–62
Blunt, Ronald 239
Boley, Joe 131, 133–135
Boston Bees 202, 206, 208, 210
Boston Braves 36, 40, 44, 51, 54–56, 72, 74, 76–78, 89, 92, 104, 113, 115, 117–119, 122–123, 127–128, 139, 147–148, 153–154, 158, 162, 164–165, 180, 185–187, 194, 199
Boston Red Sox 25, 221, 227–230, 233
Bottarini, John 208
Bottomley, Jim 51, 151, 199
Bouchard, Louis 10
Bowman, Joe 194
Brandt, Ed 162, 187
Brantford Red Sox 14
Braves Field 51
Breadon, Sam 151

271

Brickell, Fred 97
Bridges, Tommy 237
Briger, Joseph 15
Brock, Lou 238
Brooklyn Dodgers 162–163, 170, 181, 190, 198–199, 210–212, 219
Brooklyn Robins 22, 24, 36–37, 40–41, 45, 53–55, 72–74, 76, 78–79, 92, 104, 113–114, 119, 124, 127, 144, 147–149, 155–156, 158, 188
Brown, Eddie 41, 55, 104
Brown, Mordecai "Miner" 221
Brundidge, Harry T. 152
Buffalo Bisons 106, 210
Burgo, Bill 225
Burke, Kitty 199
Burns, Edward 120, 139
Burns, George 134
Burrows, John 224–225
Burrus, Dick 104
Bush, Donie 2, 10, 81–82, 84–88, 91–98, **99**, 100–104, 106–107, 114, 124, 127–128, 130, 140–141, 161, 235–236, 239
Bush, Guy 117, 120, 122, 128, 131, 133, 138, 153, 163, 169, 171, 175–176, 179, 181, 193–194
Butler, Johnny 111
Byrd, Sammy 202

Callahan, Jimmy 174
Campbell, Gilly 206
Campbell, Jimmy 181
Cantwell, Ben 158
Caplan, Maurice J. 181
Capone, Al 165
Carey, Max 19, 25, 35–36, 42–44, 53, 57–64, 66–67, 70–73, 75–80, 85, 88, 94, 98, 237–238
Carleton, Tex 189, 194, 202
Carlson, Betty Elaine 146
Carlson, Hal 145–146
Carpenter, Lew 224–225
Carpenter, Robert 229
Cavarretta, Phil 196, 221
Cermak, Mayor Anton J. 174
Chandler, Happy 225
Chapman, Ben 175–176, 179
Chapman, Calvin 201
Charleston Pals 22–24, 26, 97
Charlotte Hornets 23
Chattanooga Lookouts 26, 48–49, 213–219, 224
Chesaning, Michigan 227
Chicago Cardinals 227
Chicago Cubs 2, 10, 35, 44, 46–50, 52, 54–56, 72–73, 75, 87–90, 92, 95, 104, 106–135, **136**, 137–145, 147–167, 169, 170–171, 174–179, **180**, 181–199, 202, 207–208, 210, 214–216, 218–223, 228, 232, 235, 239–240
Chicago White Sox 25, 107, 116–117, 131, 140, 142, 150, 160–161, 174, 186, 198, 219, 221
Cincinnati Reds 31, 35, 38, 50, 52–53, 71, 73–74, 76, 86–88, 90, 96, 104, 110–111, 114, 123, 126, 146–147, 149–150, 156, 159, 164, 181–182, 184, 186, 188–189, 198–210, 212, 217, 222
Clark, Watty 127, 158
Clarke, Fred 5, 20, 33, 52–54, 56, 59, 61, 75, 77–81, 84, 94, 105–106, 234
Cleaver, Ward 239
Clemente, Roberto 1
Clemons, Verne 18
Cleveland Indians 228
Clymer, Bill 106
Cobb, Darwin 224
Cobb, Ty 10, 15–17, 82, 126, 129, 217, 232, 238
Cochrane, Mickey 129–130, 133–136
Cohen, Andy 123
Collins, Eddie 5
Collins, Jimmy "Rip" 224
Columbia Comers 23, 84
Columbus Red Birds 182
Combs, Earl 98, 176–177, 179
Comiskey Park 117, 143, 150
Comorosky, Adam 85, 96, 102
Coolidge, Pres. Calvin 59–60
Cooney, Jimmy 51
Cooper, Wilbur 46–47, 50
Coscarart, Pete 211
Cousins, Jim 70
Coveleski, Stan 58–59, 61
Crawford, Sam 10
Creedon, Connie 225
Critz, Hughie 104, 157, 191
Cronin, Joe 76, 190, 228, 233, 237
Crosetti, Frankie 175–176
Crosley, Powel, Jr. 206
Crosley Field 198–199, 202, 205, 208
Cubs Park 50
Cullings, William 6
Cunningham, Bruce 118
Cuyler, Anna Rosalind (Shirley) 6, **7**, 8, 11–12, 184, 229
Cuyler, Bertha (Kelly) 11–12, 66, **125**, 139–140, 183–184, 218, 234, 237, **238**
Cuyler, Edna May (Medor) 8–10, 140
Cuyler, George Alonzo 5–6, **7**, 8–12, 67, 162, 184, 221
Cuyler, George Canning 5
Cuyler, Harold S. 12, 53, 66, **125**, 204, 218–219, 230, 237–238

Index

Cuyler, Kelly June (Kruttlin) 114, *125*, 204, 237
Cuyler, Margaret (Gauley) 5
Cvengros, Mike 97

Dallas Rebels 226
Daniel, Dan 149
Davis, Henry 57
Davis, Dr. John F. 123, 166
Davis, Ralph S. 61, 138
Davis, Ray 200–201
Davis, Spud 188
Davison, Crozier 8–9
Day, Pea Ridge 156
Dean, Dizzy 206, 219
Dean, Paul 199
Dejan, Mike 217
Demaree, Frank 176, 179, 184, 195–196
Derringer, Paul 204, 206
Detroit Tigers 10, 15–17, 203, 207, 212, 221, 227, 229, 237
Devormer, Al 93
Dickey, Bill 175–176, 179
Dietrich, Claude 233
DiMaggio, Dom 228–229
Doerr, Bobby 228–229
Dombrowski, Frank 143
Donnelly, Charles 156
Donnelly, Charley 15
Donohue, Pete 126–127
Donovan, William "Wild Bill" 10
Doolin, Mike 33
Dooly, Bill 107
Douthit, Taylor 104, 184
Doyle, Charles "Chilly" 42
Doyle, Jack 215, 232
Dressen Chuck 201, 204–209, 213
Dreyfuss, Barney 17–18, 21–22, 31–34, 45, 48, 50, 52–53, 55, 59, 64, 68–70, 75–76, 80–84, 94–95, 97–99, 101–102, 104–107, 118–119, 128, 141, 149, 162, 234–235, 239
Dreyfuss, Samuel 59, 68–69, 75, 77–78, 97–98, 105–106, 234–235
Durocher, Leo 213, 222
Dykes, Jimmy 129, 131, 133–134, 187, 222

Earnshaw, George 129–130, 132–133
Ebbets Field 211–212
Eckert, William "Spike" 237
Ehmke, Howard 130–132, 135
Elkton, Michigan 181
Engel, Joe 214–215, 217–219
English, Woody 111, 117, 124, 130, 133–134, 141, 144, 146–147, 150, 157, 159, 164, 169, 175–179, 193–194
Ens, Jewel 34, 50, 127–128, 162, 234
Escambron Baseball Park 200

Farrington, Dick 187
Felix, Gus 56, 74
Fenway Park 227–228, 230
Ferguson, Alex 60, 62
Fewster, Chick 73
Finn, Neal 147
Fitzsimmons, Freddie 74, 93, 147
Flint, Michigan 12–13, 15, 45, 48, 67–68, 71, 80, 82–83, 103, 108, 119, 151, 181, 189, 227
Flint Halligans 14
Fonseca, Lew 52
Forbes Field 18, 21, 30–31, 35–36, 38–40, 44, 49–50, 52–59, 63, 65, 72–73, 75–78, 86, 88–93, 97, 100, 105, 111–112, 122, 128, 156, 202, 211, 235
Foster, John B. 47
Fothergill, Bob "Fatty" 15
Foulk, Dudley 28
Foxx, Jimmie 129, 131–136, 190, 221
Frankhouse, Fred 162, 194
Fraser, Charles "Chick" 21, 234
Freitas, Tony 200–201
French, Larry 194
French, Walter 136
Frey, Benny 200, 206
Frick, Ford 199, 237
Frisch, Frankie 31, 36, 40, 118, 123, 187, 192, 213, 237
Fuchs, Judge Emil 117–118, 180
Fussell, Fred 122

Gagetown, Michigan 181
Galan, Augie 191, 193, 196–197, 201
Gandil, Chick 84
Gansser, Colonel A.H. 104
Gehrig, Lou 96, 173, 175–179, 190, 236
Gehringer, Charlie 207, 217, 237
Genewich, Joe 72, 104
Gibson, George 19–21, 23, 171
Gilbert, Charlie 220
Gilbert, Larry 222
Giles, Warren 206, 209–210
Gill, Johnny 201
Glennie, Michigan 231
Gomez, Lefty 176–177
Gonzalez, Mike 114, 122–123
Gooch, Johnny 18, 21, 24, 32–33, 35, 54–55, 65, 75, 96, 98, 213
Goodman, Billy 224, 228
Goodman, Ival 208
Goslin, Goose 60, 62–64, 237, **238**
Grabiner, Harry 174
Grace, Earl 122–123, 156, 168
Graham, Skinny 72
Grampp, Harry 141
Grand Rapids, Michigan 163

Grantham, George 46, 48–49, 53–54, 72, 80, 82, 84–86, 95, 111–112
Greene, Nelson 53
Greenville Spinners 23
Griffith, Clark 84, 217
Griffith Stadium 60
Grimes, Burleigh 41, 108, 162, 170, 174–175, 179, 183–184, 210–213
Grimm, Charlie 38–39, 46, 116–117, 129, 131, 133–135, 137–138, 141–142, 144, 150–151, 156, 158, 161, 169–171, 174–179, 181–189, 192–198, 216, 222
Grimm, Marion 176
Grissom, Lefty 206
Groh, Heinie 31, 92
Grove, Lefty 129–130, 132, 134, 161, 237
Gudat, Marvin 170
Gustin Township, Michigan 140

Haas, Mule 129, 134, 136–137
Hack, Stan 164, 191, 193–194, 197, 206, 220–222
Hafey, Bud 202
Hafey, Chick 154, 164, 186, 188, 208
Haller, Frank 17
Hamilton, Jimmy 22–23, 26–27
Hamilton Tigers 14
Hamlin, Luke 211
Harper, George 52, 93
Harris, Benjamin 9
Harris, Bucky 58–59, 63–64, 71
Harris, Dave 54
Harris, Sen. Frank J. 106
Harris, Henry 9
Harris, Joe 58, 60, 63, 84–85, 89, 92
Harris, Levi 9
Harrisville, Michigan 2, 6–12, 27, 67, 139–140, 151, 162, 183, 207, 216, 221, 227, 230, 232, 234, 238, 240
Hartnett, Gabby 113–114, 119, 122–124, 126, 129, 131, 141, 144, 146, 148, 150–151, 155–156, 158, 165, 176, 180, 189, 214, 216, 218
Haslin, Mickey 223
Hassett, Buddy 211
Hayworth, Ray 212
Heathcote, Cliff 104, 127, 131, 144, 150–151
Heilmann, Harry 15
Hemsley, Rollie 156–158, 166, 169, 174, 181
Henderson, Captain J.E. 7
Henderson, Ricky 238
Hendrick, Harvey "Gink" 182, 187
Herman, Babe 104, 148, 162, 164, 181–182, 185, 187, 190, 194, 199, 202–204
Herman, Billy 159, 163–164, 170, 174–179, 213
Hernandez, Jackie 2
Herrmann, Leroy 200–201

Heydler, John A. 51, 66, 72, 74, 89, 126–127, 165
Hilcher, Walter 200
Hill, Carmen 92
Hinchman, Bill 21, 33
Hogan, Shanty 157, 180
Holden, S.M. 8–9
Holke, Walter 41
Hollywood Stars 109, 183
Hoover, Pres. Herbert 135
Hornsby, Rogers 43–44, 51, 67, 117–120, **121**, 122–126, 128–130, 132–136, 138, 141–142, 144, 146, 148–150, 152–169, 174–175, 180, 187, 213, 216
Houghton, Judge S.G. 104
Houston, Guy 237
Hubbell, Carl 128, 188–191, 194, 202–203
Hughes, Bill 18
Hughes, Harry 223
Hurst, Don 193

Indianapolis Indians 82, 235–236
Iosco, Michigan 10

Jackson, Travis 93, 99
Jahn, Art 25
Johnson, Bob 2
Johnson, Harold 161
Johnson, Jackie Boy 144
Johnson, Si 200
Johnson, Sylvester 154
Johnson, Walter 58, 60, 62–64, 219
Jones, Percy 118
Judge, Joe 58, 61, 187
Jurges, Billy 158, 163–164, 166–167, **168**, 174, 176–178, 182, 189, 222

Kampouris, Alex 207
Kansas City Blues 32–33
Keeble, Judge John Bell 234
Keen, Vic 90–91, 119
Keener, Sid 128, 160–161
Kell, Howard 10
Kelly, Arthur 12
Kelly, Clennie (Calumier) 12
Kelly, George 76, 104, 199
Kelly, Joe 113
Kessler, Gene 102
Killefer, Bill 48
Killmaster, George 227
Kincardine, Ontario 5
Kinde, Michigan 181
King George III 6
Kirksey, George 208
Kitchener Beavers 14
Klein, Chuck 147, 186–187, 189, 192–193, 195–197

Kleinhans, Ted 187
Klem, Bill 19, 74, 156, 199
Klugmann, Joe 39
Knox, Cliff 68
Koenig, Mark 169, 174–175, 186–187
Kolp, Ray 126
Kreevich, Mike 182
Kremer, Ray 32–33, 37, 39, 42, 44–45, 60, 62–63, 66, 82, 87, 89, 109, 119
Kropp, Robert 143
Kruttlin, Ted, Sr. 237

Lanahan, Dick 216
Landis, Kenesaw Mountain 28, 59, 105, 159, 169, 174, 180, 206, 214, 220
Layne, Herman 85–86
Lazzeri, Tony 175–176, 178–179
Leach, Fred 104
Legett, Lou 118
Leiber, Hank 197, 204
Leitz, Al 223
Lelivelt, Jack 218
Letchas, Charley 216
Lewis, Dr. Dean 123
Lewis, W.J. 51
Lieb, Frederick 235
Lincoln, Michigan 184
Lindstrom, Fred 105, 113, 143, 157, 180, 194, 196–197
Little Rock Travelers 27, 225
Lombardi, Ernie 202, 205
London Tecumsehs 14–15, 17
Long, James J. 128
Los Angeles Angels 48, 109
Lotshaw, Dr. Andy 140–141, 220
Louisville Colonels 71, 159
Luce, Frank 34
Ludwig, Dr. James 232
Lundgren, Delmar 28
Luque, Dolph 73, 104, 187

Mack, Connie 129–135, 217
MacPhail, Leland Stanford "Larry" 188, 200, 205–206, 210–212
Magee, Sherwood 33
Magerkurth, George 161
Maguire, Fred 106, 113, 117–118
Maines, George H. 14–17
Malone, Pat 117, 122, 129, 134–136, 144, 153, 160–161, 169, 171, 174, 178, 180–181, 183, 186, 188, 193–194
Mann, Earl 223, 225, 227
Manush, Heinie 15, 237
Mapes, Cliff 229
Maranville, Walter "Rabbit" 5, 18–19, 25, 31–32, 35, 42, 46–47, 49, 187
Marberry, Firpo 60

Marshall, Martha 119
Marshall, Dr. Roy A. 231–232
Martin, Pepper 222
Mathewson, Christy 5
Matthews, Jackson 28
Mauldin, Marshall 223
Mauney, Dick 225
Mauro, Carmen 227
Mavis, Bob 225
May, Jakie 123, 126, 147, 156, 158, 179
Mays, Carl 72
McAfee, Bill 141
McCarren, Paul 182
McCarthy, Joe 2, 106–109, 112–114, **115**, 117, 119–120, 122–123, 126–130, 133–134, 138, 141, 143, 146–150, 153, 160, 171, 173, 177, 179, 187–188, 196, 217, 227–230, 233–234
McCormick, Barry 89
McGarity, Les 225
McGill, Ralph 234–235
McGraw, Bob 73
McGraw, John 5, 18, 41, 48, 105–106, 112, 143
McInnis, Stuffy 52, 54, 63, 80
McKechnie, Bill 23–26, 28, 30–39, 44, 46–49, 52–58, 60, 62–63, 71, 73–78, 80, **81**, 85, 91, 98, 102, 186, 209–210, 234
McKechnie, Bill, Jr. 60, **81**
McMillan, Norm 130, 133, 136
McWeeny, Doug 74
Meadows, Lee 41, 58, 72
Medor, Hazen 140
Medor, Lena 10
Medor, Peter 10, 140
Medor, Shirley 184
Medwick, Joe "Ducky" 190, 199, 237, **238**
Memphis Chickasaws 26, 215, 224, 226
Meusel, Emil "Irish" 30, 42
Michaels, Ralph 26, 28
Miljus, Johnny 97–98
Miller, Bing 129–130, 133–134, 136–137
Milwaukee Brewers 33, 210, 213
Miner, Johnny 119
Minneapolis Millers 25
Miss Stedmore 50
Mission Bells 86
Mission Reds 169
Mitchell, Johnny 41
Mogridge, George 72
Mokan, Johnny 18, 21, 25
Molesworth, Carlton 21
Montreal Royals 213
Moore, Eddie 30, 32–33, 44–45, 49, 54, 57, 59–64, 71–73, 75–76, 80

276 Index

Moore, Floyd 207
Moore, Joe 190, 204
Moore, Johnny 155, 164, 169, 177, 181
Moore, Wilcy 179
Morrison, Johnny 21, 31–33, 41, 46, 54, 62, 73, 76, 89, 104
Mosolf, Jimmy 186, 188
Moss, Malcolm 141
Muehlebach, George 33
Mueller, Walter 20–21, 25–26, 34
Mullin, George 10
Munzel, Edgar 222
Murtaugh, Danny 1
Myer, Buddy 60
Myers, Billy 201, 203

Nashville Volunteers 26–28, 30, 34, 213–215, 217, 224, 227, 234
Navin, Frank J. 15–17
Neale, Greasy 123
Nehf, Art 44, 134
Neis, Bernie 41
New Orleans Pelicans 26, 215, 225–226
New York Giants 18, 24–25, 28, 30–32, 36–42, 44–45, 48, 52–56, 73–76, 79, 87, 93–97, 99, 104–106, 108, 113–114, 116, 118, 123, 127–128, 144, 147, 149, 152, 155, 157–159, 162, 165, 170–171, 180, 182, 184–186, 190–192, 194–195, 202–204, 208
New York Yankees 2, 96–98, 102, 117, 129, 140, 169, 171, 173–180, 196, 198, 228–230, 236
Newhouser, Hal 237
Newman, Albert 15
Nicholson, Bill 214–215, 217, 220, 222
Nicholson, John 7
Niehaus, Al 46–49, 52
Nieman, Butch 225
Novikoff, Lou 221–222
Nugent, Gerald "Gerry" 186

Oakland Oaks 32
O'Dea, Ken 194
Oklahoma City Indians 32, 49
Oldham, Red 64–65
O'Leary, Charley 169
Olsen, Sparky 219
Olson, Vern 220
O'Neil, Mickey 56, 73, 79
O'Neill, Steve 227, 233
Onslow, Jack 68
Ordenana, Tony 224–225
Oscada County, Michigan 10
Ott, Mel 143, 170, 204
Otto, Wayne 161
Owendale, Michigan 181

Pacific Redi-Cuts 33
Pappas, Milt 238
Parnell, Mel 228
Partridge, Jay 92
Passeau, Claude 221
Patek, Freddie 2
Patrick, J.H. 48
Paul, Robert T. 202
Pearce, Frank 187
Peckinpaugh, Roger 59, 62–63
Pennock, Herb 98, 179
Pepper, Sen. George Wharton 72
Perth, Ontario 6
Pesky, Johnny 228–229
Petty, Jesse 53, 104, 119, 239
Philadelphia Athletics 96, 129–137, 171
Philadelphia Phillies 31, 33, 36, 39, 41, 51–52, 54, 56, 74, 92, 104, 113–114, 124, 131, 139, 147, 155, 158–159, 169–170, 185–187, 190, 198, 202, 204–205, 229
Pinnebog, Michigan 181
Pipgras, George 97, 177–178
Pitts, Edwin "Alabama" 197
Pittsburgh Pirates 1–2, 10, 17–23, 25–42, 44–56, 57, 58–66, 68, 70–80, 82, 84–87, 89, 90–98, 100–109, 111–112, 114–116, 118–119, 122–125, 127–128, 135, 137–138, 140, 148–149, 152–153, 155–156, 158, 161–162, 164–165, 167–171, 173, 179–180, 182, 188, 190, 194, 198, 202–203, 206, 208, 219, 228, 233–237, 239
Plant Field 201
Polo Grounds 44, 52, 55, 95, 115, 129, 152, 155, 165, 170, 190, 204
Ponce de Leon Park 225
Port Austin, Michigan 181
Port Hope, Michigan 181
Port Huron Saints 16
Pressnell, Tot 220

Quigley, Ernest 124
Quinn, Jack 133–134

Raschi, Vic 229
Rawlings, Johnny 31, 34, 76
Raymond, Bugs 5
Reardon, Beans 79, 124
Redland Field 38, 111, 164
Reese, Bonesetter 41, 122, 126
Reese, Jimmy 93
Rehnquist, Justice William H. 239
Reinhart, Art 104
Rettenmund, Merv 228
Reynolds, H.G. 203
Rhem, Flint 104
Rhode, Dr. Richard 200
Rhyne, Hal 70, 72, 85

Rice, Sam 58, 60–61, 63–64, 237
Richbourg, Lance 181
Rickey, Branch 151, 234
Riconda, Harry 119, 239
Riggs, Lew 199–203, 206
Rigler, Charles "Cy" 60, 126
Risberg, Swede 84
Rixey, Eppa 104
Robertson, Bob 1
Robertson, Nick 236
Rochester Colts 22
Roe, Willie 6
Rogers, Lee 212
Rohwer, Claude 23
Rohwer, Ray 20
Rommel, Eddie 134
Roosevelt, Pres. Franklin D. 220
Root, Charlie 117, 124, 130–131, 133–134, 158, 163, 171, 177–178, 181, 185, 193, 219
Roush, Edd 72, 156, 237
Rudolph, Dick 89
Ruel, Muddy 63–64
Ruffing, Red 175–176, 237
Russell, Ewell "Reb" 25, 33
Russell, Fred 236
Ruth, Babe 79, 96, 173, 175–178, 182, 187, 190, 212, 217–218, 236
Ryerson, Dr. Edwin W. 183–184

Saginaw, Michigan 206, 218
Saginaw Aces 14, 17
St. Louis Cardinals 17–19, 37, 50–55, 67, 71–72, 75, 79, 88–89, 91, 95–96, 104, 111, 113–114, 116–118, 122–123, 141, 144, 147–149, 151, 154, 156, 158–159, 161, 164, 170–171, 179, 189–190, 192, 194, 196, 199, 206–207, 220
Salveson, Jack 194
San Diego Padres 215
San Francisco Seals 49, 70–71, 86, 164, 183
Scarsella, Les 204, 207
Schalk, Ray 141, 237
Schmidt, Walter 41, 44
Schott, Gene 206
Schulte, Johnny 123, 228, 230
Schumacher, Hal 195
Schwartz, Ed 144
Schwingen, Wilbert 144
Scott, Floyd "Pete" 73, 106, 115
Scott, Jack 53
Seattle Indians 49
Seattle Raniers 210, 218
Seay, Judge Ed 234
Seibold, Socks 118, 147
Sewell, Joe 175–179
Sheehan, Tom 52, 206–207
Sherdel, Bill 19, 122

Shibe Park 135
Shires, Art 140
Shirley, Martha 7
Shuster, Bill 15
Sikes, John 239
Simmons, Al 129, 131–136, 161, 190
Smayda, Frank 47
Smith, Billy 103
Smith, Bob 156, 170, 181, 206
Smith, Chester L. 80
Smith, Earl 50–51, 60, 63, 70, 88–89, 97, 104, 109
Snyder, Frank 36
Sothern, Denny 124
Sothoron, Alan "Al" 91, 210
Speaker, Tris 84
Spencer, Glenn 164
Sportsman's Park 19, 53, 71, 90, 95, 117, 144, 154, 190
Stainback, Tuck 188–189, 191, 193, 195–197
Stargell, Willie 1
Stark, Dolly 156
Statz, Arnold "Jigger" 48
Steineder, Ray 34
Stengel, Casey 230, 237
Stephens, Verne 228–229
Stephenson, Riggs 117, 122–123, 125, 129, 131, 133, 134–135, 141, 144, 148, 152, 157, 159, 169–170, 175–177, 179, 181, 187, 193
Stevens, Justice John Paul 239
Stewart, John "Stuffy" 18, 22
Stine, Lee 200
Stock, Milt 19
Stoneham, Charles 105
Street, Gabby 149
Stumpf, Benny 27
Sturgeon Point, Michigan 7–8, 27
Suhr, Gus 188, 202
Sullivan, Judge Mason S. 222
Summa, Homer 18
Sweeney, Bill 222
Sweetland, Les 156
Swetonic, Steve 122
Swope, Tom 123
Syracuse Chiefs 208, 210

Taylor, Danny 148, 158
Taylor, Zack 133–135
Teachout, Bud 159, 162
Tener, Gov. John K. 72
Terry, Bill 52, 93, 187, 190, 192, 194–195, 208, 222
Thevenow, Tommy 202
Thomas, Herb 105
Thompson, Fresco 104, 114, 124
Three Rivers Stadium 1
Tinning, Bud 179, 194

Tolson, Chick 131
Tovey, Mrs. James 6
Tracey, Bill 68
Traynor, Harold "Pie" 18, 20–21, 32, 38–39, 42, 54, 56–58, 61–63, 66–67, 70–75, 78–79, 82, 85, 93, 112, 187, 194, 198, 206, 208, 234, 237
Trippi, Charley 226–227

Ubly, Michigan 181

Valli, Violet (Popovich) 166–167
Vance, Dazzy 113
Vander Meer, Johnny 206, 212
Vaughan, Floyd "Arky" 169, 206
Vaughan, Irving 151–152, 157
Veach, Bobby 15
Veeck, William "Bill" 104, 106–107, 113, 117–118, 123, 139–140, 151, 154, 160, 162–163, 167–170, 174, 181–182, 184–186, 188, 214
Vila, Joe 105
Virdon, Bill 1

Waddell, Rube 5
Wagner, Honus 38, 52, 59, 66
Walberg, Rube 129–130, 134–135
Walker, Curt 31, 87
Walker, Luke 1
Walker, William M. 187–188, 193
Wallace, Bobby 208
Wallace, Frank 80
Walsh, Davis 52
Walsh, Ed 131
Walters, Bucky 204
Waner, Lloyd 84–87, 89, 92, *93*, 96, 102–103, 106, 111, 123, 235, 237, 239
Waner, Paul 70–74, 76, 84–87, 90, 92–93, 96, 102–103, 109, 162, 191–192, 203, 206, 235–236, 239
Ward, Dick 194
Warneke, Lon 171, 174, 176, 179, 182
Warwick, Firman 23
Washington Senators 1, 57–60, 62–63, 65–66, 70, 82, 84, 98, 133, 135, 218–219
Watters, Sam 60, 234

Weaver, Jim 194, 203
Webb, Earl 104
Weil, Sidney 186
Weintraub, Phil 207
Wenger, Cal 14–16
Wentz, Lou C. 105–106
Wheat, Zack 237
Wheeler, Floyd "Rip" 18
Whitehill, Earl 18
Whitney, Pinky 139
Whitted, George "Possum" 22
Wichita Larks 96
Wilcox, Wheeler 70
Williams, Ted 228–229
Wilson, Jimmie 213, 219–220, 222
Wilson, Lewis R. "Hack" 42, 109, 113, 116–117, 120, 122–123, 125–135, 137–138, 141, 143, 146–148, 150–153, **154**, 155–163, 187–188, 230
Wilson, Mike 22
Wilson Bugs 23–24, 26
Winship, Gov. Blanton 200
Winter, Charles A. 7
Wollen, Lou 87
Wright, Glenn 1, *32*, 33–35, 37, 39–40, 42, 45, 48, 50–51, 54, 56–57, 59, 61, 63, 66–67, 70, 72–75, 77, 82, 85, 90–91, 119, 124, 239
Wright, John 26
Wrightstone, Russ 104
Wrigley, Ada 177
Wrigley, Philip K. 163, 177, 186–188, 193, 197, 215, 220
Wrigley, William 48, 114, 130, 138–139, 149, 177, 220
Wrigley Field 90, 113–114, 116–117, 122, 124, 126–128, 130, 133, 143–144, 146–147, 150, 153, 156, 159–160, 163–165, 167, 170–171, 174, 177, 179, 181, 184, 186, 188, 191, 222

Yankee Stadium 98, 174, 176, 229–230
Yde, Emil 32–34, 37, 39, 45, 60–61, 63, 76
Yeargin, Al 44
Young, Del 182

Zarilla, Al 229

www.ingramcontent.com/pod-product-compliance
Ingram Content Group UK Ltd.
Pitfield, Milton Keynes, MK11 3LW, UK
UKHW041929140426
5217IPUK00014B/392